The Economics of
Growth and Development

The Economics of
Growth and Development

PETER HALL

St. Martin's Press   New York

All rights reserved. For information, write:
St. Martin's Press, Inc., 175 Fifth Avenue, New York, NY 10010
Printed in Great Britain
First published in the United States of America in 1983

ISBN 0-312-23663-8

Library of Congress Cataloging in Publication Data

Hall, Peter (Peter H.)
The economics of growth and development.

Bibliography: p.
Includes index.
1. Economic development.   I. Title.
HD82.H236   1983   338.9   83-13955
              ISBN 0-312-23663-8

To Jenny

Contents

Acknowledgements

My greatest debt in the writing of this book is to Peter Sinclair, for it was his unflagging vitality in teaching economics that first drew me into the discipline. To him, further, I owe the insight that the study of economic development should not be undertaken without initially acquiring a thorough grounding in the central tenets of general economic analysis. Familiarity with the principles of the discipline at an introductory level is therefore assumed here, but basic analyses are none the less revised and incorporated in the text where necessary.

In the course of writing the book I have drawn heavily upon those authors' works whose expositions I have found particularly clear and enlightening—in the hope that this, in itself, will guide readers towards rewarding literature beyond.

The following publishers and authors have kindly consented to the use in this book of copyright material. Oxford University Press: *World Development Report* (produced in collaboration with the World Bank) for statistical information in tables in chapters 3, 6 and 7; *Industry and Trade in Some Developing Countries* (1970) by I. Little, M. Scott and T. Scitovsky, for a quotation in chapter 7; *On Economic Inequality* (1973) by A. Sen, for a quotation in chapter 8; *Oxford University Papers*, vol. 23, p. 158, for figure 5.3, from F. Stewart and P. Streeten, 'Conflicts between Output and Employment Objectives in Developing Countries'; *Readings on Malaysian Economic Development* (1975), ed. D. Lim, for a quotation in chapter 3. Basil Blackwell Publishers: H.G. Johnson, *The Theory of Income Distribution* (1973), for figures 8.5(a) and 8.5(b). Pergamon Press in relation to quotations in chapter 5 and the Conclusion, respectively, taken from *World Development*, vols 4 (p. 786) and 7 (p. 542). The International Monetary Fund in respect of material from *IMF Staff Papers*, vol. 26 used in table 4.4 and a quotation taken from the same source. John Wiley in respect of the *Quarterly Journal of Economics* (1971) for a table used in the

Introduction taken from an article by Sherman Robinson. Van Nostrand Reinhold and Dr J. Jones in respect of figure 2.2, taken from Jones's *An Introduction to Modern Theories of Economic Growth* (1975). Macmillan Publishers in relation to quotations in chapter 5 taken from A.K. Dasgupta and D.W. Pearce, *Cost—Benefit Analysis: Theory and Practice* (1972). Cambridge University Press in respect of a diagram and quotation in chapter 7 from R.A. Batchelor, R.L. Major and A.D. Morgan, *Industrialization and the Basis for Trade* (1980), and several quotations in chapter 8 from Gary S. Fields's *Poverty, Inequality and Development* (1980). University of Chicago Press in respect of material used in chapter 6 taken from a paper by Samuel Preston in R. Easterlin (ed.), *Population and Economic Change in Developing Countries* (1980). Princeton University Press in respect of a quotation in chapter 5 taken from Becker's paper in G.S. Becker (ed.), *Demographic and Economic Change in Developed Countries* (1960). The Economic Society of Australia and New Zealand and the author in respect of table 4.3 taken from an article, 'Personal Saving in Developing Nations: An Intertemporal Cross-Section from Asia', by J. Williamson in *Economic Record*, vol. 44. The National Westminster Bank in respect of table A7. taken from their *Quarterly Review* for August 1981. George Allen and Unwin in respect of diagrams adapted for use in chapter 6 taken from H.G. Johnson, *Essays in Monetary Economics* (1969). Prentice-Hall, Inc. in respect of figure 4.6 adapted from G. Brunhild and R. Burton, *Macroeconomic Theory* (1974). The North-Holland Publishing Co. in respect of table 3.3 based on work in an article by F. Lysy, which appeared in the *Journal of Development Economics*, vol. 7. The American Economic Association and various authors in respect of quotations and tabulated information used in chapters 4, 6 and 8 taken from the *Journal of Economic Literature* (1973, 1974 and 1978) and the *American Economic Review* (1961); Penguin Books in respect of quotations, diagrams and tabulated information in chapter 6 taken from M. Blaug, *An Introduction to the Economics of Education* (1970). Professor R.I. McKinnon in respect of quotations in chapter 4 from a mimeographed paper, 'Money and Credit in Semi-Industrial Less Developed Countries', which, in revised form, has since appeared in S. Grassman and E. Lundberg (eds), *The World Economic Order: Past and Prospects* (1981).

Peter Drake provided most helpful comments upon chapter 4, not all of which (regrettably) I have been able to incorporate. Geoff Harris was a tireless sounding-board on a wide range of issues and was especially supportive in reading and discussing chapter 5. I am also indebted to an anonymous reviewer for, among other things, persuading me to write a separate chapter on agriculture. None of these, of course, must bear any of the blame for remaining errors.

This was a book written in the shadow of a pressing publisher's deadline. That deadline could never have been met without the generous secretarial assistance of Jayne Bourke (who, beyond the call of duty, typed early and final drafts of chapters 2–6), and Rosalie Hall, with Cathy Sevil (who turned round the rest of the typescript with an alacrity worthy of the best Fleet Street copy-takers).

Finally, my wife has suffered bravely throughout the gestation of this book, and without her unselfish support its production would have been inestimably more difficult.

P.H.H.

1

Introduction

The aims of this book are to make the economics of development manageable, and to build a bridge between 'standard' economic theory and the branch of economics that particularly considers the problems of developing countries.

The first aim springs from hearing (with sympathy) students complain that they can see no underlying structure or framework within the study of development economics. It is tempting to say to them that the whole of economics is in the melting pot at present, and that one can hardly hope for the developmental arm to have a firmer and less ambiguous structure than the main body to which it is attached. Alternatively, one could argue that the context of development has become a testing ground for almost any new economic idea that comes to light in the main discipline, so that no coherent structure or ordered research programme should really be expected—particularly when it is realized that additional hypotheses also derive directly from the experience of development itself. But these are, in a sense, counsels of despair.

To take a more positive approach, this book starts from the premise that, however economic development is defined, growth must be an essential part of it. Alleviation of poverty and reduction in inequality are generally agreed to be other important elements of economic development, but a substantial body of evidence now suggests that growth in any case is usually associated with diminished impoverishment and by no means always implies increasing relative inequality. Suffice it to say at this stage that growth is assumed an integral part of development, and to take comfort from the fact that the extent of absolute poverty is probably of greater concern in most developing countries anyway than the degree of relative inequality.

Given the importance of growth to development, it seems important to present at the outset a fully integrated yet simple growth model—that constructed by Robert Solow in 1956. This strategy should accustom you to thinking in growth terms rather than the more familiar comparative static, and in terms of the sort of ratios and magnitudes that seem to determine how rapidly economics grow. Since this model was built in and for the mainstream of modern macroeconomics, we have here the first link between the body of the discipline and its developmental arm.

More importantly, from the point of view of manageability, however, this model can concentrate and organize our thoughts in two ways. On the one hand, the model identifies explicitly the elements of an economy that deserve special attention when we come to consider how it might be made to grow. On the other, we have to ask whether the simplifying assumptions of the model, so valuable in helping us to concentrate our thoughts, are so simple that they obscure factors that we really should consider if we are to understand how economies actually do grow. Having considered the model at the outset, therefore, we then go on to use its assumptions as a means of organizing some of the mass of analysis that has been brought to bear on developmental issues. By questioning each of the assumptions, we will open doors upon particular areas of work that have contributed to the study of development. By the end of the 'Basic Model' chapter (chapter 2), you should have a clear picture of the factors influencing growth in the simplest of economies. By the end of the book you may feel you want to discard the model as a coherent unit, but it should continue to act as a memory aid and general tool for organizing your thoughts. This is a factor of increasing significance in an age when research in journals often has to be presented so succinctly that little perspective, or placing within the bigger picture, is possible.

Before proceeding to the basic model, let us consider two areas of general significance: the meaning and definition of development; and the nature of the aggregate production function, a general form of which is embedded in the basic model but which, in various guises, has been used to identify the wellsprings of growth in economies of all kinds.

DEVELOPMENT

CONCEPTS AND CONTENT

Since the Second World War, the study of the economic problems of less developed countries (LDCs) has, from a tiny base, grown rapidly to generate an enormous literature. Precisely what economic development is, however, is still to some extent open to debate. The commentators of the 1940s and 1950s saw 'economic development' as 'virtually synonymous with growth in per capita income in the less developed countries', says Arndt (1981) in a paper tracing the semantic history of the term. This in turn implied a focus almost exclusively upon raising the rate of provision of material goods and services (averaged out over the population).

Yet, as Arndt reminds us, this approach tends to neglect what both before and since has often been regarded as an important distinction. The growth-of-real-output view conforms fairly closely with a perception that economic development has to do with extracting, employing and upgrading a country's natural resources. On the other hand, this perspective leaves unconsidered the welfare of the people: resources may be developed while the people whose land contains the resources remain largely unaffected.

To attend to this point, the distinction between natural resource development and changes in human well-being needs to be made explicit. Further, if, as is the current tendency, we wish to see development primarily from the point of view of its impact upon the people in a LDC, then we must go further, and either define development in such a way that the welfare of the people is incorporated in it, or show that material growth is a sufficient condition for an unambiguous improvement in human welfare.

In the conventional economic analysis of welfare, the most widely used standard of reference has tended to be the Pareto optimum—named after the Italian social scientist who devised the analysis on which it is based. An optimum in this view occurs when no individual can be made better off without making someone else worse off. Once such a position is reached, no change from it can be considered an unambiguous improvement. For developmentalists, the implications of this have seemed unfortunate.

By construction in this model, individuals in an economy start off with a random endowment of human and material resources which each is allowed to employ in the course of attempting to maximize individual utility. At the optimum, those poorly endowed at the outset may finish up starving while those better endowed initially may well finish up in sumptuous luxury. On the other hand, no unambiguous Pareto welfare improvement can be achieved from this state of affairs: it is already an optimum, and any attempt to improve the lot of, say the poorest must involve taking income from the less poor, who will, as a consequence, be made less well off.

Such a view of welfare optima has appealed to those in search of 'value-free' economic judgements. In the economics of development, however, theorists have been much more ready to express a view that is anything but value-free. They have argued that a poverty that is so intense that it threatens life and reduces to misery every day of existence must be a matter of fundamental concern. The absolutely poor, it is implied, must be viewed as special cases and every effort made to ensure that their suffering is eased. A view of development, which stresses human well-being must, then, contain a strand particularly addressed to the absolutely poor.

More generally, such a perspective will see development as the vehicle for allowing an increasing realization of human potential. This is achieved through widening the extent and scope of material consumption at the same time as expanding the opportunities to allow human aspirations to be fulfilled. Such aspirations may include supporting and rearing a healthy family; education as a means, an end or both; particular types of employment; the opportunity to manage or own a business; and so on. The rate of expansion of opportunities to fulfil human aspirations of this kind are necessarily bound up with growth, but for such growth to be development-serving, it must also proceed along a path on which access to its benefits is widely distributed. Thus if the idea of 'economic development' is to include the ideal of realizing human potential to the full, we must expect distributional objectives to be installed alongside any others.

Let us make, explicitly, the normative statements that development must include the achievement of poverty-alleviating and distributional objectives. Where, then, does growth fit in? Clearly, if a whole population is desperately poor, growth is the only way any of them (let alone all) will ever be able to see their plight eased. If only a part of the population is desperately poor, growth permits the suffering of the poor to be alleviated without penalizing the non-poor as much as would have been the case without growth. It also allows their position to be tackled more quickly than in the absence of growth. We cannot say, *a priori*, whether reducing the extent and intensity of poverty must also reduce relative inequality, that is, the dispersion of incomes around the mean. But even if it does not, growth offers the potential, not available under non-growth, of shifting the whole distribution upwards.

I examine these relationships in much more detail in chapter 8, but the point here is that, even with a view of development which emphasizes human well-being, making increased and effective use of a country's resource base to raise the level of real incomes through growth seems to make good sense in principle, in serving general developmental ends. As it turns out, most of the evidence demonstrates a positive association between growth and the alleviation of poverty but is much more mixed on the association between growth and relative inequality. This leads to a final point in this general overview.

Governments should be prepared to allocate weights to each objective, indicating what they consider the relative social desirability of each goal. If alleviating absolute poverty were given the heaviest weight, then, even if the relative inequality of the whole distribution were to increase in the course of a growth-oriented strategy that reduced poverty, the government could justifiably remain unworried. (It could hope in any case that the trend might be reversed in the longer run, or that a general rise in absolute incomes might compensate for widening income relativities.) On the other hand, if a government were to place at least as much weight on relative equality as on alleviating poverty, it might find itself tempted by radical, short-term redistributive measures which could threaten the prospects for growth and, in turn, the prospects for assisting the absolutely poor. Given the economic conditions —natural resources, comparative advantage, skill base, institutional flexibility and so on—within which an economy is constrained to develop, it is important therefore that objectives be chosen to reflect not only preference, but also feasibility of achievement.

We turn now to measures or indices of development.

MEASURES[1]

GNP per Head
The commonest indicator of development is gross national product (GNP) per head. If GNP per head grows over time in a country, real output is growing faster than population and there is therefore an increasingly large income, on average, for all potentially to enjoy. The measure can also be used to rank countries from 'poorest' to 'richest' and to group countries, as we often will in this book, according to whether they are 'low-income' or 'middle-income' developing countries, or 'industrialized countries'. (The income levels chosen to divide these groups will always be to some extent arbitrary. We follow the guidelines laid down in statistics published in the World Bank publication, *World Development Report*.)

In relation to individual countries, use of growth in GNP per head to measure the rate of development assumes either that poverty and distributional objectives will always be associated with growth, or that developmentalists should not be concerned if they are not. Now, while individual governments may sometimes be prepared to ignore poverty and relative inequality, we shall take the view that, in general, the plight of the absolutely and relatively poor should count for something. Given that basic judgement, we have to note that growth in GNP per head has not always been associated with the alleviation of poverty and has often been linked with increasing relative inequality. Evidence to this effect means that we cannot accept unquestioningly the assumption that benefits can be relied upon to 'trickle down' from sectors of the economy where the seeds of growth and modernization first start to flourish. Belief in the 'trickle-down effect' is one reason why the GNP per head measure became deeply entrenched. Yet the fact that the benefits of growth have not always trickled down as expected is an argument neither against growth as such (a faster growth rate might, after all, have been what was needed—not no growth at all) nor against using a growth measure of development. On the latter point, what is needed is a measure or measures that capture more information. We look at these in a moment.

Even in using GNP per head, note that a range of problems must be resolved in calculating the measure. Among other things, the effects of inflation in monetary measures must be removed to reveal real changes only; and efforts must be made to capture the value of output in sectors where money is not the medium of exchange and where formal accounts may not be kept.

Turning to GNP per head as a comparative measure among countries, notice that use of the official exchange rate to convert GNP per head in local currency to that in a common currency is seriously misleading. This is because we really want to compare the real purchasing power of the average consumer in each country, one with the other. Yet parts of GNP are not traded (and domestic prices are thus importantly determined by local costs), and tariffs and quotas often distort nominal exchange rates. In these conditions, the official exchange rate is a poor guide to relative purchasing power. What should be used to overcome these difficulties are purchasing power parities of the kind generated by Kravis and his associates (1978).

Adjustments for Poverty and Distribution
One way of meeting the objection that GNP per head ignores distributional goals is to make the index of development dependent specifically upon the income growth enjoyed by different components of the population. This is the approach proposed by Ahluwalia and Chenery (1974). They suggest giving increasingly heavy weights to the income growth experienced by lower and lower portions of the income distribution— explicitly discriminating, in terms of welfare, against the relatively

well-off. And should absolute poverty be a prime concern, they go on to suggest that only the income growth of the poorest (say, the lowest 20 or 40 per cent) be allowed to count towards development.

While the advantage of this approach is that it makes explicit distributional considerations, one problem lies in the difficulty of assigning appropriate weights in practice. Further, selecting the poorest 20 per cent, say, for special notice implies employing a poverty line—the income line below which this 20 per cent fall. Such an approach is insensitive to variations in the intensity of poverty, a matter taken up at greater length in chapter 8.

Direct Measures of Relative Inequality
A wide range of measures of relative inequality is available to set alongside an index of growth. These measures are examined in depth in chapter 8.

Social Indicators and Quality of Life Indices
If we wish to focus more directly upon the way in which social welfare changes, we can attempt to use measures identified with particular dimensions of poverty or need. These tell us more about the ends of development than the means—expanding real output per head—employed to achieve them. Thus in its *World Development Report*, the World Bank lists among basic indicators of development not only GNP per head but also an index of food production per head, life expectancy at birth and the adult literacy rate.

A number of issues arise in this connection. First of all, if poverty and its alleviation take centre stage in development programmes, then development strategies are described as being directed towards meeting basic needs. The basic needs approach, however, must in turn be founded on a view of which needs really are basic. Nutritional, health, shelter and perhaps educational needs are obvious candidates, but if programmes are constructed to attack them, each should be further weighted relative to the other so that priorities in expenditure and effort can be established. Both the selection of a group of basic needs and a ranking of them are issues that policy-makers must face.

Second, once each need has been identified and ranked, an appropriate measure for the degree of need must be found. Broadly speaking, measures here can reflect either resources made available and put into certain areas of need, or the effects of such efforts. Input measures, the former, include daily calorie supply per head (for nutrition), doctors or hospital beds per 1000 head of population (for health), or secondary school enrolments as a proportion of a given age group (for education). Measures of result, on the other hand, might relate to observed mortality and longevity, to literacy rates achieved and to effective reductions in disease rates. As these output measures give a direct indication of the success of development in influencing basic needs, there is a strong case for their use. On the other hand, input measures should not be ignored. If we know how many resources are being put into given areas, we can work out how effectively such resources are achieving desired results, and try to understand how efficiency of use might be increased (Hicks and Streeten, 1979, pp. 571–2).

As a third point, suppose we are convinced of the merit of such measures; how should we view them? Should they be taken as alternatives to GNP per head or supplements to it? If GNP per head were, in practice, related to basic needs or other poverty indices in a simple and predictable way, then there would be little need to calculate the latter. From a resource allocation and efficiency point of view there would be a case, but from the perspective of monitoring development there would not. The evidence suggests that higher average GNP levels are, in general, associated with other changes betokening the alleviation of basic needs and an easing of the grip of poverty. But the relationship is not a simple one. Some basic needs respond to rising real incomes earlier in some countries than others, and the response rate can be much faster at some points in the course of growth of real incomes than at others. (For a summary of evidence see Hicks and Streeten, 1979, pp. 572–4.) This sort of result is encouraging in the main but points to the fact that varying economic conditions will be associated with variations in the developmental concomitants of growth. Particular countries will want to know precisely what the relationships are in their individual cases, and from the perspective of general understanding we might also want to know why such inter-country variation arises. Thus we can conclude that estimates of basic needs measures are worthwhile, and should be used to supplement GNP per head.

Finally, notice that some indices of development go well beyond measuring the most fundamental dimensions of absolute poverty. Such wider-ranging, composite measures are sometimes called 'quality of life' indices. At a modest level of ambition they may extend to cover factors such as leisure and security, but in other instances the tally of indicators has risen well beyond that to take in the socio-cultural and political as well as 'purely' economic. While this sort of index contains information on poverty alleviation, it can concentrate on fundamental impoverishment only by allocating those elements a decisively heavy weight in the overall composition.

Structural Measures

As a final note on measures, it should be said that development can be viewed not so much from the angle of the objectives it achieves but from the point of view of various changes in economic structure. A highly generalized picture of development sees it as a transition from static economic dependence upon traditional agriculture, with little outside contact through trade, to self-sustaining growth built on international trade, capital-intensive techniques, technical progress and adaptation, and an ever-changing sectoral composition of employment and output in light of changing world conditions. The work of some commentators (Chenery, 1960; Chenery and Syrquin, 1975; Chenery and Taylor, 1968) suggests that countries tend to pass through a common sequence of structural changes with first one type of industry then another growing most rapidly, different sectors accounting at different times for the majority of non-traditional output and applying the greatest impetus to overall growth. This leads to suggesting development indices based on measures such as the share in overall output accounted for by manufacturing (often the most dynamic sector), the share in total income earned from manufactured exports, the share of manufactured exports or the share of manufacturing output occupied by certain types of activity.

Related to this view of development is the idea that differing degrees of economic maturity can be identified. 'Maturity' depends upon the extent to which a country can match its natural resources with the most efficient production techniques to ensure full employment for its population in the prevailing market conditions. Generally, we might expect that maturity should bring with it the alleviation of poverty and so feed back on our earlier criteria. On the other hand, if a country is very poorly endowed with natural resources there may be relatively little scope for it to advance at all. Its best hope would probably lie in a strategy of expanding local, distinctive craft industry, tourism and other service industries—and seeking economic links with neighbouring countries.

We have said enough to give a feel for the content and measurement of development and its connection with growth. Let us now turn to a basic tool in the analysis of both growth and development—the aggregate production function.

THE AGGREGATE PRODUCTION FUNCTION

In the next chapter I shall present a model of growth that incorporates an aggregate production function. A function is merely a rule that defines the relationship, in more or less general terms, between one variable (or set of variables) and another. The production function at the level of an individual process defines the relationship between inputs (land, labour and capital, for example) and the output(s) they combine to produce. In general from this relationship can be written:

$$Y = F(D, L, K) \tag{1.1}$$

where Y is output, D land, L labour, K capital and F should be read 'is a function of'. Similarly, we can think of all national output—aggregate output—being produced by means of combining all the land, labour and capital employed by each production unit (or aggregates of each input) in the economy. From now on, (1.1) and all other formulations of the production function in this section will be taken to refer to the aggregate.

If interest is restricted merely to any two inputs of the three included in (1.1), we can derive an isoquant map which represents the production function in diagrammatic form. In figure 1.1 we have selected L

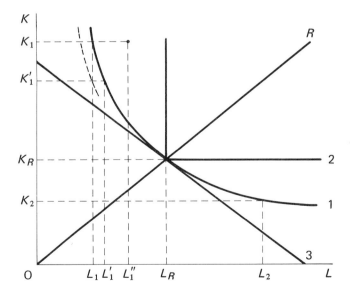

Figure 1.1 Isoquants for aggregate output $\bar{Y}$

and K as our two inputs and will assume that each is homogeneous in quality. The properties embedded in specific types of production function can be illustrated by reference to this figure. In the figure three different types of isoquant, labelled 1, 2 and 3, are shown. Each one relates to a given level of output, $\bar{Y}$, and shows all the combinations of capital and labour that are needed to produce that output, assuming that efficient use is made of the existing technology.

Look first at isoquant 1. Any of the combinations (K_1, L_1), (K_R, L_R) and (K_2, L_2) will produce $\bar{Y}$ on this isoquant—as would any other combination of inputs that could be found by reading off the points on the axes corresponding to a given point on the isoquant. The isoquant reflects technical efficiency in the sense that the given output level $\bar{Y}$ could not be produced using any less of a given input without at the same time adding in more of the other. For example, if $K = K_1'$, then either L would have to rise to L_1' to maintain output at $\bar{Y}$, or else output, given $L = L_1$, would have to fall to a level below $\bar{Y}$, represented by the dotted segment of isoquant drawn in for reference. These constraints are enforced by the technology.[2]

Now, every isoquant reflects technical efficiency in this way, but why might they vary in shape? The answer is that such variations represent differences, as between one production function and another, in the degree of substitutability between inputs. In the case of isoquant 2, $\bar{Y}$ can be produced efficiently only by the input combination (K_R, L_R)—capital and labour employed in the fixed proportions shown by the slope of the ray OR. If the given capital stock were K_R, any amount of labour less than L_R would lead to a lower output level and, because labour and capital must be employed in fixed proportions, to under-utilization of available capital. Similarly, even if labour were available in excess of L_R, no more output than $\bar{Y}$ could be produced if capital were limited to K_R. While the isoquant is conventionally drawn in the L-shape shown, the only relevant, efficient point on it is the corner point itself. In the case of isoquant 3, the production function is characterized by perfect substitutability between inputs: for any unit of capital removed from production the addition of equal amounts of labour will permit the same output to be produced as before—irrespective of whether we start with much capital or little.

Isoquant 1 lies between these extreme cases. For each successive unit of capital removed, more and more labour must be added in to compensate for its loss. This reflects the intuition that, if L and K are imperfect substitutes, but substitutes none the less, then the less capital that is available, the more labour will need to be 'topped up' as the ever-shrinking capital stock becomes increasingly small. Looked at another way, successive unit additions to labour can be associated with the given output level $\bar{Y}$ only if capital inputs are reduced by less and less as the process continues. All of this is represented by changes in the slope of the isoquant. The slope at any point represents the rate of substitution, at the margin (i.e. when we consider one-unit changes), of labour for capital. From what we have said, and by observation of isoquant 1, this marginal rate of substitution will diminish as we move down the curve: less and less capital can be sacrificed at the margin as unit additions to labour occur.

In the case of isoquant 2, the marginal rate of substitution is zero; in the case of isoquant 3 it is constant, not diminishing, and is reflected in the fixed slope of the line.

A widely used term that captures the substitutability between inputs and thus the flexibility of the production processes is the elasticity of substitution. This is written σ and is defined along any given isoquant as:

$$\sigma \equiv - \left(\frac{\text{\% change in the capital–labour ratio}}{\begin{array}{c}\text{\% change in the marginal rate of substitution between}\\ \text{labour and capital}\end{array}} \right).$$

Changes in the marginal rate of substitution can be observed by looking at changes in the slope of tangents to the isoquant at different points on the curve, each of which is associated with some values of K and L, and hence some value of K/L, the capital–labour ratio. If such tangents are extended as far as the axes they can be called isocost lines, and show all the combinations of K and L that can be used for a given level of expenditure. The slope of the isocost line is given by the relative prices of the inputs, the rent–wage ratio, r/w. In profit-maximizing equilibrium conditions, where the isocost line is tangent to the isoquant, changes in the marginal rate of substitution can thus be equated with changes in (r/w). With a flexible technology, changes in relative input prices will be associated with larger changes in the capital–labour ratio than in the case of an inflexible one. The elasticity may be as low as zero (isoquant 2) or as high as infinity (isoquant 3). The implications of this are explored further in chapter 8.

In figure 1.2 we take the shape of an isoquant between the two extremes as the general case and construct a map of such curves, each one representing a different output level, the lowest output levels nearest the origin and the highest farthest out. A map like this gives us all the information we need about the relationship between inputs and outputs, in other words the production function. It is sometimes assumed that every isoquant is parallel to its fellows—in the sense that

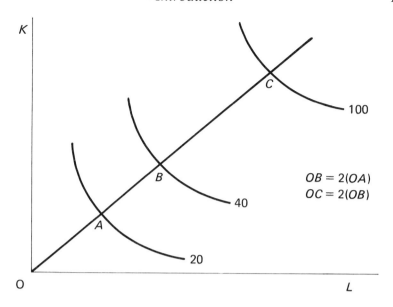

Figure 1.2 Returns to scale

a ray from the origin would pass through each curve at a point of equal slope. In this case we have a homothetic production function and any one isoquant can be taken as representative of all. Homothetic or not, each production function will be characterized by returns to scale. The nature of these returns is conventionally observed by permitting each input to be multiplied by some number (say 2, to double them) and asking what then happens to output. Diagrammatically, this is equivalent to moving, in our example, twice as far out along a ray from the origin and seeing what difference it makes in terms of isoquant levels. If output were to double exactly we would have constant returns to scale; if it rose more than two-fold we would have increasing returns to scale; if it rose less than two-fold we would have decreasing returns to scale. In figure 1.2 constant returns to scale prevail between A and B since $OB = 2(OA)$ and $40 = 2(20)$, but between B and C increasing returns set in because, although $OC = 2(OB)$, $100 > 2(40) = 80$.

Finally, notice that the concept of diminishing returns to a variable factor can also be illustrated. This idea asks us to consider how output will be influenced if we add more of a variable factor while holding at least one other fixed. If K is fixed at $\bar{K}$, then it can easily be seen in figure 1.3 that unit additions of labour must eventually be associated

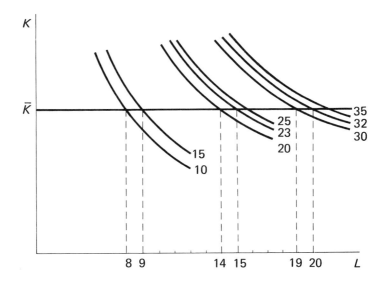

Figure 1.3 Diminishing marginal productivity of labour when capital stock is fixed. Notice that when labour input rises by 1 unit, from 8 to 9, output rises by 5 units. When labour input rises from 14 to 15, output rises by 3 units: more than 1 labour unit is required to raise output by 5 units at this point, given K = K̄. *When labour rises by 1 unit from 19 to 20, output rises by less still—by 2 units.*

with diminishing returns in terms of output. This is called 'diminishing marginal productivity'.

This rapid review of basic theory will be useful later in the book and also enables us to assess better the empirical work that has been done on growth and development using the aggregate production function. As it stands, (1.1) says merely that inputs are needed to produce output. This is irrefutable but not very useful if we want to know how much of an influence on output each of the inputs has. It is the latter question we want to address if we wish to examine the relative performance of (and potential for) each input as a source of growth.

To tackle this assignment, the production function is given a more precise form which enables us, in turn, to derive estimates in quantitative terms of this potential. One of the most widely used formulations is the Cobb–Douglas production function:

$$Y = AK^{\alpha}L^{\beta} \tag{1.2}$$

where A captures influences on output not derived from quantitative changes in K or L and α and β are parameters that, under perfectly competitive conditions, can be shown to equal the respective shares in income of capital and labour. This particular formulation has the desirable theoretical properties of a positive but diminishing marginal productivity for each variable input, and can be constrained, by assumption, to embody constant returns to scale or can be permitted to reflect a wider range of return to scale possibilities. Unfortunately, it also embodies the condition that the elasticity of substitution be equal to unity—a constraint for which we have neither theoretical nor empirical justification.

To ease this constraint in formulation, the constant elasticity of substitution production function was devised by Arrow, Chenery, Minhas and Solow (1961). It may be written:

$$Y = \gamma [\delta K^{-\rho} + (1 - \delta)L^{-\rho}]^{-(1/\rho)} \tag{1.3}$$

where the elasticity of substitution is equal to $1/(1 + \rho)$, and γ and δ are efficiency and distribution parameters. While the elasticity of substitution may take any value in this formulation, this value is none the less still a constant, again a condition that is more restrictive than either theory or evidence permit.

It is beyond the scope of this text to report on the work that has been done to provide other and less restrictive formulations, but it is clear that, the more in-built restrictions that any given formulation is permitted to carry, the less likely it is that we shall gain an undistorted picture of how output changes are related to those on the input side.

A number of production function studies have been used to estimate the contributions of various factors to output growth, famous among them Denison's (1967) nine-country study of advanced industrial nations using a Cobb–Douglas form. For evidence on LDCs, table 1.1 summarizes the findings of Robinson (1971), whose conclusions from a cross-section study of data from 39 developing countries give a good impression of general results in the area. For the period 1958–66 the average annual growth rate of GNP in the countries he studied was 4.95 per cent. Of this, he estimates that capital input growth accounted for 1.56 per cent (32 per cent of the total) and labour input growth for 0.95 per cent (19 per cent of the total). Items (c) and (d) are included separately to try to capture the effects of resources shifting from low-productivity agricultural to high-productivity urban employments. These resource shift influences on growth require a refinement of the basic production function technique but are necessary if some of the

TABLE 1.1 Sources of growth in LDCs: 39-country average, 1958–66

Contributions to growth by	Estimate	Share of contributions
	%	%
(a) Labour	0.95	19
(b) Capital	1.56	32
(c) Change in share of agriculture in GDP	0.22 ⎫	18
(d) Change in urban population share	0.68 ⎭	
(e) Net foreign balances as percentage of GNP	0.70	14
(f) Residual	0.84	17
Total	4.95	100

Source: Robinson (1971, p. 405)

important effects of structural change are to be identified separately in the process of development. Robinson estimates that 18 per cent of total growth derived, on average, from this source. Item (e) reflects the role that foreign exchange availability might have in assisting growth, and item (f) is the contribution of factors otherwise unidentified and often called 'total productivity'.

While other studies vary in the relative importance attributed to capital as opposed to labour, there is widespread agreement that growth in LDCs springs dominantly from quantitative increases in factor inputs. A point that needs to be made is that factor inputs also tend to improve in quality over time, either as technical advances are embodied in new machines or as higher standards of education, health and nutrition raise the productivity of labour. For poor countries in particular, evidence suggests that improved health conditions can play an important role here. The residual 'total productivity' element captures the effects of increasing returns to scale if, as in some studies, a constant returns restriction is built into the justification. It also reflects gains made from making better use of plant, equipment and other inputs as distinct from improvements embodied in the inputs. Where Robinson estimates that this contributed about 17 per cent, on average, to growth in the countries he studied, he allocated 35 per cent to this element for the USA, and 54 per cent to it for north-west Europe. While other studies necessarily vary widely in the precise size of the residual (it must always depend upon the range of factors they have already identified, the specification of their production function and the accuracy of their data), it seems that developed countries generally benefit rather more than LDCs from such 'total productivity' elements.

This chapter has paved the way to our basic growth model in chapter 2 by pointing up the central role of growth in the development process. A frequently used device for studying the wellsprings of growth has been the aggregate production function, and we have examined briefly the theory and application of this tool. Analysis along these lines has not been taken very far here, however, because the production function represents only a part of even the simplest models of economic growth. Rather than working from a partial foundation, it is intended to make a proper start with a fully integrated growth model. Our study of the production function here will help in this endeavour, but ultimately it can be seen only as a stepping-stone towards it. It is to the basic model that we now turn.

Arndt's brief paper mentioned in the chapter can be supplemented in a number of ways. Higgins (1959) discusses the meaning of 'under-developed' and the characteristics of underdeveloped countries in the opening chapter of an early text in the area. Seers's paper in Baster (1972) should be consulted for a more recent statement defining development in terms of the conditions for realizing human personality. Nugent and Yotopoulos (1979) should be read for a flavour of arguments that suggest that inequality and unemployment are logical consequences of growth if excessive reliance is placed on the market mechanism early in the development process. Papers by Baster, Drewnowski and McGranahan in Baster (1972) are particularly enlightening on the measurement issues, but a good place to start in this area is Hicks and Streeten (1979)—from which a number of the points made in this introduction were drawn. Finally, on the aggregate production function, see Henderson and Quandt (1980) for the micro-economic foundations and general properties of the tool; Solow (1957), Jorgenson and Griliches (1967), and Denison (1967) for classic studies in its application in developed countries; and Maddison (1970) for a supplement to Robinson's work on LDCs.

NOTES

1 Not surprisingly this area is frequently covered at the start of texts on development, and this section shares common features with the discussion for example in Ghatak (1978) and Thirlwall (1978), either of which might provide instructive further reading. A further most helpful reference is Hicks and Streeten (1979).

2 It is quite probable that $\bar{Y}$ could also be produced using K_1 and more than L_1 of labour, say L_1'', to generate a point like N. This is a technically inefficient point, however, since we know we can obtain $\bar{Y}$ with K_1 and less than L_1'' labour—i.e. L_1.

2

A Basic Model

Without growth there cannot be development. Development is more than just growth and different from it, but there are few countries in the world so well off already that they can afford to give anything but top priority to growth as their primary objective. Only self-cultivated, self-sustaining growth has the capacity to alleviate the widespread and desperate poverty that characterizes so many LDCs. As we shall see later, growth may have to be cultivated in a particular way and/or its benefits redistributed to ensure that the most desperately poor enjoy some share in the fruits of expanded production. But all the same, growth comes first.

To examine how growth occurs, we shall work initially with a model invented by Robert Solow in 1956. This model has been selected here for the following reasons. First, development cannot occur without growth. But growth is a dynamic process (it is necessarily concerned with changes in the economy) and can be approached appropriately only by means of models designed specifically to explain how and why economies do grow. Unfortunately, the theory of economic growth is often quite difficult, but the Solow model is relatively simple, and easy to understand in commonsense terms.

Second, this model is entirely self-contained and internally consistent. The great advantage of this is that the model can be viewed as a 'box' or a framework of self-supporting scaffolding, each part of which can be examined in relation to every other part. Given that the model is a relatively simple one, the student should therefore be rapidly able to grasp what, in terms of the model, conditions are necessary and sufficient for an economy to grow.

The simplicity and logical consistency of the model make it ideal, in the third place, as a means of organizing all the material we shall want to consider as the subject matter of economic development. Rather more needs to be said, however, to justify the use of the Solow model as the organizational vehicle for exploring the whole of development economics.

No one is likely even to pretend that a simple, one-sector, full-employment equilibrium growth model represents the conditions prevailing in most LDCs. But now turn the problem on its head. Suppose we look at the varying and complex patterns of change occurring in economies throughout the world and wish to gain some understanding of, some insight into why, in perfectly general terms, economies grow. The project as it turns out is an ambitious (and absolutely fascinating) one, but for every student it has to start somewhere. Usually, the best place to start is with a relatively simple sort of explanation. Such explanations often turn out to be inadequate in all sorts of respects, but as learning devices they have a vital purpose to serve: they open the door to coping with more complicated theories later—theories that would never have been devised in the first place if the simple model had not come first.

Turning next to the characteristics of the theory of economic development, the student may well be forgiven for thinking, upon first acquaintance, that the area is a rag-bag of unconnected fragments. And, indeed, there is no general and uniformly applicable model of economic development. Instead, both micro- and macroeconomic theories (as well as many sub-branches of the discipline) have been drawn upon to aid in the analysis of particular issues, and such theory has also been extensively adapted to meet particular developmental conditions. All of this presents a confused and confusing picture, but by adopting a model like the Solow growth analysis it becomes much easier to organize and to fit together the many apparently unconnected pieces—not only with each other to illuminate the development of an economy, but also with the main body of economic theory. This should make it not only satisfying to learn the material involved but also much easier to remember.

All economic models take the form of outlining a set of assumptions and then building upon them to reach conclusions. (Not all model-builders make all of their assumptions explicit, but they can always be found if you look hard enough!) In the case of the neoclassical growth model, most of the assumptions are quite explicit and easy to understand. We shall derive the conclusions of the model later in this chapter. Having said this much, there are two broad alternatives for judging or testing the model.

As one approach, we may look at the assumptions and see if they constitute a fair representation of the economic world as we know it. If we think they do not, we can always ask whether the conclusions of the model are likely to change in any important way if the assumptions are changed. (A warning is in order here. Students often believe assumptions paint a picture that is an over-simplification of the real world—and react by demanding assumptions that achieve 'greater reality' by importing new elements of complexity. Such demands can, of course, easily be met. But there is always a price to pay: the structure of reasoning built up on the foundations of the assumptions must become more complicated, too, and the result is that the argument becomes more difficult to understand and insights harder to glean. This then starts to defeat the object of constructing a model in the first place—which is to *simplify* the world enough to be able to understand *something* about it, rather than trying to account for everything, which is always going to be beyond the comprehension of any of us.)

An alternative approach is to ask whether the conclusions of the model conform with the experience of real-world economies. If the conclusions are at variance with actual economic experience, then it could be the case that one, some or all of the assumptions fail successfully to represent elements of the economic world, which are in fact important for explaining the operation of the economic mechanisms under scrutiny. Another possibility is that the assumptions, taken individually, might be well founded, but that some further assumption, which is quite crucial, has been omitted and so the model reaches conclusions that do not reflect real world experience. Finally, of course, it is quite possible that a model might reach conclusions that appear perfectly reasonable empirically and yet the model is built on assumptions about which we are rather doubtful. In that case we have to search for other mechanisms that generate the same conclusions.

In using the basic model to organize development theory we shall have resort to each of these methods. Sometimes experience will be found to conform to the predictions of the model despite its assumptions—which directs us at once to look for alternative mechanisms that must have been at work; sometimes experience will be found that fails to reflect the conclusions of the model—which, of course, casts doubt upon the assumptions, but has the entirely constructive consequence of forcing us to ask *which* assumption or assumptions were to blame, or might have been omitted.

It should by now be clear that, even if the Solow model of growth turned out to oversimplify or even misrepresent the processes of change in LDCs, it would still be far from useless. For in its simplicity and logical coherence it provides a sound and accessible first step in the business of learning about economic dynamics, while the clarity and sharpness of its assumptions and mechanisms make it self-evident what questions have to be asked on the road to building up a better understanding of actual development paths. In short, it gives us an agenda for action.

The presentation and analysis of Solow's model given here is slightly different from Solow's own. We follow instead the approach taken by Hywel Jones (1975, especially p. 72–82). Students are strongly recommended to consult this text should they wish to extend their knowledge of growth theory.[1]

ASSUMPTIONS OF THE MODEL[1]

(1) THE SINGLE-COMMODITY ECONOMY

The model concerns itself with an economy producing only one good, or commodity. Production of this good per period is denoted Y, and, since its rate of production per period will change in a growing economy from one period to the next, it is explicitly made a function of (i.e. to depend on) the period, t, when this rate is observed. Thus the rate of production is written $Y(t)$. In some ways the single-commodity assumption may seem more suited to simple economies producing only a few goods than to the advanced industrial economies Solow had in mind. There are in any case two ways that may make this assumption appear acceptable.

First, suppose this single commodity is corn. Corn has the advantage that it can be used either for consumption (it can be eaten) or for investment (saved from consumption this year to be sown to grow next year's corn). Consumption is the end to which all economic activity is directed, and investment today is the means of ensuring that consumption can be enjoyed in future. This distinction is not only central to macroeconomics in general but is of particular importance to models of macroeconomic growth. That it can be made even in the single-commodity world of Solow's model, imagining corn to be that one commodity, is a source of considerable comfort.

Second, even if two or more different goods are produced, it is possible to consider all output as a single good if each and every product is the output of an identical technology. If this is so, every good will have the same production function and so will be 'perfectly substitutable in production' (Meade, 1962, p. 71).

(2) CONSTANT PROPORTIONAL SAVING

In any period, output can be either consumed or saved. Here it is assumed that the fraction of output saved is a constant proportion, s (e.g. 0.2 or 20 per cent). The rate of saving per period, S, can therefore be shown algebraically:

$$S(t) = s\ Y(t); \qquad 0 < s < 1 \qquad (2.1)$$

where the inequality condition simply says that saving per period must fall somewhere between 0 and 100 per cent of the value of output.

(3) EQUALITY OF NET INVESTMENT AND SAVING

When corn in any period is not consumed, it automatically goes to supplement the stock of corn that has accumulated when, in previous periods, corn production has not all been consumed. This accumulation of unconsumed corn forms the economy's capital stock in any period, denoted $K(t)$. The rate of increase of this capital stock is called net investment. The difference between net investment and gross investment per period is that gross investment counts in all additions to the capital stock in a period whereas net investment subtracts from this amount any corn required to make up for depreciation in the existing stock. For simplicity (it makes no difference to the important results of our analysis) we shall assume that corn does not depreciate so that net and gross investment are both the same.

Now, we already know that what is not consumed is saved, and we have now observed that uneaten corn adds to the existing stock of capital. Thus we may write:

$$I(t) = \frac{dK(t)}{dt} = \dot{K}(t) = sY(t) \qquad (2.2)$$

which says that investment (net and gross) in period t equals the change in the capital stock associated with the passage of a (short) period of time, which, purely as a matter of alternative notation, can be written $\dot{K}(t)$, and which equals the rate of saving in the period.

(4) WELL-BEHAVED, CONSTANT RETURNS TO SCALE, AGGREGATE PRODUCTION FUNCTION

Solow himself assumes that aggregate output and two inputs, labour and capital, can be related to each other by an aggregate production function:

$$Y(t) = F[K(t), L(t)] \qquad (2.3)$$

or dropping, but not forgetting, the arguments of time,

$$Y = F(K, L). \tag{2.3a}$$

This function can be re-expressed in what is called the 'intensive' form, given the assumption that the function has the property of constant returns to scale (CRS). Under CRS, the multiplication of all inputs by a given amount (say, doubling, or halving) will result in a similar change (doubling or halving, respectively) in output. By multiplying all inputs by $(1/L)$ here, CRS ensures that the resulting change in output can be found by also multiplying it by $(1/L)$; i.e.,

$$\frac{Y}{L} = \frac{F(K, L)}{L}.$$

This can be simplified and rewritten in lower-case letters which represent per-unit-of-labour forms of each variable:

$$y = f(k, 1) = f(k). \tag{2.3b}$$

In other words, output per worker is simply a function of capital per worker.

Following Jones, we shall go a little further than simply specifying CRS in the production function. We shall also assume a positive but always diminishing marginal product of capital and the impossibility of producing output without capital. This ensures that the production

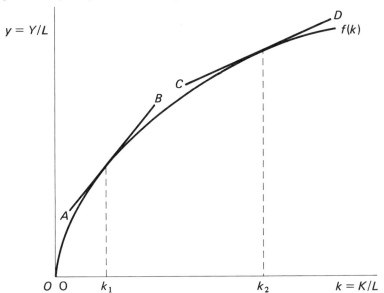

Figure 2.1 The aggregate production function per worker (intensive) form

function, in its intensive form, can be drawn as in figure 2.1. We shall call this form 'well behaved' because it enables us to reach the results of the analysis in the most clear-cut fashion. In the figure, the slopes of tangents *AB* and *CD* measure the marginal product of capital at points on $f(k)$ where the capital–labour ratio is k_1 or k_2.[2] *CD* is 'flatter' than *AB*, in line with our assumption of a diminishing marginal product of capital.

(5) CONSTANT LABOUR FORCE GROWTH RATE

Solow assumes that the growth rate of the labour force, n, is constant and is not determined by any elements of the model; in other words, it is exogenous. By definition,

$$n = \dot{L}/L = \frac{dL/dt}{L}. \tag{2.4}$$

(6) PERFECT FACTOR MARKETS

The model operates in the general framework of costless and instantaneous adjustments in the wage paid to labour and rate of profit paid to capital. An important consequence of this is that both inputs will always be fully employed.

(7) CLOSED ECONOMY

At no point in his model does Solow introduce the possible effects of international trade on growth.

If these assumptions are understood, the rest of the work follows rather naturally.* To make it even easier, I shall state at the outset the main propositions that I am going to demonstrate.

(1) Given any specified saving propensity, s, and labour force growth rate, n, the capital–labour ratio will always adjust, whatever its initial value, to bring the economy on to a steady-state growth path. On such a path output, capital and the labour force will *all* grow at the same rate, n.

---

* Solow's model is often described as 'neoclassical' because of its smooth and 'well-behaved' aggregate production function and the trouble-free market clearing and adjustment mechanisms implicit in it. While the term 'neoclassical' will often be used here from now on, it should be noted that the fixed proportional saving assumption actually abstracts from the choice theoretic problems that would be posed in a fully fledged neoclassical approach.

(2) If, *ceteris paribus*, the saving propensity, s, increases (falls), permanently higher (lower) output per worker will result, but in the long run the growth rate will be the same as before.

(3) If, *ceteris paribus*, the rate of labour force growth increases (falls), output per unit of capital and employment per unit of capital, L/K, will rise (fall) but output per worker will fall (rise).

(4) An increase in the rate of technological progress raises both output per head and the rate of growth.

Even without further comment or analysis, the content of these propositions makes them of self-evident interest to developing countries, crucially interested in isolating the factors that will raise income per capita over time, and that may also raise the rate of growth of income per capita.

We now turn to figure 2.2, which depicts the whole of the model at work. This figure actually builds on figure 2.1 and uses just three lines (two curved, one straight) to represent all the important relationships in the model.

First, notice that the production function, in its intensive (i.e. per worker) form $f(k)$, is exactly what we saw in figure 2.1.

Second, the line labelled $sf(k)$ represents the savings-per-man function. Recall from assumption (2) that s is the (fixed) proportion of

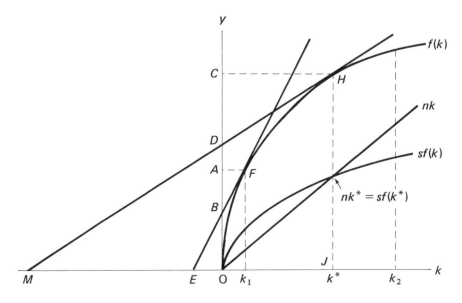

Figure 2.2 Equilibrium, and wage and profit rates in the neoclassical model

income saved per period, so the savings rate per worker is $sy(t)$, or $sf(k)$. Since s always lies between 0 and 1, $sf(k)$ must always lie below $f(k)$ and is derived, in fact, simply by scaling down each value of $f(k)$ by the factor s.

Lastly, assumption (5) requires population (and the workforce) to grow at the *constant* rate of n per cent per period. Although its usefulness will not become clear immediately, the expression nk can therefore be shown by the third (straight) line.

Let us now derive the main results of the model.

THE MECHANICS OF EQUILIBRIUM GROWTH

By definition, output is divided between consumption and investment (corn is either eaten or kept for next year's sowing), so output per man must be equal to the sum of investment per man and consumption per man:

$$\frac{Y}{L} = \frac{I}{L} + \frac{C}{L}. \tag{2.5}$$

Now, purely as a matter of definition, we know that

$$k = K/L. \tag{2.6a}$$

Since our first proposition suggests that it is *changes* over time in k that enable the economy to adjust, we want to focus on finding out about such changes. Remembering that a dot over a variable indicates the change in it associated with the passage of a (short) period of time, write $dk/dt \equiv \dot{k}$. Further, to denote the rate of change of the variable k in relation to its initial or base value, write $(dk/dt)/k$, or $\dot{k}/k$. This measures the proportionate rate of change of k.

All the variables in this model are dependent on the period at which they are observed, so rewrite (2.6a) as

$$k(t) = \frac{K(t)}{L(t)}. \tag{2.6b}$$

Now by the rules of logarithms we know that

$$\ln \frac{K(t)}{L(t)} = \ln K(t) - \ln L(t).$$

The equality of (2.6b) is is no way disturbed by taking the natural log of both sides of it. So:

$$\ln k(t) \equiv \ln \frac{K(t)}{L(t)} = \ln K(t) - \ln L(t).$$

The only further piece of information we need in order to examine changes over time in k is the rule that tells us what happens when we differentiate the natural log of a time-dependent function (like $k(t)$) with respect to t itself. This mathematical operation is saying nothing more complicated than that we are watching how the natural logarithm of a variable changes when a short period of time passes. This rule (which may be checked in any basic text) is:

$$\text{If } x = f(t), \text{ then } \frac{d \ln x(t)}{dt} = \frac{1}{x(t)} \frac{dx(t)}{dt} \text{ or } \frac{\dot{x}(t)}{x}.$$

Suppose we differentiate each of the above logarithmic terms with respect to t—which we may again do without disturbing the equality. Then:

$$\frac{d \ln k(t)}{dt} = \frac{d \ln K(t)}{dt} - \frac{d \ln L(t)}{dt}$$

which can be rewritten:

$$\frac{\dot{k}(t)}{k(t)} = \frac{\dot{K}(t)}{K(t)} - \frac{\dot{L}(t)}{L(t)} = \frac{\dot{K}(t)}{K(t)} - n(t). \tag{2.7}$$

This tells us something of considerable value. We saw earlier on that $\dot{k}/k$ measures the proportionate growth rate of k. Now we have found that $\dot{k}/k$ is found by *subtracting* the growth rate of the labour force from the growth rate of the capital stock.

Examples 2.1 and 2.2 may help to demonstrate the truth of this.

Example 2.1
Suppose that K and L both grow at 5 per cent per annum, and that the initial values of K and L are 400 and 100 respectively. According to our result, the growth rate of $k(t)$ is $K(t) - L(t)$, which in this case is $(5\% - 5\%) = 0\%$. Let's see.

	Yr 0	*Yr 1*	*Yr 2*	*Growth rate*
$K(t)$	400	420	441	0.05
$L(t)$	100	105	110.25	0.05
$k(t) (= K(t)/L(t))$:	4	4	4	0.00

Example 2.2

Now suppose $K(t)$ grows at 5 per cent but that $L(t)$ grows at 3 per cent. Initial values are as in Example 2.1. Here, we expect $k(t)$ to grow at $(5\% - 3\%) = 2\%$.

	Yr 0	*Yr 1*	*Yr 2*	*Growth rate*
$K(t)$	400	420	441	0.05
$L(t)$	100	103	106.09	0.03
$k(t)$ $(= K(t)/L(t))$:	4	4.08	4.16	$0.0194 \approx 0.02$

Dropping now the function-of-t notation, and remembering that $k \equiv K/L$, (2.7) can be rearranged to yield

$$\frac{\dot{K}}{L} = \dot{k} + nk \tag{2.8}$$

or

$$\frac{I}{L} = \dot{k} + nk. \tag{2.9}$$

Since

$$\frac{I}{L} = \left(\frac{Y}{L} - \frac{C}{L}\right) = \left|f(k) - \frac{C}{L}\right| = \frac{S}{L}$$

it must also be the case that:

$$f(k) - \frac{C}{L} = \dot{k} + nk$$

or

$$\dot{k} = f(k) - \frac{C}{L} - nk \tag{2.10}$$

and

$$\dot{k} = sf(k) - nk. \tag{2.11}$$

In words this can be interpreted as saying that the proportionate change in capital per worker equals savings per worker minus the investment required to keep an initial level of capital per worker constant. Clearly, if savings per worker (which automatically become invested) provide more capital than that required to maintain the existing capital–labour ratio as the workforce grows, then capital per worker will grow. This is merely saying in words that, if $sf(k) > nk$, then $[sf(k) - nk] > 0$

and so $\dot{k} > 0$. The converse is also true. (Think it through!) Finally, of course, if savings per worker are translated into just the exact amount required to maintain the growing labour force in capital, then $sf(k) = nk$ and $\dot{k} = 0$; in other words, capital and labour are both growing at the same rate, and so the ratio of capital to labour must be constant. (Refresh your memory on this by reference to numerical example 2.1.)

With this understanding firmly in place, look again at figure 2.2. Suppose an economy were to find itself with a capital–labour ratio of k^*. (In mathematical notation, a star usually means something special. Let us see what that is.) Associated with k^* we notice that $sf(k)$ takes a value $sf(k^*)$ and that nk takes a value nk^*. What is more, we notice that $sf(k^*) = nk^*$ so that, substituting into equation (2.11),

$$k^* = sf(k^*) - nk^* = 0.$$

Put another way, if we observe a value of k associated with the intersection of the $sf(k)$ and nk schedules, then we know that, at that level, k is not changing—which is the same as saying that K and L are growing at the same rate. Further, we know that, because of the CRS assumption, output must also be growing at the same rate. Finally, we can easily find out what this rate of growth is because we know that L is growing at n per cent per annum. If all inputs and outputs are growing at the same proportionate rate, as they are here, we have what is called a 'steady-state growth equilibrium'.

We can now look again at the propositions on pp. 25–6. Proposition (1) suggests that, eventually, the economy described in this model will 'home in' on levels of the capital–labour and output-per-man ratios at which capital, labour and output will all be growing at the same rate, n—a steady-state equilibrium.

To show this, suppose that in figure 2.2. capital per worker is not at the starred point, k^*. If $k > k^*$ (say at k_2), then you will observe that $sf(k) < nk$; that is, savings per worker are *less than* the amount required to maintain the capital–labour ratio at the level k_2, given that the labour force is growing at rate n. As a result, k will fall—which is precisely what we would expect from inspecting equation (2.7). In that equation, the fact that $sf(k) < nk$ means that $[sf(k) - nk] < 0$, or that $\dot{k} < 0$—which, of course, means that k itself is falling. (As an exercise, suppose now that $k = k_1 < k^*$ and explain to yourself why the capital–labour ratio must rise until k^* is again reached.) What this means is that, whatever values of s and n occur in an economy of the Solow type, the capital–labour ratio can be relied upon to change until a steady-state equilibrium is achieved. This, of course, implies that, in aggregate, the technology is sufficiently flexible, in the long run, to permit substitution between capital and labour inputs. It also implies that changes will occur in the ratio of rewards paid to the providers of capital and labour services. To see this look at figure 2.2 again.

Given the underlying assumption in this model of perfectly competitive factor markets, the marginal product of capital (MPK) will equal the rate of return on capital (rate of profit or interest), so the slope of a tangent to $f(k)$ tells us the rate of profit at that point.

Now for a little simple geometry.[3] Look at the tangent at H associated with k^*. The slope of this tangent, and thus the rate of profit, can be measured by the ratio DC/CH. But $CH = OJ = k^*$. Thus $r = DC/k^*$, and $rk^* = DC$. Since, by definition, $rk^* = r(K^*/L)$, DC represents the rate of profit times the capital stock divided by the labour force, in other words, the profit per labourer. We know that, with constant returns to scale, the returns to each factor (the incomes paid to them) exactly exhaust (or account for) total product available for distribution. Since labour is the only other input to production in the assumptions, wages per worker (the wage rate) must be what is left from output per man once capital has been paid. Since capital is paid DC, labour must be paid OD.

The ratio between wage and profit rates can therefore be observed by comparing OD with DC. It is even more easily observed by noting that the slope of the tangent, r, can also be measured by the ratio OD/OM. We know that OD is the wage rate w, so $r = w/OM$, and $OM = w/r$.

Returning to proposition (1), notice now what happens to the ratio w/r if k were to be at k_1 rather than k^*. A new tangent, at F, becomes the relevant one for analysis and by argument exactly analogous to that in the last two paragraphs we notice that the ratio w/r is now OB/BA or, simply, OE. Clearly, $OE < OM$, so w/r is lower than before: with a lower ratio of capital to labour, the wage rate has fallen relative to the profit rate.

CHANGES IN THE SAVINGS RATIO

Let us now examine proposition (2). This will give us the first important clue we need in understanding how a country may, by its own efforts, raise its real standard of living. If the proportion of per capita income saved rises, s becomes larger and the whole savings-per-worker schedule, $sf(k)$, swivels upwards and to the left. The factor s now scales down $f(k)$ by a lesser amount than before. With an unchanged value of n (and thus a fixed nk schedule) the result is clear: in the new equilibrium $sf(k)$ now intersects nk at a higher value of k than before, and the intersection is associated with a higher value of y than before. The economic reasoning here is also easy to grasp.

If savings per man rises from one period to the next, and is maintained for ever at this new higher level, then more investment per worker can take place each period. This in turn means that, in the new equilibrium, there will be more capital per man since labour is still continuing to grow at the same old rate, n. Given more capital per man, it is entirely predictable that the economy should be able to produce more output per man. Predictable as it is, however, the result is of great interest, for it draws our attention to raised savings ratios as a potentially important element in the development process.

Notice two points about this result. First, the new equilibrium is characterized by a higher level of income per man, but a steady-state growth rate of output and inputs, which is just the same as before: n. This must be so, because in a steady-state equilibrium (which the economy, by proposition (1), must reach, with the new savings ratio, given sufficient time) labour, capital and output are all growing together at the same rate. Second, nothing has yet been said about how the economy travels from one equilibrium to the other. In fact, such a journey (technically, a traverse) may take a very long time,[4] and during this period it will be the case (because $sf(k)$ lies above nk throughout) that savings per man generate investment at a faster rate than that required to maintain the existing capital–labour ratio in face of labour force growth. Thus K is in fact growing faster than L, and so Y/L can also grow, as clearly it must if y is to rise to new, higher, level. If the savings ratio is initially very low, then successive upward shifts in $sf(k)$ may thus not only have the desired effect of raising equilibrium levels of income per capita, but also, during periods of adjustment, lead to higher growth rates.

CHANGES IN POPULATION GROWTH

Proceeding now to proposition (3), we may rapidly obtain a second valuable clue about raising standards of living. If the rate of growth of the labour force were to fall overnight from a value n_1 per cent per annum to n_2 per cent per annum, the slope of the nk line would become less steep. (Every value of k is now multiplied by a smaller number than before, so the corresponding values of nk, measured on the vertical axis, will be lower.) If the savings per man schedule, $sf(k)$, is held constant the result will again be that, in the new equilibrium, k will be higher than before and so also income per capita will be higher. The intuitive appeal of this is that, if savings per man remain as high as before, then investment per man will not fall, but, since the labour force now grows at a slower rate than before, the ratio of capital per man must rise. Notice, though, that while the pay-off to the economy is again a higher level of income per capita, the consequences for the growth rate are that, on the new equilibrium path, inputs and output must all be growing less quickly than before, because the equilibrium growth rate is always the rate of growth of the labour force and that is now lower than before. (As an exercise, you might like to consider what happens to the growth rate of output and income per capita during the period over which the economy is adjusting to this sudden downward shift in labour force growth rate. Remind yourself, also, of what must happen to the w/r ratio.)

TECHNICAL PROGRESS

Finally, it has been recognized since the days of the early classical economists—Adam Smith, Ricardo and Malthus—that the rate of technical progress could be a crucial determinant of the rate at which an economy grew and developed. The simplest way of understanding how the effect of technical progress can be shown in our simple model is to ask what it means, in physical terms, to say that technical progress has occurred. Whatever the cause of technical progress, the effect is the same: with a given number of units of input, more output can be produced than was the case before. Thinking now in terms of figure 2.2, this means that, for any given number of capital units per worker (any chosen value of k), the value of output per man will rise over time if technical progress is occurring. Supposing this to be true for all values of k, the production function, $f(k)$, will rise steadily over time. Thus, without any change in the savings ratio or labour force growth rate, income per capita will rise steadily so long as technical progress takes place. This is clearly a most important result, and it is of great interest to developing countries to know how the rate of technical progress might be raised and what forms it might take.

The questions surrounding the measurement and impact of technical progress are many and profound, but at this stage it is well worth recognizing one important distinction that is often made. On the one hand technical progress may be 'disembodied', which means that it raises the productivity of an input without there being any qualitative change in the input itself; on the other hand, technical progress may be 'embodied', which means that a given quantity of an input becomes more output-productive *because of* some qualitative change. A good example of disembodied progress is the higher output per unit of capital input that can be derived from altering the way in which it is applied. In our simple world, where the only capital available is seed corn, a helpful analogy might be to think of a sower who casts his seed randomly over stony ground, land spoiled by weeds and fertile ground. Disembodied technical progress would involve finding better ways of distributing the seed so it fell in increasing proportions on the best of the land. (In a more complex world of many capital goods, higher output may be derived from a given number of machines involved in a production process by rearranging their positions on the shop floor so that time is reduced in carrying the unfinished product from one machine to another.) Embodied progress is perhaps more easily appreciated. With seed corn capital, embodied technical progress would take the form of improving (maybe by simple selection processes) the quality of the seed so that a greater proportion survived to grow, or more ears of corn grew on each stalk. In the more complicated world of many capital goods, it is clear that research and development effort is always improving the design of machines so that they might work faster, or in some other sense better.

The implications of this distinction are that, even if it is too poor to undertake research itself, a developing country may still increase output per unit of input, either by improving the methods by which its resources can be applied or by taking advantage of trade (see chapter 7) to import capital goods in which the research done abroad has already been embodied.

CONCLUSION

The analysis of our basic growth model is now complete. It suggests that savings, population growth and technical progress rates are all likely to play an important role in the development process. How they play their parts, and how other factors need to be incorporated alongside them, forms the substance of the rest of the book.

NOTES

1 Other recommended reading in this area is Hacche (1979); Sen (1970), which includes Solow's original article; and Solow (1970).
2 The slope of a line touching $f(k)$ (a tangent to $f(k)$) is equal to the slope of the curve at that point. The slope of a tangent to $f(k)$ is the distance between two points on the axis measuring $y(\Delta y)$ divided by the distance between the two associated values of $k(\Delta k)$; in other words, the slope of tangent $= \Delta y/\Delta k = \Delta Y/L/\Delta K/L = \Delta(Y/L) \times \Delta(L/K) = \Delta Y/\Delta K$. When the distances between points becomes very small, this measures the rate at which Y changes in response to a small change in K—which you will recognize at the definition of the marginal product of capital (MPK).
3 The analysis is developed by Jones (1975, pp. 29–33).
4 Jones (1975, p. 95) cites the work of R. Sato (*Economic Journal*, 1964) in reporting that, with 'plausible' values of the parameters adjustment to a new equilibrium might take at least 100 years.

3

The Dual Economy

Embodied in Solow's model are the explicit assumptions of a single-commodity economy and associated single production function, and the implicit assumption of full employment. As many commentators have pointed out, these assumptions are very far from accurately describing the conditions that prevail in LDCs, and analyses that have sought to provide explanations for the high observed rates of unemployment in LDCs have often done so in frameworks that also introduce a division of the economy into two distinct sectors. It is a discussion of these dual-economy (two-sector) models, and their relevance for understanding the unemployment question, that will concern us in this chapter.

THE TWO SECTORS

An economy can be divided into two parts on the basis of any one of a wide range of criteria. One sector may perform all of its transactions with money while the other uses little or no money; one sector may be 'urban' and the other 'rural'; one sector may produce only consumption goods (foodstuffs) while the other produces both consumption and capital goods (such as ploughs). While any one of these distinctions might have special relevance to one particular line of enquiry or another, we shall make use principally of a distinction that is essentially technological—to do with how production takes place. As it turns out, this criterion suggests a division that in many instances will have much in common with the divisions identified under the criteria mentioned above.

Although it is still oversimplifying matters to say so, it seems reasonable to assume that, while one part of many LDCs (the 'traditional' sector) produces output with much labour, an important land input and the assistance of little or no capital, another part (the 'modern' sector) produces its output with an important element of physical capital (machines and factories), some labour and only the bare essential amount of land.[1] In technical terms, the production functions relating inputs to output in each sector are quite different. This being the case, it is simply not permissible to use a one-sector model to represent the activities of the economy (see chapter 2, p. 22). Even if an economy did have more than one sector, it would still be permissible to use the one-commodity assumption—but only so long as the output of every commodity derived from an identical production function. In other words, the single-commodity assumption is 'safe' in a multiproduct economy only if inputs can be switched freely from one production process to another without making any difference to output. Clearly this is not the case where production functions vary from one sector to another. We therefore need to examine explicitly what might happen once we assume that two distinct sectors exist.

A SIMPLE DUAL ECONOMY MODEL

In work that later helped him to a Nobel Prize in economics, W.A. Lewis (1954, 1958) proposed a model of LDCs that Ranis and Fei (1961) later built upon, and which has proved enormously fruitful as a basis for considering the problems of developing countries. Here we shall simply integrate Lewis's model into that of Ranis and Fei (RF).

The framework of the model is a two-sector economy. The traditional sector differs from the modern primarily in that only the latter uses reproducible capital. Also we assume that the traditional sector produces only foodstuffs while the modern sector produces only 'manufactures'.[2] Assume now that this economy has a surplus of labour in the traditional sector. Strictly, a labour surplus is said to exist in a sector when an individual worker can be withdrawn from it without output in that sector falling as a result. The general reason for the existence of surplus labour is that, with the existing technology and institutional arrangements (for example, land tenure system), the labour force in a sector is so large relative to other factors of production (in the case of the traditional sector, mainly a fixed amount of land) that, at the margin, the contribution of labour is negligible or zero.[3] A further assumption is that each member of the agricultural labour force is, by social convention, provided with a food income equal to the average product of labour. This is called the subsistence wage. The situation in the traditional sector can be represented by an aggregate production function that is only a slight variation of the version with which you are already familiar (see figure 3.1). Output rises at a decreasing rate from O to $\bar{Y}$ as labour input rises from O to L_0. Notice that the horizontal axis measures men (or workers) and not man-hours, and that, once L_0 men are employed, the addition of any further labourers yields no further output. If the labour force is OL_x, therefore, L_0L_x is surplus labour. Given that total output is $O\bar{Y}$, and the total labour force OL_x, the average product of labour is $O\bar{Y} \div OL_x$, which is represented by the slope of the line OX.

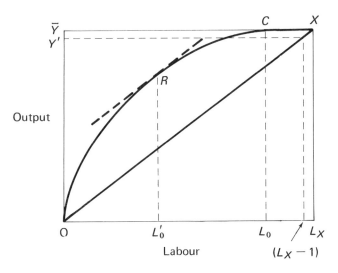

Figure 3.1 The aggregate production function and surplus labour in the traditional sector

There are two points to notice here. First, in an important way the economy seems to be under-utilizing its resources: L_0L_x men could be withdrawn from the traditional sector without its output falling; even if such men appear to be doing something, their contribution is actually nothing at all, or at least nothing that the remainder of the workforce could not easily do for them. In this sense we may say they are in *disguised unemployment*. Second, at the subsistence wage and with the given technology, a food surplus will appear if labour migrates elsewhere. Define *total agricultural surplus* (TAS) as the excess of total production over basic or subsistence consumption. Then, to measure the size of this surplus, notice that if one man left the sector, $(L_x - 1)$ men would be left and would receive OY' food in total for producing $O\bar{Y}$ output. The vertical distance $Y'\bar{Y}$ is thus left as the total agricultural surplus. For every man in the range $L_0 - L_x$ who leaves output remains at $O\bar{Y}$, so the total agricultural surplus increases by the amount he would have received if he had remained, a vertical distance equal to $Y'\bar{Y}$ each time. Once the labour force is at L_0, removal of further labour results in a fall in total output, but TAS continues to rise as long as each man's contribution at the margin (shown by the slope of a tangent to $ORCX$) continues to be less than what he would have received as a food wage. This is true over the range $L_0' - L_0$ associated with points between R and C on the production function. Once the labour force falls below L_0', TAS also starts to fall.

What is clear, then, is that an economy like this has both a labour surplus and a surplus of food produce with which it could work—if only there were another productive sector of the economy to which agricultural labour could be transferred. With this in mind, it is time to examine the modern sector.

Here it is assumed that profit-maximizing entrepreneurs are actively engaged in putting reproducible capital to work. They are capitalists. To attract labour from the traditional sector, modern sector employers offer a wage that must in real terms at least equal the subsistence wage.[4] (Modern sector employers face an infinitely elastic supply of labour at such a wage.) Since the traditional sector is large relative to the modern, the number of workers in disguised unemployment is likely easily to meet the initial requirements of the modern sector. The number of men employed is determined by the profit-maximizing condition that firms hire up to the point at which the output produced by the marginal man equals his real wage. This can best be seen in a diagram (see figure 3.2). Suppose W_M, the modern sector wage, equals the subsistence wage. Then the horizontal line at that level represents the supply curve of labour to employers. Firms' demand for labour can now be found by supposing that they have a fixed stock of capital and that the marginal product of the variable factor, labour, thus eventually falls— and at an increasing rate as shown by the marginal product of labour (MPL) schedule, AB. Now, if a labour force of less than L_1 is hired, the contribution to output of the last man is greater than the real wage paid to him, which means that there is still scope for making more profit by hiring more men. When the L_1th man is hired, however, his contribution to output is just what he is paid; and were another man to be hired, the employer would have to pay him, the $(L_1 + 1)$th man, more than he contributed to output, which would only start to reduce profits. Thus, it maximizes profit to hire just L_1 men.

Turning to the mechanics of the model, notice first that it must be to

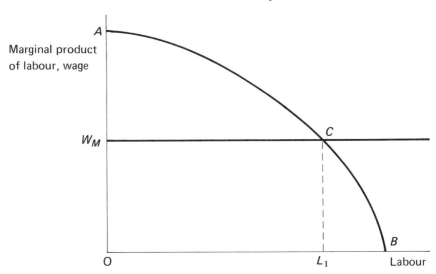

Figure 3.2 Profit-maximizing equilibrium in the modern sector

the advantage of the economy for labour to move from the traditional to the modern sector, since the availability of mechanized capital there enables it to become more productive. Indeed, so long as the MPL of labour in the modern sector exceeds that in the traditional (irrespective of whether labour's marginal product in the traditional sector is zero or not), the economy will gain by labour transferring.

Look again now at figure 3.2. The area $ACL_1 0$ under the MPL curve represents the total output produced by L_1 men. Clearly, the rectangle beneath the labour supply curve shows the total wages earned by all labour (because it is the wage per man, W_M, times the number of men, L_1), so the remaining part of output must go to the employers of labour. This residual, left after wages have been paid, is often referred to as the capitalist surplus, or just the surplus, and must not be confused with surplus labour.

The next step is absolutely crucial to understanding how the model works. It is assumed that capitalist entrepreneurs *reinvest* their surplus, in other words that capitalist income is spent wholly on buying new machines and factories. Notice the implications for employment here. In general, an expansion of productive capacity increases not only the level of output but also the number of people employed in contributing to its production. An increasing supply of capital is thus in this view the essential ingredient for ensuring a continuous expansion in employment. This can be seen diagrammatically when we notice that an

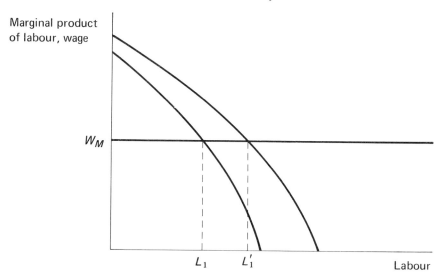

Figure 3.3 The effect of increasing the capital stock in the modern sector

increase in the capital stock must result in an outward shift of the MPL curve. At the given wage, W_M, this will mean a rise in employment offered from L_1 to L_1' (see figure 3.3).

Although we began by assuming that businessmen would reinvest the surplus, we should note that Lewis believed they would actually be induced to do so on the basis of expected results. He believed that technical advances embodied in new capital would generate productivity gains, which, because of the fixed wage, would accrue entirely to capitalists. He also believed that the capitalists' share of overall national income would rise if they reinvested, partly because their share of modern sector income would increase, and partly because the modern sector would account for an increasingly large portion of aggregate income.

It cannot be stressed strongly enough that reinvestment of the capitalist surplus is the key, in this model, to soaking up surplus labour and putting it to more effective use. The cycle of reinvestment and further hiring goes on unimpeded until the capitalist surplus is threatened and/or surplus labour is exhausted.

We can now link figures 3.1 and 3.3 together to see exactly how far this process can be expected to go and what might interrupt it.

Going back to the traditional sector, recall first that the vertical distance between OX and the production function measures total agricultural surplus. Notice now that we can also define *average*

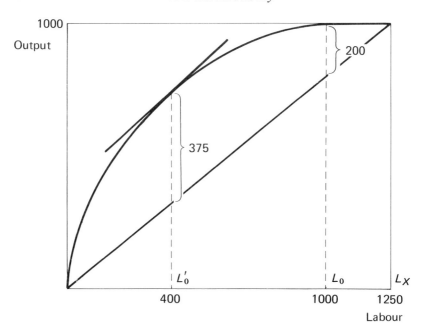

Figure 3.4 Labour migration and changes in the agricultural surplus.

Withdrawal of traditional agricultural labour from:	Total agricultural surplus changes from:	Average agricultural surplus
L_X to L_0	0 to 200	0 to 200/250 = 0.0 to 0.08
L_0 to L_0'	200 to 375	200/250 to 375/850 = 0.8 to 0.44
L_0' to 0	375 to 0	375/850 to 0 = 0.44 to 0

agricultural surplus (AAS) as the result of dividing TAS into equal parts among the non-agricultural (or modern sector) workforce. In the labour force range $L_X - L_0$, TAS rises each time a worker leaves by the amount he would have received if he had remained. Thus, for each withdrawal of labour in this range the average agricultural surplus remains constant at the subsistence food wage. Once the traditional labour force falls to L_0, however, total output starts to fall with further withdrawals, and the inevitable result is that average agricultural surplus must also fall. This is true even though total agricultural surplus continues to rise over a range. (See figure 3.4, for example.)

The significance of this should immediately be apparent. A fall in the AAS means that the food available per worker in the modern sector is diminishing. Thus the growth of the modern sector, built on the transfer of labour from the traditional sector, must, in the absence of other changes, eventually bring with it a growing scarcity in food supplies. This growing scarcity, relative to the availability of goods produced in the modern sector, generates market pressures which drive up the price of food relative to 'manufactures'. When this happens it is said that the internal terms of trade between the traditional and modern sectors turn against the modern sector. To see this, denote the price of 'manufactures' by P_M and the price of traditional sector goods by P_T. Then the internal terms of trade faced by the modern sector are defined by the ratio P_M/P_T. When P_T rises relative to P_M, this ratio falls; a given quantity of 'manufactures' will now buy less food than before. When this occurs, the wage paid in terms of modern-sector goods must rise to maintain at a constant level the wage in terms of goods consumed by labour. As soon as this starts to happen, the capitalist surplus is threatened and as a result so are the rates of reinvestment, modern sector growth and the absorption of surplus labour. This is reflected in the up-turn of the labour supply curve at C' in figure 3.5.

Another look at figure 3.5 reveals that this curve becomes even steeper at C''. The point C'' is associated with the point R on the traditional sector total product curve. Here, the marginal product of labour in the traditional sector is exactly equal to the average product, which is the subsistence wage. This is called the 'commercialization point'. If labour is withdrawn beyond this point, the agricultural real wage begins to rise in line with marginal productivity, and modern sector employers must offer higher wages if they are to compete with landlords for labour that is now increasingly scarce. (Rising agricultural wages also reduce the TAS from this point on.) Together, the worsening terms of trade and the rising agricultural wage combine to threaten the capitalist surplus even further and slow down the rate at which surplus labour is absolved.

One potential solution to these problems is to promote technical advance in the traditional sector. This would have the effect of raising the whole production function, and, whatever the form of the technical progress, must raise TAS and AAS in the early stages and increase the AAS compared with that formerly available. On the other hand, the subsistence wage must also necessarily rise, in the framework of the model, so that once again the modern sector is put under pressure.

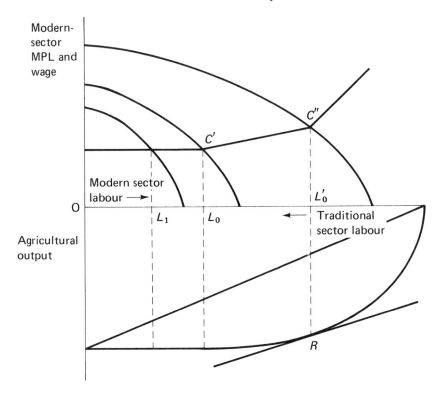

Figure 3.5 Modern sector expansion in a two-sector framework

THE DUAL ECONOMY TRADITION: EXTENSIONS AND CRITICISMS

The type of model we have been considering has proved enormously influential in leading economists to perceive the problems and characteristics of development in a specifically dualistic framework. But this approach is not without its critics. A particularly virulent attack by Griffin (1969, pp. 19–31) argues that the dualistic division is unhelpful, that the assumptions of the model are erroneous, and the predictions of the theory incorrect. As for the RF model itself, 'in its country of origin [Pakistan] it remains pathetically irrelevant'.

Criticisms of this kind cannot be ignored, and for the rest of the chapter we shall be concerned with some of the reasons why the model, as it has been presented, must be considered inadequate, and with evidence from Malaysia.

First, we shall consider an extension of the model which helps to explain better the incidence of urban unemployment. Second, we shall ask whether a two-sector view should be abandoned in favour of a more ambitious degree of division. Third, we shall see that capital may not be the only important constraint on development, as the model implies, while technical progress may also have a central role. And lastly, we shall examine the argument that demand factors are inadequately represented.

MORE ON INTERNAL MIGRATION

One over-simplification embedded in the basic model is the view that, implicitly, it conveys of internal labour migration. From an essentially rural traditional sector, a member of the surplus labour force is viewed as transferring speedily into gainful employment in the modern sector at the real wage employers offer there. As Todaro (1969) pointed out, however, migration might well, as a matter of fact, involve having to spend an initial period in what he called the 'urban traditional' sector, probably unemployed. This is the case because unskilled workers, newly arrived, need time to find out where jobs are and how to apply for them. The longer they stay in the urban traditional sector, the more likely they are to be absorbed into the modern sector.

The length of time a migrant must wait for a job will clearly depend on the difference between the rates at which supply of and demand for urban sector labour are growing. On the supply side, the urban labour force grows at a rate made up of its natural rate of increase and the rural–urban migration rate. We will assume that the death and birth rates in the modern sector are exactly equal, so that the natural growth rate is zero. The migration rate in any period is influenced by two elements:

(1) the probability of being selected for a job from the pool of unemployed in the period; and
(2) the percentage difference between the urban and rural real wage.

The probability of being selected for a job in a given period is defined by a ratio—the ratio of new modern sector employment openings (the job creation rate times total existing jobs) to the number of job-seekers already in the pool of urban unemployed (that is, the total urban labour force minus the number employed). For example, say new modern sector jobs are being created at a rate of 5 per cent a year and 10,000 members of the urban labour force already have jobs while 1000 are in the urban traditional sector, waiting. Then the probability of being selected for a job is:

$$\frac{0.05 \times 10,000}{1000} = \frac{500}{1000} = 0.5.$$

In other words, there is a '50–50 chance' that the typical migrant will be selected for a job during this year. Notice that the probability of being selected for a job in this period would be greater if: (a) the job creation rate were faster—given the existing stock of jobs and job-seekers; (b) the existing level of employment were greater ($> 10,000$)—given the job creation rate and number of job-seekers; (c) the number of job-seekers were less (< 1000)—given the job creation rate and existing jobs. The higher the overall probability of selection for employment, given the other determinants of migration, the faster migration will be because the more optimistic a migrant will be about being selected quickly for a job.

Now, turning to the second determinant of migration, it is also assumed that, the greater is the difference between urban and rural wages, the faster will be the migration rate. To find the impact of this differential it has to be 'weighted', or multiplied by the probability factor. The theory thus suggests that migration might be rapid either if the probability of selection is high (even if the wage differential is not large), or if the urban–rural wage differential is substantial (despite a relatively small probability of selection from the pool), or of course if both are high.

On the demand side, new jobs are created at a rate equal to the growth rate of modern sector output minus the rate of growth of labour productivity. (Clearly, if labour works more efficiently, or if labour-saving processes are introduced as output grows, then new employment cannot grow as fast as output itself.)

Now, suppose that this year modern sector output is growing rapidly, that businessmen offer a substantial premium to rural labour to induce it to migrate to work for them, but that, as yet, the pool of job-seekers is still small. Under these circumstances, both the probability of being selected for a job and the wage differential will be high and migration will be rapid—much more rapid, let us assume, than the rate at which jobs will be created for them. In other words, this year supply of migrant labour will exceed the demand for it.

Notice the effect of this. Because migrant labour is arriving more quickly than it can be absorbed, the number seeking employment in the urban traditional sector next year will have risen. But this in turn must *reduce* the probability, next year, of being selected for employment. To return to our example, 10,500 will be employed next year if new jobs are created at 5 per cent per year, so it will only require the number of job-seekers to rise above 1050 (a growth rate of > 5 per cent) to make the probability element fall. If the wage differential and job creation rate are fixed, this must bring about a slowing down of migration. If the new job creation rate is faster than the migration rate, the number seeking jobs will be less than 1050 next year, and since the probability element would thus rise, the migration rate would speed up, other things being equal.

The probability factor can be seen to act as an equilibrium factor. It should thus be apparent intuitively (and Todaro shows it formally) that, if we know the rate of new job creation, the size of the wage differential and the quantitative response of rural labour to given differentials, we can calculate the proportion of the urban labour force that, in equilibrium, will be employed and the proportion that will be waiting.

As our example suggests, there is no guarantee that new job creation will prevent an increase in the size of the urban traditional sector, even with a fixed wage differential; and if the wage differential in fact increases, even an increase in the rate of growth of new employment might be insufficient to prevent the absolute number of urban unemployed from rising.

Todaro has also shown that, in the long run, an increase in the rate of urban job creation may (and, he believes, usually will) work through more optimistic expectations of employment to induce an increased rate of rural–urban migration—resulting in a rise in the number of urban unemployed. This effect is often called the 'Todaro Paradox' (see Todaro, 1971b, 1976).

TWO SECTORS OR MORE?

One of the clear advantages that the dual-sector model offers over Solow's growth model is that it enables us to consider the workings of an economy that, in a very obvious way, is not homogeneous. But as some authors point out, whether descriptive accuracy or real understanding is our aim, a simple two-way division may also be inadequate.

The main argument here (Dixit, 1973) is that a third quite distinct sector can be identified in most LDCs—the service sector. This sector contains financial institutions, transport services, radio and tele-communications, government services, entertainment, wholesaling and retailing, personal services (like hairdressing) and so on. Given that the dual economy model was set up to examine employment, as much as anything, it seems unhelpful for it to ignore the service sector,

TABLE 3.1 Labour force structure, 1978

	Agriculture	Industry	Services
	%	%	%
Low-income countries	72	11	17
Middle-income countries	45	23	32
Industrialized countries	6	39	55

Source: *World Bank World Development Report* (1980).

since as table 3.1 suggests, employment in this part of the economy often forms an important proportion of the whole, and an increasingly important proportion, the higher the per capita income a country has.

It might be argued (Dixit, 1973, p. 326) that for analytical purposes the service sector can be absorbed into the modern sector, since, as borne out by the figures in table 3.1, both seem to expand at the same proportionate rate. This certainly makes for simplicity. On the other hand, to the extent that service sector activity actually influences, permits or induces modern sector growth, this strategem may deny us insights into why economies develop at different rates and in different ways.

For example, we shall see later that the growth of financial institutions may have an important role to play in raising the saving rate and directing investible resources into growth-generating employment. Growth in an economy may be slow, therefore, because this particular part of the service sector has been shown to expand. Again, an absence of reliable and efficient transport services may seriously hamper the physical transport of goods between markets within the economy, or to and from ports in the case of traded goods. This may slow down or disrupt growth. As a final example, consider radio. In countries with scattered populations and generally low levels of education, radio services are ideal for providing information that may assist in the adoption and spread of new farming methods, for encouraging participation in public health campaigns and for advertising in general.

This is also perhaps the most appropriate point to discuss what has been called the 'urban informal sector'. This usage springs from a type of dualistic classification that divides the economy into an 'informal' sector—an extension of the concept of 'traditional'—and a 'formal' sector—more or less analogous to 'modern' (Bromley, 1978, p. 1033). Although definitions in this area are fuzzy and contentious, the main characteristics of the informal sector may be taken to be the significance of self-employment; small, labour-intensive, family owned enterprises; and operation outside government rules, regulations and statistical surveillance. These features are to be compared with the formal sector's corporate structures, capital-intensive and often foreign-owned, operating within the framework of government regulations (Bromley, 1978, pp. 1033–4). The informal sector can, in turn, be divided into urban and rural elements—the former essentially similar to Todaro's 'urban traditional' sector.

The descriptive appeal of this approach is that it seems to relate to the large 'shanty towns' that can be observed on the outskirts of many cities in developing countries. From an analytical point of view, however, the usefulness of the distinction seems to be limited by its fuzziness. If we do focus on the characteristics of productive activities, as above, then the division cannot be drawn even over individuals, much less over families or neighbourhoods. The reason is that an individual (and, more so, a family or community) may 'commute' between formal and informal sector activities seasonally, or even during the day. Given that members of the urban informal sector cannot, either, be considered as uniformly poor (for example, self-employed artisans might well be better off than wage-paid labour working for corporate bodies), it is hard to know precisely what extra insights might be generated in respect of the connections between growth, employment and poverty (Bromley, 1978, p. 1035).

While definitional problems beset the debate, we should in fairness note that the originator of the distinction (Hart, 1973) was genuinely concerned to ask whether the informal sector could offer a hitherto unrecognized source of independent growth and employment in a developing economy. Given this concern, there may be something to be said for concentrating on the role of 'petty commodity production' (Moser, 1978, p. 1057), a form of activity describing much of the work undertaken by the small-scale enterprises envisaged as characterizing the informal sector. The urban petty commodity sector, says Moser (1978, p. 1058), includes artisan production and trading, providing goods and services not only for its own consumption but, importantly, for the formal sector, where it has concerned itself with activity considered unprofitable by foreign or larger-scale enterprise. As artisan skills become more varied, activity in the sector can grow and diversify, thus providing new sources of income as well as more and cheaper household goods and services to the relatively poor. On the other hand, it has also been argued that, precisely because the sector provides goods more cheaply than would otherwise have been the case, formal sector employers are able to continue paying low wages to their workers. From its own point of view, moreover, the petty commodity sector may have to obtain its raw materials at inflated prices from the formal sector upon which it depends and yet not be able to gain access either to credit or more sophisticated technology. The sector may therefore find any upward movement in its standard of living much impeded (see Moser, 1978, pp. 1058–9).

We have looked at two different ways in which a developing economy may be divided into more than two parts: in one case separating out the service sector, in the other suggesting that an 'informal' sector as distinct from the formal might be divided into urban and rural sub-sectors. Is there any case for yet further subdivision? There are really two answers to this question. On the one hand, if we want to know the precise interrelationships between every industry in the economy, then as the economy becomes more diversified, further disaggregation will be necessary. But, then, what purpose would it serve to know about such relationships? Admittedly, planners may be able to use this information if they want to know how the expansion of industry A might influence the demand for the output of industry B, imports of inputs into industry A (and B), and the labour requirements of each. On the other hand, it might be quite sufficient to know in principle that such linkages and repercussions are likely to occur without needing to know much about them in detail. Detailed knowledge of all the interrelationships might, indeed, obscure a more general understanding of the whole. In other words, we use models to simplify the world in a way that enables us to understand it better. The more divisions we introduce into a model, the more complicated and inaccessible it becomes—and the less likely it is to generate illumination.

SUPPLY-SIDE FACTORS

The Wage
It was stated earlier that a rise in the real wage of labour at an early stage in the development process could prematurely slow down the rate at which surplus labour was absorbed.

Consider now the circumstances under which the wage, which in the model is assumed constant in terms of modern sector output, might rise. In many countries, the wage is actually fixed in money terms. If, in these circumstances, an increase in output resulting from an expanded capital stock is associated with a fall in the price of modern sector goods, then the wage, fixed in money terms, will rise if calculated in terms of modern sector goods. Clearly, this effect is even more marked if the money wage itself rises. Alternatively, imagine that the wage is actually fixed in terms of the goods that labour consumes—goods derived from both sectors. Then, if the internal terms of trade shift against the modern sector, as we observed earlier, this too will raise the wage measured in terms of modern sector goods. Trade union activity and government minimum wage legislation can act independently of or together with non-institutional factors to raise labour's wage.

Technology and Technical Progress
A factor that may slow the rate at which labour is absorbed as output increases is the nature of the production function. It is by no means impossible that, even with a given factor−price ratio, it might be profit-maximizing to move towards techniques with a higher capital−labour ratio. This possibility is illustrated in figure 3.6, where at the low levels of output Q_1 and Q_2 it is profit-maximizing to use a relatively labour-intensive technique (i.e. a low K/L ratio represented by the slope of the ray $OABN$), while at higher levels of output such as Q_3 it becomes profit-maximizing to use a technique with a higher K/L ratio (represented by the slope of the ray OCM). This reflects the possibility that certain 'labour-saving devices' are available on larger machines, which it is possible to install only when output levels are high.

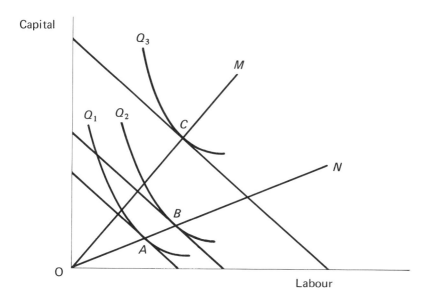

Figure 3.6 Increasing capital-intensity with higher output levels

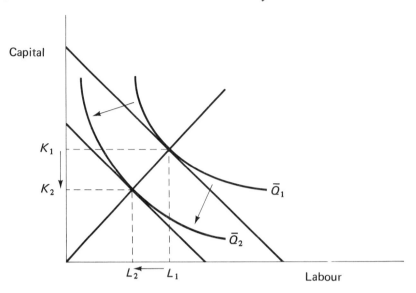

Figure 3.7 Hicks-neutral technical progress

This picture may become even more threatening to the rate of employment creation if technical progress occurs over time, as Lewis envisaged. Technical progress can be represented by the inward shift of an isoquant, proclaiming the fact that a given output level can be achieved with less of either or (usually) both inputs. This reduction in the use of inputs reflects the fact that technical progress permits more effective use to be made of them. The extent and nature of the technical progress can be observed by examining, at a given rent–wage ratio, the changes in capital and labour used, and the ratios in which they are used, in the pre- and post-progress situations.

Look first at figure 3.7. Here it will be observed that the isoquant relating to the production of output level $\bar{Q}$ has shifted inwards from $\bar{Q}_1$ to $\bar{Q}_2$ in such a way that *equal* proportionate savings are made in the employment of both capital and labour. Less of each input is thus used in producing $\bar{Q}$, but the ratio in which they are used is the same in each case: $K_1/L_1 = K_2/L_2$. When this occurs, *Hicks-neutral technical progress* is said to have taken place (after the economist Sir John Hicks).

Now turn to figure 3.8. In this case output $\bar{Q}$ is produced with substantially less labour (as a percentage of the original amount, L_2) but only a small proportion less of capital than before. Clearly, $K_2/L_2 >$

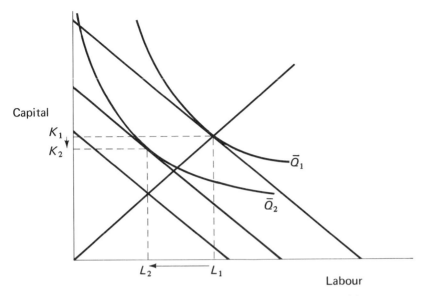

Figure 3.8 Technical progress with a labour-saving bias

K_1/L_1. Since the capital–labour ratio is taken as a measure of capital intensity, the new technique clearly involves a much higher degree of capital intensity than the old, and technical progress, given the unchanged wage, is said to have a *labour-saving bias*.

The purpose of this discussion is to draw attention to the fact that, if reinvestment in equipment occurs over time, it is almost unavoidable that design and other improvements will occur which might well reduce the employment opportunities associated with producing a given output level. This need not necessarily be so, of course: technical progress could just as logically have a capital-saving bias as a labour-saving bias, and figure 3.9 illustrates how such change could imply no loss of employment at all.

Despite the logical soundness of this argument, however, it has often been pointed out that technical improvements tend to be made predominantly in advanced industrial nations, where capital is much more plentiful relative to labour than in LDCs. This leads, it is said, to a general bias towards labour-saving technical change.

Two further points must be made before we leave this important area. First, the employment-displacing effects of labour-saving technical progress will be magnified to the extent that new techniques are embodied in replacement investment as well as in net additions to the

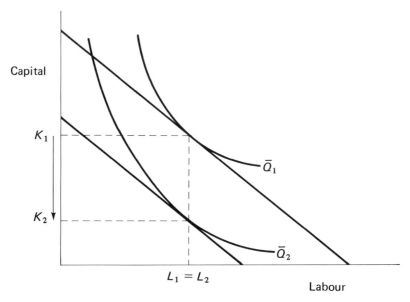

Figure 3.9 Purely capital-saving technical progress

capital stock. But, second, technical progress always brings with it the potential for creating employment as well as displacing it. It is extremely important to realize this.

Employment-creating potential is the result of technical progress raising the productivity of an industry. Increased productivity permits an industry to reduce the price of its product, and, indeed, under competitive conditions it will be forced to do this. The faster a firm's, an industry's, a sector's or an economy's rate of productivity increases relative to those of other firms, industries, sectors or economies, the faster it will also be able to reduce its relative price, and the more attractive its product will thus become in the market. Given price-elastic demand, a larger market will thus be created. To compensate for the job losses noted earlier, therefore, there will be a job-creating effect derived from expanding demand. The crucial question (which can be answered only empirically) is, which effect dominates? Most evidence suggests that those industries that show most rapid productivity gains are also those that generate the highest employment growth rates.

Co-operant Factors
In the basic model it is capital that is represented as the major constraint

upon development. Increase the saving rate, it suggests, and (assuming it is invested domestically with productive results) the economy can and must proceed to grow. Missing from this story, however, is a sufficient emphasis on the fact that physical capital, by itself, cannot do the job. Labour with certain skills is required to operate it; energy inputs are needed to make it work; entrepreneurs must be on hand to identify profitable areas to invest in and then to organize all the inputs in the productive process so that firms and industries run efficiently. All of these factors are called *co-operant inputs*.

The role of education and training in providing human capital is discussed in chapter 6. Notice here that certain manual and administrative skills are self-evidently necessary to make machines effective in their contribution to output, and in ensuring that material inputs flow in smoothly when needed while a record of all transactions is kept, bills are paid and accounts collected. In subsistence agricultural economies substantial mechanical maintenance and administrative skills are unlikely to exist. There is thus an immediate impediment to growth. In the context of our model, this can be resolved in two obvious ways. First, modern sector businesses may provide on-the-job training. Second, businesses may collaborate, or government act on their behalf, to set up educational institutions. In either case, the consequences are worth noting. On-the-job training will, at least initially, result in businesses incurring real costs in addition to the wage: materials will be spoiled and wasted; inexperience will be reflected in inefficient methods; senior staff will have to spend time on instruction that they could have spent doing other tasks. The higher the turnover rate of employees and the slower the learning rate, the more severe will these costs be. The result is that the much-needed surplus is eroded, and in the short run the rate of reinvestment and growth thus threatened. Similarly, colleges are costly to build and run, and whether each firm pays a training levy or a government tax to finance education, its surplus is again reduced. Even in order to make use of a given capital stock, therefore, the modern sector must incur substantial costs to obtain necessary skills, and this in turn will result in a growth rate initially less rapid than that which could have been achieved with an already skilled labour force.

A co-operant input even more basic to the needs of industry is energy. By definition, economically productive activity involves adding value. But value can be added to physical objects in only one of three ways: changing their shape (material transformations, examples of which are forming regularly shaped bricks from naturally occurring clay or stamping out car bodies from steel sheets); changing their location (for example, driving agricultural products to market); or storing them over time (as when letting newly brewed beer stand until it is at its most palatable). Such value-adding activity almost invariably requires inputs of energy,[5] but not all countries have energy in the form or quantity they require.

In countries richly endowed with energy resources usable in existing technologies this is not a problem—or at least, it is a problem only to the extent that some energy forms can be used, at present, only with capital-intensive techniques which do not absorb much labour. The worst-off countries are those whose energy resources are of a kind for which existing technologies have not yet been extensively developed (such as solar, wind and wave energy). In between are countries with some energy endowments suitable for use in existing technology, but insufficient or of too poor quality to meet all their needs. For these countries, the ever-present realization must be that they are drawing on an exhaustible resource. There is a clear limit to the coal, oil or gas deposits in a country, and a limit also to the hydro-power that a country's dams and rivers may generate. LDCs may therefore find themselves faced with an absolute physical constraint, imposed by their usable energy resources, on the rate at which they can employ capital. In the effort to ease such constraints, surplus-eroding costs will be incurred in searching for new deposits of fossil fuels and in seeking ways of slowing down the rate of energy consumption—in other words, by research and development activity to develop more efficient techniques of energy use.

The final co-operant input, a severe scarcity of which may upset the smooth running of the model, is entrepreneurship. Our basic model assumes the existence of a class of entrepreneurs to make the necessary investments, but it has often been suggested that this implies too optimistic a view. The definition of entrepreneurship is in some ways elusive. While it 'clearly refers to the capacity for innovation, investment and activist expansion in new markets, products and techniques'[6] (Leff, 1979), some commentators have in addition stressed the managerial component of a businessman's activities (Kaldor, 1934). Here we shall concentrate broadly on two general aspects of entrepreneurial activity: the ability to see and grasp risky business ventures in an environment of poor information and limited markets, and the capacity to organize inputs efficiently once the venture is set up.

In a world of perfect certainty (or, alternatively, in a world with such a wealth of markets that contracts could be made to take account of anything that might happen in an uncertain future), the risk-taking role of the entrepreneur could not exist. But as we all know, the world is an uncertain place (no one can with certainty predict the future), and also it lacks a market structure that, to any more than a limited extent, can cope with that fact.[7] These statements are particularly true for LDCs. An important implication of this is that businessmen can only guess at what their future costs and sales revenues will be and therefore at whether the profitability of an investment over time will make it worthwhile having laid out the capital to set it up initially. There is, quite simply, risk involved.

As it happens, a businessman in an LDC probably faces much more uncertainty than his counterparts elsewhere. Information about the size of the domestic market and potential production costs will be particularly difficult to assemble if important parts of the economy do not use money to make transactions; if the quantity and quality of skilled labour available at any given wage is uncharted; if supplies of materials are unreliable, as may particularly be the case in landlocked countries; if the price and availability of financial capital are arbitrarily determined outside the market; and so on.

The special significance of the entrepreneur for development is, in terms of this stage of the argument, twofold. First, he has and uses a special aptitude for seeing a potentially profit-making and income-generating opportunity, despite the fog of uncertainty that surrounds him. The country benefits from the entrepreneur's developing and following up his 'hunches'—either to the extent that resources are successfully combined in production that would not otherwise have occurred, or, if he was wrong, to the extent that it learns more about the way its economy is structured. Second, the more that an entrepreneur uses his own capital, the more he himself bears the risks we have talked about. The less well developed are financial institutions (banks, stock markets and so on), therefore, the more a country must rely on the risk-bearing proclivities of a class of enterprising individuals if it is to benefit in the ways just described, and the more it needs such willingness to take risk to ensure development.

Until about 20 years ago there was considerable pessimism about the entrepreneurial capacities of most LDCs. It was believed that, for primarily socio-cultural reasons, entrepreneurial attitudes and aptitudes were unlikely to develop at the rate required to permit rapid growth and structural change to occur. To some extent these fears have been allayed. There is widespread evidence now of entrepreneurial behaviour in a great variety of cultural settings. One important explanation for this is that the economic framework changed in ways that reduced the risks perceived by the would-be investor. Protective and pricing policies implemented by governments, for example, brought new elements of certainty into the economic future, by apparently guaranteeing a market for the investor's product. This in turn stimulated the supply of entrepreneurship.[8]

Two other supply responses should also be noted. First, there has been the emergence of the 'group'—'a large-scale firm that invests and produces in several product lines that involve vertical integration or other economic and technological complementarities' (Leff, 1979, p. 52). Group capital is often derived from an interlinking network of family and institutional wealth. Its mobilization reflects the perception that single-product firms are at much greater risk than diversified businesses, and that the inadequacy of financial capital markets can be overcome partially by a pooling of wealth and information within a group framework. The second, perhaps more obvious, response has been for government itself and its agencies to act as entrepreneur.

While the supply of entrepreneurship in its risk-taking role may not have turned out to be an insuperable problem, it remains the case that much productive activity in LDCs is inefficiently managed. Capital, supposedly scarce, is none the less often grossly underutilized;[9] stocks of material inputs are frequently allowed to fall below the level required to keep a business in continuous production; theft and corruption may go unprosecuted; and the labour force is in many cases insufficiently closely supervised to prevent its members from doing what they prefer more than what is profit-maximizing. (This last, which betokens a failure to extract and direct the profit-maximizing effort from labour, is often called *X-inefficiency*, a term invented by Leibenstein, 1978.)

We shall not pursue this any further, but it is worth noting that those same policies that can be said to stimulate the initial flow of entrepreneurship may also be to blame for allowing inefficiency to have developed and survived subsequently.

DEMAND-SIDE FACTORS

An important implication of the basic dual-sector model is that an increase in the capital stock will bring with it an increase in employment of equal proportions—assuming a homothetic production function, the availability of co-operant inputs, and no tendency to invest in increasingly capital-intensive equipment. But there is a fundamental question of which this view fails to take account: why should capitalists invest in the first place? It makes sense to reinvest the surplus in capital goods only if it is clear that the additional output that will be produced can be sold. In other words, it is being implicitly assumed that there will be a demand for the extra goods produced. It has long been realized that this demand-side problem could be serious. Nurkse, for example, states:

The trouble is this: there is not a sufficient market for manufactured goods in a country where peasants, farm labourers and their families, comprising typically two-thirds to four-fifths of the population, are too poor to buy any factory products, or anything in addition to the little they already buy. [Nurkse, 1959, p. 41]

The obvious answer to this is to promote higher incomes in the farm sector by introducing more efficient production techniques and higher-yielding varieties, and by land reform. Higher agricultural productivity should raise real purchasing power and thus stimulate demand and modern-sector investment. On the other hand, moves of this kind may well also drive up modern sector wages and thus reduce, on the supply side, the amount of capital available for reinvestment.

A different approach is to argue that, with given prices, money wage and any capital stock, the demand for labour and level of output can be determined through the production function. Aggregate demand comprises aggregate consumption and aggregate investment. The consumption element can be found by applying a consumption function to real income generated in producing the known output. If it is now assumed that anything not consumed is saved and immediately invested, then demand exists for all that has been produced.

As much of modern economics has been at pains to show, however, supply does not instantaneously create its own demand in this way. In particular, if some output is not 'snapped up' at existing prices, the prices of goods left on the shelf will in due course fall as the seller attempts to get rid of them. Faced with these conditions upon having expanded capacity once, producers are unlikely to install yet more capital—and take on more labour—even if there is a surplus available.

The important conclusion to emerge from discussions of this kind is that overall growth and development in a two-sector economy cannot be achieved simply by looking at supply-of-capital considerations. If the modern sector is to rely on domestic sources to feed its workforce and to provide it with a reservoir of investible resources, only the agricultural sector can do the job. Expansion of the modern sector therefore creates demand for primary products. On the other hand, the rate of expansion also depends on the rate at which demand for modern sector output grows. If the agricultural sector increases its capacity to supply the modern sector by undertaking productivity-raising advances, modern sector products will be used in making these advances and the additional incomes generated will also create further demand for the output of the modern sector. Efforts to raise agricultural productivity are therefore important for both sectors—although it must not be forgotten that higher incomes in the agricultural sector will put upward pressure on industrial wages at the same time.

THE DUAL ECONOMY: AN EXAMPLE

A developing country within which many of the features of dual economies can be identified is Malaysia. Malaysia actually comprises West Malaysia (the Malayan Peninsula south of Thailand but excluding Singapore, which seceded from the Malaysian Federation in 1965), Sarawak and Sabah, but we shall focus in places on developments in the west, formerly Malaya.

Historically, Malaya followed a pattern common to many LDCs, seeing its modern sector established on the basis of primary products intended mainly for export. Until the late 1950s it would have been reasonable to describe the modern sector as an 'enclave' producing the primary commodities rubber and tin. Coexisting with this sector was a low-productivity subsistence sector, growing rice and coconuts and catching fish.

In recent decades, West Malaysia has experienced rapid population and labour force growth rates (with the fastest natural increase in population occurring in rural areas). Since the 1950s, the labour force has been growing at an average of about 3 per cent per annum. Although definitional problems surround estimates of magnitudes, open (as opposed to disguised) unemployment grew between 1962 and 1972, as shown in table 3.2. On the other hand, rural underemployment appears to be dominantly seasonal. One study of West Malaysian villages revealed that, although the rate of underemployment among men was

TABLE 3.2 Growth of unemployment in West Malaysia, 1962–72

	Urban unemployment rate	Rural unemployment rate	Overall
	%	%	%
1962	8.9	5.0	6
1967/8	9.9	5.4	6.8
1972	10.2	6.0	7.5

Source: Blake (1973); reprinted in Lim (1975).

well over 30 per cent for the whole year, it varied with rice cropping demands from an effective rate of zero during peak harvesting months to over 50 per cent at other times (Purcal, 1975). Female employment rates fluctuated even more widely with season. The study concludes, however, that, while no single farm could maintain output levels if labour were permanently withdrawn from it, the whole sector's rice production total could be produced with fewer workers. This is because rice harvesting seasons occur at different times in the year across West Malaysia. Were a part of the labour force to migrate regularly from one harvesting location to another, each worker in this fraction could be fully employed while releasing the remainder. In other words, instead of 100 per cent of the workforce working, say, at 70 per cent of its 'fully employed capacity', 70 per cent of the workforce could do the same amount of work by being fully employed throughout the year—releasing 30 per cent of the workforce, which could be described as the surplus.

The experience of Malaysia illustrates many of the points we have made in relation to the supply side of a dual economy's development. The manufacturing sector accounted for 21 per cent of GDP in 1980—representing a 50 per cent increase on its 14 per cent share in 1970. This growth was built on an active investment programme: commercial banks' loans and advances to the sector grew at an average of almost 20 per cent per annum between 1974 and 1980. Further, Malaysia has become a major world producer of palm oil, importantly as the result of capital funds pumped into setting up infrastructure and mills for the industry by the government-sponsored Federal Land Development Authority. As a result of this and other capital investment, many thousands of new jobs have been created. In manufacturing alone, employment was rising by 40,000–50,000 new jobs a year in the late 1970s.

On the other hand, while the rapidly expanding petroleum industry accounted for 12 per cent of private investment in 1980, it is by nature so capital-intensive that it has created relatively few jobs. And even in manufacturing, the growth of demand for unskilled labour is slowing—officials believe as a result of increasing capital intensity in techniques used.

The services sector is, as usual, an important employer, representing 37 per cent of the total employed in 1980. As far as supply-side constraints are concerned, Malaysia's domestic oil and gas reserves have helped it ward off any energy constraint, and with 60 per cent of its population aged less than 24 the country has concentrated on educating and training its youthful potential labour force to avoid skill bottlenecks. Comparing Malaysia with other middle-income developing countries, it has a higher proportion of eligible age groups in primary and secondary school than the average, although its 60 per cent adult literacy rate is somewhat below the average.

On the question of entrepreneurship, this class of input has been dominated historically by the Chinese, and in an effort to promote indigenous Malay business operation, official assistance (loans and technical advice) has been proffered. While this may have an impact in the long run, entrepreneurial spirit cannot be fostered by these means alone, and one commentator has suggested that other elements that have contributed to the growth of such aptitudes are mixing with the Chinese and experiencing periods of personal hardship (Popenoe, 1973).

Given the rapid growth of employment opportunities in service and manufacturing industry, it should not be surprising to find that there has been evidence of an increasing flow of net internal migration to the urban areas. In fact, urban population has grown more quickly than rural, even though natural population growth is faster in rural areas.

The role of demand-related factors in ensuring modern sector growth can be seen from a number of angles. Aggregate demand derives from foreign sources on the one hand, generating the export component, and domestic sources on the other—for consumption and investment goods and services. In 1957 exports accounted for 47 per cent of GDP and the bulk of this demand comprised orders for rubber and tin. Since the early 1960s, however, the demand for rubber has been undermined by synthetic substitutes, and between 1970 and 1980 the share of rubber in agricultural output (itself a declining proportion of overall production) fell from about 50 per cent of value added in agriculture to 30 per cent. In the case of tin, technological developments have permitted economies in the use of the metal for plating, and where 74,000 tonnes were produced in 1970, the total dropped to 62,500 tonnes in 1980. With declining demand here, derived demand for labour in these industries was also reduced, and it has been necessary to turn to other sources of international demand to maintain employment in the export sector. (See earlier for the supply-side efforts here and chapter 7 for linkage effects.)

While international factors are certainly important, recent work also suggests that low levels of domestic demand could also help explain why injections of capital cannot always be expected to generate new employment opportunities of similar proportions.

In a study based on Malaysian data for 1970, Lysy (1980) investigated

TABLE 3.3 Simulated changes in employment and value added for Malaysia under varying wage, technology, and export price elasticity assumptions.

Equation no.	Description	Capital change	Elasticity of substitution	Export price elasticity	Change in value added	Change in employment
		%			%	%
Money wages fixed						
(A1)	Benchmark	+ 10	1.5	3.0	+ 3.45	− 3.23
(A2)	Variations in price elasticity	+ 10	1.5	0.3	− 2.87	− 15.44
(A3)		+ 10	1.5	6.0	+ 5.77	+ 1.39
(A4)		+ 10	1.5	10.0	+ 7.13	+ 4.12
(A5)	Variations in elasticity of substitution	+ 10	0.3	3.0	+ 8.15	+ 6.30
(A6)		+ 10	3.0	3.0	+ 0.26	− 9.79
(A7)		+ 10	5.0	3.0	− 2.21	− 14.90
Wage fixed in terms of goods labour consumes						
(B1)	Benchmark	+ 10	1.5	3.0	+ 7.0	+ 3.87
(B2)	Variations in export price elasticity	+ 10	1.5	0.3	− 5.65	− 20.62
(B3)		+ 10	1.5	6.0	+ 8.44	+ 6.80
(B4)	Variations in elasticity of substitution	+ 10	0.3	3.0	+ 9.30	+ 8.57
(B5)		+ 10	3.0	3.0	+ 4.87	− 0.50

Source: Lysy (1980, pp. 552, 562).

the effects of a 10 per cent rise in the capital stock on employment, making alternative assumptions about the way in which the modern sector wage might be fixed, and under a range of assumptions relating to the substitutability of capital for labour (reflected in varying values of the elasticity of substitution) and to the price elasticity of demand for exports. A summary of his results is presented in table 3.3.

The conclusions from this table are instructive. In the Malaysia of 1970, value added and employment would both have risen most (though not equiproportionally), with a 10 per cent increase in capital stock if the elasticity of substitution between capital and labour had been low, given a price elasticity of demand for exports taking a value (3.0) characteristic of a small open economy (see (A5) and (B4)). Higher values of the elasticity of substitution, on the other hand, would have generated reduced employment-creating effects following a capital injection, given the export elasticity. The reason for this lies in the influence that variations in the substitution elasticity have upon domestic consumption demand—reflecting the importance that we placed upon the role of domestic demand in our analysis. The employment-creating production of output increases, assuming no input constraints, in response to increased demand—made up of consumption demand from wages and profits, investment demand and export demand. We treat investment demand as exogenously fixed, export demand as determined by the export price elasticity and consumption demand as determined simply by wage or profit incomes.

As Lysy formally shows, the price of adding value (made up of payments to capital and labour feeding through the cost function) falls when the capital stock increases, and this has a twofold effect. On the one hand, it raises demand for exports, but on the other, it will also reduce the large and important element of labour's consumption demand if the elasticity of substitution is high and the increased supply of capital merely substitutes for capital. Thus the optimistic results reported at the start of the previous paragraph suggest that technical inflexibility not only may inhibit labour–capital substitution, but also is required to maintain at a relatively high-level labour consumption demand. In the Malaysian case, increased export demand could by no means have been guaranteed to offset reduced domestic labour consumption demand.

A further finding in the study is that increasing exogenous demand (investment and government expenditure), even if only by an amount that would not have worsened the balance of trade, would have been particularly effective in raising employment.

CONCLUSION

In this chapter we have examined some of the implications of moving from a single-commodity full-employment growth model to a two-sector model in which unemployment is explicitly dealt with. We have found that a conventional type of dual economy model stresses the importance of reinvesting the capitalist surplus to build up the capital stock in the modern sector. The results are that new sources of employment are created and overall economic growth is promoted as labour, whose contribution to output was formerly negligible, moves to a sector where its productivity is much greater. Notice here that, despite an apparently different framework of analysis, the importance of saving for investment to increase the capital stock is just as great as it was in the one-sector model. As a consequence, anything that endangers the capitalist surplus poses a constant threat to the dynamism of the economy.

Just as Solow's model must be scrutinized for shortcomings, so must the basic dual economy model. We have noted that migration behaviour may well lead to urban as well as rural unemployment; that omitting a service sector from explicit analysis could be dangerous; that capital accumulation, by itself, is not a sufficient condition for growth from a supply-side point of view because of the additional requirement of co-operant inputs. It has been suggested that a fuller analysis should also include a demonstration of how demand for modern sector output can be guaranteed to grow at the same rate as output itself.

In the same way that Solow's model was suggestive and fruitful, however, so has the basic dual economy model been. Although in its simplest form it probably is *too* simple, it none the less has led naturally into other avenues of enquiry which have done much to illuminate developmental problems.

FURTHER READING

The seminal papers in this area are due to Sir Arthur Lewis (1954), and Ranis and Fei (1961). The former, like all of Lewis's work, is extremely readable and actually contains the seeds of much of the work done since. The latter presents essentially the same arguments with the aid of an extensive diagrammatic treatment of both sectors and their relationship to one another. Dixit's article (1973) critically summarizes most of the dual economy literature in a valuable, albeit condensed and somewhat mathematical, form. He also presents a helpful summary of the contribution of Jorgenson in this area. More recent analytical papers worth consulting include Fei and Ranis (1975); Bertrand and Squire (1980); and Lele and Mellor (1981).

The migration literature has now taken on a life of its own, and in addition to the Todaro references noted in the text, it would be useful to consult Harris and Todaro (1970). While Todaro's approach essentially focuses upon the disequilibrium and adjustment features of the dual economy, his work with Harris concentrates more on the characteristics of a dual economy that has already attained equilibrium with a certain level of unemployment. The latter approach is perhaps best appreciated by reading Corden and Findlay (1975). This paper contains a most helpful diagrammatic exposition.

More on the service sector can be found in Galenson (1963) and Bhalla (1971).

Finally, on the issue of entrepreneurship, a wide variety of viewpoints and perspectives can be found in Kilby (1971), the preface to which, by Kilby himself, is particularly good value.

NOTES

1 If the modern sector comprises commercial agriculture, land will play a more important role.
2 This is very much a label of convenience for the purposes of making a clear distinction. In fact, as Lewis points out, the modern sector might well produce agricultural commodities too, but on commercial estates or plantations using mechanized capital.
3 Notice that at least two obvious alternative interpretations of this condition are possible. In one case there might simply be no way, technically, in which labour can contribute further to output. In the other case, when a labourer leaves the traditional sector, those remaining behind work a little harder or longer to make up for his departure.
4 Lewis assumed that a substantial premium must be offered above the subsistence wage to overcome fears of moving and to compensate for the higher cost of living in towns. RF incorporate no such premium, and neither shall we.
5 Only some forms of storage might be exceptions.
6 It is Leff's approach that we follow in the ensuing paragraphs.
7 Examples of markets that have been set up to cope with future uncertainty are insurance markets.

8 We shall see later (chapter 7) that these types of policy are anything but an unmixed blessing, however. Protected business is almost always inefficient business.

9 A substantial literature on this topic exists. See Winston (1975); Kim and Kwon (1977); Lecraw (1978).

4

Domestic Resource Mobilization

As we observe at several points in this book, the accumulation of productive capital assets is one of the major keys to economic development. The mobilization of resources for this purpose is the subject of this chapter: the process of investment and criteria for effective investment are discussed in the next.

In Solow's model, saving is set at a fixed proportion of real income in a world abstracting from governments and international trade. With a one-commodity economy, any abstention from consumption is automatically investment in the one good that the economy possesses. Furthermore, with perfect factor markets, any change in the parameters of the model (say, a fall in the population rate) sets in motion price adjustments that ensure that, at the existing saving rate, a changing capital–output ratio, reflecting changing techniques, will take the economy to a new equilibrium.

This begs many questions. To start with, how is the savings ratio determined at any point in time, and should we expect it to be a constant? Since, all other things equal, changes in the savings ratio lead to changes in income per capita and, for a while, changes in the growth rate, what can be done to influence it? We shall see that a wide range of influences operate upon the voluntary saving behaviour of individuals and these are examined in a simple two-period consumption framework. Evidence relating to the savings ratio in LDCs is also discussed. Governments often believe that the savings ratio should be raised, and we shall look at the weapons available to them: persuasion, education, and inducement, through extending and liberalizing savings institutions. If such encouragement of voluntary saving fails, governments can turn to more forceful means: taxation, or manipulation of the domestic terms of trade. Finally, if domestic sources of saving prove inadequate, foreign savings can be tapped, by looking to private capital inflows or seeking aid. This aspect of resource mobilization is not developed fully in this chapter but is left until later in the book.

BASIC SAVINGS THEORY

Suppose all consumers in a society are utility-maximizers: they want to reach the highest indifference curve they can, given the constraints they face. Initially, assume that utility is to be maximized over only two periods, this year and next. Utility will be derived from consumption in each period, C_0 and C_1, and income in each period, Y_0 and Y_1, given the opportunities available for borrowing and lending at some positive rate of interest, r. To simplify the analysis, we will assume $Y_0 = Y_1$ unless otherwise stated.

If a consumer lends all Y_0 at the beginning of the year, he will receive $Y_0 + r(Y_0)$ at the end, which he can add to Y_1 to use for consumption next year. The potential purchasing power available to him next year is thus

$$Y_1 + (1 + r)Y_0.$$

Notice now that the consumer could also borrow in the market, again at r. We have already seen that Y_0 will next year be worth $(1 + r)Y_0$ if lent for a year at rate r, so the value today of $(1 + r)Y_0$ not received until next year we know to be Y_0 today.

Y_0 is called the *present value* of $(1 + r)Y_0$ in this simple two-period case: it is the amount that, if lent at r for a year, will generate $(1 + r)Y_0$. The exact relationship between Y_0 and $(1 + r)Y_0$ is clear: $(1 + r)Y_0$ must be divided by $(1 + r)$ to bring its value back, or *discount* it, to today's value. To find the present value of any amount Y_1 received next period, we must divide that amount by $(1 + r)$. If the consumer borrows in the market, the most he can expect to raise now is the present value of the income he will receive next period since, looking at the question from the lender's point of view, next year's income is all that this consumer will have available to pay back the loan, principal and interest. Since the consumer expects to receive Y_1 next year, the most he can borrow is thus $Y_1/(1 + r)$. It can easily be checked that this is right by looking at it from the lender's position. At year-end he will receive:

$$[Y_1/(1 + r)] + [Y_1/(1 + r)]r = [Y_1/(1 + r)](1 + r) = Y_1.$$

Thus, the potential purchasing power available to the consumer this year—assuming he uses all next year's income, as soon as it arrives, to pay off his debts—is:

$$Y_0 + \frac{Y_1}{1 + r}.$$

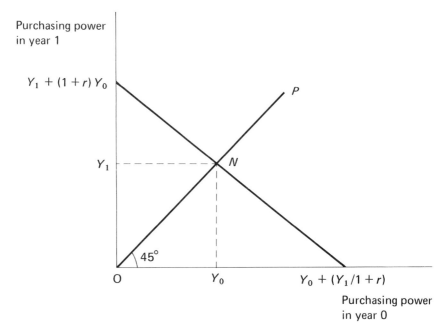

Figure 4.1 The two-period budget constraint

All this can be represented on a simple diagram (see figure 4.1). Here, we see that the purchasing power available in period 0 is measured on the horizontal axis and that in period 1 on the vertical. If no borrowing or lending were done, the consumer would be at N. Notice that, since $Y_0 = Y_1$, by assumption, N lies on a ray OP exactly bisecting the quadrant. The slope of the budget line is $-(1 + r)$ since if the consumer were, say, to lend one of today's dollars, we know he would receive $(1 + r)$ times that dollar next year, an 'exchange rate' over time of $(1 + r)$ to 1. (The minus sign simply reflects the fact that present income is reduced by \$1 while future receipts are increased by $(1 + r)1$: a ratio with terms of opposite sign.)

This line can be interpreted as a budget constraint on consumption in each period where the dimensions of the constraint are determined by Y_0, Y_1 and r.

To see how the individual maximizes utility, we must now examine the indifference curves representing his preferences over present and future consumption. Assume that the indifference curves take the usual shape—downward-sloping and convex to the origin. Then, looking at

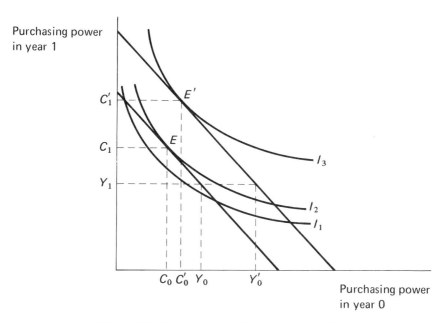

Figure 4.2 Maximizing utility over two periods

figure 4.2, we see that utility is maximized, given the budget constraint, on I_2. The individual maximizes utility over the two periods at E by consuming less in 0 than the income he receives (note that $C_0 < Y_0$) so that savings in period 0 is ($Y_0 - C_0$). He lends this at the rate r so that in period 1 consumption exceeds income ($C_1 > Y_1$). (As an exercise, assume that the budget line reached the highest indifference curve at a point south-east of N: what then?)

Given the consumer's preference pattern (that is, his indifference curve map), the exact amount of consumption shuffled between periods depends upon income in each period and the interest rate. If year 0 income rose to Y_0', for example, with no change in r or Y_1, the present value of overall income would rise, the budget line would shift outwards parallel to itself, and the new utility maximum would be achieved at E' on I_3. More would be saved in period 0 and more consumed in period 1. A similar result could be obtained by allowing Y_1 to increase (try it).

If income before borrowing or lending remains unchanged but we consider a higher interest rate, the slope of the budget line would be steeper, and, in all probability, saving would change. A higher interest rate is equivalent to making it relatively more costly to undertake current consumption, and, as with all price changes, its overall effect can be broken down into an income and a substitution effect. Because current consumption has a higher relative price attached to it at the higher interest rate, the substitution effect must operate in favour of future-period consumption; in other words, it will raise current savings. But the higher income offered by the higher interest rate will raise present consumption (reduce current savings) if it is a normal 'good' and will reduce current consumption if it is an inferior 'good'—and in advance we cannot tell which way this effect will go, or how large it will be relative to the substitution effect. In figure 4.3 initial equilibrium is at A, where there is zero savings: the income effect of the interest rate change on current consumption is zero, and the substitution effect, BD, is associated with saving of $C_0{'}C_0$. Notice that the size of the substitution effect will depend upon the curvature of the indifference curves. The more sharply they are curved, the less will be the substitution effect.

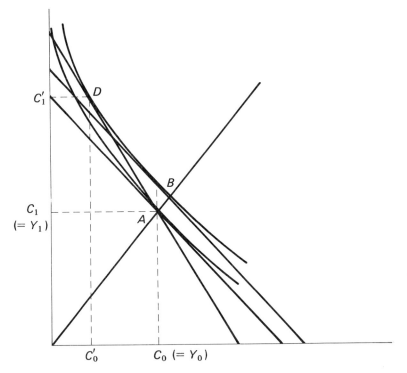

Figure 4.3 Consumption and saving at different interest rates

What we have now seen is that individuals' saving behaviour depends upon their present income, their future income and the interest rate. These conclusions can be expected to hold, in aggregate, for all individuals together, and this is discussed on pp. 77–81. Notice, however, that we have implicitly assumed that everyone faces the same interest rate when borrowing or lending, that the institutional framework to permit borrowing and lending exists and works smoothly, and that everyone knows their future income and the future interest rate. Particularly in LDCs, these assumptions need to be questioned and we shall turn to them now.

THE THEORY IN LDCs

Let us start by noticing that the amount saved in any LDC depends, first, upon the capacity to save and, second, upon the desire to save. One reason why very poor countries may find it hard ever to develop much is that they may not have any surplus upon which to build (that is, to invest). Looking at it from the point of view of a typical individual in such a country, his income in each period might be only just sufficient to keep him alive, even though he consumes all of it. This 'survival income' is marked by the distances OY_{S0} and OY_{S1} in figure 4.4. Point

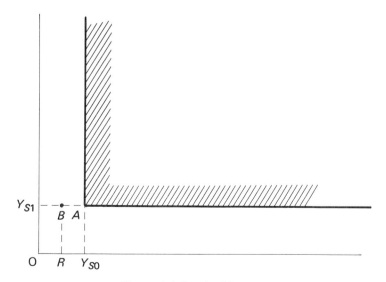

Figure 4.4 Survival income

A represents the survival incomes received; and, since all income must be consumed in the period it is received to permit life to go on, it also represents the pattern of consumption. Since at least OY_{S0} must be consumed in period 0 and at least OY_{S1} in period 1, the only relevant (or life-preserving) region of the graph is the cross-hatched area with *A* at its bottom left-hand corner. Unless income in either period permits us to move into (or along the boundary) of that region, no saving is even possible.

In LDCs in particular it is not uncommon for some people to face the prospect of receiving income below the survival level—for example, to find themselves at a point such as *B*, where period 0 income, *OR*, would be insufficient to keep the individual alive until period 1, even though he was promised a survival income then. In such cases, individuals must rely upon gifts to survive. If members of the community act as an extended family and choose to look after the unfortunate in period 0—perhaps because they fear facing a similar plight in period 1, then the individual may expect to receive RY_{S0}. It is easy to identify the circumstances when this will not occur. If everyone in the country faces below-survival incomes (because of natural disaster, for example) then the only solutions are to hope for gifts from outside the country or to wait until so many have died that the country's 'gifts of nature' provide a survival income for those still living. On the other hand, some parts of the population might fall below the survival income simply because other parts of the community who could supply their needs simply refuse to. All in all, we cannot even expect saving from the very poor. This is just another way of saying that a surplus, above the minimum income needed to survive, must exist before saving can even occur.

Once the 'survival' income level is passed, increasingly high levels of current income will permit increasing saving. To what extent and in what form individuals actually do save more as their income rises depends upon a variety of factors, some of which are not immediately obvious from the general analysis.

In his text *Theory of Economic Growth*, Lewis (1955) suggests (p. 229) that the amount of saving done in a community depends, at least in part, upon the ease of access to savings institutions. This implies that saving activity responds positively to the security offered by such institutions and that it may be influenced by the interest payments offered on deposits held with them. Further, these influences will be reinforced by the wide-ranging spread of branches and agencies of savings institutions so that all may gain easy access to them. These arguments deserve closer inspection.

The term 'savings institutions' carries with it the idea of formal arrangements, initiated and conducted by the governmental and corporate sectors of the economy. These institutions are exemplified by banks and similar financial intermediaries. Yet such institutions are certainly not required to permit income not currently consumed to be saved for future use. Drake (1980, pp. 122–3) identifies *informal* financial activity to include saving, which derives from the household sector (including simple businesses and family farms) and flows into non-institutional assets. Such assets permit value to be stored from one period to another and may be either instruments of hoarding (such as precious metals and stones) or informal financial assets.

Drake suggests that the demand for precious metals and stones reflects the ease with which they can be turned into cash (in other words, their *liquidity*). Such assets are held mainly as a precaution against unexpected income shortfalls, and to permit them to perform this role effectively, it must be assumed that dealers are always on hand to purchase valuables of this kind on demand. The assumption is easy to meet where (as in Malaya, for example) both pawnbroking and buy-back arrangements by jewellers are widespread. Despite the superior claim that banks may make to security,[1] the financial assets offered by them may not be regarded as superior stores of value, particularly if illiteracy and unfamiliarity breeds fear or mistrust of them, and if formal financial institutions are thinly spread and inefficiently operated (Drake, 1980, p. 126).

Although hoarding of this kind may generate a capital gain, we have seen that it is the promise of liquidity in times of trouble that is the main motivation to save here, rather than the hope of increasing income over time. When we turn to informal assets, however, we can find evidence of interest, which may indeed influence decisions with respect to consumption over time.

Informal financial assets may be created by quite a wide range of persons, generically identified as 'moneylenders'. Such people might be pawnbrokers, traders and their wives, or landlords (see Rozental, 1970, for one treatment). They see in informal loans—to households, small businessmen, farmers and traders—the opportunity to earn higher rates of return than they could on formal securities, the possibility of avoiding taxes (since loans are often secret and sometimes unrecorded), and the advantage of minimizing administrative transaction costs (Drake, 1980, pp. 128–9). Notice that, particularly in rural areas, these loans may be contracted and paid for in commodities rather than money, and that 'the usual textbook conditions for a perfect market are completely non-existent: lenders and borrowers do not know the rates at which loans are being transacted in other parts of the country' (Wai, 1957, p. 82).

As for the actual interest rates that such lenders can command when they choose to save in the form of making informal loans, these are often observed to be relatively high. Wai, for example, notes that moneylenders' rates ranged from 10.6 to 36.4 per cent per year in Ceylon in 1951 and from 22 to 44 per cent per year in Thailand in 1952–53 (Wai, 1957, pp. 99–100). The usual reason given for this is that informal loans are often unsecured and therefore contain a significant element of risk of default in respect of which the lender simply cannot obtain redress. Bottomley (1963) concludes that in rural areas high rates of interest are inextricably bound up with low levels of agricultural productivity. Since risk of default is greatest when the borrowing farmer's surplus of production over subsistence requirements is least, the effect of raising productivity will, other things being equal, be to increase this surplus and thus the ability of the farmer to repay the loan. This in turn should lead lenders to require less by way of a 'risk premium' in the interest they charge—where the premium is the element of interest charged to induce the lender to make the loan under such risky conditions. On the other hand, it should be pointed out that lenders of this kind are generally intimately acquainted with the credentials and characteristics of potential borrowers since they tend to operate within closely defined geographical areas. This helps to reduce to a minimum the risk element introduced by imperfect information.

Moneylenders are not the only creators of informal financial assets. The other common source is what may be called money loan associations (Drake, 1980, p. 134). Those associations operate widely in both Asia and Africa[2] and enable groups of individuals to pool their (individually) small amounts of saving into larger sums which can achieve more when spent. Contributions are made to the pool on a regular basis, as are 'draws' (that is, appropriations) of the whole pool (Drake, 1980, p. 135). The question of who draws the pool may be decided by an auction within the group, or by lottery. The precise mechanics of the operation of these associations is described by Freedman (1961) and is quoted at length in Drake (1980, p. 136). Implicitly, auctioning the pool enables contributors to receive interest while those drawing it must pay interest. In general, the longer a contributor waits before drawing the pool, the better the return he enjoys.

Notice that, on the question of security, associations like this depend crucially upon mutual trust. So long as each member is trustworthy and each also, with good reason, trusts the other not to abscond upon drawing the pool, then there is nothing to fear. Formal institutions gain an advantage in terms of security to the extent that they are (or are perceived to be) more trustworthy than personal acquaintances with whom such an association may be set up.

The operation of the informal capital market discussed in the last few paragraphs serves to suggest that, even without a wide-ranging structure of secure, interest-offering formal saving institutions, we might expect to see individuals organizing among themselves to save— and to save in a way that may reflect sensitivity to interest rates. Banks may certainly offer security, but security may also be sought, in varying degrees, in the informal arrangements described and may be offset by factors such as fear of large institutions and the perception that banks are not interested in, or efficient at dealing with, very small amounts. On the other hand, as education spreads, fear founded on ignorance and illiteracy can be expected to recede, and as development proceeds, incomes will rise and experience of financial transactions will grow. These factors can then combine with the spread of banking institutions to encourage participation in formal banking activity, and this is likely to occur. As banking functions are better understood and monetary sums involved reach a size more appropriate to formal banking operations, it may indeed be the case that increasing their accessibility will encourage the saving habit.

One final point needs to be made. Socio-cultural factors may importantly influence saving behaviour. Status in many societies is associated with conspicuous consumption, often among the relatively well off who could afford to save substantial amounts. Such consumption may involve buying expensive imports, taking holidays abroad and so on. This sort of behaviour can have repercussive effects among the less well off, too. They also will consume much (or all) of their incomes in an effort to associate themselves with the rich. Under these circumstances, an important element of development strategy, via education, must be to change the cultural premises upon which consumption behaviour is based.

CONSUMPTION AND SAVINGS FUNCTIONS

We showed earlier how individual consumption and savings depend upon income and the interest rate. Let us now convert that framework into the consumption function form familiar in macroeconomics. To do this we start by deriving an individual's consumption function.

If we consider a set of budget lines, all parallel to one another (see

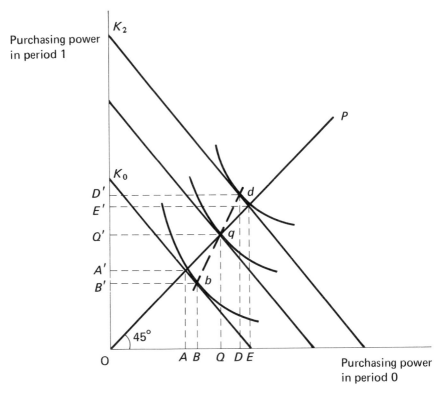

Figure 4.5 The individual's consumption decision at different income levels
(Based on Brunhild and Burton, 1974, p. 231).

figure 4.5), we can say these represent different income levels at a given interest rate. Examining the tangency points between indifference curves and parallel budget lines will tell us how consumption and saving behaviour change with income, assuming we know income in each period. By assumption, $Y_0 = Y_1$, so all we need do is compare the consumption in each period implied by tangency points with points on *OP*.

In figure 4.5 a low level of current income *OA* and future-period income *OA'* generate the budget constraint K_0, assuming an interest rate shown by the slope of the budget line. With this income, utility is maximized at *b*, where the individual consumes *OB*, beyond his present income by an amount *AB*. Such negative saving activity is called *dis-saving* and could be achieved by borrowing. At the higher income level (*OE*, *OE'*), the individual faces budget constraint K_2 and maximizes

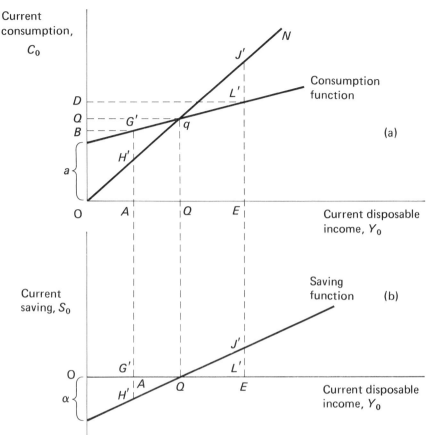

Figure 4.6 The individual's consumption and saving functions

utility at d. Here he chooses to consume OD and to save DE this period, to give him additional purchasing power of $E'D'$ in the next period. With income OQ now and OQ' next period, the individual operates at q and neither saves nor dis-saves. This is all represented in a different form on figure 4.6(a). Here a 45° line ON shows all points at which current income Y_0 and current consumption C_0 are equal. When current income is OA, we recall that current consumption is OB, the dis-saving in figure 4.6(a) being represented by the vertical distance $G'H'$. When current income is OE, current consumption is OD and current saving shown by the vertical distance $J'L'$. Finally, by joining up points like G' and L', we can find the individual's whole consumption function, one point on which will be the intersection between the function and *ON*. Since $C_0 = Y_0$ at this point, we know that on figure 4.6(a) it is shown as q.

The individual's saving function is derived directly from the consumption function (see figure 4.6(b)), bearing in mind that income can be allocated only to either consumption or saving. Since current income equals current consumption at income level *OQ*, it is at this value of Y_0 that current saving, S_0, is zero. S_0 is positive when $Y_0 > OQ$ and negative when $Y_0 < OQ$.

The point at which the consumption function meets the vertical axis depends upon the consumption required when current income is zero. If positive, this presupposes the availability of gifts, borrowing or accumulated wealth to draw on. The slope of the functions at any level of current income depends upon the additional consumption and saving that is undertaken when small changes are allowed to occur around that level. Thus the slopes tell us the marginal propensities to consume and save (MPC and MPS) at given income levels. In figure 4.6 these marginal propensities are constant at all income levels, but it can be argued that, as income levels rise, so individuals will choose to add to present consumption at a decreasing rate because of the diminishing marginal utility associated with equal additions to consumption. If this is so, the MPC will fall and the MPS rise. An implication of this view is that people on high incomes save more than people on low. This is one basis for a formulation of saving behaviour which assumes that wage-earners save nothing but profit-earners save all of their income—because wage-earners have much lower incomes than profit-earners. Such a formulation is not always helpful for LDCs where wage- and salary-earners are sometimes among the best off in a community and enjoy sufficient security of income to undertake long-term savings plans. On the other hand, if income (however derived) is related in this way (or other ways) to variations in consumption and saving propensities, then it is easy to see that the distribution of income among persons may have an important influence on overall savings achieved.

The average propensities to consume and save (APC and APS) are by definition C_0/Y_0 and S_0/Y_0 and can thus be found, for any income level, by examining the slope of a line from the origin to the associated point on the functions. So long as the consumption function has a positive intercept with the vertical axis and the $0 < MPC < 1$ (whether MPC is constant or falling), the APC will fall as income rises and the APS will rise. Further, APC > MPC and APS < MPS.

Finally, notice that more saving will be done at all but the lowest income levels if there is a spread of savings institutions or a successful campaign to reduce conspicuous consumption. Factors such as these, and also changes in the interest rate, will shift or change the slope of the functions.

We shall now assume that individuals' consumption and saving functions can be added together without difficulty to obtain aggregate functions. One problem about this assumption is that, in order to aggregate, we must assume each person to act quite independently of everyone else. We have already noted, however, that some consumption and saving behaviour may be the result of a desire to imitate others and thus cannot be considered independently determined. Another difficulty arises from the possibility that different groups of individuals might have different consumption and saving propensities. Thus, a given increase in aggregate income could have quite different results depending upon which group received it. We ignore these complications for the moment and simply assume that aggregate functions with characteristics similar to those of individuals can be derived.

AGGREGATE SAVING BEHAVIOUR IN LDCs: EVIDENCE

The aggregate consumption and saving functions are often viewed as relationships between current consumption or savings and current disposable (i.e. after-tax) income alone.[3] In Solow's formulation, savings are simply a fixed proportion of income. Thus, however low (or high) income might be, a fixed percentage of it is always saved. Note, however, that Solow (1956, pp. 87–9) considers the possibility of a variable savings ratio as an extension to his basic model. For very poor countries, however, it might well be necessary to dis-save for periods as a reflection of the need to consume some positive amount even when current income approaches zero. This implies that saving might well change as a proportion of income, as income rises. The simplest formulations which allow for this possibility are

$$C_0 = a + bY_0$$

where a gives the value of the consumption function intercept with the vertical axis and b is the MPC, and a saving function:

$$S_0 = \alpha + \beta Y_0$$

where α is the dis-saving done at zero current income and β is the MPS. The important point for developmentalists is that, if saving is related simply to current income, with α assumed negative (reflecting a positive value of a) and β, the MPS, assumed positive but less than 1, then the APS will rise (reflecting a fall in APC) as income increases.

To test for the values of α and β, and to draw conclusions from the findings, it would seem a simple matter of collecting observations on aggregate savings and a national income magnitude such as GNP over a number of years for a country, and regressing the one on the other. It must be recognized, however, that, while we have tended to view saving as if done by private sector household individuals, saving is also done by governments and corporations. Aggregate saving contains all of these elements, and yet each group might react in quite different ways to the factors that stimulate or discourage saving if only because the forms in which different groups may save themselves vary widely. Further, observations on actual savings may be a good measure of the saving that was intended and so may not illuminate clearly what savers had tried or wished to do as their contribution to national saving effort. Finally, national income data in LDCs are often unreliable even when they are available at all,[4] and when data from many countries are employed, there is the added difficulty that different statisticians use quite different definitions of the magnitudes measured.

Bearing these comments in mind, let us now examine the findings of researchers in this area. An important reference, upon which we rely heavily here, is a survey paper by Mikesell and Zinser (1973). Table 4.1 reports their findings on the relationship between overall aggregate saving and GNP. They found that α took a negative value in only 8 of the 18 countries they studied. Across these countries, the APS ranged from 5.9 per cent (Bolivia) to 25.6 per cent (Venezuela), bearing out Snyder's remark (1974) that the APS 'is particularly erratic in developing countries, many of which are undergoing rapid structural changes plus evolution in attitudes towards work consumption and thrift' (p. 140). This should be seen against the general tendency for middle- and higher-income countries to have higher savings ratios than low-income countries (see table 4.2). The MPS in Mikesell and Zinser's work is positive in all cases but one (Dominican Republic) but was by no means found always to exceed the APS, a condition needed to ensure that the savings ratio will rise with aggregate income. The MPS range is from 3.5 to 29.4 per cent, ignoring the Dominican Republic.

In a village study of primitive South Pacific economies, Blyth (1969) discovered that the MPS increased significantly and substantially with income. He was also able to conclude tentatively that, with the introduction of money into village life, cash income increased at the expense of subsistence income within the total of income. Examining village-to-village variations in the cash income proportion, he found to his surprise that 'at the aggregate level, differences in cash income appear to account adequately for differences in the propensity to save'.

TABLE 4.1 Saving functions: Latin America

Country	Period	α (intercept)	β (MPS)	APS
Argentina	1950–68	– 100.82	0.294	0.182
Bolivia	1953–68	537.02	0.097	0.059
Brazil	1950–67	4.15	0.140	0.147
Chile	1960–68	1.64	0.047	0.146
Columbia	1950–68	0.73	0.151	0.187
Costa Rica	1953–68	– 165.14	0.107	0.139
Dominican Republic	1953–68	193.71	– 0.114	0.132
Ecuador	1953–67	1.22	0.035	0.126
El Salvador	1958–68	42.72	0.087	0.112
Guatemala	1953–68	– 68.15	0.163	0.100
Honduras	1953–68	– 27.67	0.148	0.101
Mexico	1950–67	– 4.54	0.159	0.135
Nicaragua	1953–68	– 98.17	0.164	0.128
Panama	1960–68	– 59.95	0.238	0.129
Paraguay	1962–70	– 4.76	0.190	0.120
Peru	1950–68	4.67	0.122	0.198
Uruguay	1955–68	0.82	0.076	0.125
Venezuela	1950–68	1.41	0.186	0.256
Average			0.132	0.139
Median			0.150	0.130

Source: Mikesell and Zinser (1973, table 2)

TABLE 4.2 Gross domestic saving as proportion of GDP

	1960	1978
	%	%
Low-income countries	11	15
Middle-income countries	20	22
Industrialized countries	22	22

Source: World Bank *World Development Report* (1980, table 5, p. 118)

Turning to studies of household saving alone, Johnson and Chiu (1968) found a positive correlation between private saving and private household income when they examined the experience of 30 LDCs and DCs. In only five cases was $\alpha < 0$. Houthakker (1961) found private saving from employment income to be negligible. Many researchers agree that the private MPS is an increasing function of income, particularly at lower levels of development. In particular, Gupta (1970) finds the household MPS rising with per capita income in both rural and urban areas.

Earlier it was noted that future as well as current income should be considered a potential determinant of current saving, and of changes in the savings ratio. In a formulation that incorporates this insight, the permanent income hypothesis (Friedman, 1957) suggests that people make their consumption and saving decision in relation to a two-part view of their income. One part of their income they regard as permanent; while an individual might expect his income to vary over his lifetime, he takes as his permanent annual income an *average* of what he expects to receive in each year of his life. The exact shape of the earnings profile (that is, of when he expects to receive the income during his lifetime) is not important: the year-by-year average based on his expectations is. Clearly, an individual's expectations may change over time, but it is in relation to his present perception of what his permanent income is that he decides what to consume—and it is assumed that he will consume (and save) a fixed proportion of this component. Another way of putting this is simply to say that households strongly resist departures from their preferred time pattern of consumption (Williamson, 1968, p. 197).

When the actual income differs from the permanent annual income, the difference (positive or negative) is called *transitory income.* If consumption out of permanent income is to be kept at a steady level, incomes received in excess of permanent income must be put aside to permit consumption to be maintained even if actual income falls below the permanent level. Thus, it is suggested, individuals will save almost all of their positive transitory income and dis-save most negative transitory income. The more variable a group's actual incomes are around the average (permanent) level, the higher the proportion in aggregate they will save.

Difficulties in measuring savings from each of the components of income arise from the fact that any individual's view of what his permanent income actually is must be subjective—because related to his expectations of what income he will receive in future and when he will receive it. It is divergencies from what he perceives as his permanent income that constitute transitory income. But, of course, expectations and subjective perceptions cannot be observed. Williamson (1968) effectively assumes that expectations are formed exclusively on the basis of recent income experience and takes as his proxy for permanent income a three-year moving average of disposable income. Transitory income is expressed in terms of the deviations of actual annual disposable income from the moving average. Savings are defined as the difference between income and expenditure in the household sector. Williamson's results, based on observations in the period 1950–64, are shown in table 4.3. As can be seen, the Burmese and Koreans seem to have saved nothing, at the margin, from permanent income, but their marginal propensities to save or dis-save from transitory income were substantial. The Japanese and Philippinos saved much more, at the margin, from transitory than from permanent incomes. Only the Taiwanese and Indians fell outside the predicted pattern. Other studies have also found savings from transitory income to exceed that from permanent, with Argentina and urban India providing exceptions (see Friend and Taubman, 1966; Friend, 1966; Gupta, 1970). All this suggests, therefore, that observed savings will in all probability depend upon the extent to which incomes diverge from what is perceived to be a norm.

TABLE 4.3 Marginal saving propensities out of permanent and transitory income

Country	MPS out of permanent income	MPS out of transitory income
Burma	0.09	0.37
India	− 0.23	− 0.14
Japan	0.29	0.46
Korea	− 0.07	1.12
Philippines	0.30	0.50
Taiwan	0.27	− 0.17

One obvious way in which such divergences might occur is through an increased growth rate of income. Suppose a 2 per cent per year trend is replaced by a 3 per cent per year trend as the result of introducing more efficient technology. Given that most savers are unlikely to have built the expectation of such a trend shift into their perceptions, they will view some of the higher income they receive as transitory income— at least until they are used to the new growth rate. Thus, average aggregate saving should rise *as the result of* a higher growth rate in addition to being a potential cause of it. Singh (1971), Houthakker (1965) and Modigliani (1965) are among researchers to have found evidence supporting this view.

Turning now to the influence of interest rates, recall that savings might be either positively or negatively related to interest rate changes, depending on the relative strength of the substitution and income effects. Gupta's (1970) study of Indian household data found per capita saving from disposable income positively related to changes in the interest rate: Williamson (1968) found a predominance of negative relationships in examining the countries listed in table 4.3, but his method of testing has been criticized by Gupta.

A final point worth noting in the evidence is the influence of income distribution. Defining their division in terms of the functional distribution of income between property and labour income, Houthakker (1961, 1965) and Williamson (1968, 1969) conclude that property income explains much more inter-country variation in saving than does labour income. Kelley and Williamson (1968) also find Asian entrepreneurs to have higher saving propensities than non-entrepreneurs. More will be said on definitions of income distribution, and the savings implications, in chapter 8.

RAISING THE DOMESTIC SAVING RATE

LIBERALIZING THE CAPITAL MARKET

Domestic savers can be persuaded to increase their voluntary saving activity by education, and by easing their access to savings institutions and permitting such institutions to offer attractive interest rates on deposits. We shall first examine the potential for the latter type of operation and later in the chapter consider the scope for forms of forced saving, taxation dominant among them.

In this section, we examine the ways in which a country's financial system can be best organized to mobilize savings and direct them to the most productive investment uses. To provide motivation, let us note the experience of a group of countries whose rapid growth has been associated with—and may be attributable to—a much expanded role for financial intermediation, namely, marrying savers' activity to investors' needs. Over recent decades Japan, Taiwan and Korea have all experienced rapid real growth (ranging from an average of 8.5 to 10.5 per cent per year during the 1960s and from 5 to 9.7 per cent in the 1970s). At the same time, there has been a remarkable growth rate in each case in the ratio to GNP of banking system liabilities—including, importantly, demand deposits and interest-bearing time deposits. Although this ratio is a rather rough-and-ready proxy, it provides an acceptable measure of the size of a banking system and an indication of the success achieved in mobilizing voluntary financial saving, which can be made available as credit (loans) to investors. Over the period 1960–75 this ratio rose from 0.105 to 0.369 in Korea, 0.198 to 0.641 in Taiwan and 0.67 to 1.141 in Japan. Comparing this with the experience of some semi-industrial LDCs over the same period, Argentina, Brazil, Chile, Colombia, India, Philippines, Sri Lanka and Turkey (with a mean 1960s annual growth rate of 4.2 per cent and mean 1970s annual growth rate of 4.9 per cent) saw the mean value of their ratios rise from 0.233 to 0.255 (see McKinnon, 1981, on all of this).

This comparison is suggestive. Countries that have recently grown quickly have also seen the rapid growth of their formal financial institutions. It is also true that advanced industrial economies in general have more extensive financial systems than LDCs. What is the connection?

It has often been claimed that the very existence of a spreading bank network should be sufficient to encourage saving. Miracle *et al.* (1980, p. 702) note that, while over 70 per cent of the population of most tropical African countries is rural, banks are found almost exclusively in the larger urban areas. These are among countries that in relative terms have often found growth hardest to achieve. Again, Drake (1980, p. 169) cites evidence in relation to Thailand that suggests that that country's development has gone hand in hand with the spread of bank offices. In 1945, he says, Thailand had 24 bank offices of which 16 were in Bangkok; by 1967 the total had risen to 535, with only 182 of them located in Bangkok.

Even though formal banking institutions offer interest rates that are observably positive, less savings may be mobilized through such channels than might be expected, for a variety of reasons. First, profit-seeking banks will not go into areas whose remoteness imposes high costs of operation upon them, where accounts are likely to be small (and the administration costs of handling are thus high), and where loan activity may be very risky. Even though resources may well be available for saving in such areas (as we noted earlier), banks may simply not see it in their financial interests to seek such funds. Second, so long as individuals remain poorly educated and lack experience of financial transactions, the mere presence of banks may not be sufficient to induce individuals to use them. Third, there may simply be an income constraint: savings cannot be increased by spreading the banking network unless incomes are high enough (and preferably, growing) so that the opportunity to save more is also present.

Positive interest rates can be offered to savers if the institutions with which they hold deposits are able to charge borrowers an interest rate that more than suffices to cover the administration costs of such institutions. Such borrowers will usually be seeking funds to finance capital investment. We shall explore the determinants of investment in the next chapter, but broadly speaking an economy with a promising growth potential and little existing capital stock should offer substantial returns to investors. Even if the interest rates they must pay on borrowed funds to make the investment is high, therefore, it may well still be worthwhile to take a loan.

Now, in many LDCs it has long been appreciated that machines and other capital stock will be accumulated by profit-maximizing businessmen in any given period until the rate of return promised by such investment has fallen to the interest rate level that businessmen must pay to finance it. A typical government response has been to subsidize the interest rate or, more usually, to operate a range of financial institutions that offer a variety of subsidized interest rates to borrowers whose projects are considered in some way desirable.

But there is a catch here. If borrowers are allowed to pay an artificially depressed rate of interest, the institutions that supply their loan finance can also offer only a low rate of interest to depositors. As a consequence, individuals are offered little encouragement to save voluntarily and only limited resources are then made available for investment. As McKinnon puts it:

Governments in semi-industrial LDCs . . . intervene in an extremely detailed and pervasive way to reduce the cost of credit (interest rates) and influence its availability to various classes of potential borrowers . . . These interventions— together with the government itself tapping the money system as a revenue source—are responsible for the phenomenon of 'financial repression': where the lending capacity of the banks is inordinately reduced. This squeezing of the banking system occurs because these credit subsidies . . . reduce earnings . . . and thus reduce the yield to the holders of money (savers) . . . . [McKinnon, 1977, p. 15]

McKinnon cites Colombia as providing one example of all of this. Here, savers' deposits with commercial banks and savings banks are in large measure put at the disposal of the central (i.e. government) bank through the operation of central bank deposit requirements. These resources are then channelled through specialized credit agencies (such as agricultural, industrial development and mortgage banks) so that they might lend to their clienteles at artificially depressed interest rates—starting (in 1972) at 2 or 4 per cent. Under these circumstances, it is not surprising to learn that savings deposits carried a low (5 – 8 per cent) interest rate for small depositors—which, given 18 per cent per year inflation, implied a real yield on savings in this form of minus 10 per cent. It can be guessed that this did little to encourage saving and resulted in a much smaller amount of banking activity based on deposits —in particular, lending to finance productive investment—than would otherwise have been achieved. Finally, a consequence of subsidizing interest rates to investor-borrowers is that it becomes worthwhile to undertake projects of very little promise—projects, indeed, that offer a negative rate of return in an inflationary environment. Given that low interest rates under-realize potential savings, this could well mean that high-yielding projects were not undertaken because of a shortage of resources.

Turning now to the example of Korea, we can see what can happen when government intervention is removed. Before 1965 savers faced low interest rates on deposits (again, negative in real terms) and bank deposits fell to only 9 per cent of GNP in 1964. Borrowers, similarly, faced low interest rates, but with deposits at such a low level were subject to the rationing of funds. In the wake of reforms in 1965—essentially involving a move away from government control of the interest rate (the price of money) to control of the monetary base (the quantity of money)—both savers and borrowers saw interest rates rise sharply as a reflection of market forces. From 1964 to 1966, the real rate of return rose by about 11 percentage points on demand deposits and by about 26 percentage points on time deposits.

McKinnon (1976, p. 76) reports that 'the response of savers was enthusiastic'. The flow of private savings rose from almost nothing to about 8 per cent of GNP by 1969. On the other side of the balance sheet, the expansion of loanable funds from savings permitted large-scale financing of investment for the first time in many industrial and agricultural enterprises. That such lending occurred at high real rates of interest was an indication of the opportunities that had formerly gone untapped through lack of funds. This in turn contributed to Korea's rapid growth, says McKinnon.

Savings, then, as we noted in our basic analysis, may respond to changes in the interest rate, and in a dramatic way. But such a response is premised on the accessibility of savings institutions and upon a willingness of governments to let the market for savers' funds operate freely. Because of many governments' desire to appropriate banks' funds for its own purposes, and because of essentially political forces at work in lobbying for subsidized credit for special groups, such a willingness is not widespread in the developing world. In the absence of such willingness, governments have turned to forced saving to try to mobilize resources.

FORCED SAVING

If voluntary saving in a country fails to generate sufficient resources for investment to achieve a desirable growth rate, governments may force households and firms to save. We shall consider here coercion through manipulation of the domestic terms of trade, and taxation.

Domestic Terms of Trade

Suppose we view the structure of an LDC's economy as essentially divided into two parts: an agricultural sector, using traditional labour-intensive techniques of production, producing food and other primary products as its main output; and a sector using modern, capital-intensive techniques of production to produce consumer goods (perhaps including food), non-food primary products and capital goods. Now, the principally capital-using sector—the 'modern' sector—is generally seen as the dynamic part of the economy, mainly because it employs machines with other labour and non-labour inputs to a much greater extent than the traditional sector. This in turn permits it to be much more productive and growth-oriented.

This thumbnail sketch of what underlies the whole of chapter 3 needed to be drawn so that we can understand why LDCs have often acted in a way that explicitly operates to the immediate disadvantage of their traditional sectors. According to the views above,[5] for the whole economy to grow most rapidly, capital must be injected into the modern sector. But such resources can be generated in the first place, and their expansion sustained later, only by drawing on an 'economic surplus' of production over consumption. True, the modern sector should in due course be able to generate its own surplus from profits, but, particularly in the early stages of development, the largest potential source of such surplus is the traditional sector. If traditional producers grow more food than they need to eat, then there is a surplus that can be used to assist modern sector growth.

An obvious way of mobilizing this surplus is to organize the structure of agricultural production in such a way that producers have any surplus physically removed from them; in other words, they may be required to deliver all produce to collection centres, where they are given back sufficient to live on, and the balance is taken to feed industrial workers or to be sold in world markets to buy machines. This is forced saving with a vengeance.

A more subtle form of forcing agricultural producers to save is seen in turning the domestic terms of trade between traditional and modern sector goods against the traditional sector. Households in the modern sector must eat, but do not produce food. Suppose their income is fixed in terms of the goods they produce (or that, at least, it cannot fall). Then, if there is a rise in the amount of food from the traditional sector that each unit of modern sector output can buy, the real value of their incomes will increase. This is precisely the effect of turning the domestic terms of trade against the traditional sector: reducing the price of traditional sector goods relative to modern sector goods.

Such an effect can be gained by legislating, or operating through marketing boards to depress the relative price of traditional sector output. It can also be achieved by protecting modern sector industry by a tariff that permits it to charge to local market buyers higher prices than they would have to pay by importing similar goods from lower-cost producers abroad. The purpose of the strategy is to raise real modern sector incomes with the aim of raising modern sector saving.

Whichever form of forced saving mechanism is used against traditional agriculture, the dangers are clear. Peasant producers may simply rebel and refuse to grow or deliver food in the quantities of which they are capable. The surplus is therefore diminished. Further, by concentrating on mobilizing resources from traditional agriculture to assist the modern sector, opportunities for investing in the traditional sector itself, to make it more productive, may be missed. This is unfortunate for that sector, which usually contains the largest proportion of an LDC's population, but it is also a potential barrier to overall development. This is because modern sector growth cannot continue unabated unless the traditional sector itself becomes more productive—and, indeed, increasingly modernized in its production techniques. Resources from the surplus, and incentives, have to be left in the traditional sector to encourage this.

Bearing all this in mind, we turn now to the question of taxation, making no distinction in relation to its sectoral target.

Taxation

Taxation is saving that the private sector is forced to undertake by government legislation. A widely used index of the extent to which countries are actually taxed is the *tax ratio*—total tax revenues as a fraction or percentage of GNP (see table 4.4). We must note at the outset that tax revenue collected by a government in a given year is not in itself a measure of saving. Governments engage in recurrent expenditure (analogous to the consumption expenditure of households) all the time, and only if tax revenues exceed such expenditure can we talk about net saving having occurred by the government. Further, additions to government saving achieved by higher taxation constitute additions to aggregate saving only to the extent that the extra tax burden is met out of sacrificed consumption expenditure. (For more on this, see 'The Please effect', pp. 97–8 below.)

Taxation Potential: Theory. Of central importance to discussions of taxation's contribution to development is the notion of taxation

TABLE 4.4 Tax ratios for developing countries

Country	Total tax over GNP	Direct tax over GNP	Indirect tax over GNP
	%	%	%
Afghanistan	5.66	0.95	4.55
Algeria	39.83	26.37	13.47
Bangladesh	5.80	0.57	4.14
Benim	16.02	3.75	11.97
Bolivia	11.84	1.44	10.07
Brazil	18.10	3.85	13.39
Burma	7.56	2.73	3.98
Burundi	9.28	3.09	6.14
Cameroon	16.16	3.07	12.48
Central African Empire	15.90	4.81	9.79
Chile	18.36	6.24	11.44
China, Republic of	19.94	5.31	14.51
Colombia	11.61	4.47	4.91
Congo	19.82	8.12	11.70
Costa Rica	13.58	3.21	10.28
Dominican Republic	15.04	3.39	10.84
Ecuador	12.02	3.14	8.59
Egypt	18.15	6.02	11.89
El Salvador	11.53	2.98	8.55
Ethiopia	10.11	2.92	7.07
Gambia, The	14.94	2.17	12.63
Ghana	14.24	3.61	10.54
Guatemala	8.12	1.48	6.59
Guinea	22.08	6.11	14.45
Guyana	31.27	10.28	20.03
Honduras	11.52	3.26	8.25
India	13.87	2.52	9.81
Indonesia	16.26	11.50	4.52
Iraq	37.60	32.68	4.59
Ivory Coast	20.60	3.90	15.84
Jamaica	19.02	9.67	8.17
Jordan	19.34	1.89	8.96

potential, or taxable capacity. It is assumed that we can obtain some idea of the resources that governments *could* remove from consumers, and that amount can be compared with the amounts that they actually *do* remove. A broad approach to this question is taken by Kaldor (1963), and in more recent years specified elements of taxation potential have been closely examined by Chelliah, Baas and Kelly (1975), Lotz and Morss (1967), and Tait, Gratz and Eichengreen (1979).

TABLE 4.4 *continued*

Country	Total tax over GNP	Direct tax over GNP	Indirect tax over GNP
	%	%	%
Kenya	19.23	7.71	11.30
Korea	13.57	4.42	8.71
Liberia	14.37	6.04	7.94
Malawi	10.05	4.31	5.68
Malaysia	22.48	6.89	12.19
Mali	13.00	1.63	7.82
Mexico	8.63	4.70	3.70
Morocco	18.62	5.62	12.32
Nepal	5.37	1.21	4.17
Nicaragua	11.09	2.27	8.55
Pakistan	11.39	1.86	8.78
Panama	11.58	5.44	5.61
Paraguay	8.76	2.00	5.54
Peru	14.04	4.72	8.64
Philippines	10.13	3.45	6.27
Rwanda	10.02	2.23	7.11
Senegal	20.20	4.28	13.83
Sierra Leone	17.01	5.66	11.20
Sri Lanka	17.97	3.43	14.54
Sudan	18.92	2.35	14.47
Swaziland	23.09	6.82	15.74
Syrian Arab Republic	11.29	2.86	6.05
Tanzania	18.94	5.96	12.99
Thailand	13.96	3.14	10.82
Togo	12.38	2.05	9.73
Tunisia	20.68	4.49	11.38
Turkey	16.19	7.20	8.99
Upper Volta	11.34	2.17	8.77
Yemen Arab Republic	7.67	0.43	6.60
Zaire	27.19	6.86	20.22
Zambia	30.80	16.74	14.06
Average	15.80	5.15	9.81

Source: Tait, Grätz and Eichengreen (1979, table 15)

It should be said at the outset that taxation almost always brings with it disincentive effects—effects that are reflected in a reduced supply of effort or other productive resources in areas affected by the taxes. As a matter of emphasis, Kaldor believes that it is not inadequate incentives but a shortage of resources that limits the pace of economic development. In his discussion of taxation potential he thus focuses

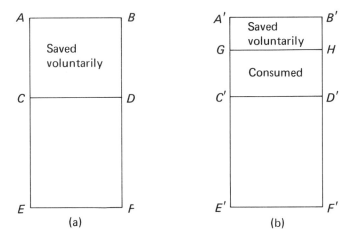

Figure 4.7 Varying bases for taxation potential (a) thrifty; (b) profligate.

on the factors that might assist or inhibit a government in playing its part to mobilize resources.

As a matter of broad definition, Kaldor suggests that 'the taxation potential of a country depends on the excess of its actual consumption over the minimum essential consumption of the population'. Clearly, the absolute amount of tax revenue that could be raised in a country will depend first on real income per capita. But suppose we take two countries of similar real income, population and income distribution. The real income of each country can be represented by boxes of equal height, shown in figure 4.7. In each country—call them T for 'thrifty' and P for 'profligate'—a similar quantity of real income is considered the biologically essential consumption minimum. This is represented by the areas $CEDF$ and $C'D'E'F'$. In T, all income in excess of this is voluntarily saved, but in P an additional $GHC'D'$ is consumed and only $A'B'GH$ is saved. In T there is clearly no taxation potential: nothing is actually being consumed beyond the bare subsistence minimum. In P the first idea we might have is that $GHC'D'$ must be the taxation potential, but as Kaldor points out, this is unlikely to be the case. If consumers in P have been for some time consuming well in excess of the subsistence minimum, they will have become accustomed to this standard of living—and will expect it to be maintained. Even if a government knows for a fact that the population could live on consumption of $C'D'E'F'$, it still could not count the area $GHC'D'$ as taxation potential. This is because the population do not perceive $C'D'E'F'$ as their essential minimum—or, perhaps more accurately, will not permit the government to interpret it as the essential minimum. If the government were to try to tax away all of $GHC'D'$ the people would either dislodge it or refuse to cooperate. The minimum essential consumption level is thus, at least partially, determined by political feasibility.

Turning now to the influence income distribution, Kaldor states:

> As between two countries with the same real income per head, the accustomed standard of living of the bulk of the population will evidently be the lower in the country in which a larger share of total incomes accrues to a minority of wealthy individuals: and it will be this country that has the higher taxation potential. [Kaldor, 1963]

Now, it is possible to argue for this point of view on the grounds of pure equity, but it takes its strongest form when it can be shown that the wealthy minority derives most of its incomes from property rents rather than wage labour and spends most of its income on consumer goods, particularly if imported. Bearing this in mind, the almost entire absence of property-owning classes in some African countries gives them a lower taxation potential than many Latin American countries, where the share of national income accruing to property owners is relatively high.

What is clear also is that even those who are not wealthy, materially speaking, may provide a useful target for a government anxious to raise the overall saving ratio. Families in the traditional agricultural sector might be choosing to produce only enough to cover their immediate needs and be taking an important part of their real income in the form of leisure. If a way can be found to tax them, they will need to raise their total output in order to maintain a rate of consumption that just meets their needs. In other words, they will have to offer greater effort to finish up consuming the same amount as before, their extra production going to the tax collector in the form of forced savings. This dimension of taxation potential offers more promise where land is plentiful (Africa) than where it is already worked to the limits (parts of Asia).

One realistic (if unfortunate and economically unjustified) reason why governments may choose to tax the relatively less well off, materially, is that they may simply not be able to extract taxes from the wealthy. The wealthy are often also the politically powerful, and so can influence the nature and coverage of fiscal legislation. It is unlikely that they will agitate for a tax structure and tax rates that are directed heavily against their own interests. Further, the wealthy are often also the best educated and have readiest access to professional advice on how to avoid taxation. While the consumption of such groups therefore might considerably exceed not only the subsistence level but also the level that most of the population would be happy for them to have, it might be almost impossible to tap this apparent potential.

Related in some ways to the last point, the taxation potential of a country will depend upon the competence of the tax collectors. While the wealthy and educated will always battle with the bureaucracy, a poorly educated, poorly motivated and dishonest tax-gathering force will imply a smaller potential tax catch from any distribution of income than will a revenue department that is highly literate, active and honest.

Finally, countries that engage heavily in trade will tend to find themselves, all other things equal, in a better position to raise taxes than countries that do not. The reason for this is that taxation revenue is most easily raised through customs duties (an indirect tax) levied at borders when compared with the problems associated with collecting, for example, income tax (a direct tax).

As must be clear from this discussion, taxation potential is by no means simple to identify in a country. Apparently plausible objective estimates can run foul of political infeasibility; estimates that strain too far to take account of 'political realities' can be criticized on the grounds that such historical and institutional factors should not be allowed to count as real constraints but should be viewed as removable in the interests of development.[6]

Taxation Potential: Evidence. While there is no reason to believe that LDCs have a better voluntary saving record than DCs (and, indeed, there is evidence to the contrary), the first point to note is that the average level of taxation in developing countries is still well below that in developed countries. As table 4.4 reveals, the average tax ratio (total tax/GNP) for 63 LDCs, 1972–76, was 15.8 per cent. In 1975 the average tax ratio for 23 DCs in Europe and North America was 26 per cent net of social security and 34 per cent including social security (Tait, Gratz and Eichengreen, 1979, p. 31). Variation among LDCs is substantial: Algeria 39.8 per cent, Guyana, Iraq and Zambia all exceeding 30 per cent, Afghanistan, Bangladesh and Nepal hardly exceeding 5 per cent. The interesting question, though, is how much of this variation can be explained in terms of the sort of factors discussed above.

On the basis of data drawn from the 63 countries listed in table 4.4, Tait *et al.* conclude that almost 60 per cent of the variance in tax ratios can be explained by non-export income per capita, the share of mining in GDP and the share of non-mineral exports in GDP experienced in each country. The first of these explains very little, but impressive explanatory power attaches to the share of mining, which is used to stand for the sectoral composition of the economy, and the share of non-mineral exports, which gives an indication of the extent of trade done by the economy. When Tait *et al.* divided the countries they studied into three annual per capita income ranges ($0–$250, $250–$500 and $500 +), they found support for the hypothesis that mining and foreign trade (both easy targets for taxation) matter relatively more for countries with per capita GNPs in the lowest range. Both Malaysia and Papua New Guinea are classic examples. Their findings, in general, suggest that, at the earliest stage of development, the mix of domestic and foreign trade is the most important determinant of taxable capacity. That said, it is worthwhile noting their warning that:

Not only economic parameters but such social variables as attitude toward egalitarianism . . . and the influence of various private interest groups upon the formation of economic policy affect the extent to which a government can exploit a potential tax base. For example, the capacity of two otherwise identical economies to tax the external trade sector would differ significantly, depending on whether the relatively wealthy consumers of imports had enough political clout to discourage import duties or whether the poorer classes were able to initiate income redistribution programs. [Tait, Gratz and Eichengreen, 1979, pp. 140–1]

Considering that it is the aggregate saving ratio we wish to discuss, we finally present two rather different types of argument that bear upon the question of how taxation might influence this magnitude.

The 'Please effect'. The first line of argument suggests that increased taxation might actually reduce overall savings because of the relationship between the saving propensities out of current income of private and government decision-makers. Suppose, to fix ideas, that the government has a MPS of zero; in other words, it devotes to ends analogous with consumption all the extra income it raises from taxation (for example, it might simply hire more public servants with the tax revenue). If all tax payments are financed by private individuals and firms by reducing consumption, the money value of the forced saving that they have done will be exactly offset by the additional consumption done by the government—so there will be no net gain in overall savings. If the private sector finances increased tax demands by reducing its own saving to any extent (by running down interest-bearing bank deposits, for example), then overall savings will actually be reduced: the private sector will have reduced its consumption by less than the government increases it. This sort of result is generally called the 'Please effect', after the economist Stanley Please (1967).

Evidence on this point is mixed. Landau (1969), cited in Mikesell and Zinser (1973, p. 15), performed a cross-sectional study of 19 Latin American nations and found a tendency for increased government saving to be more than offset by a decrease in the rate of private saving. Bhatia (1967), on the other hand, in a cross-section study of 20 African countries, found evidence of a net increase in overall savings, with 1 per cent rises in the tax ratio reducing private consumption by 0.21 per cent of GDP and increasing public consumption by only 0.05 per cent of GDP. Singh (1971) concluded that, as Please suggested, governments do have low propensities to save, and also that one-unit additions to government saving were achieved at the cost of 0.57 units of private saving. Given these results, it is not surprising that he finds that the ratio of tax revenue to GNP would, on average in LDCs be studied, have to rise by about 6 per cent to achieve a 1 per cent increase in the overall saving ratio.

Having said all this, it should be added that in this debate it is of considerable importance to identify the form that saving takes. The most favourable complexion that can be put on the matter is that, even though governments save less at the margin than the private sector, their more extensive information base enables them to engage in capital purchases that have a higher social-welfare-generating potential than, for example, investment in foreign securities, a form of saving that the private sector wealthy might undertake. On the other hand, the point has often been made that, while taxation removes, particularly from businesses, the opportunity to buy productive equipment, it may also put funds in government hands that are then used for capital outlays of a quite unproductive nature—such as palace building.

The 'isolation paradox'[7]. Turning now to the second argument, we shall assume that equally good use could be made of savings, whether privately employed or used by the government. Returning to the basic premise that LDCs may often need to raise their savings ratios, governments may be able to appeal to the so-called 'isolation paradox' to justify increasing rates of taxation. The argument here is that individuals, left to make their decisions as isolated independent units, may well in aggregate finish up saving less than if they made their decision collectively. Taxation makes up the difference. To see this, assume that, in a society with perfectly equal income distribution, each individual has identical preferences as between present and future consumption and faces the same interest rate. Suppose now that, left to make decisions independently, each individual chooses to save $10 out of $100. It could well be, however, that, if told that everyone else would increase their savings to $11, each individual would be equally happy to save $11 himself. The difference between the two cases is that in the latter instance individuals take other individuals' actions into account in formulating their own preferences: they no longer act in isolation.

A concrete example might help to illustrate this. If a population of one million collectively decide each to save $1 more than they would choose to save as independent decision-makers, they will have $1 million extra with which to provide something worthwhile (a dam or a school) for themselves and their children collectively. It is barely far-fetched to imagine that each individual would be quite happy to sacrifice an extra $1 of present consumption so long as he knows for sure that his $1 will be added to another $999,999 collected from his fellow countrymen. On the other hand, viewing the benefits that he or his children might gain from the extra $1 of postponed consumption taken in isolation, it is quite consistent that he should prefer not to save it. Governments, by ensuring that everyone joins in, can bridge this gap between isolated individuals without the community incurring any loss of welfare as a result of the marginal extra sacrifice of present consumption. From a practical point of view, this argument is likely to carry weight only so long as the taxation system is perceived by all contributors to be fair— in that everyone without exception is forced to save more, according to some generally agreed set of criteria defining eligibility for taxation. Clearly, the argument also requires that a consensus exist on the desirability of the uses to which the taxes are put. So long as these criteria are met, there should not be any conflict between private saving and taxation.

Inflation

If governments are unable to find a sufficient tax base or consensus to raise tax revenue from it, one further avenue available to them is an inflationary development policy. The effects of inflation have been widely discussed, particularly in relation to South American countries, but here we shall focus upon the two main channels through which inflation is said to assist in raising domestic saving.

The first mechanism assumes that wage-earning workers and peasants have a low MPS while capitalist entrepreneurs have a high MPS. The effect of inflation, it is then said, will be to reduce the real value (the purchasing power) of wage incomes, leaving to entrepreneurs an increased surplus in the form of the real value of profit. If entrepreneurs save more at the margin than workers, this will raise the overall saving rate. Assuming these increased savings are invested effectively domestically, the economy should benefit through a higher growth rate. Clearly, the efficacy of this approach depends upon the different groups actually having different marginal propensities to save. It also requires that wage-earners do not or cannot fight back to preserve the real value of their income. If wage-earners are paid a fixed money wage, or a wage the money value of which is rising less quickly than prices, they may for a while not notice the erosion of their wage in real terms. This so-called 'money illusion' will help an inflationary policy. Further, any opposition to such a policy is likely to be weakened by the availability of a large pool of under- or unemployed labour outside the wage-earning pool of the economy, or by access to migrant labour. In the end, however, we must expect wage-earners to start to learn and to build inflationary expectations more accurately into their dealings with employers. And ultimately, such actions may be reinforced by the exhaustion of surplus labour. Once this happens, this channel for raising savings will cease to have any potential.

The second mechanism fully admits that everyone will before too long come to adjust all of their economic behaviour to an expected inflation rate. Its crucial assumption is that those in the monetary sector have a target level of real money balances that they wish to maintain—importantly, because of the convenience that money provides in ease of transaction-making. When inflation occurs, the number of transactions per period that can, on average, be made with a given sum of money starts to fall—unless institutions adjust to permit money to flow with ever-increasing speed around the economy. In order to maintain the transaction-making power, or real value, of their money balances, money holders attempt to build up their stock of money in nominal terms each period by an amount that offsets the inflation rate. This simultaneously requires them to sacrifice consumption of a certain quantity of non-monetary, real resources—saving is forced upon them through the medium of an 'inflationary tax' which now become available for development. Notice, though, that, since inflation reduces the usefulness of each unit of money, transactors may eventually start to cut down on their real balance holdings and take action (for example, storing goods instead), which tends to waste resources from an economic point of view.

It should be noted, however, that spiralling inflation eventually leads to a collapse of confidence in money and a demise in the willingness to hold both money itself and money-denominated assets. This in turn impedes the spread of money-use (monetization) in a developing country and can, in turn, be expected to reflect negatively upon the growth of savings.

In concluding our discussion on domestic resource mobilization, it is well worth noting that the question needs also to be viewed from an open economy perspective.

On the one hand, it should be pointed out that, even if the domestic savings ratio rises markedly, the direct usefulness of this trend will be inhibited to the extent that such savings subsequently find their way into investments abroad. We can think of several ways in which this might occur. Savings might be deposited in banks that prefer not to invest locally because they perceive opportunities to be limited by the early stage of development or believe too much risk attaches to the prospect of future returns. Wealthy individuals may make similar judgements, and respond to the prospect of higher returns abroad by buying foreign securities or depositing savings with foreign institutions. Again, multinational corporate enterprises may remit profits to the country where their headquarters are based rather than reinvest locally. To the extent that the process of development opens up the potential for private investment and reduces the risks associated with returns, not only should saving increase with rising income, but these resources should also be locally deployed to a greater degree.

On the other hand, developing countries have also often been the recipients of foreign capital inflows, both from private and governmental sources. Such inflows (the results, of course, of saving activity abroad) have led to the growth of primary (extractive or agricultural natural resource) industry and the importation of equipment embodying new techniques, or, as aid, have helped build up both physical infrastructure and the technical skill base. These in turn have the potential to promote development in a way that encourages both increased local saving and the conditions favourable for its domestic use. (Later—in chapter 6 and appendix 2 to that chapter—we shall explore the implications of admitting international aspects in much greater depth. We shall also look at a 'two-gap' model, which suggests that, if domestic saving is insufficient to permit a desired growth rate, then foreign capital inflows may be able to help meet the deficiency.) It should be said, however, that LDCs cannot expect private investors to 'fill the gap' unless they make the effort to provide a stable growing economic environment, and that, further, aid donors are likely to be unimpressed by nations that 'underperform' in mobilizing their own resources. That puts the onus of cultivating growth once more on the LDCs themselves—and so points up the importance, once again, of raising domestic savings rates.

CONCLUSION

Resource mobilization through saving, voluntary or enforced, is one of the keys to development. We know that technical progress, improved skills and reduced population growth can all contribute to development independently of the savings effort. But positive contributions from these directions will be supplemented and reinforced by a higher savings ratio, and, by itself, such an increase offers at least the potential for advance. Savings, of course, must be put to good use, which is why investment criteria are important (see next chapter). In countries where higher savings ratios have had disappointing consequences in terms of development, other productive inputs (especially skilled labour and managerial ability) may have been in short supply; resources, once mobilized, may not have been put to work where the economic returns were greatest; or domestically mobilized resources may have found their way into investments abroad. For all these types of reason, raising the saving rate is not a sufficient condition for raising domestic living standards in an LDC. The distributional consequences of increasing the savings rate must also be considered (see chapter 8).

The fact remains however that, if LDCs do not find ways of mobilizing resources themselves, they can hardly expect other countries to assist them, particularly when potential aid donors are themselves facing what they perceive to be insuperable economic problems. One way or another, learning to abstain from consumption today to increase consumption in years to come is an essential part of the development process.

FURTHER READING

The shifting of consumption over time is treated in many intermediate texts, for example Brunhild and Burton (1974, chapter 8); Branson (1979, chapters 3 and 10); and Laidler (1974, chapter 8).

Helpful references on the question of saving behaviour in developing economies are the wide-ranging survey by Mikesell and Zinser (1973), noted in the text, and Miracle, Miracle and Cohen (1980), which assembles much more recent evidence of the institutions underlying 'informal' saving activity. Snyder (1974) is another useful compilation of evidence from LDCs.

On capital market liberalization, McKinnon's contributions (1973, 1976, 1981) are central. The general question of financial institutions and their role in development is extensively treated in Drake (1980).

In the area of taxation, Kaldor (1963) remains the best starting-point for considering the issue of taxation potential, while the IMF and its staff (see references in text) provide comprehensive surveys of evidence.

Finally, much has been written on inflation and saving, and readers are directed to Thirlwall (1974) for a full treatment.

NOTES

1 As Miracle, Miracle and Cohen (1980, p. 708) point out, precious metals and stones kept domestically are, and are often perceived to be, subject to theft. Hoarded cash, not considered here, may also be eaten by insects.
2 For Africa, see Miracle, Miracle and Cohen (1980).
3 In terms of the more general framework we have adopted, this requires us to ignore the effect of interest rate changes. Such effects will be small if indifference curves are sharply curved (reducing intertemporal substitution effects to a minimum) and income effects can be ignored.
4 Blades, in Matthews (1980), points out that 25 per cent of LDCs still do not regularly publish national income statistics. In a study of five African countries he concludes that the 'two-sigma error range' for GDP is, on average ± 20 per cent, where this range has the meaning that 'if 100 national accountants were provided with the same basic data, 95 of them would produce estimates with the ranges shown'.
5 The surplus can, of course be reinvested within the agricultural sector— with the effect of transforming traditional agriculture into modernized agriculture. The 'instrumental' role of agriculture and its surplus, serving modern industry, is taken up in chapter 9. There, it is also pointed out that overemphasis on this approach may lead to a neglect of the agricultural population itself. To encourage agriculture to invest in itself, it may be necessary to encourage the spread of financial intermediaries into rural areas and the establishment of rural credit cooperatives; to provide infra-structure to raise rates of return on agricultural products and, further, to give general and specific forms of education and training; and perhaps to engage in land reform programmes. 'Green Revolution' techniques have significantly altered the prospects for agricultural investment (see chapter 9).
6 Colin Clark (1945) once argued that the critical limit of taxation was about 25 per cent of national income. Excessive taxation, reflecting budgetary

expenditure, he suggested, would weaken employers' resistance to wage increases, while policy-makers and bankers would become more reluctant to restrict rising wages and prices (p. 373). Inflation would be permitted to occur until the burden of the budget became 'bearable' again, a point that empirically, Clark calculated might be at the 25 per cent point.

7 The seminal work here is by A.K. Sen (1967).

5

Investment in Physical Capital

In this chapter we explore the determinants of how saved resources are put to use. We first construct a simple yet fairly general model which explains the logic behind the PV (present value) criterion for undertaking investment, and from this are able to identify factors that lead to varying investment rates. The lesson here is that investment has a multiplicity of determinants. One such determinant—changes in expected demand—has received special attention in the accelerator model and we examine this as a stepping stone to understanding the destabilizing potential of expectations in Harrod's model of growth. Next, we show the parallels and some of the major differences between private and public sector investment analysis. Finally, we take up the theme of intertemporal trade-offs in examining the long- and short-term consumption, output and employment consequences of adopting different techniques.

In the previous chapter we noted that the present value of an amount Y_1 received next year is $Y_1/(1 + r)$. It is easy to extend the analysis there to show that a dollar lent today for two years grows by the end of that period to:

$$\$1 + \$1(r) + \$[1(r)]r = \$1 + r + r^2$$
$$= \$(1 + r)^2.$$

By simple extension, $\$A$ lent at rate r will offer $\$A(1 + r)^2$ in two years' time. Further, $\$1$ lent for any number of years, say n, will, by then, offer a receipt of:

$$\$1 + r + r^2 + \ldots + r^n = \$(1 + r)^n$$

and
$$\$A \text{ will offer } \$A(1 + r)^n.$$

Similarly, the PV of $1 received in two years' time is $[1/(1 + r^2)]$ and in n years' time is $[1/(1 + r)^n]$, while the PV of A received in two years' time is $[A/(1 + r)^2]$ and of A received in n years' time $[A/(1 + r)^n]$. We are now in a strong position to examine investment theory. We shall concern ourselves solely with additions to the existing capital stock, or *net investment*. This enables us to ignore machine purchases made solely to replace existing machines that have physically worn out.

Firms make investments to increase the future consumption available to their owners. Firms may be entirely owned and run by a single individual, or owned by shareholders whose interests the managers of the company serve. When an investment is considered, the consumption that owners forgo in this period when buying an additional machine has to be compared with the consumption they will gain in future as a result of the investment.

To see how this fits in with our earlier section on saving, notice that, if we restrict our attention to two periods again, it is possible to draw a transformation curve which shows how consumption forgone (that is, saved) and invested in a piece of equipment can generate consumption in a future period.[1] In figure 5.1 we suppose that the firm has available to it today resources worth Y_m. If it adds one new machine to its stock, this will cost $(OY_m - OP_0)$ today. Putting this machine to effective use will, in the next period, earn net revenue of OE where $OE >$ $(OY_m - OP_0)$. If it adds a further machine this year at a cost of $(OP_0 - OP_0')$, it will earn a further EE', where EE' is a sum smaller than OE as it is assumed that each additional unit of capital will be associated with a diminishing return. This process can be continued until the complete transformation curve has been constructed. This curve summarizes the technical possibilities faced by the firm in generating future income and consumption from present capital outlay. The question is, 'How much present consumption should be forgone?'; in other words, 'How far should investment proceed?'

The answer to this question is that additions to the capital stock should be made until the PV of the marginal project falls to zero. Staying still with two periods, the PV of a two-period income stream we know to be $Y_0 + [Y_1/(1 + r)]$. In this case r is given by the market, but the firm can vary Y_0 and Y_1 by choosing different points on the transformation curve. Looking back at figure 4.1, recall that, with given values of Y_0 and Y_1 and given r, the present value of both periods' income was shown on the horizontal (year 0) axis where it was cut by the budget line. Utility-maximizing consumers wish to reach the highest indifference curve they can, and at any given r the means of achieving

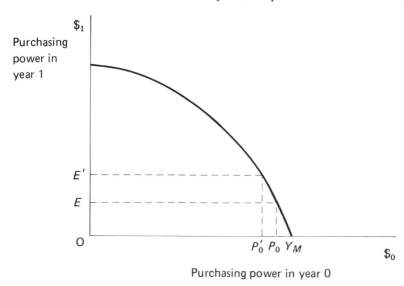

Figure 5.1 The two-period transformation curve

this is to require that the budget line be as far out from the origin as possible. Since the budget line cuts the horizontal axis at a point representing the PV of any combination of Y_0 and Y_1, this is equivalent to seeking the highest PV available.

Looking now at the transformation curve, note that each point upon it represents a combination of Y_0 and Y_1. The highest PV, given r, that can be achieved from all the possible combinations of Y_0 and Y_1 is that associated with a point on the transformation curve that just touches the *highest* (farthest out) budget line. The firm can vary Y_0 and Y_1 at will, but the particular combination it chooses must be the one at which PV is maximized—otherwise the owners as consumers will not be maximizing utility.

It is irrelevant that the particular combination of Y_0 and Y_1 chosen is not exactly that required by the owners. So long as the combination chosen lies on the budget line associated with the highest PV of two-period income, the owners can borrow or lend in the market at interest rate r and thereby move up or down the budget line to their utility-maximizing point. Notice that it will be a feature of the chosen investment point that the slope of the transformation curve must be the same as that of the budget line, namely $-(1 + r)$, otherwise it would not be true that the transformation curve was *just touching* it, which is the condition required to tell us that the highest budget line has been

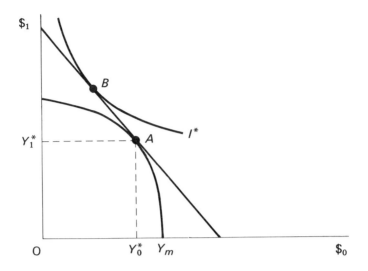

Figure 5.2 Equilibrium investment

reached. Also, as we saw earlier, this is at the same time the slope of the highest indifference curve attainable, given the budget constraint, at the point where the two just touch. In figure 5.2 resources worth $\$(OY_m - OY_0^*)$ are invested in capital stock and generate $\$OY_1^*$ next period. At A, the transformation curve touches the highest attainable budget constraint, given the interest rate r which determines its slope. At B, the budget constraint touches the highest attainable indifference curve, I^*, given the interest rate and the transformation possibilities. Even though saver−owners do not most prefer current and future income divided in the proportions OY_0^* to OY_1^*, they can trade up and down the budget line until they reach B.

It can now be seen why net investment should occur until the PV of the marginal machine is zero. So long as PV > 0 for the marginal machine, the PV of overall consumer expected incomes can be increased. Since increasing PV is the only way to increase consumer utility, firms can ensure owner utility maximization only by increasing investment until PV = 0 for the marginal machine. The firm then has an optimal capital stock. If, however, investment funds are a constraint, projects should be ranked with the highest PV project at the top, the second-highest PV project next, and so on down. Projects should be undertaken, starting from the top, until available funds are exhausted.

In general, the PV of a project is simply the result of adding up all the (discounted) receipts and subtracting the sum of all present and (discounted) future costs. The cost of the machine now, P_0, does not need to be discounted because it is already expressed in terms of today's dollars. Future receipts—$R_1, R_2, \ldots, R_n$ for the n years of the project— and future operating costs—$C_1, C_2, \ldots, C_n$—do need to be discounted, however, so that they can be compared on equal terms with each other and with P_0. Thus:

$$\mathrm{PV} = \left[\frac{R_1}{1 + r} + \frac{R_2}{(1 + r)^2} + \ldots + \frac{R_n}{(1 + r)^n} \right]$$

$$- \left[\frac{C_1}{1 + r} + \frac{C_2}{(1 + r)^2} + \ldots + \frac{C_n}{(1 + r)^n} \right] - P_0$$

or, equivalently,

$$\mathrm{PV} = \frac{R_1 - C_1}{1 + r} + \frac{R_2 - C_2}{(1 + r)^2} + \ldots + \frac{R_n - C_n}{(1 + r)^n} - P_0. \tag{5.1}$$

We can now see how net investment might vary from time to time.

(1) If r falls, all else constant, then each of the terms $(R_1 - C_1)/(1 + r), (R_2 - C_2)/(1 + r)^2, \ldots$ will rise for every project and so all projects will see the PV of their expected income stream rise. Some projects that formerly had a negative PV will now have a positive PV and so will become worth undertaking. This explains why a fall (rise) in the market rate of interest is usually assumed to stimulate a rise (fall) in investment.
(2) If some or all of the R terms rise (fall) in relation to a project, all else constant, then the PV of the project will also rise (fall).
(3) If some or all of the terms $C_1, C_2, \ldots, C_n$ rise (fall) in relation to a project, all else constant, then the PV of the project will fall (rise).
(4) If the P_0 term rises (falls) in relation to a project, all else constant, then the PV of the project will fall (rise).

Notice that, armed with a PV ranking, each firm knows what its optimal capital stock is—it is that stock whose size is such that the PV of the marginal unit is zero. When, owing to factors (1)–(4), some or all of the ranking changes, an adjustment to this optimum stock must be made. If we start with a position where all firms have an optimum capital stock, then it is clear that changes from that optimum must define net investment (or disinvestment—if negative), which is why investment is often called a stock adjustment process. Nothing we have said above, however, indicates how quickly this adjustment will occur.

An alternative procedure, called the internal rate of return (IRR) method, sets up the problem by asking what value i must take to solve the following equation:

$$P_0 = \frac{R_1 - C_1}{1 + i} + \frac{R_2 - C_2}{(1 + i)^2} + \ldots + \frac{R_n - C_n}{(1 + i)^n}$$

where the symbols have the same meaning as in (5.1). In other words, a value for i, the internal rate of return of the project, is being sought that will equate the value of the expected profit stream to the value of the initial outlay. Here the decision rule is to invest if IRR is greater than the rate of interest. So long as $i > r$, the project will offer a better rate of return on resources valued at P_0 than can be obtained in the financial market. Another way of looking at the meaning of the rule is to see that, if funds were borrowed in the market at rate r, then a project for which $i > r$ would generate enough profit to pay off the loan and still leave something over for the owners of the firm.

Although this method is widely understood and applied, it unfortunately cannot be relied upon to provide unique solutions. We note it here partly because it is so widely used and partly because by drawing attention to the market rate of interest as an opportunity cost it provides a natural opening to the discussion (pp. 122–5) of the appropriate discount rate to use in social cost–benefit analyses.

Notice that, in a two-period framework, i can be represented in figure 5.1 by looking at the slopes such as $OE/(OY_m - OP_0)$ and $EE'/(OP_0 - OP_0')$ Clearly, the numerator in each of these cases exceeds the denominator, so future purchasing power is greater than the current purchasing power that was put into capital rather than consumption goods. The percentage amount by which the numerator exceeds the denominator represents the internal rate of return generated by the project in each case. If ratios such as these were, for example 1.5/1.0 or 1.32/1.0, they could alternatively be written $(1 + 0.5)$ or $(1 + 0.32)$ and in each case i would be 50 per cent and 32 per cent.

One implication of examining investment in a two-period framework is that, if conditions change in one period, any adjustment to the optimum capital stock that needs to be made can and will be made in the next period. This is clearly an over-simplification. The rational firm will make the adjustment at the speed that maximizes profit. If there are no costs associated with the adjustment, the whole of the change required to obtain a new optimum stock will indeed occur in one period. But in fact, adjustment costs are usually positive. In particular, new capital stock has to be properly integrated into the existing set-up. This may require reorganization of existing arrangements and perhaps elements of training to accustom labour to any new design features. It may therefore be profit-maximizing to adopt a more gradual adjustment to the new optimum rather than attempting to rush changes through at once.

In general, all of the analysis carried out so far at the level of the individual business can be applied to explain aggregate investment behaviour. For example, a change in the interest rate should influence all firms whose optimal capital stock changes as a result. There will then be an economy-wide shift in investment demand. Again, a change in expected aggregate demand should raise or lower the return expected from many firms' projects. A change in expected operating costs— arising, say, from oil price changes or minimum wage legislation— should have the same widespread effect.

As changes such as these work through changes in the optimal capital stock to induce aggregate investment demand changes, so we might also expect the price of capital goods themselves to vary. If aggregate investment demand rises and the suppliers of capital goods are near to full-capacity production, then excess demand for capital goods may occur and the price of such goods will rise. Along with positive adjustment costs, this element will tend to slow down the rate at which it is profit-maximizing to undertake investment.

Even ignoring adjustment costs and capital goods price inflation, it should finally be noted that lags are an integral part of the investment process. It takes time for businesses to realize that their existing capital stock is no longer optimal, either in size or in the nature of its composition, given that patterns of demand are changing all the time and new techniques of production are becoming available. This period of dawning realization is called the 'recognition lag'. Once the realities of the new situation have been recognized, a decision has to be made on what to do about it. Information has to be gathered relating to the price and quality of capital available on the market. Meetings may have to be held to decide how the investment should be financed. All this defines the 'implementation lag'. Finally, orders for machines cannot immediately be met, particularly if the equipment is being purchased abroad. This lag, often substantial in LDCs, is called the 'delivery lag'.

There is then a multiplicity of factors at work in determining the optimum capital stock at any moment, changes in that stock, and the rate at which the change might occur. Any theory that relies upon a single explanatory variable, therefore, can be treated only as a partial theory. On the other hand, such theories can be useful in directing our attention to particular facets and consequences of investment behaviour, and we shall develop one such theory here: the accelerator. It is by no means a complete model of investment, but we shall see that it can be incorporated in a model of growth to give a quite different perspective on the way economies change from that which is embedded in Solow's model.

ACCELERATOR MODELS

In the general model of investment presented in the last few pages, we noted that an increase in expected revenues (either in the absence of other changes, or if faster than expected cost increases) would have the effect of setting off an upward adjustment in the capital stock. A less general but very influential model of investment, based on the so-called accelerator principle, stresses the change in expected revenue to the exclusion of all other elements. Increasing revenue is assumed to flow from increasing demand, and more capital is required to produce the output to meet increased demand if existing capital is already at or near full utilization and no substantial substitution in production is available between capital and labour. Looked at formally, it is assumed that, in aggregate, a fixed number of capital units is required by the technology in producing one unit of output. Thus, denoting that fixed ratio by v, and expressing the relation in aggregate terms,

$$K_t / Y_t = v \qquad (5.2a)$$

or, equivalently,[2]

$$K_t = v Y_t. \qquad (5.2b)$$

This is a mechanical relationship in more senses than one. It can be converted into an investment relationship by noting that, if the capital stock is fully adjusted in line with the technical requirements during one period,

$$K_t = v Y_t$$
$$K_{t-1} = v Y_{t-1}$$

Thus

$$K_t - K_{t-1} = v Y_t - v Y_{t-1} = v(Y_t - Y_{t-1}). \qquad (5.3)$$

Since by definition[3] $K_t - K_{t-1} = I_t$, then

$$I_t = v(Y_t - Y_{t-1}). \qquad (5.4)$$

This says that net aggregate investment will be determined by the *change* in demand-generated output and will be directly proportional to it. In general, we would not expect the whole of the capital stock adjustment to be made in one period, so that the effect of the determining elements in (5.3)—output change and the technical coefficient, v—must be scaled down, by a factor with a numerical value of less than one. Let us call this factor β. Then[4]

$$I_t = \beta[v(Y_t - Y_{t-1})] \qquad 0 < \beta < 1.$$

It is now time to introduce the crucial element of *expectations*. Investment decisions are made with an eye to what the future is expected to bring. Suppose all firms in an economy make their investment decisions on the first day of the financial year. A year we shall enumerate '2' stretches before them (it might be 1992) and a year enumerated '1' (say 1991) lies behind them. Investment in year 2 (I_2) will depend, according to (5.3), on demand generated output in year 2, Y_2 and the demand based output of year 1, Y_1; put another way,

$$I_2 = v(Y_2 - Y_1).$$

But the only observable magnitudes here are v and Y_1: Y_2 is an *expected* variable and in future we shall denote it Y_2^e to remind ourselves of the fact. The investment decisions actually made thus depend upon how demand is expected to change. Clearly, net investment will occur only if businessmen expect demand in year 2 to outstrip that in year 1.

Merely stating this fact, however, tells us nothing about how expectations are formed. It is usually suggested that past experience is taken as the best guide to the future, with the recent past providing the most influential weight. On the other hand, it must be recognized that the future is always uncertain and investors must always expect to 'get it wrong' sometimes.

For LDCs, this view of investment behaviour needs to be treated with care for a number of reasons, mainly associated with v. This coefficient represents the belief that capital, in aggregate, bears some fixed proportional relationship to output. As we have already seen, the most obvious way of interpreting this is to view the nature of the aggregate production as such that, irrespective of relative factor prices or anything else, the only technologically available way of producing output is by using capital goods in fixed proportion to it. This seems highly implausible, certainly in the longer run. It is a feature of real economic life that technical progress permits, in the longer run, progressively *less* capital to be used per unit of output, and thus v should fall over time. It is also observably true that in many production processes a unit of output can be produced with varying proportions of capital and labour, and no empirical study has ever claimed that the elasticity of substitution between capital and labour is in actuality zero in the aggregate. Another interpretation of fixed v is however available —that the market never gives any justification or incentive for it to change. Clearly, if relative factor prices never change, then, no matter how rich the technology in its variants, there will never be any inducement for profit-maximizing entrepreneurs to change the proportions in which they employ capital and labour, and thus the ratio of capital to a unit of output.

Two other points about v should be noted here for future reference. Even if v is observably fixed over time at the aggregate level, it is by no means impossible that the capital–output relationship in firms and industries may change. Aggregate v is merely a weighted average of a host of micro-level ratios, so that important structural changes might be occurring in the nature and composition of the economy that do not show up in the aggregate measure. Second, if the ratio of capital to output is fixed at every moment, then the ratio of the *change* in capital to the *change* in output must also be fixed. This also is implausible, particularly in LDCs. At an early stage of development, this ratio of changing variables—the incremental capital–output ratio (ICOR)— can be expected to be higher than it is later. This is because, as labour becomes more skilled and managerial inputs increase in number and quality, so successively smaller additions of capital should be needed to increase output by similar increments.

THE EFFECT OF INVESTORS' EXPECTATIONS ON GROWTH: HARROD'S MODEL

Armed with this view of investment, we can proceed to a brief review of the Harrod growth model to see the sort of general conditions under which instability, largely ignored in Solow-type models, can arise through the impact of imperfect guessing in an uncertain world.

(The following analysis takes its approach from Sen, 1970, Introduction.)

Elementary analysis of national income determination permits derivation of the simple multiplier relationship,

$$Y_t = \frac{1}{s} I_t \qquad 0 < s < 1 \qquad (5.5)$$

where s is the MPS and assumed constant, and thus equal to the APS.

Now, if we assume investment is accelerator-determined,

$$Y_2 = \frac{1}{s} I_2$$

$$= \frac{1}{s} [v(Y_2^e - Y_1)] = \frac{v}{s}(Y_2^e - Y_1). \qquad (5.6)$$

Further, we can find the relationship between what is expected to happen and what actually does happen to income in year 2 by dividing both sides by Y_2^e:

$$\frac{Y_2}{Y_2^e} = \frac{v}{s}\left(\frac{Y_2^e - Y_1}{Y_2^e}\right). \qquad (5.7)$$

Now, the term in brackets represents the expected growth rate of income, which we will write g^e. If what happens is what investors actually expected, $Y_2 = Y_2^e$ and so $Y_2/Y_2^e = 1$. But this ratio is determined by what happens on the right-hand side of the equation. Since exact fulfilment of expectations is represented by the equality $Y_2/Y_2^e = 1$, and $Y_2/Y_2^e = (v/s)(g^e)$, we must ask what conditions the various parts of $(v/s)(g^e)$ must fulfil in order that the whole expression be equal to 1. The obvious answer is that s/v must be the same as g^e. That growth rate which exactly fulfils investors' expectations is called the 'warranted growth rate'. Businessmen invest in line with their expectations of future demand for their output. This is the accelerator. The actual value of future demand is determined by the multiplier and how much they invest. If the demand they observe (resulting from the investment they undertook to meet the demand they expected) actually turns out to be what they expected, then they will feel warranted or justified in having invested as they did. This will occur only when businessmen's growth expectations exactly match s/v.

This is equivalent to saying that the growth rate of demand for which businessmen plan (and on which they base their investment decisions) must be s/v, or else the actual growth rate that results from their investment decisions will differ from that for which they planned. In fact, it can be shown formally that

$$\begin{matrix}\text{Actual} \\ \text{growth}\end{matrix} \gtreqless \begin{matrix}\text{expected} \\ \text{growth}\end{matrix} \quad \text{according as} \quad \begin{matrix}\text{expected} \\ \text{growth}\end{matrix} \gtreqless \frac{s}{v}.$$

Here we will give a simple numerical example. Investors make decisions in light of given data on s and v, which are fixed by the terms of the model, observed demand in the last period Y_1 and expected demand in the next period, Y_2^e. Below we look at three cases: the first with expected demand implying an expected growth rate of aggregate output in line with s/v, and the second and third with expected demand implying expected growth rates above and below s/v. In each case $s/v = 0.05$,

	s	v	$\dfrac{s}{v}$	Y_2^e	Y_1	g^e	Y_2	g^a
(1)	0.2	4	0.05	160	152	0.05	160	0.05
(2)	0.2	4	0.05	161	152	0.056	180	0.156
(3)	0.2	4	0.05	159	152	0.44	140	−0.086

or 5 per cent. In case (1), if expected demand is 160, the accelerator principle requires investment in four machines for every unit of expected increase in required output: 32 in all. Through the multiplier, this generates actual demand for output of 160, so expectations are exactly fulfilled, and the actual growth rate, g^a, is the same as the expected growth rate and s/v. This is clearly the warranted growth rate. In case (2), investors expect demand to require output of 161 from them and so invest in 36 machines. But through the multiplier this generates actual output demand of 180—and a growth rate of 15.6 per cent. Since this actual growth rate, $(180 - 152)/180 = 15.56$ per cent, is greater than the rate $(161 - 152)/161 = 5.59$ per cent, that businessmen had expected, they will be left feeling that they did not undertake enough investment. Notice the paradox: even though they invested more than the amount required for the economy to achieve a growth rate that would have made them feel warranted (or justified) in their decision, businessmen finish up with the perception that they did not invest enough. In the absence of outside intervention not allowed for by the simple specifications of the model, businessmen will in this case invest in the next round at a rate that is again in excess of that associated with the warranted growth rate. What is more, there is no way in which the economy can get back on an even keel. In case (3), businessmen under-invest with respect to the rate that would achieve the warranted growth rate but in the end feel they should have invested even less. Once again, the economy sets off on an apparently irreversible path away from the warranted growth rate.

This account suggests that the world might be a much more unstable place than could ever be conceived in a Solow type of framework. The inevitable tendency of a Solow-type model to achieve equilibrium disappears because of the perfectly reasonable requirement that invest-ment activity be modelled as the result of decisions made on the basis of guesses about an uncertain future. Meeting this requirement supplants the assumption that all intertemporal resource allocation occurs with a perfect knowledge of the future, or as if such knowledge were possessed by decision-makers. In a Solow-type world, expectations cannot be disappointed; in a Harrod-type world, we are directed to notice not only that they might be, but also that, if they are, instability on a substantial scale results.

It takes very little in the realistically drawn world of an uncertain future to introduce instability into the growth of an economy. The extreme degree of instability in Harrod's model arises from the equally extreme simplicity of his specifications: a crude accelerator interacting with a crude multiplier mechanism. In a more rounded model, a government could intervene, automatic fiscal stabilizers could get to work, and so on.

But let us not be deceived. Instability and the disappointment of expectations are prevalent features of real economies. Even if the mechanisms we have examined here oversimplify the picture, they capture a crucial element of truth: businessmen's inability to predict the future accurately can have potentially serious effects in destabilizing the economy. In the field of development economics, the question of market instability, penetratingly revealed by Keynes, has tended to be ignored (see Nugent and Yotopoulos, 1979, p. 549). This section has been a modest attempt at least to draw attention to it.

Before we finally leave this area, it is worth noting that the apparently irreconcilable predictions of Solow- and Harrod-type models may not after all be entirely at odds. Harrod was concerned more with the short run, Solow with the long. In a long-run model, fluctuations around a trend (explained by Harrod-type mechanisms, supplemented by economic 'buffers' to prevent completely irreversible divergences from the warranted growth path) would be relegated to a position of secondary importance behind the growth trend itself.

PUBLIC SECTOR INVESTMENT

So far in this chapter we have dealt with the analytical foundations of private investment behaviour. In general, we saw, rational utility-maximizing firms' owners would require that investment proceed until the net present value of expected profit was reduced, at the margin, to zero. In the last chapter, however, we noted that, if private saving proved inadequate to generate capital investment sufficient to achieve some desired higher growth rate, then governments could force the private sector to save by taxation, manipulation of the domestic terms of trade or inflation. Assuming now that governments wish to invest public funds in productive capital projects, how should they go about their task? The approach, in principle, is not all that different from that of the businessman's, but the perspective is wider. We shall look at this question next, and then complete the chapter with a discussion of the way in which varying the stated objectives may in turn lead to different decisions with respect to the types of technique adopted.

COST–BENEFIT ANALYSIS

In equation (5.1) we summarized the calculation that a private sector business would make in working out the present value of a capital project. This PV was calculated from the point of view of the firm's owners and represented the present-day value to them of the expected financial profit stream that the project would generate. We saw that a firm owned by utility-maximizing owners would be motivated to maximize the overall PV of the business and so would be rational to continue expanding until the PV of the marginal project fell to zero. Assuming that the owners are utility-maximizers, this tells us how firms might be expected to act and what sort of factors we might therefore expect to influence investment.

We viewed this sort of analysis from the perspective of the firm, which we then aggregated up. But suppose now that we wish to view the stream of profit generated by a project from the point of view of the economy as a whole—the social point of view. We would then need to take into account not only (and perhaps not all of) the elements included in the businessman's calculation, but also elements representing the effect of the project on other parts of the economy—effects external to the project itself. Further, if we wish to value the project in terms of its success in meeting developmental objectives and also want to take account correctly of the relative scarcity of developmental resources, we may not be able to use market prices. Adjustments can be made, if necessary, to any purely financial calculation in relation to any private sector project with a view to assessing its value from an overall economic point of view. But the need to carry out an analysis of costs and benefits from a social perspective—a cost–benefit analysis (CBA)—becomes particularly acute when governments come to decide how to allocate the resources that they have forced the private sector to save. Such decisions should, after all, be guided by clearly defined developmental aims.

Having said this, governments must still decide, once they have resources mobilized for investment, how to rank potential projects so that they may be compared with each other. In a CBA, a government will try to find the social present value (SPV) of a project according to a calculation:

$$\text{SPV} = \frac{B_1 - SC_1}{(1 + r)} + \frac{B_2 - SC_2}{(1 + r)^2} + \ldots + \frac{B_n - SC_n}{(1 + r)^n} - K \qquad (5.8)$$

where $B_1, \ldots, B_n$ are the social (that is, economy-wide) benefits, $SC_1, \ldots, SC_n$ are the social costs, K is the initial capital cost, $1/(1 + r)$ is the discount factor at rate of interest r, and n is the number of years of the project's life. The rule is to proceed from the project with the highest SPV down the list to the project with the next highest SPV, and so on until SPV = 0. The similarity of (5.8) with (5.1) should be carefully noted, but so should the differences underlying its calculation.

WHICH BENEFITS? WHICH COSTS?

While the firm will find it relatively easy to identify the particular items that will bring it revenue and involve it in cost, the government must exercise great skill and foresight in 'catching' the full range of items generating benefit and cost in relation to a potential public investment, from the point of view of the economy. A firm, for example, should include as a cost taxes that it must pay. Yet this is not a resource cost to the economy as a whole (it is a transfer payment) and should not be treated as a cost in a CBA. On the other hand, a firm will exclude from consideration externalities. An externality exists when:

(a) economic activity in the form of production or consumption affects the production or utility levels of other producers or consumers; and

(b) the effect is unpriced or uncompensated. [Dasgupta and Pearce, 1972, p. 118]

Two examples of how a CBA would have to adjust for externalities are given here.

Consider first a firm that trains young apprentices who, at the end of their training period, leave and set up in business on their own account, or work for other firms in the economy. Here, other producers, or the young as producer–consumers, gain valuable skills from their training, but while the firm incurs the costs of the training we can assume that it will not have appropriated many of the benefits accruing from the training (in the form of skilled workmanship) which in future years the economy as a whole will enjoy. There is a benefit, external to the firm, which a CBA should capture when assessing the training programme as a project.

On the other hand, a firm might adopt a particularly 'dirty' technique in its manufacturing process and perhaps pollute or poison water that, downstream, is used by consumers to bathe or wash clothes in, and by producers as an input into another process. The costs of pollution and, perhaps, of purifying the water before re-use will not be borne by the firm (and thus will be external to it) unless compensation is claimed from it by legal action. They will not therefore occur in the firm's private analysis of the project. But a CBA, taking the broader view, should incorporate these costs.

SHADOW PRICES AND VALUATION

A major difference in the method by which a CBA proceeds, compared with a purely financial analysis, lies in the prices that are used to value costs and benefits. Since CBA attempts to value expected *social* costs and *social* benefits, and their difference (if positive) is expected *social* profit, it is important that all of the elements of the calculation be valued appropriately. To put the appropriate social value upon costs and benefits, we need to know a country's developmental objectives and to be sure that the relative scarcity of resources in meeting these objectives is properly reflected in the prices used to decide how resources should be allocated. Even more explicitly, a CBA is an attempt to put a value, from the point of view of the economy as a whole, upon any planned project. Such a value must incorporate the aspirations of that economy and the constraints that limit the freedom of the economy to meet these objectives. Prices constructed to do these jobs are called 'shadow prices'.

Shadow pricing is itself a large and complex topic and we can only touch on it here, drawing on work done at the World Bank by Squire and Van der Tak (1975). Other important references are Little and Mirrlees (1974), UNIDO (1972), a symposium published in the *Bulletin of the Oxford University Institute of Economics and Statistics* (1972), and Scott, Macarthur and Newbery (1976).

Suppose we start with the shadow price of labour—the shadow wage rate (SWR). The cost incurred by the economy as a whole through employing a unit of labour on a project is the marginal contribution that that unit of labour would have made to producing output elsewhere. In the case where a unit of labour would have been unemployed if not working on this project, the opportunity cost to the economy of employing him would be zero. Since LDCs are often supposed to be characterized by a labour surplus, or widespread disguised unemployment where the marginal product of labour is at or near zero, the SWR employed in CBA calculations is often much below the actual wage paid to the worker on the project.

It may be asked why the actual wage is so far above labour's social opportunity cost. The reasons could be institutional; equity-motivated minimum wage legislation or trade union activity may both introduce distortions for which the shadow calculation corrects. On the other hand, we should beware of concluding that a high actual wage necessarily betokens the presence of distortions. Scarce skilled labour may have a high marginal product elsewhere in the economy, and both its actual wage and the shadow wage might therefore also be high.

While this discussion has focused primarily upon the relative scarcity aspect of shadow pricing, it is essential to bear in mind the developmental objectives of the economy. Suppose the government is committed to faster growth, but that administrative and political factors (of the kind discussed in the section on taxation, pp. 94–7 above) prevent it from bringing about forced saving at the rate desired to 'top up' voluntary savings. If employing additional labour on a project increases labour's overall income, one expectation might well be for overall consumption to increase, since labour's MPC is often assumed to be higher than that of entrepreneurs (for evidence see p. 86). With savings at a premium where faster growth is an objective, this addition to consumption should in some way be accounted a cost of the project and included in the shadow price of labour. By increasing the SWR in this case, a price signal is incorporated in the analysis that should make the cost incurred in terms of the growth objective clear.

It is quite probable, on the other hand, that governments will have objectives that potentially conflict with the faster growth aim. In particular, governments in LDCs will probably have the objective of improving the standard of living of the worst off. Assuming once again that fiscal means cannot do the job, a project evaluation that provides jobs and incomes for the unemployed poor should contain an element reflecting the fact that the project helps meet this objective. The obvious way to do this is to adjust the SWR downwards.

That the adjustments in these cases are of opposite direction is quite consistent with realizing that growth must often be traded off against income distribution objectives.

This discussion has centred on the shadow price of labour, but a similar type of analysis can be conducted for any scarce input. When the cost of intermediate or produced inputs is determined solely by current operating costs, as will be the case when capacity is fully utilized, the current price is the short-run marginal social cost. But when capacity is fully utilized, such inputs may start to earn a scarcity rent. Any factor in fixed supply may earn such a rent, reflecting its scarcity, and since the purpose of a CBA is to identify and follow up the implications of such scarcities, they will be embodied in the shadow price of these factors. But rents, along with interest and profit income on capital, accrue to individuals or classes of fixed factor and capital owners. In the same way that the SWR could be adjusted in light of how labour income was used and who received it, so also must shadow prices for non-labour factors reflect the social value attached to generating income for, say, landowners as opposed to the landless, or potentially heavy savers (perhaps entrepreneurs) as opposed to committed consumers.

Finally, if a project is relatively large, it can often be expected to reduce the price paid domestically for the output(s) of the project. This means that there will be an increase in consumer surplus which should be incorporated in the benefits of the project. The reason is that consumer surplus measures the difference between what consumers would be prepared to pay for a given quantity and what they are actually charged. If price per unit falls, then for each quantity consumers might consider buying, the amount they would be prepared to pay now exceeds the actual price by a greater extent than before. Using the same criteria as with costs to judge the value, in terms of developmental objectives, of additional incomes according to their recipients, such growth in the consumer surplus can be given a social value.

THE DISCOUNT RATE

Consider, finally, the rate r at which the social profits of the project should be discounted. One approach is to examine the opportunity cost to society of undertaking the project. It requires us to examine points on the transformation curve representing the technical capacity of the economy to convert forgone current consumption into future consumption. A second approach requires a direct appeal to society's preferences between present and future consumption and calls upon us to look at the social analogue for an individual's indifference curves.

To understand the first approach go back to figure 5.1. There we noted that amounts of resources like $(OY_m - OP_0)$ and $(OP_0 - OP_0')$ could be invested in capital stock rather than consumed today, with the result that consumption possibilities next period could be increased by OE and EE' respectively, compared with what would have been available in the absence of sacrificing these amounts of present consumption. We also noted (see p. 110) that slopes like $OE/OY_m - OP_0$ and $EE'/OP_0 - OP_0'$ could be used to find the internal rate of return on a given resource investment. If ratios like these are written in the form $OE/(OY_m - OP_0) = (1 + i)$, then i represents the project internal rate of return.

Now imagine figure 5.1 to represent all private sector projects. If we concern ourselves solely with public sector investment we should examine the slope of this now-sectoral transformation curve at various points to find the internal rate of return (IRR) of any chosen private project. Bear in mind that the government 'can be thought of as competing in the capital market for funds which would otherwise go to private investments' (Dasgupta and Pearce, 1972, p. 145). Then, of particular interest to us will be the IRR of the project *not* undertaken by the private sector, at the margin, because the public sector is using resources that would, alternatively, have been invested privately.

If this view is taken, we have a measure of the opportunity cost of the public sector investment. To make sure it is a true social opportunity cost, however, we must also calculate the social costs and benefits of the private sector project and, if the IRR then implied is different from that in the financial calculation, adjust accordingly. This social opportunity cost of capital can then be used either as the standard of comparison by which to judge the IRR on any public sector project or as the value to be taken by r in the SPV formula. The IRR of a public sector project is found by writing

$$K = \frac{B_1 - SC_1}{(1 + i)} + \frac{B_2 - SC_2}{(1 + i)^2} + \ldots + \frac{B_n - SC_n}{(1 + i)^n}$$

and solving for i.

An alternative approach is to adopt a direct welfare measure of the rate at which society *wants* to substitute consumption in one period for that in another. Here, we have to define a social welfare function

$$W = W(C_0, C_1)$$

where overall economic welfare is made to depend upon overall consumption in each of the periods. Now, this is analogous to writing down individual utility as a function of individual consumption, and, as in the individual case, we may draw an indifference curve showing the combinations of C_0 and C_1 that generate a given level of social welfare. The slope of this social indifference curve at any point shows the marginal rate at which society considers it desirable to substitute C_0 for C_1. It is a welfare term and can be found algebraically by noting, first, that along a social indifference curve the value of W will be held fixed (by definition) but that, second, any value of W is determined by both C_0 and C_1. Allowing C_0 to change by a small amount and C_1 to change (in the opposite direction) by an amount that keeps W constant ($dW = 0$) allows us to identify the marginal rate of substitution; that is,

$$dW = 0$$

along any social indifference curve. But

$$W = W(C_0, C_1)$$

so

$$dW = \frac{\partial W}{\partial C_0} dC_0 + \frac{\partial W}{\partial C_1} dC_1$$

by the rules of total differentiation, and, rearranging,

$$\frac{\partial W}{\partial C_0} dC_0 = - \frac{\partial W}{\partial C_1} dC_1$$

or

$$\frac{\partial W/\partial C_0}{\partial W/\partial C_1} = - \frac{dC_1}{dC_0}.$$

By definition, the marginal rate of substitution between consumption in the two periods is $-(dC_1/dC_0)$ and is thus equal to the ratio of the welfare derivatives. As we said, therefore, the slope of the indifference curve is a welfare term.

Suppose $dC_1 > dC_0$. Then $dC_1/dC_0 > 1$ and can be written in the form $(1 + \rho)$, where ρ represents the percentage by which dC_1 exceeds dC_0. In fact, ρ is called the social rate of time preference between periods 0 and 1, and also the social rate of time discount. Of interest to us is what determines ρ.

It turns out that ρ is made up of two elements. First, suppose that $C_0 = C_1$. If, none the less, society prefers C_0 to C_1 at the margin (in which case $(dC_1/dC_0) > 1$ along the indifference curve at this point), society is said to have pure time preference or to be impatient. Some commentators have attributed such social behaviour to a weakness of imagination or even to pure rapacity. On the other hand, governments (which must decide what ρ is in order to make decisions) are subject by election or threat of coup to the short-run preferences of their constituents. And even if society takes the long view, the threat of extinction by natural causes or nuclear war may make it rational to put a premium on early-period consumption—or to discount on later-period consumption.

Now suppose that $C_1 > C_0$, and that population is growing less quickly than aggregate consumption. Then there is the further argument that an additional unit of consumption in period 0 has more social value than the same additional unit in period 1, since society will in any case have more consumption in period 1. This also would tend to make society discount future consumption, at the margin, at a positive rate.

In LDCs, it is usually found that the rate of return on capital exceeds the time preference rate. In this situation, sacrifice of an extra unit of C_0 will generate, through investment, $(1 + r)$ units of extra C_1. This is more than the $(1 + \rho)$ extra units that society actually wants, according to its social welfare function, to make up for its sacrifice of a marginal unit of C_0 while being maintained at a given level of social welfare. Thus the opportunity to achieve a higher level of welfare exists—and will continue to exist until ρ and r are brought into equality.

Deciding on which of these to use is not by any means straight-forward, but readers interested in further discussion on this point should consult Marglin (1967). In principle, however, if $r > \rho$ a higher rate of investment would achieve a higher level of social welfare. Since investment derives from saving, this suggests that, of the incomes generated by a project, any elements that are saved should be valued more highly than those that are consumed. This is one of the features of the Little–Mirrlees approach, which goes to some pains to put a shadow price on savings. As Dasgupta and Pearce (1972) show, the social opportunity cost and social time preference rates can be used together to derive this shadow price. If benefits are expressed in terms of consumption, they can be discounted using the social time preference rate (STPR) (which was built on a consumption trade-off), and the value of any savings, appropriately shadow priced, can be discounted at the social opportunity cost (SOC) since this represents the next-best alternative rate of return that such savings could earn.

THE CHOICE OF TECHNIQUES

The importance of raising the saving rate and putting those unconsumed resources to productive use is now generally appreciated. Given that widespread unemployment is a feature of many LDCs, a question that on the other hand has received more attention recently is whether we should worry about the nature of the techniques adopted in the course of capital investment. A technique is defined as the ratio of capital to labour (K/L), used in a project where we shall assume that both can be considered homogeneous. The higher the value of this ratio, the more capital-intensive the technique is said to be; the lower the value, the more labour-intensive it is.

Now, in an economy that is relatively abundant in labour and suffers a capital scarcity, the most rational course of action would seem to be to adopt in any project the technique that maximizes output per unit of capital, in other words minimizes the ratio of capital to output, K/Y. Thus, the most rational decision criterion might seem to be to select investments in terms of this ratio, irrespective of their K/L ratio.—In fact, such a criterion—the so-called 'rate of turnover criterion'—is suggested both by Polak (1943) and Buchanan (1945). Buchanan says: 'If investment funds are limited, the wise policy, in the absence of special considerations, would be to undertake first those investments having a high value of annual product relative to the investment necessary to bring them into existence' (p. 24).

We argued in the last section, however, that LDCs tend to place emphasis on precisely those type of objectives that Buchanan might regard as 'special considerations'—the alleviation of poverty and equalization of the income distribution by project choice when other policy measures are impotent or weak. In fact, the ramifications are even wider. The choice of technique influences not only the achievement of such objectives now but the potential for achieving them and other objectives in future.

To see this, assume that a given (quite large) quantity of resources is available for investment in physical capital. If a relatively labour-intensive technique is chosen, present-day employment will be much increased and the income generated by the project spread over many recipients, thus directly alleviating poverty and probably introducing greater equality into the income distribution. This would seem in a short time to meet important developmental objectives. On the other hand, a relatively capital-intensive technique would employ only a small amount of extra labour and because, as a result, the share of wages in the overall value of output produced would be relatively small, a larger surplus or profit should be generated. This surplus would accrue not to labour but to the owner or small group of owners, in the case of a private sector project, and would not in the short run serve the developmental objectives referred to above.

But does this constitute a watertight case for adopting the labour-intensive technique? As it turns out, it does not. First of all, there will be variation from one LDC to another in the actual incidence of unemployment and the seriousness of income inequality. Further, there will be variation in the degree of concern with which different LDCs view such factors. Even ignoring those points, though, adjusting our perspective from the short to the long term throws quite a different light on the whole question.

The labour-intensive project will generate income for a group of people who may be expected to consume a high proportion of what they earn. And since what they earn constitutes a relatively large proportion of the income generated by the project, much of the project-generated income will be spent on consumption goods. On the other hand, the relatively capital-intensive project will put a larger proportion of project-generated income into the hands of a group—entrepreneurs —that may be expected also to save at a higher rate. If their savings are reinvested domestically and effectively, a higher rate of investment will be achieved than had the labour-intensive technique been adopted. As a result, a higher growth rate of output will also be achieved and the long-term prospect of growing employment will be created.

The labour-intensive technique thus achieves a higher level of employment and consumption in the first period, but because it is associated with a lower saving and investment rate, the longer-term implication is that output will grow less quickly than it would in the wake of a capital-intensive investment. If output grows more slowly, so also will the potential for consumption and employment. In the case of a capital-intensive technique, initial employment created will be less, but growth in employment, as well as output, will be faster. In due course the overall employment created by capital-intensive techniques should 'overtake' that created by labour-intensive techniques, and the various advantages associated with higher employment levels can thus, eventually, be enjoyed in addition to the faster growth rate of output. Only if techniques adopted in future periods are increasingly capital-intensive might this conclusion be endangered.

The argument about the right technique to adopt turns out to hinge, therefore, upon the urgency with which an LDC wishes to achieve one type of objective rather than another and the constraints it believes to be operating upon it. If a country prefers to increase current consumption, even at the expense of future growth in consumption potential, it should adopt relatively labour-intensive techniques. Further, should it believe that income redistribution or the alleviation of poverty could not be effectively achieved in the short term by taxation and subsidy, then it will also tend to look to the choice of techniques of production as an alternative means of achieving these ends. It should be said, however, that 'using' the choice of techniques in this way may not always be justified. It may simply be the case that governments prefer to try to persuade businessmen (and their own planners) to adopt labour-intensive techniques rather than to take unpalatable decisions about rates of and targets for higher taxation. The former, after all, looks to be a purely technical matter while the latter is more obviously perceived to have political implications which might be unpopular.

We assumed at the outset of the discussion that a given amount of capital was to be put to work and that the choice was between a capital-intensive and a labour-intensive technique. One dimension of the problem we suppressed at that stage was the capital–output ratio. Some schools of thought suggest that employment-creating, labour-intensive techniques not only pose problems for future output growth, but in the short run also offer less current output per unit of capital. This would lead the rate-of-turnover criterion to reject them. If we maintain our fixed capital assumption, that also means that the labour-intensive technique must produce less output in total than the capital-intensive technique both now and in future. In other words, current employment is receiving an extremely strong emphasis. Figure 5.3 summarizes the position. In this case we would need overwhelmingly strong reasons to lead us to believe in the labour-intensive technique, reasons that justified sacrificing current output (relative to what the capital-intensive technique could produce) and long-term employment growth prospects, as well as future output. Current employment, in other words, would have to be at a substantial premium. Stewart and Streeten (1971) list four reasons underlying such a premium:

(1) income redistributive objectives;
(2) the preservation of self-respect;
(3) the intrinsic merit of work;
(4) the potential for staving off political instability.

The first of these is relevant only if fiscal policy cannot do the same job; the rest seem to be very much a matter of judgement.

On the other hand, the realities might not be quite as we have represented them. One penalty of adopting a capital-intensive technique now might be to reduce the opportunities for keeping a pool of skilled and semi-skilled labour in employment for long enough periods in future to maintain their skills. If this happens, there might not be sufficient skilled labour on hand in future to work with the growing capital stock once it is large enough to offer them all employment. A counter-argument to this is that skilled labour is the scarcest of all resources in many LDCs. By adopting a capital-intensive technique now, demand for such skills is kept within the limits of present domestic availability while continuing programmes of education and training can provide a growing pool of skilled workers in line with economic growth later.

Finally, notice that there is no reason in logic, nor is there empirical evidence to support the proposition, that low capital–labour ratios must be associated with high capital–output ratios. One reason why

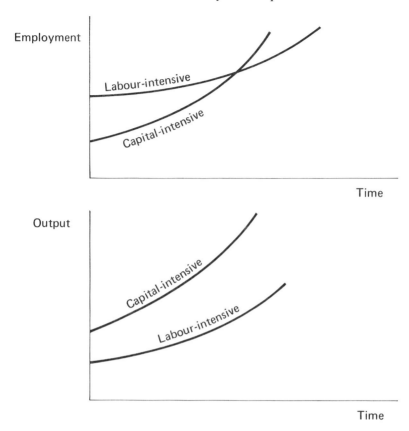

Figure 5.3 Growth paths for employment and output given labour-intensive or capital-intensive choice of technique

the (low K/L–high K/Y) and (high K/L–low K/Y) relationships are so often supposed to exist as a general feature of economic life is that old techniques co-exist in most economies with new ones, because, contrary to perfect world assumptions, old machines are not immediately replaced by new and more efficient ones as soon as technical advances occur. Thus *old* labour-intensive processes appear relatively inefficient, with a relatively high K/Y ratio, because *new* processes, which have the same K/L ratio but use less capital (and labour) per unit of output, have not yet been introduced.

A second and associated reason is that labour-intensive techniques with relatively low K/Y ratios may not even have been invented. The reason for this is that, historically, most technical changes in industrial processing have been researched and developed in the advanced industrial nations where labour has been becoming scarcer relative to capital than in LDCs, and for this and other reasons, labour's wage has become much higher relative to capital's income than is the case in LDCs. Given labour's increasing wage relative to capital, it has been rational to search over time for new techniques that are more labour-saving. When LDCs looked to the industrial nations for their capital goods, therefore, they often found that such labour-intensive techniques as were available were less efficient, in terms of their output per unit of capital, than newer but more capital-intensive techniques. Had the incentive been there, it is quite likely that techniques with a lower K/L *and* a lower K/Y ratio might have been developed. Innovations that both increase labour intensity and reduce capital per unit of output may be described as *capital-stretching*, and it is clearly to the advantage of LDCs to promote research in this area.

One extensive study of techniques, carried out in relation to the food processing industry in LDCs, shows that actual experience is very mixed (see Baron, 1980[5]). It was concluded that capital-economizing techniques are available in maize-milling, baking, grain storage, gari manufacture, the drying of fish, fruit and vegetables, rice milling, corn-beer brewing and open-pan sulphitation (OPS) sugar milling. In each case, a large-scale modern technique using more capital was also available, though this should not necessarily be taken to imply that the modern technique would have a higher ratio of capital to output. Even so, the capital-economizing techniques were 'not paralleled by high direct labour intensity, which is only found in hard rice mills, small bakeries, and OPS sugar mills' (Baron, 1980, p. 196). This leads to the conclusion that capital-economizing techniques cannot empirically be linked directly to labour intensity in production and substantial employment creation. Their principal advantage, the study concludes, is to provide cheaper supplies of processed food to the poor (though the argument could extend to the output of any industry).

Another widely quoted study by Sen (1968) suggests that the most labour-intensive technique in cotton-weaving, the fly-shuttle hand loom, has a capital–output ratio only two-fifths of that associated with the most capital-intensive technique, the automatic power loom.

CONCLUSION

In this chapter we have shown that any observed investment rate is the result of many factors, and that the consequences of investment can be of great importance for the way the economy itself changes. Much of the 'smoothness' of the Solow model is called into question (at least in the short run) once an independent investment function is introduced. Further, decision-makers not only face an uncertain future in reality but may make decisions that have important consequences for socially desirable objectives. In constructing policy for influencing private and making public investments, government must therefore make explicit their preferences for current and future consumption and employment possibilities, in addition to considering how their decisions may influence such variables.

FURTHER READING

The basic analysis of investment given here was pioneered by Fisher (1930) and Hirschleifer (1958). It can also be found in standard macroeconomic texts such as Branson (1979). Harrod's work appears in his 'An Essay in Dynamic Theory' (1939) and *Towards a Dynamic Economics* (1948). Public investment criteria and CBA have been widely discussed in the literature, but a good starting point would be Squire and Van der Tak (1975) and their bibliography. A useful text in the area is Dasgupta and Pearce (1972). On the question of techniques, Stewart and Streeten's paper (1971) is important, and the question is discussed analytically by Sen (1968). Myint (1973, chapter 8) provides a succinct discussion of the area and his influence on the section in this chapter is acknowledged.

NOTES

1 The analysis here is in the style pioneered by Hirschleifer (1958). A standard textbook analysis upon which the analysis here also draws can be found in Branson (1979, pp. 214–18).
2 Suppose 4 units of capital (i.e. machine hours) are required to produce a unit of output; then $K_t = 4$, $Y_t = 1$ and $v = 4$.
3 Suppose $Y_{t-1} = 150$, $Y_t = 160$ and $v = 4$: then $I_t = 4(10) = 40$.
4 If only three-quarters of the adjustment can be made (or is most profitably made) in the period, $\beta = 0.75$ and $I_t = 30$.
5 See especially chapter 3, which gives a wide range of case studies collated by Keddie and Cleghorn.

6

Human Resources: Population Growth and Education

In Solow's basic model, labour joins with capital to produce output. The labour force grows at the same constant rate, n, as the population and is of uniform quality. Yet, by observation, the population growth rate may vary substantially at different points in the development process. Moreover, because the forces determining population growth spring from socio-cultural as well as economic considerations, population growth rates in different countries at the same stage of development may also vary widely. Theories relating to population growth fashion our thoughts on the size of the potential labour force. But notice also that the *quality* of labour is an important element governing its contribution to development. In fact, many commentators have suggested that, with the shortage of skills a major bottleneck to development, the improvement of labour through education, training and better nutrition is at least as important as the accumulation of physical capital. Naturally, a variety of skills will be required in an economy with two or more types of productive activity, and this in turn requires us to set aside the homogeneous labour assumption of Solow.

In this chapter we examine, within the Solow framework, the way in which variations in population growth rate with per capita income may interact with a given savings ratio to condemn an economy to a low-equilibrium standard of living. However, the population growth rate is likely to be sensitive to a wider range of factors than simply income; we examine how some of these factors may operate, and also consider the costs of reducing population growth.

In the second part of the chapter we look at the individual and economy-wide costs and benefits of education in the framework now familiar from the theory of capital investment. We shall see that the general term 'human capital' is applied regularly to knowledge, skills, health and other factors that can be embodied in labour to raise its productivity.

DEFINITIONS AND OVERVIEW OF EVIDENCE

It is first necessary to understand the component factors of population changes in a country. The natural rate of growth of a country's population is found by subtracting the death rate (deaths per 1000) from the birth rate (live births per 1000) over a year. There will be a positive natural rate so long as the birth rate exceeds the death rate. The overall growth rate of the population also needs to take account of international migration patterns. Even if births and deaths exactly balanced, a country would experience a positive population growth rate if immigration occurred more quickly than emigration.

As table 6.1 shows, both the crude birth and death rates in recent times have been highest in low-income LDCs and lowest in the industrial nations. When death rate is subtracted from birth rate, however, the resulting natural population growth rate is highest on average in the middle-income developing countries, primarily because the death rates are relatively lower in these nations than in the average low-income LDC. The small differences between the natural population growth rate (shown for 1960 and 1978) and the average annual population growth rates for 1960–70 and 1970–78 may be the result partly of international migration and partly of comparing single-year estimates with longer-period averages. Table 6.2 provides a more detailed survey of these statistics for the low- and middle-income developing nations.

It is often assumed that the growth in the size of the labour force bears an exact proportional relationship to the population growth rate. It should be noted, however, that the size of the labour force depends not only upon the size of the population but also upon the participation rate—that is, on the proportion of a given population that wants (or is permitted) to be in the labour force. For example, a rise in the school-leaving age, or a general spread in compulsory education, would have the effect of reducing the participation rate among the young. A case in point is the Philippines, where the proportion of the population aged 10–24 in the labour force fell sharply from 77.8 to 70.6 per cent between 1968 and 1969 entirely because of increased education participation rates (see International Labour Organization, 1974, p. 396). Again, a change of attitude in relation to women at work could have important consequences here.

Bearing these points in mind, it is of interest to compare the population growth figures with actual and projected labour force growth statistics. Average annual labour force growth in the period 1970–80 was, for both the low- and middle-income developing countries, never faster than the average annual population growth rate in either the 1970s or the 1960s. On the other hand, ILO estimates for the period 1980–2000, shown in tables 6.1 and 6.2, suggest average annual labour force growth more or less in line with recent population trends. Country-by-country data are provided in table 6.2.

DEMOGRAPHIC TRANSITION AND THE LOW-LEVEL EQUILIBRIUM TRAP

Demographers—scholars working on population change—have for many years had a view of variations in fertility and mortality that, in its most basic form, provides a simple relationship between population growth and development. This view, usually called the 'theory of demographic transition', is formulated in three stages, each with implications for the birth and death rate. In stage I, societies are assumed primitive and technologically unorganized. As a consequence, death rates are assumed to be high and the survival of the society is based upon customs and institutions that ensure a birth rate at least equally as high. Stage II sees the first evidence of modernization, bringing with it cleaner water, sanitation, mass immunization against common but eradicable diseases, and improved dietary habits. While childbearing decisions, rooted in custom, remain unaffected at this stage, infant and child mortality is much reduced and the longevity of the population increased. The death rate falls but the birth rate remains constant— and a population explosion results. Only in stage III does the birth rate start to fall. Motivation to reduce the rate of childbearing derives from a number of factors associated with continuing income growth and modernization. Increased education opportunities lead both men and women to postpone marriage, which reduces youthful childbearing. The breakdown in traditional beliefs and customs removes at least one social pressure to reproduce. Women start to find jobs in the non-agricultural labour force, which reduces the relative importance for them of their childrearing role. Higher incomes all round reduce the need to use children in family productive activity. In addition, modernization brings with it a wider range of contraceptive devices, which permit these motivations to be more easily translated into action.

TABLE 6.1 Birth and death rates, and population and labour force growth rates in LDCs and industrialized countries

	Crude birth rate per 1000 population (1)		Crude death rate per 1000 population (2)		Natural population growth[a] $(3) = \dfrac{(1) - (2)}{10}$		Ave. annual population growth (4)		Ave. annual labour force growth (5)	
	1960	1978	1960	1978	1960	1978	1960/70	1970/78	1970/80	1980/2000
					%	%	%	%	%	%
Low-income countries[b]	48	39	24	15	2.4	2.4	2.5	2.2	1.9	2.2
Middle-income countries[b]	40	35	14	11	2.6	2.6	2.5	2.4	2.4	2.5
Industrialized countries[b]	20	14	10	9	1.0	0.5	1.0	0.7	1.1	0.6

[a] Birth and death rates are measured per 1000; to convert their difference into percentage terms, the measures of columns (1) and (2) must thus be divided by 10.
[b] Figures shown are weighted averages for each group of countries.

Source: World Bank World Development Report (1980, tables 17, 18, 19)

TABLE 6.2 Population and labour force growth rates for low- and middle-income developing countries

	Average annual growth of population		Crude birth rate per 1000 population		Crude death rate per 1000 population		Average annual growth of labour force	
	1960–70	1970–78	1960	1978	1960	1978	1970–80	1980–2000
Low-income countries								
Bangladesh	2.5	2.7	51	46	25	18	2.4	2.5
Lao PDR	2.2	1.3	44	45	23	22	0.3	2.0
Bhutan	2.0	2.1	46	44	28	23	2.0	1.9
Ethiopia	2.4	2.5	51	49	28	25	1.8	2.2
Mali	2.4	2.5	50	49	27	22	2.2	2.5
Nepal	2.0	2.2	46	45	29	21	2.0	2.1
Somalia	2.4	2.3	57	48	29	20	2.3	2.4
Burundi	2.4	2.0	48	47	27	20	1.6	2.3
Chad	1.8	2.2	46	44	29	21	2.0	2.3
Mozambique	2.2	2.5	46	46	26	19	1.7	2.2
Burma	2.2	2.2	43	39	22	14	1.5	2.0
Upper Volta	1.6	1.6	49	48	27	22	1.4	2.3
Vietnam	3.1	2.9	47	37	21	9	1.9	2.6
India	2.5	2.0	43	35	21	14	1.7	2.0
Malawi	2.8	2.9	53	52	27	20	2.4	2.8
Rwanda	2.6	2.9	51	51	27	19	2.5	2.8
Sri Lanka	2.4	1.7	36	26	9	6	2.1	2.1
Guinea	2.8	2.9	47	46	30	21	2.2	2.1
Sierra Leone	2.2	2.5	47	46	27	19	1.8	2.3

Zaire	2.0	2.7	48	46	24	19	2.1	2.4
Niger	3.3	2.8	52	51	27	22	2.6	2.9
Benin	2.6	2.8	51	49	27	19	2.2	2.1
Pakistan	2.8	3.1	48	45	23	15	2.5	2.9
Tanzania	2.7	3.0	47	48	22	16	2.3	2.7
Afghanistan	2.2	2.2	48	48	30	22	1.8	2.5
Central African Rep.	2.2	2.2	42	42	26	19	1.6	2.3
Madagascar	2.2	2.5	47	45	27	19	2.0	2.3
Haiti	1.5	1.7	45	43	23	17	1.4	2.4
Mauritania	2.5	2.7	51	50	27	22	2.3	2.7
Lesotho	2.0	2.3	40	40	23	16	1.9	2.1
Uganda	3.7	2.9	45	45	21	14	2.5	2.5
Angola	1.5	2.3	50	48	31	23	1.9	2.4
Sudan	2.2	2.6	47	45	25	18	2.3	2.7
Togo	2.7	2.7	51	50	27	19	2.1	2.6
Kenya	3.4	3.3	51	51	19	14	2.8	3.3
Senegal	2.4	2.6	48	49	27	22	1.9	2.2
Indonesia	2.2	1.8	47	37	23	17	2.1	1.8
Middle-income countries								
Egypt	2.5	2.2	45	37	19	13	2.2	2.3
Ghana	2.4	3.0	49	48	24	17	2.4	2.9
Yemen, PDR	1.9	1.9	54	48	30	21	1.3	2.8
Cameroon	1.8	2.2	43	42	27	19	1.3	1.7
Liberia	3.1	3.3	51	51	25	18	2.6	2.9
Honduras	3.1	3.3	51	47	19	12	3.0	3.3
Zambia	2.8	3.0	51	49	24	17	2.4	2.8
Zimbabwe	3.9	3.3	47	48	19	14	2.6	3.0
Thailand	3.0	2.7	46	32	17	8	2.9	2.3
Bolivia	2.5	2.6	48	44	23	15	2.4	2.9

	Average annual growth of population		Crude birth rate per 1000 population		Crude death rate per 1000 population		Average annual growth of labour force	
	1960–70	1970–78	1960	1978	1960	1978	1970–80	1980–2000
Philippines	3.0	2.7	45	35	15	9	2.4	2.7
Yemen Arab Rep.	1.8	1.9	49	48	29	25	1.4	2.3
Congo, People's Rep.	2.1	2.5	46	45	27	19	2.0	2.7
Nigeria	2.5	2.5	52	50	25	18	2.0	2.9
Papua New Guinea	2.3	2.4	44	41	23	16	1.9	2.0
El Salvador	2.9	2.9	48	39	17	9	2.8	3.3
Morocco	2.5	2.9	52	45	23	13	2.9	3.3
Peru	2.8	2.7	47	39	19	12	3.0	3.1
Ivory Coast	3.7	5.6	50	50	27	19	4.5	2.4
Nicaragua	2.9	3.3	51	45	19	13	3.3	3.6
Colombia	3.0	2.3	46	31	14	8	3.2	2.6
Paraguay	2.6	2.8	43	39	13	9	3.1	3.4
Ecuador	3.1	3.3	47	44	14	10	3.2	3.2
Dominican Rep.	2.9	2.9	50	37	16	9	3.4	3.3
Guatemala	2.8	2.9	48	41	18	12	3.0	2.8
Syrian Arab Rep.	3.2	3.2	47	45	26	13	2.9	3.5
Tunisia	1.9	2.0	49	32	21	12	2.9	2.6
Jordan	3.0	3.3	48	46	20	13	2.9	3.2

Malaysia	2.9	2.7	39	29	9	6	3.0	2.8
Jamaica	1.4	1.7	39	29	9	6	2.4	3.3
Lebanon	2.8	2.5	43	33	14	8	3.0	2.8
Korea, Rep. of	2.4	1.9	41	21	13	8	2.8	2.0
Turkey	2.5	2.5	44	32	17	10	2.2	2.1
Algeria	2.4	3.2	50	48	23	14	3.5	3.5
Mexico	3.3	3.3	45	38	12	8	3.3	3.5
Panama	2.9	2.6	41	31	10	6	2.8	2.6
Taiwan	2.6	2.0	39	21	7	5	1.9	1.6
Chile	2.1	1.7	37	22	12	7	2.6	2.1
South Africa	2.6	2.7	39	38	15	10	2.6	3.0
Costa Rica	3.4	2.5	47	28	10	5	3.6	2.7
Brazil	2.9	2.8	40	36	11	9	2.8	2.9
Uruguay	1.1	0.3	22	20	9	9	0.2	1.1
Argentina	1.4	1.3	24	21	9	8	1.2	1.2
Portugal	0.0	1.0	24	18	8	10	0.8	0.9
Yugoslavia	1.0	0.9	23	18	10	8	1.1	0.7
Trinidad and Tobago	2.0	1.2	37	22	7	6	2.6	2.2
Venezuela	3.4	3.3	45	36	10	7	3.0	3.2
Hong Kong	2.5	1.9	35	19	7	6	3.0	1.3
Greece	0.5	0.7	49	15	8	9	0.6	0.5
Singapore	2.4	1.5	38	17	8	6	2.7	1.4
Spain	1.1	1.2	21	18	9	8	1.2	0.9
Israel	3.4	2.7	26	26	8	7	2.4	2.1

Source: World Bank *World Development Report* (1980, tables 17, 18, 19)

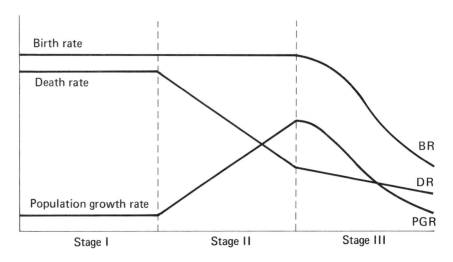

Figure 6.1 Demographic transition

Putting all this together in a diagram (figure 6.1), we see that population growth is expected to be zero or only at a small positive rate in stage I, rapidly rising in stage II, and then steadily falling in stage III.

Neat as this view undoubtedly is, historical record shows it to be a gross over-simplification. As Cassen (1976) remarks, 'There are too many varieties of experience for the ... theory to accommodate. Nowadays, the phrase "demographic transition" is used mainly to refer simply to the change in both mortality and fertility from high to low rates.' Given the desire of family units, tribes and nations to survive, it should not be surprising to find that, where death rates are high, birth rates are high also. The evidence shows that cases of major fertility decline in the absence of a fall in death rate are in fact so rare in LDCs that reducing child mortality must almost be considered a prerequisite for significantly reducing the birth rate. On the other hand, while declining mortality has typically preceded declining fertility, the two have sometimes declined simultaneously (contrary to stage II predictions), and, in Africa and parts of Brazil, fertility has risen while mortality declines (contrary to any portion of figure 6.1) (Cassen, 1976, p. 788). Table 6.3 provides a wide cross-section of recent evidence on relative rates of decline of both birth and death rates. The death rate decline in general exceeds diminution in the birth rate.

Despite the variety of historical experience, it is by no means unusual, as table 6.3 suggests, for population to grow rapidly as rising income per head denotes developmental advance and brings with it a more rapidly declining death rate than birth rate. What many developmentalists have feared is that, should this occur, we might observe not a transition to higher incomes with falling birth rates, but instead a reversion to lower incomes.

This can be shown in the framework of Solow's model (see figure 6.2). Solow himself (1956, pp. 90–1) considered this possibility in an extension to his basic model. Suppose that at low levels of income per head the birth rate only barely exceeds the death rate. Then n will be very small and the slope of the line nk, which we examined in the basic model, will be rather flat. Now assume that, as income per head rises, population growth rises quickly but then, at high levels of income, falls back to some constant, positive rate. The slope of the line nk will then vary, with y, in the general sort of way suggested by the curve nk in figure 6.2. If all the other elements of the basic model remain unchanged, then, as the diagram also shows, nk could, as one possibility, 'weave around' the savings-per-head curve $s_1 f(k)$. (Ignore $s_2 f(k)$.) If this represents the economic conditions in an LDC, then the condition

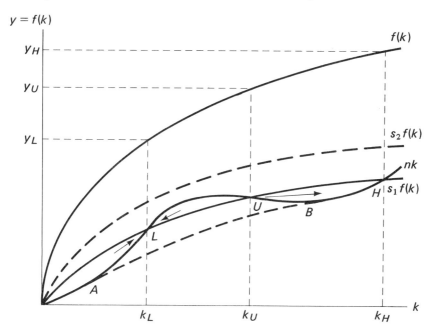

Figure 6.2 The low-level equilibrium trap.
(This figure combines and builds upon Johnson, 1969, p. 158, figures 5 and 6)

TABLE 6.3 Relative rates of decline in birth and death rates in LDCs, 1960–78

	Change in			Change in	
	Crude birth rate 1960–78	Crude death rate 1960–78		Crude birth rate 1960–78	Crude death rate 1960–78
	%	%		%	%
Low-income countries					
Bangladesh	– 9.8	– 28.0	Zaire	– 4.2	– 20.8
Lao PDR	2.3	– 4.3	Niger	– 1.9	– 18.5
Bhutan	– 4.3	– 17.9	Benin	– 3.9	– 29.6
Ethiopia	– 3.9	– 10.7	Pakistan	– 6.3	– 34.8
			Tanzania	2.1	– 27.3
Mali	– 2.0	– 18.5			
Nepal	– 2.2	– 27.6	Afghanistan	0.0	– 26.7
Somalia	– 15.8	– 31.0	Central African		
Burundi	– 2.1	– 25.9	Republic	0.0	– 26.9
Chad	– 4.3	– 27.6	Madagascar	– 4.3	– 29.6
			Haiti	– 4.4	– 26.1
Mozambique	0.0	– 26.9	Mauritania	– 2.0	– 18.5
Burma	– 9.3	– 36.4			
Upper Volta	– 2.0	– 18.5	Lesotho	0.0	– 30.4
Vietnam	– 21.3	– 57.1	Uganda	0.0	– 33.3
India	– 18.6	– 33.3	Angola	– 4.0	– 25.8
			Sudan	– 4.3	– 28.0
Malawi	– 1.9	– 25.9	Togo	– 2.0	– 29.6
Rwanda	0.0	– 29.6			
Sri Lanka	– 27.8	– 33.3	Kenya	0.0	– 26.3
Guinea	– 2.1	– 30.0	Senegal	2.1	– 18.5
Sierra Leone	– 2.1	– 29.6	Indonesia	– 21.3	– 26.1
Middle-income countries					
Egypt	– 17.8	– 31.6	Papua New		
Ghana	– 2.0	– 29.2	Guinea	– 6.8	– 30.4
Yemen, PDR	– 11.1	– 30.0			
Cameroon	– 2.3	– 29.6	El Salvador	– 18.8	– 47.1
Liberia	0.0	– 28.0	Morocco	– 13.5	– 43.5
			Peru	– 17.0	– 36.8
Honduras	– 7.8	– 36.8	Ivory Coast	0.0	– 29.6
Zambia	– 3.9	– 29.2	Nicaragua	– 11.8	– 31.6
Zimbabwe	2.1	– 26.3			
Thailand	– 30.4	– 52.9	Colombia	– 32.6	– 42.9
Bolivia	– 8.3	– 34.8	Paraguay	– 9.3	– 30.8
			Ecuador	– 6.4	– 28.6
Philippines	– 22.2	– 40.0	Dominican Rep.	– 26.0	– 43.8
Yemen Arab			Guatemala	– 14.6	– 33.3
Republic	– 2.0	– 13.8			
Congo, People's			Syrian Arab Rep.	– 4.3	– 50.0
Republic	– 2.2	– 29.6	Tunisia	– 34.7	– 42.9
Nigeria	– 3.8	– 28.0	Jordan	– 4.2	– 35.0

TABLE 6.3   *continued*

| | Change in | | | | Change in | |
| | Crude birth rate 1960–78 | Crude death rate 1960–78 | | | Crude birth rate 1960–78 | Crude death rate 1960–78 |
	%	%			%	%
Middle-income countries						
Malaysia	– 25.6	– 33.3		Uruguay	– 9.1	0.0
Jamaica	– 25.6	– 33.3		Argentina	– 12.5	– 11.1
Lebanon	– 23.3	– 42.9				
Korea, Rep. of	– 48.8	– 38.5		Portugal	– 25.0	25.0
Turkey	– 27.3	– 41.2		Yugoslavia	– 21.7	– 20.0
Algeria	– 4.0	– 39.1		Trinidad and		
Mexico	– 15.6	– 33.3		Tobago	– 40.5	– 14.3
Panama	– 24.4	– 40.0		Venezuela	– 20.0	– 30.0
Taiwan	– 46.2	– 28.6		Hong Kong	– 45.7	– 14.3
Chile	– 40.5	– 41.7				
				Greece	– 21.1	12.5
South Africa	– 2.6	– 33.3		Singapore	– 55.3	– 25.0
Costa Rica	– 40.4	– 50.0		Spain	– 14.3	– 11.1
Brazil	– 10.0	– 18.2		Israel	0.0	– 12.5

Source: World Bank *World Development Report* (1980, table 18)

for equilibrium, $sf(k) = nk$, seems to be satisfied not just at one point but at three! In fact, a few moments' thought should make it clear that the characteristics of these equilibria are not actually identical.

Look first at the point L, where nk cuts $s_1f(k)$ in association with capital per head of k_L and income per head of y_L. Now, if k took a value below k_L, we can see from the diagram that $s_1f(k)$ would exceed nk so that k would necessarily be rising. Also, if k took a value between k_L and k_U, nk would exceed $s_1f(k)$ and k would be falling. Thus, if the capital-per-head ratio were to lie anywhere between zero and k_U (but not including k_U), the economy would move to the equilibrium point L where income per head is y_L.

Now look at point H. Here, if k were to take any value above k_U but below k_H, $s_1f(k)$ would exceed nk and k would rise until it reached its equilibrium at k_H. Similarly, if k were to lie above k_H, k would fall to k_H in due course. The point H is associated with income per head of y_H.

Finally, look at point U. If by pure chance, k were to take the value k_U, then nk would equal $s_1f(k)$ and we would have some sort of equilibrium. The equilibrium is, however, most unstable. If k were to fall only a tiny amount below k_U, then $nk > s_1 f(k)$ and k would continue to fall, irreversibly, until it reached k_L. Similarly, if k were to rise only fractionally above k_U, $s_1 f(k) > nk$ and k would continue to rise until it reached k_H.

The points L and H represent stable equilibria, in the sense that, even if k takes value quite different from k_L or k_H, the internal workings of the system will drive it back to one of these two points. The point U represents an unstable equilibrium, because once k takes any value different from k_U, there is nothing in the internal workings of the system to allow it to regain this position. Indeed, everything works to drive the system away from U. The arrows in figure 6.2, pointing away from U but homing in on L and H, remind us of all this.

The meaning of the letters used in the diagram can now be explained. The point L is called a low-level equilibrium, and is to be compared with the high-level equilibrium established at H. The point U is an unstable equilibrium. Because of the way in which the dynamics of the model drive it towards L so long as $0 < k < k_U$, an economy is said to be caught in a low-level equilibrium trap (LLET) if it has nk and $s_1 f(k)$ schedules as shown and if it is unable to find any way of raising k to a point above k_U. This way of looking at development provides one explanation for attaching importance to aid. If a country cannot, by its own devices, achieve a value of capital per head above k_U, provision of aid to lift k to a point above k_U should have a long-term beneficial effect. Once k lies above k_U (which, in the simplest terms, could be achieved by a gift of capital), the economy should be set right on the path towards the high-level equilibrium under its own steam.[1]

Getting an LDC past a point like U is not the only way of solving its problem, though. Why not change the conditions under which the economy operates so that the LLET disappears altogether? If the 'bump' in the solid nk line could be removed, or flattened to some extent, as shown by the dotted line between A and B, for example, then the LLET would cease to exist. The 'bump' reflects the population explosion that in many instances has characterized the transition from a high birth rate–high death rate to a low birth rate–low death rate regime. Where the rates fall at a similar speed, simultaneously, the problem does not arise. But where they do not, or threaten not to, then family planning programmes and related policies must be considered. This point is developed later.

Notice, on the other hand, that attacking the birth rate head-on is not the only way of eradicating the LLET. As figure 6.2 shows, if the given solid nk line remained unchanged but the savings ratio could be raised so that $s_1 f(k)$ were replaced by $s_2 f(k)$, then again the problem would disappear.

Recall, finally, that the early economists also recognized the possibility that rapid population growth might outstrip the rate of capital accumulation and result, as we have just seen, in falling values of capital and income per head. On the other hand, they also realized that technical progress had the effect of making each successive generation of capital more productive than its predecessor. A given saving rate thus proved increasingly effective, once productively invested, in generating output. And if technical progress was fast enough, it could hold at bay and perhaps even reverse the influence of population growth on income per head. In this context, as in so many others, the importance of making use of technical advances is once again manifest.

An element ignored in the foregoing analysis was that population growth and saving behaviour might be related to each other. One analysis that incorporates this important possibility is that of Coale and Hoover (1958), a summary account of which is given in Cassen (1976, p. 804). They compare a high-fertility (HF) with a low-fertility (LF) economy and assume that the savings ratio in the first will be lower than that in the second. The reasoning behind this is that the HF economy has a higher proportion of non-productive young dependants to support so that consumption increases at the expense of saving over time when compared with the experience of the LF society. Coale and Hoover also suppose that an HF-type economy will tend to invest more, proportionately, in 'unproductive' social capital than will an LF-type. Finally, they assume that, in the short run, output is a function of capital alone (in the fashion of Harrod—see chapter 5), while in the longer run labour may be substituted for capital according to a Cobb–Douglas production function. Within this framework, total output grows more slowly in an HF-type economy than in an LF-type in the short run. In the longer run, the HF type wins in terms of total output but loses again in terms of output per head: the larger labour force has made its impact as a productive input, but not by enough to offset its growing consumption requirements.

There are many variations that can be played on the principles and degrees of interaction between population growth and other determinants of economic change. These are left to the reader to consider. We now focus more precisely on the factors determining population growth at the microeconomic level.

DETERMINANTS OF POPULATION GROWTH

The so-called 'theory' of demographic transition is at worst no more than an attempt to generalize from historical experience, and at best a listing of the factors that tend to link advancing development or 'modernization' with changing population growth rates. In this section we shall examine population growth rate changes analytically from a number of economic perspectives.

CHILDREN AS CONSUMER GOODS

One way in which a child can be viewed is as a consumer good: he or she generates utility for his or her parents. This insight at once invites the employment of consumer demand theory. The microeconomic theory of demand postulates that, so long as a good is not inferior, an increase in real income will bring with it an increase in the demand for that good. Let us suppose that a given money income can be spent either on a bundle of material goods or upon children. Then we can draw the usual budget constraint from consumer demand theory with material goods on one axis and children on the other, as shown in figure 6.3. If the parents' indifference map reflects their perception of children as normal goods, then, as the figure attests, an outward shift of the budget line, reflecting a rise in their real income with relative prices fixed, will bring with it an increased demand for both children and material goods.

If an increased real income is observed to be associated with a falling

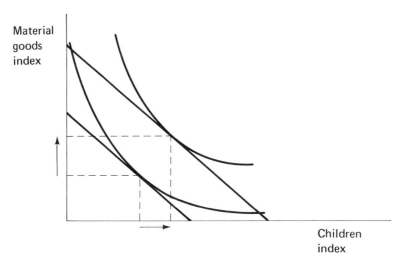

Figure 6.3 The income effect and the family size decision.
(Source: Leibenstein, 1974, p. 464)

demand for children (lower birth rate), we may, in this framework, draw one of two conclusions. Either children are, or have become, inferior goods, or so-called 'price' effects—in fact, mostly opportunity cost elements—have begun to dominate income effects. (A further possibility, based on interdependent preferences, is taken up below.) Let us consider what these 'price effects' may comprise. First, children must be fed, clothed and educated. This requires direct outlays on goods and services. Second, parents must spend time with their children. This requires them to sacrifice other types of activity to which they may impute a positive utility value, or to sacrifice the possibility of earning wage income. If higher real incomes are associated with child-rearing costs that rise more rapidly than all other prices, then the budget line will steepen at the same time as it shifts outwards, and this may account for a reduction in the number of children families plan to have (see figure 6.4). As it happens, there is evidence that this might tell at least one part of the story. This is because, as real incomes rise throughout an economy, more and better job opportunities for both parents arise, a wider range of goods and services may be purchased, and a wider spectrum of activities opens up for the use of non-working time. This means that each child will impose greater costs upon his or her parents, the higher the average income level.

The question of education costs needs to be treated with care. Direct

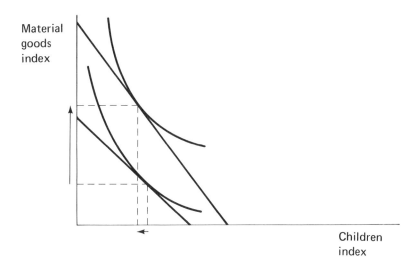

Figure. 6.4 Income and price effects and the family size decision.
(Source: Leibenstein, 1974, p. 464)

education costs will rise if compulsory education to a certain age replaces a voluntary system and if parents are generally required to contribute towards fees or pay for books. On the other hand, the cost of educating a child to a given standard within an established system is unlikely to rise as development proceeds at a rate much in excess of other prices. Thus, once-for-all, government-instigated changes in the nature and financing of education can influence education costs; but, it should be noted, such changes often also imply an attempt to raise educational standards—whereas the argument in the last sentence related to a given standard. In general, it is often suggested that education costs influence the parents' desired family size not so much because education to a given standard becomes more costly with development (although it might), but rather because they want their children to reach higher standards. This desire for a better educated, better 'quality' of child reflects changing attitudes and opportunities which the parents experience as development proceeds and leads to a commitment to spend more on the education of each child. This in turn implies that the desire to have more children, associated with a positive income effect, could be offset or more than offset by the desire to rear higher-quality children as per capita incomes rise.

A rather different focus on the choice of family size is offered by Leibenstein (1974). He assumes that individuals aspire to reach target levels of consumption or living standards. Each household belongs to what he calls a social influence group (SIG), and each SIG operates on the status sensibilities of decision-makers in the family to determine the target consumption level to which it aspires. Notice that inter-household competition and emulation within SIGs are relied upon to exert social pressure here, whereas it is an assumption of standard demand theory that all households act independently of each other. Leibenstein rounds off his assumptions by saying: 'it is not argued that the proportion spent on commitment goods is *necessarily* higher in status α than in β (where the average income in α is higher than in β) but that empirically it frequently turns out this way ...' (p. 473). Given this general relationship, the implications for family size are twofold. On the one hand, families in higher-level SIGs will tend to allocate a higher proportion of their resources to material consumption than to child-rearing when compared with lower-level SIG households. On the other, families within a given SIG will tend to spend more on children as their income rises and they move from the 'bottom end' of the SIG towards the top. Leibenstein concludes: 'if we choose socio-economic groups ... as proxies for SIGs, we find that the empirical evidence supports the generalization that the higher the income level of the groups . . . the fewer the average number of children per family, but within such groups, the reverse holds' (Leibenstein, 1974, p. 474).

While the consumption framework offers one set of insights into the motivations operating to determine family size, it is probably true to say that more value can be derived, in the case of many LDCs, from viewing human reproduction decisions from a production perspective. To this we now turn.

CHILDREN AS INVESTMENT GOODS

An aspect of the family size decision ignored until now is the fact that children, from quite a young age, may contribute to the family's overall work effort. Further, children are also seen as serving the important socioeconomic function of caring for their parents in sickness and old age. A child therefore is a parental investment. The parents sacrifice consumption to feed and rear their child while it is still wholly or partially dependent on them. On the other hand, the family benefits as a whole from the child's productive efforts, from the prospect that the child may remit funds for family use even if it moves away to town or emigrates, and from the security in adversity and age that a large family is seen to offer. In fact, just as the costs and benefits returned by a physical capital investment are calculated by a businessman, so parents may engage, even if only implicitly, in a similar calculation when considering whether to have another child.

In this case, the benefits must be seen as the contributions that a child might be expected to make to family real income and in particular to the fraction going to the parents: the value of its later caring services, and the money value of utility that the child offers as a consumption good. With the exception of the last of these, it can usually be reckoned that such benefits will decline at the margin for each successive child. The costs involved include the earnings and money value of utility forgone in devoting time in bringing children up, and the direct costs of feeding, clothing and educating the child. This whole stream of expected values must then be discounted at an appropriate rate so that a present value (PV) of the child-as-investment-good can be found and compared with the PV of other available income streams.

Although little quantitative work has been done in this area, White (1976), in a Japanese village study, and Caldwell (1977), using Nigerian survey data, both conclude that children have a positive PV as far as their parents are concerned. Cassen (1976), on the other hand, reports that, to obtain a positive rate of return on a child investment using Indian data, he had to build in an early starting age for child earnings, a low level of child consumption, a high share of child earnings for the parents and a low discount rate. Such conditions may by no means always be plausible—and in addition a particular problem may arise with respect to the discount rate. As we saw in our chapters on investment and saving, a discount factor is applied to future income streams to reflect the fact that any capital investment considered today represents a commitment of resources to a particular use when they could also have been employed to earn interest elsewhere. In the poor village economy, however, it may be hard for the parents to identify any alternative investment opportunity whose real rate of interest could be used as the discount rate. Indeed, none may exist.[2]

Still considering family size as the outcome of decision-making processes analogous with investment in physical capital, recall now that we said that net investment (additions to the capital stock) could be described as a capital stock adjustment in the direction of some perceived optimum. Similarly, Schultz (1980) suggests that reproductive goods can be 'summarized in terms of a desired lifetime stock of children'. In a study drawing on Taiwanese data, he finds confirmation of a positive relationship between fertility and child mortality that has often been observed elsewhere. If parents harbour some idea of an ideal family size, as Schultz and others suggest, their response to a high level of mortality may be twofold. On the one hand, they may wish to make good an infant death by attempting to have another child ('replacement investment'). On the other, even if they escape infant or child deaths in their early marriage, the high level of mortality they observe around them will encourage them to continue having children to ensure that they will achieve their desired lifetime stock of children if deaths occur later. With this in mind, it is interesting to note that Schultz also finds that, when women are completing the formation of their families (are 35 or older), in regions where recent child mortality has been high, his dynamic stock adjustment model implies a 'compensating higher current flow of births' in this age bracket.

OTHER FACTORS INFLUENCING FERTILITY

Because of the deliberately analytical approach we have taken in looking at fertility, some specific determinants of fertility have to some extent been 'played down'. Here we summarize the more important of them.

Education
It has often been said that the general level of education of potential parents influences the birth rate, usually negatively. Schultz (1980),

for example, found that, on a cross-section of Taiwanese families, a sharp reduction in total fertility rates occurred among women who had gone beyond primary school. When he compared educational attainment levels of both men and women with fertility, he found that women with higher education were about half as fertile as illiterate women. Among men, total fertility rates were higher for primary school graduates than illiterates but lowest among those with higher education. Such findings are commonplace both within and between countries. One reason might be that, within countries, higher educational attainments place parents in a different 'social influence group', to use Leibenstein's phrase, so that, while they may have higher incomes, they also aspire to higher levels of material consumption. More generally, higher education levels will usually alert parents to the possibilities of contraception, help them to consider rationally the implications of varying family sizes, and assist them in understanding how to make effective use of contraceptives. If widespread education has the effect of delaying marriages, it may also work through that channel to reduce fertility—assuming that premarital intercourse, unattended by contraception, does not have an offsetting effect.

Urbanization

Despite some evidence to the contrary, it is usually found that urban fertility is lower than rural. Perhaps this should not be a surprise since, in an urban population, men far outnumber women, education levels are generally higher, and women are widely employed in wage-earning occupations.

FERTILITY: AN ECONOMIC QUESTION?

The microeconomic theory of fertility presented in the last few pages is most at home in an economic text. But it is easy to object that the question of human reproduction is influenced only partially, and perhaps only slightly, by economic considerations. And how much, in any case, do we actually learn from the type of economic analysis we have presented?

To take the second point first, a full-blooded theory of fertility would certainly want to investigate the factors determining the slope and position of indifference curves such as those in figures 6.3 and 6.4. Importantly, it would also need to explain whether, and under what circumstances, the indifference curves might shift. Yet these are questions that may need to be answered in essentially psychological or anthropological terms, and to go beyond the general arena in which economists operate. The same comments could be made about the determinants of the 'optimum stock' of children in a family.

Notice, further, that almost all of economic theory is built upon the presumption of rational behaviour, and often of sufficient, if not perfect, information. Yet not all births are the result of decisions taken with an eye to longer-term consequences, and even if consequences were considered by the parents, we cannot be sure that it was economic consequences that were uppermost in their mind.

Finally, we could never know for sure how much of the decision to have another child is influenced by measurable, economic factors and how much by non-measurable, probably non-economic, factors—precisely because we accept that some potentially important elements are non-measurable. All we can say is that changing economic conditions do appear to have partially predictable consequences for population growth, and we can infer that fertility must in all probability be affected to some extent by economic factors. The economist must be satisfied to concentrate on those.

FAMILY PLANNING

Until now, the emphasis in this section has been upon the motivations to reproduce. In countries where effective contraceptives are widely and cheaply available, this makes a good deal of sense. Individuals can use such devices to plan with some accuracy, whether we view them as utility-maximizing consumers or as long-sighted investors. The less widely available contraceptives are, the less they are understood and the more expensive they are, the more we are also driven to consider those factors explored long ago by Malthus as bearing on fertility. Malthus felt that fertility was determined largely by the age of marriage and the frequency of intercourse during marriage. To quote a leading neo-Malthusian,

In societies lacking knowledge of contraception, control over the number of births can be achieved either through abortion or abstinence ... Other things the same, couples desiring small families would marry later and have more abortions than the average couple. Yet the room for decision-making would be uncomfortably small, given the taboos against abortion, the strong social forces determining the age of marriage, and the relative inefficiency of reductions in the frequency of crition. Chance would bulk large in determining the distribution of births among families. [Becker, 1960, p. 210]

Now, in the battle to control their own destinies, LDCs need to reduce as much as possible such chance elements. Today, the means to do so are readily available. What LDCs need to consider, therefore, is what their optimum population might be and how it might best be achieved.

The question of optimum population growth can be considered fully only in the context optimal growth models. Such models generally operate at a rather high level of abstraction and present technical difficulties beyond the amibitions of this text. At a less abstruse level, though, we have already seen how a population explosion can pose the problem of a low-level equilibrium trap, and this alone should motivate us to consider the question of population control in a little more depth. We shall also see whether society can put a value on an extra life within its midst. If so, this marginal net benefit can be compared with the cost of preventing it through a family planning programme. We are back to cost–benefit analysis again.

If a government considers introducing a family planning programme, it should have some broad idea of the social costs and benefits likely to be associated with it. A fairly rough-and-ready way of deriving guidelines here is to compare the value of the consumption resources diverted to preventing a marginal birth with the PV of future consumption gains expected to accrue from having prevented the birth. If a population is large relative to other productive resources, and/or growing fast relative to their growth rates, labour's marginal product may well be low or negligible. Further, each individual consumes without producing early in life and continues to consume throughout his life. Consumption covers goods and services both privately and publicly provided. Any excess or surplus of lifetime production by the individual over and above his lifetime consumption requirements is likely to be small, if positive, and might easily be negative. Suppose it is negative: then it will be well worth the rest of society—with an eye to its future consumption expectations—working out the marginal cost of preventing the child's being born at all. If the consumption forgone today in preventing the birth is less than the extent to which the PV of the child's lifetime consumption would exceed that of his lifetime production, then a consumption-oriented society would clearly have a case for thinking in terms of fertility control. The birth control programme in this framework should proceed until marginal consumption costs associated with the programme equal marginal expected consumption benefits.

A more wide-ranging set of considerations is presented by Haveman (1976). He notes that the contribution to production of the marginal individual should be adjusted to reflect his effect on the productivity of other persons. He also points out that benefits should include the consumption value of the marginal child to others, and that long-term costs might include not only his consumption but also congestion and pollution costs. Summarizing his method elsewhere, he says:

> Additional individuals resulting from higher fertility rates absorb both consumption and investment goods that would be available to others and impose both congestion and environmental pollution costs on others. To the extent that such costs exceed the value of the production stream yielded by the individual and the consumption value that his/her existence affords others, there is a net social willingness to pay to avoid the marginal birth (Berelson and Haveman, 1980, p. 228).

Partly because of the extreme difficulty (see below) of measuring many of these elements satisfactorily, Berelson and Haveman (1980) have adopted an alternative approach. Here, the means of reducing fertility were identified first, and the effectiveness of each strategy was assessed in relation to different social settings and degrees of government commitment and capacity to implement programmes of this kind. The relative fertility-reducing effectiveness of each combination of strategy, social setting and implementation strength was then worked out, and from this it was possible to find the marginal effectiveness of any additional expenditure in this area. What is important here is that no monetary value is attached to the fertility reduction achieved, as in the earlier frameworks. As Berelson and Haveman state, their approach focuses on fertility reduction as a determinant of the ultimate objectives of socioeconomic development. It is simply implicit in their work that fertility reduction is positively related to gains in education and literacy, health and nutrition, jobs and housing, and development and modernization in general—and is thus desirable. Its desirability, therefore, no longer needs to be demonstrated.

Their judgement here is supported by Cuca (1980), who, in a study of 63 countries, concluded that 18 out of 20 'relatively developed' countries had large reductions in birth rate while only 10 of the 23 'middle-level' countries and none of the 20 'low-level' countries had a large drop in fertility. ('Levels' here refer to an index of social setting based on measures of adult literacy, school enrolment, life expectancy, infant mortality, men in non-agricultural activities, GNP per head and urbanization.)

What more can be said, empirically, about social costs, social benefits and the results of family planning programmes? On the cost side, it is generally considered developmentally damaging to think in terms of birth control programmes administered by coercion or other unreasonable means. The point is made because enforced castration at birth, for example, would be both cheap and effective, and yet we would generally not wish to admit it as an alternative. Looking at the implications more positively, effective programmes require not only the apparatus of birth control (condoms, intra-uterine devices, birth control pills and so on) but also education programmes to give motivation and instructions on effective use. Such programme costs are fairly easy to estimate and can be related to the number of acceptors won by a programme. What is much more difficult to know is how many births the acceptors of birth control methods would have had without the programme and how many they actually finish up having. This is vital information for calculating the cost of preventing a birth. Blaikie (1975) estimated that the cost could be less than $10 or as much as $115 per prevented birth when he carried out a study on Bihar.

On the benefits side, the easier items to measure include resources saved that would have been absorbed by the child in its use of publicly provided health and education services, but are now released for other uses. These savings could be quite substantial, and in themselves may make it worth undertaking a cost–benefit exercise. Much more difficult to assess are the consumption value to society of a child, and the impact he and his descendants might make upon the productivity of others—this last being an important element of a full calculation.

Let us turn now to evidence on the extent and effectiveness of birth control programmes. As table 6.4 suggests, the percentage of married women using contraceptives (more precisely, women acceptors in the childbearing age bracket 15–44) varies widely among countries. Given that the lowest-income country tops the list and that national incomes rise going down the list, what is clear is a generally positive correlation between higher incomes and higher contraceptive use. We can, however, go further. Cuca, in his study based on similar data, shows that significant reductions in fertility generally require not only relatively medium to high levels of income per head and social development, but also, 'as a minimum, a favourable official attitude toward family planning if not a positive commitment to reducing the birth rate' (Cuca, 1980, p. 38). While India, Sri Lanka and Vietnam are low-income countries, and thus exceptional on this count in their fertility-reducing success, they are fully committed to birth rate reductions and are relatively well developed in social terms. Other less successful countries, such as Ghana and Kenya, failed to affect birth rates substantially, Cuca suggests, because their clear official commitment to fertility decline was not followed through in effectively implemented programmes. Much of this ties in well with the Berelson–Haveman (1980) work mentioned earlier.

Population Growth and Education

TABLE 6.4 Percentage of married women using contraceptives, latter half of 1970s

	%
Low-income countries *	
Bangladesh	9
Nepal	4
India	17
Sri Lanka	41
Pakistan	6
Afghanistan	1
Haiti	5
Kenya	4
Indonesia	19
Middle-income countries *	
Egypt	21
Ghana	4
Honduras	9
Zimbabwe	5
Thailand	40
Philippines	22
Papua New Guinea	3
El Salvador	22
Morocco	5
Peru	1
Nicaragua	19
Colombia	36
Paraguay	16
Ecuador	6
Dominican Republic	31
Guatemala	3
Tunisia	18
Malaysia	36
Jamaica	40
Korea, Republic of	44
Turkey	38
Mexico	21
Panama	44
Taiwan	65
Costa Rica	67
Hong Kong	77
Singapore	71

* Ranked according to per capita income, lowest-income country at the top of the list

Source: World Bank *World Development Report* (1980, table 18)

MORTALITY

Particularly in countries where contraception is widely practised, the decision-making powers of individuals to influence the birth rate are considerable. Purely individual behaviour can do rather less to affect the death rate, but that does not mean that this part of the population growth equation is devoid of interest. The main issue here is whether it is rising private living standards, the by-product of social and economic development, or deliberate social policy based on public health programmes that best accounts for the world-wide decline in mortality evident in table 6.3.

To examine this issue, let us start with a brief review of the main causes of death in LDCs and the extent to which their effects have been reduced. Here we draw on an illuminating paper by Preston (1980).

Preston finds that, in the early twentieth century, the major killers in a small cross-section of LDCs yielding relevant data were respiratory diseases, dysentry and malaria. The influenza/pneumonia/bronchitis group accounted for between 3.2 deaths per 1000 per year in Mexico and 8.2 in Taiwan: respiratory tuberculosis, for between 0.65 in Mexico and 2.4 in Chile: dysentry-type diseases, for between 1.7 in Taiwan and 2.8 in Guyana: and malaria for between 0.03 in Chile and perhaps more than 8 in India. Preston then looks at the percentage of overall mortality decline brought about by reducing the impact of each of these diseases during the ensuing 50 years. He suggests that the largest reductions in mortality rates have been achieved in the influenza-type group (down by 9.4 per cent of the total in Mexico and by as much as 27.8 per cent in Taiwan), dysentry (from a 5.4 per cent decline in Taiwan to a 25 per cent fall in Mexico), and malaria (from 0 per cent in Chile to perhaps 35 per cent reduction in India). Table 6.5 gives Preston's summary of conclusions on the relative degrees of influence each type of disease has had on overall mortality in LDCs during this century.

Having identified these major causes of death and the decline in their impact, what can be said to have reduced their effect? To start with, we must expect mortality from every one of the diseases listed in table 6.5 to fall with rising living standards. Under this general umbrella poor nutrition is generally agreed to be a major factor underlying high death rates, with a WHO study in 1974 attributing to it well over half the deaths of children under five in 13 Latin American areas. As table 6.5 again makes clear, the preventive weaponry of immunization, water purification and hygienic sewage disposal can do much to drive

TABLE 6.5 Diseases responsible for LDC mortality declines and methods that have been used against them

Dominant mode of transmission	Diseases	Approximate percentage of mortality decline in LDCs, 1900–70, accounted for by disease	Principal methods of prevention deployed	Principal methods of treatment deployed
		%		
Airborne	Influenza/pneumonia/ bronchitis	30		Antibiotics
	Respiratory tuberculosis	10	Immunization; identification and isolation	Chemotherapy
	Smallpox	2	Immunization	Chemotherapy
	Measles	1	Immunization	Antibiotics
	Diphtheria	2	Immunization	Antibiotics
	Whooping cough			
	Total	45		
Water-, food-, and feces-borne	Diarrhea, enteritis, gastroenteritis	7	Purification and increased supply of water; sewage disposal; personal sanitation	Rehydration
	Typhoid	1	Purification and increased supply of water; sewage disposal; personal sanitation; partially effective vaccine	Rehydration, antibiotics
	Cholera	1	Purification and increased supply of water; sewage disposal; personal sanitation; partially effective vaccine, quarantine	Rehydration
	Total	9		
Insect-borne	Malaria	13–33	Insecticides, drainage, larvicides	Quinine drugs
	Typhus	1	Insecticides, partially effective vaccines	Antibiotics
	Plague	1	Insecticides, rat control, quarantine	
	Total	15–35		

down the mortality level, while curative treatments are now increasingly widely deployed.

This brings us back to our basic issue. Within countries, higher private living standards are indisputably associated with the lower mortality rates. But in deciding upon the impact of public health programmes, relative to private consumption, at an international level, there is a real difficulty of identification. 'Richer countries not only have richer people but, in general, have larger and more effective social programmes' (Preston, p. 291).

To demonstrate that declining mortality is not just a by-product of higher living standards, it must be shown that important changes in commitment to public health (incorporating better techniques for attacking disease) have raised the level of life expectancy above that which would have been predicted in light of other development indicators. This is what Preston does. For LDCs as a unit, he estimates that, if life expectancy had borne the same relationship to selected development indices in 1970–75 as was observed in 1940, then life expectancy in the latter period would have been 8.7 years less than that which was actually experienced. This provides an estimate of the increase in longevity attributable to factors other than national income, literacy and calorie consumption. In general, Preston concludes that conscious health policy implementation must divide the honours about equally with overall socioeconomic development in accounting for reduced mortality.

HUMAN CAPITAL

We have already noted that even a fixed rate of capital accumulation, measured in purely physical terms (say, machine-hours per year), can make an increasing contribution to growth if new design features reflecting technical advance are embodied in it. Similarly, a fixed growth rate in the size of the labour force should be able to make an increasing contribution to output growth if its quality is improved. Such labour productivity increase can be achieved by educating labour in a general sense and by training it in specific skills and tasks (and also by increasing nutritional intake and health). All such activities involve incurring costs in the form of using current resources for purposes that, conceptually, are separate from current consumption. They are thus said to be incurred in installing human capital.

Notice first how education and training are very much in the nature of an investment in capital. From the point of view of an individual, direct and indirect costs are incurred (in relation to fees, travelling expenses, forgone earnings and the like) in education or training. The motivation for incurring such costs is the prospect of achieving a higher earning and consumption stream than could otherwise have been obtained. From the point of view of society, costs are again incurred in education (schools must be built and staffed; production is sacrificed while individuals learn; and so on). Societies are prepared to incur such costs because they perceive that an increasingly well educated labour force should be able to contribute increasingly effectively to production and the potential for future consumption.

We shall consider, to start with, the factors that enter into an individual's assessment of the costs and benefits of education and find that these perceptions underlie the demand for education in a society, however it is provided. Assuming that government is a major provider of education, we then have to compare the costs and benefits to individuals with those to society as a whole. It is now widely understood that in the course of development, conditions may change in ways that lead scarce resources to be badly misused. We shall therefore also need to consider the framework of manpower planning, which tackles this problem head-on. Finally, we shall say a few words about nutrition and health.

THE DEMAND FOR EDUCATION AND TRAINING

Seen from the perspective of cost–benefit analysis, an individual assesses the value of each extra year of education or training programme entirely as if he were a businessman contemplating the revenues and costs to be included in making an investment decision in physical capital. For some people, of course, it cannot be denied that education is taken as a consumption good—that is, it is taken partly or purely because the individual enjoys it for its own sake. Such consumption benefits will, however, be ignored here in our direct analysis. However, if individuals are found to be volunteering for education that offers, at the margin, a negative PV or low (perhaps negative) rate of return, we shall be able to surmise that one possible reason for this apparently irrational behaviour is that they simply treat education as consumption.

Two other points should be cleared up at the outset. First, the individual really has the freedom to exercise choice over education only after he has passed beyond a compulsory minimum school-leaving age. While costs certainly occur before this age, and prospective benefits accrue, we have no way of observing individual choice at work. Second, we need to distinguish 'education' from 'training'. The former may be equated with formal schooling (at schools, universities, colleges) while the latter is usually associated with an individual's actual or potential employer. As Blaug (1970) puts it, '"training" is actually a somewhat vague term. It may comprise one or all of three things: (a) "on-the-job learning from experience" ...; (b) "on-the-job training" under ... supervision ...; (c) "off-the-job training", involving the provision of formal training programmes inside the factory' (pp. 191–2). Cutting across these distinctions (originally devised by Machlup, 1962) is the important difference, noted by Becker (1964), between specific and general training. Specific training increases the future productivity of a trainee in the firm providing it, but does not raise his productivity by the same extent should he go to another firm. General training enhances a trainee's productivity by the same extent, irrespective of employer.

In fact, from the point of view of the individual, the same decision-making framework can be applied either to education or to training. From the point of view of firms, the quantity and types of training offered may vary according to their perception of it as either specific or general in nature. From the point of view of the economy, the distinction between education and training, and between different types of training, are important to the extent that the private returns to each form of human capital reflect social priorities.

We start with the individual's demand for education. As in the analysis of physical capital investment, it is possible to define either the PV of an extra period of a certain type of education, or its rate of return. In the education literature it is conventional to use the rate of return, and we shall do likewise. The internal rate of return, then, on investment in education is the discount rate that equates the PV of the extra lifetime earnings attributable to a certain period of additional education (after the legal school-leaving age) to the PV of the costs of that extra education (Blaug, 1970, p. 169). The individual's private rate of return is calculated on the basis of after-tax expected future earnings, out-of-pocket costs and the individual's earnings forgone while taking education. While we talk here about 'the individual', it should be noted that many of these decisions are made by families, or by parents on behalf of their children. Whoever makes the decision, however, the criterion is: the child shall remain at school/college/university if the private rate of return on the next increment of education exceeds the yield of the best alternative investment.

There are a number of important points about the elements in this calculation. The benefits—after-tax expected future earnings—require the family or individual to make judgements, for each future year, on: (a) how likely it is that the individual will actually be alive to receive

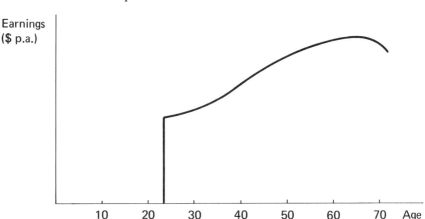

Figure. 6.5 Age—earnings profile of a university graduate

the benefits; (b) how likely it is that he will be employed; (c) whether the presently observed rewards to this increment of education can be expected to persist, and if so, for how long. The costs involve an assessment of government subsidies (if any) on fees, and of the impact on his and his family's income resulting from withdrawing him from productive activity.

The rate of return on an increment of education will increase if an individual believes that he will be alive longer to enjoy the rewards of further education, or that his chances have increased of being employed in a position requiring this level of education, or that the earnings attaching to such employment will rise. It will also rise if the costs of acquiring the education fall.

The effect of different levels of education upon earnings streams can be demonstrated with the aid of age—earnings profiles, two examples of which are shown in figures 6.5 and 6.6. Such profiles are derived by examining the income per period of individuals of different educational attainment at similar periods in their life. The individual in figure 6.5 pursues study until his early twenties, eventually graduating from university. He has zero earnings throughout his early life, while people who leave the education system earlier (see figure 6.6) are all able to start earning before he does—unschooled illiterates starting earliest of all. On the other hand, the higher the educational standard achieved, the higher is the initial starting point for earnings, the more rapidly earnings tend to rise, and the higher the peaks eventually reached.

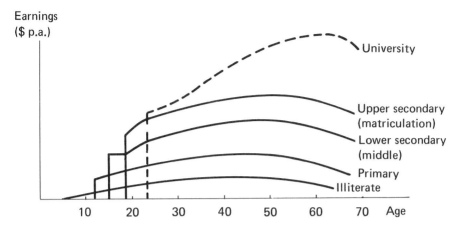

Figure 6.6 Age–earnings profiles of graduates of various levels of educational attainment.
(Adapted from Blaug, 1970, p. 25)

Earnings are only one side of the story, though. Individuals (or their families) must pay directly for education, unless it is wholly government-subsidized, and must also forgo earnings while receiving education. To obtain a complete picture, therefore, we need to draw in the negative dollar amounts representing the costs per period associated with each level of education. To see this, look at figure 6.7. Here the

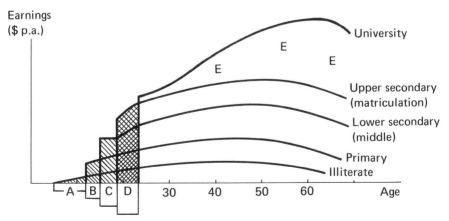

Figure 6.7 Private costs and benefits associated with various levels of education.
(Adapted from Blaug, 1970, p. 48)

direct costs of primary, lower secondary, upper secondary and tertiary education are represented by areas A, B, C and D, respectively. These comprise teaching fees, books, and travelling expenses and the like, minus any subsidy or scholarships. They are assumed to rise with each increment of education. The indirect (opportunity) costs of education are the earnings forgone by taking education instead. For a university graduate these amount to what he could have earned had he been working since the earliest period possible until the time he graduates. This is the area hatched by single and double diagonal lines. What individuals are most likely to be interested in is the incremental opportunity cost—that is, the earnings forgone by taking one more year or stage of education. The opportunity cost incurred by a university graduate compared with an upper secondary school matriculant is just the area hatched by crossing diagonal lines.

Finally, notice that area E represents the extra lifetime income that a university graduate can expect compared with an upper secondary school matriculant. Suppose for a moment that the student (or his family) is well informed about these observed costs and benefits. Then, in deciding whether to take a university degree, a student should compare this area—representing marginal benefits—with the incremental direct costs (area D) and indirect costs (double cross-hatched area) of taking the degree. If, further, he applies a discount factor to each of the annual benefits and costs, this is equivalent to the procedure described verbally earlier on. The discount rate that equates the incremental benefits to incremental costs is the internal rate of return on a university education.

It is most important to notice that, particularly in LDCs, where in many societies children participate in production from an early age, the indirect costs of education are likely to be substantially higher than the direct costs. As Blaug points out, this helps to explain why the drop-out rate after the school-leaving age is everywhere inversely related to household incomes. Families with low incomes cannot easily afford to sacrifice their children's earnings (Blaug, 1970, p. 49).

Of course, students actually have to make an assessment of age-income profiles and educational costs for themselves. They might lack the information that we have used to draw up our diagrams, however. And, more seriously, cross-section data relating to a population today may not apply to a country's population 20 years hence. In particular, the peak earnings received by, say, a graduate or matriculant in mid-life in real terms may lie well below the presently observed levels by the time the student has himself reached that age. Indeed, that is to some extent what we might expect. If the high peak earnings reflect a current relative scarcity of graduates in heavy demand by employers, then a tendency to pursue education to enjoy those high earnings can, in the end, only alleviate the scarcity. In the absence of market imperfections, this should reduce the rate of return offered on increments of higher education.

This sort of argument contributes to an understanding of the phenomenon, in some countries, of a pool of highly qualified unemployed persons. Attracted by the perceived prospect of a high rate of return, individuals pursue their studies to a high level. But if a great many follow the same path, an excess supply of the highly educated emerges. It is this excess supply that should eventually drive down the private rate of return on at least some types of higher education and discourage others from taking it—unless solely for consumption purposes.

If we now turn to the individual and training, we can see that he can make a perfectly analogous calculation. In this case, however, the cost to the trainee needs to be examined with particular care. We follow here the argument of Becker (1964). Assume initially that perfect competition prevails in the labour markets. Then, in equilibrium, the wage rate will be equal to workers' marginal productivity in all firms in the industry. If a firm provided a general training, as defined earlier, all firms would benefit from the higher labour productivity to which it would lead. Further, all wages in the industry would rise to the same level. Any individual firm could capture some of the return from its training effort only if its marginal productivity rose more than the wage it paid. Since, by assumption, the wage will rise in line with marginal productivity, no return on general training can be captured by the firm. The result is that firms would provide general training only if they did not have to pay any of the costs. On the other hand, people receiving such training would be willing to pay such costs because the training would raise their future earnings prospects. Thus, so long as firms can pass on training costs to trainees, in the form of reduced current earnings, they may still, rationally, offer training programmes from which all firms benefit.

With specific training the story is different. Here, by definition, individual firms can benefit from the training they offer. It is therefore rational for them to bear some or all of the financial burden of providing the training. The cost in forgone earnings to the individual is therefore less than in the general case.

An important gloss on this theory is that the relative generality or specificity of a training often turns out to hinge not on the nature of the training itself but rather on the mobility of labour. To see this, we have only to recognize that a training in a useful and widely applicable skill—an apparently general training—would actually benefit only the firm in which the training was given if ex-trainees could never move elsewhere. Since the firm that provided the training could, under these circumstances, be sure of reaping productivity gains from the trainee, it could treat the training as specific and would not require that workers be prepared to pay for it in terms of much reduced earnings.

It is easy to see from this survey that the sum of individuals' demands for education and/or training must in important respects be related to the private costs and prospective benefits that they attach to each increment of such human capital investment. We need to ask now how social costs and benefits need to reflect divergences from the private individual's view.

In a social rate of return calculation the obvious elements to be included on the cost side are the values of equipment and teaching materials used, of teachers' and administrators' time and effort expended, of output forgone by the economy while students acquire education rather than work, and finally the imputed value of the rent on educational buildings. The societal valuation of benefits, on the other hand, will start off by taking the pre-tax earnings stream of the individual. Whereas private rates of return include the effects of subsidies (such as scholarships and grants) and taxes, social rates of return ignore such flows since they represent only transfer payments. This factor alone can introduce an important divergence between measured private and social rates of return. Much evidence suggests that high-level state subsidies may never be completely recouped from taxes paid in later life by the more highly educated.

Further issues need to be considered, however. First, it is widely recognized that the externalities associated with education are potentially considerable. In the education literature a very wide range of so-called 'spillover' effects are discussed. Most amenable to measurement, and most obvious to the economist, is the increased income enjoyed by others as a result of an individual receiving an increment of education or training. The additional knowledge and skills obtained might, for example, enable an individual to organize productive inputs more effectively as a supervisor or manager, or might supply him with productivity-raising innovative ideas from which everyone benefits. Other externalities are harder to identify quantitatively. To make one point, education can contribute importantly to the ease with which information flows through an economy. An educated and literate population, for example, can understand and use banks and their financial instruments (such as cheques). This economizes on transaction costs. Still in the information area, education qualifications can be used by potential employers as a 'screening device': instead of having to use their own or their firm's (or a government department's) time and effort in assessing the relative merits of applicants for jobs, they can use the educational performance of candidates as a time-saving guide to quality. Finally, among the more clear-cut economic externalities, schools not only educate but act as child-caring institutions. Parents who might otherwise have had to care for children at home may therefore work productively.

Taking an even broader social view of externalities, it has also been suggested that more education promotes lawful behaviour, greater participation in the political process, greater awareness of the country's culture, leading to increased social cohesion, and, in general, changes from traditional to newer attitudes, which can in turn assist in raising savings and introducing new techniques. The strength of such arguments will vary from country to country and from one period to another. What is clear is that they cannot be satisfactorily valued in monetary amounts. Given that this last point applies with equal strength to many of the economic externalities, no comprehensive measure of social return can be expected.

Even if externalities were more amenable to measurement, other factors reflecting social aspirations should be included in a cost–benefit analysis. For example, education is often said to be one of the most promising means of engendering a more equal distribution of incomes since it offers the opportunity of advancement to higher-income employment that many would otherwise have been denied. To the extent (a) that this is true, and (b) that a country values greater equality of distribution, it may place a premium upon the earnings expected to accrue to the education of the poor.

Evidence on social and private rates of return to education remains fragmentary and must be interpreted with care. In particular, it would be dangerous to suppose that, if the observed earnings of a university graduate exceeded those of a high school matriculant, the whole differential could be attributed to the increment of education. Some of the difference may reflect innate ability and/or family background—and these need to be winnowed out, although many LDCs lack sufficient information to permit this to be done. In table 6.6 we reproduce some of the findings of Blaug, Layard and Woodhall (1969). Here private and social rates of return are given for increments of education for Indian urban males in 1960. The adjusted rate shown in each case assumes that education in itself, as opposed to background and ability, accounts for 65 per cent of observed income differentials. It will be noted that in all instances the private rate lay above the social rate (to

TABLE 6.6 Private and social rates of return, urban India, males, 1960

Level of education	Private rates		Social rates	
	Unadjusted	Adjusted	Unadjusted	Adjusted
	%	%	%	%
(1) Primary over illiterate	24.7	18.7	20.2	15.2
(2) Middle over primary	20.0	16.1	17.4	14.2
(3) Matriculation over middle	18.4	11.9	16.1	10.5
(4) First degree over matriculation	14.3	10.4	12.7	8.9

Source: Blaug, Layard and Woodhall (1969); reprinted in Blaug (1970, p. 228)

the extent that relevant factors could be incorporated in it) in this case. As noted earlier, this is in fact a commonly found result where such studies have been performed. Also more generally applicable are the findings of a particularly high social return on primary education in LDCs and a tendency for both private and social rates of return to decline as students pass from one level of education to the next.

CONFLICTING SIGNALS IN EDUCATIONAL INVESTMENT

The coming of political independence from former imperial powers brought with it a great and sudden social demand for 'localization' or 'indigenization', that is, the replacement of expatriate public servants and private sector staffs by locally born and bred personnel. Indigenous people already fortunate enough to have a relevant training or education often enjoyed relatively high salaries, embodying an important element of scarcity rent. Given the substantial social benefits perceived to be associated with indigenization programmes, large-scale expenditure on and subsidies for education and training to alleviate scarcities were felt to be socially justified. Both private and social rates of return on most levels of education were high.

Once the initial 'stocking up' on appropriately educated local personnel was completed, however, the social need for education and training changed in important ways. Continuing economic growth, replacement needs and the demands for new skills call for an education system growing at perhaps the rate of growth of the size of the labour force. But this rate is much slower than that which was required to meet the demands of the unique occasion of post-independence 'stocking up'. What is more, the alleviation of scarcities was already under way and thus was steadily reducing at least some elements of the social benefits flowing from education.

Individuals' perceptions do not take account of all of this, however. Their private costs of education often lie well below social costs because of subsidies continued from the immediately post-independence years. Their estimate of the benefits that they believe they will enjoy in, say, 10 or 20 years' time may be based on the current earnings paid to a cousin or friend who received his education (or the relevant portion of it under review) one or two decades ago. Yet observed current earnings may overstate what the individual can realistically expect in future for himself. The inflated expectations of return that private individuals come to harbour lead them to demand even more education, despite declining social returns to education expansion. This problem deserves special attention, and we examine it in light of the analysis of Edwards and Todaro (1973).

It is widely agreed now that students and their families view education as a 'passport for entry' into the modern sector where high-paying employment opportunities are available (see Edwards and Todaro, 1973, p. 109). As Harbison (1977) puts it, 'Even in the most remote rural areas, the aspiration of poor families is to have their offspring "get book" (primary education) or "big book" (higher education) so that they may escape a life sentence in traditional agriculture' (p. 129). This in itself can hardly be criticized. The real problem is that private individuals may well perceive the existence of a significant, positive rate of return on additional increments of education while the corresponding social benefits may be low or negative.[3]

To see this, recall that individuals (or their families) may be supposed to make an educational investment decision according to their expectations of the benefits it will bring compared with the costs. The benefit can be summarized by the differential between the traditional sector wage for an illiterate or basically educated person and the modern sector wage accruing to a person with the level of education (say, primary) that qualifies him for a modern sector job. This differential has often been observed to be large, sometimes because scarcity rents to education have been institutionally maintained despite subsequent alleviation of the scarcity, sometimes because of minimum wage legislation, sometimes because multinational companies may wish to 'buy off' criticism by paying high salaries to local employees. On the one hand, therefore, the modern sector wage often overstates the social value of the person's employment. On the other hand, it continues to induce heavy demand for education, even though graduates from some or all levels may exceed the number of jobs for which their qualification is the usual prerequisite. This in turn only perpetuates a supply of graduates that may be in excess of the jobs available for them.

Suppose now that employers use the education system as a screening device to help them save time in making hiring decisions in face of an excess supply of applicants for jobs. Then there will be a tendency to hire individuals of higher educational attainment than a job really requires, even though, in the long run, institutional pressures may force employers to pay a higher wage to reflect educational attainment rather than the minimum educational requirement.

Recall finally that individuals are often subsidized throughout their education—increasingly so as they reach higher levels. On the cost side, this means that private costs often lie well below social costs and are, for the individual, relatively insignificant.

Edwards and Todaro believe that these conditions have prevailed widely in LDCs and point out that they lead to a peculiar irony. As primary education ceases to give any certainty of modern sector employment, so the demand for higher levels increases. But secondary education cannot be undertaken without primary, so that, despite the falling return to primary education in itself, more of it is demanded as a way up the ladder.

Attention has already been drawn to the ways in which private and social costs and benefits diverge under these conditions, and Edwards and Todaro are able to identify the misallocation of human resources that results. First, 'frictional' unemployment arises when school-leavers find that jobs for which they are qualified are being taken by 'over-qualified' individuals from further up the ladder. Second, the 'over-qualified' either do jobs for which they are overpaid (compared with the wage that would be paid to the 'just qualified' individual), or are unemployed. Finally, there is a natural tendency for the more highly educated to migrate to cities, since the modern sector jobs for which they aim are often urban jobs. This draws away young talent from the rural areas where educated manpower is actually needed most.

Another aspect of this discussion is that educational needs, both in quantity and nature, change during the course of development. Cost—benefit calculations may be able to cope with the economy-wide repercussions of incremental changes—such as raising the school-leaving age by a year, or building a new school or university, or measuring the effects of taking an extra level of education. But cost—benefit analysis seems to be able to handle less well issues bearing on the changing place, role and shape of the whole education system within the developing economy. To quote Anderson and Bowman (1967),

Rate of return analysis does not incorporate systematic assessment of linkages between educational and economic developments over time. Rate of return estimates use cross-section age–income data to measure the life-income streams associated with one or another level or kind of schooling, but the time patterns used in this way are not historic or development time.

This latter point is closely related to the discussion earlier on in this section. The social rate of return on an increment of education, calculated on the basis of earnings in different age groups now, is likely to be quite different from the rate of return on that same increment that society will in fact enjoy as the individual or individuals concerned actually pass through life. The reason is that the economy will grow and change in ways that will alter its demands for skills as compared with the existing composition of demands. This is precisely the problem that manpower planning attacks.

MANPOWER PLANNING

Manpower planning attempts to take account of the future structure of the economy in determining the size and sort of education system an economy should have. Anderson and Bowman identify the common essential ingredients of any manpower plan as follows:

(1) a specification of the composition of manpower requirements at some future date or sequence of dates;
(2) a specification of manpower availabilities now and in future (involving the subtraction of retired and deceased workers from new entrants into the labour force);
(3) a reconciliation of manpower demand in (1) with manpower supply in (2).

Notice that the idea of manpower requirements is more a technological than an economic one in the sense that it presupposes a fixed proportional relationship between target levels of output and labour inputs of various kinds. The economic implication of this view is an assumption of zero or near-zero elasticity of demand for skills—which, of course, is a proposition that would have to be tested. Unlike cost–benefit analysis, it avoids the necessity of gauging a worker's contribution by his projected earnings. Underlying the whole approach is a view of education primarily as a supplier of manpower, with the added rider that instilling necessary skills must often take protracted periods of time.

The manpower planning approach is, however, open to criticism. It explicitly omits consideration of the consumption benefits and externalities of education that can, in principle, be included in a cost–benefit analysis—although they often are not. Further, it is sometimes employed in a way that ignores the costs of education and training. Finally, by taking a fixed coefficient stance, manpower planning has often turned a blind eye to the substitution possibilities between different skills in production that could be achieved by allowing relative wage rates to change.

Summarizing this debate, Blaug (1968) concludes that the rate of return and manpower planning approaches are in fact complementary: 'unless we assume that the production of highly qualified manpower is the only economic purpose of an educational system, even the most accurate manpower forecasting would not dispense with the need for rate of return analysis' (p. 259).

OTHER FORMS OF INVESTMENT IN HUMANS

Although education has usually been at the focus of the human capital debate, it has long been recognized that health measures, additional food and better shelter can also improve the quality of human resources. While indices relating to health, nutrition and shelter have received much more attention recently in relation to identifying basic needs in LDCs, the point here is that improvements in these areas can also be regarded as investments. The resulting increased earnings represents the yield on the investment.

In relation to nutrition, Schultz (1961) comments: 'On the "hungry" steppes and in the teeming valleys of Asia, millions of adult males have so meagre a diet that they cannot do more than a few hours of hard work ... Under such circumstances, it is certainly meaningful to treat food partly as consumption, and partly as a current "producer good" ...' (p. 5). It may seem odd to think of food as a producer good when it is so often regarded as consumption. But the extent to which it has this attribute falls as food intake rises, since there will come a point, before long, when nutritional improvements lead to only very small positive gains. At this point, additional food may indeed be regarded as a consumption good.

Evidence in this area is still being assembled, but according to a World Bank (1979) study, malnourished workers have been shown to lose 30 per cent of their muscle strength and 15 per cent of their precision of movement. Poor nutrition also reduces the desire to take advantage of ideas for innovation, increases absenteeism in general, and prolongs absence through illness.

In relation to health, we have already looked at this area from a different angle when examining mortality earlier in the chapter. Preventive and curative health measures not only prevent death but also reduce the severity and incidence of debilitating afflictions. For example, the parasitic group—malaria, schistosomiasis and Chagas's disease—is receiving considerable attention in Brazil, where government programmes are being directed against their principal vectors ('carriers'), the mosquito, a fresh-water snail and a nocturnally active blood-sucking insect (see World Bank, 1979, vol. II, p. 14). The aim of this type of programme can certainly be seen, partially at least, as improving the contribution of labour to production.

Finally, on housing, adequate shelter from the elements reduces susceptibility to extremes of climate, and adequate internal housing space and space between dwellings assist in reducing the spread of disease. The worst housing conditions are associated with poor or non-existent sanitation and thus contribute to the debilitating effects of disease.

CONCLUSION

Changes in the growth rate of population and labour force are among the least predictable in economic theory, and yet we can predict for certain that such changes will occur. The simplest assumption, that Solow's n is fixed, must be challenged. While the degree of such changes is unpredictable, however (depending as it does on socio-cultural as well as purely economic factors, themselves ambiguous in effect), the nature of their influence on development is also dependent on other economic variables such as saving and investment rates. In particular, labour both contributes to production and must consume much of what is produced in order to live. The balance between these two establishes whether incomes per head can rise steadily or are forced to remain at a low level.

While the quantity of human resources is a central element in the development process, the quality of those resources determines the contribution they can make to production, and improved quality has the potential to benefit all. Indiscriminate expansion of all types of education, especially if subsidized, can however lead to a misallocation of scarce resources, and governments must take care to ensure that the returns to investment in human capital—via education or other means —do not fall out of line with returns that could be earned elsewhere.

FURTHER READING

Demography is a discipline in itself and its literature is vast. Particularly useful recent contributions drawn on in this chapter include Cassen (1976); Easterlin (1980)—which contains much of the most recent thinking in the area—and Perlman (1981), which puts this work in perspective in a particularly illuminating and succinct fashion.

On the question of human capital, a good all-round introduction is Blaug (1970). The readings in Blaug (1968) cover most of the basic theoretical groundwork as presented by pioneers in the field.

NOTES

1 As has been realized with the passage of time, this is a rather too simple solution. Recall that the Solow model is built on the assumption of a single-commodity world. To ensure self-perpetuating growth as described above, it may well not be sufficient to think in terms of an injection of capital. Physical capital of the right kind for the country's particular needs and stage of development should be considered of prime importance. However, physical capital, even of the right kind, will not guarantee automatic success unless other inputs (such as skilled labour and entrepreneurship) are also available.

2 Cassen (1976) also makes the point, relevant to our discussion of saving in chapter 4, that children might in some cases act as a form of forced saving. If having fewer children means merely that parents and the existing offspring consume at a higher level and do not (or cannot) put to alternative investment use the consumption costs that would have been incurred in rearing an extra child, then the marginal child forces the parents to save.

3 In table 6.6, private rates are uniformly higher than social rates, but social rates are still well above zero. The specific numbers given there, however, refer to one country at one date, and elsewhere at other times social rates could well be lower and the differential between private and social rates greater.

7

International Trade

Our basic growth model assumes a closed economy. Yet one of the most obvious facts of economic life—and one of the most important facts for growth and development—is that nations engage in international trade. In this chapter we start by examining the benefits that any country should, according to a wide range of theories, be able to enjoy by engaging in trade. Some of these theories abstract from growth and point to the improved resource allocation that trade promotes by encouraging specialization. Other theories argue directly that trade is an engine of growth. We also look at the arguments of critics who have suggested that trade may be detrimental to development, and assess theory and evidence here.

With this background we are in a strong position to examine industrialization. Thus far, industrialization has largely been viewed in a framework of a closed dual economy, although it was hinted in chapter 3 that open-economy aspects could not be ignored. Defining industrialization rather loosely as the adoption of mechanized means of production, and defining mechanized means of production as reproducible capital, we can see that the urges to industrialize and to accumulate capital have much in common.[1] Both can be seen as key developmental strategies. Whether we think in terms merely of acquiring capital, or in terms of the nature of the industries on which development is built, the influence of trade is likely to be considerable.[2]

THE BENEFITS OF TRADE

STATIC RESOURCE-ALLOCATIVE ARGUMENTS

In this section we shall show that every LDC stands to gain from trade by fully employing its resources in the specialized production of the good or goods in which, relative to other countries, it has a comparative advantage. The central point here is that trade permits a country to achieve a level of consumption that lies above and beyond any level that production possibilities under autarky (no trade) would permit.

It can also be shown that, under certain assumptions, a by-product of international trade should be a tendency to equalize incomes.

Let us start with one of the most fundamental principles of economics: the concept of comparative advantage. This principle pervades all situations in which trade might occur—between persons and between sectors, for example, as well as between nations.

Consider the simplest possible conditions in which trade might take place. Two countries, an LDC and a DC, each produce two commodities, say rice and metal boxes. Producing a unit of either of these goods involves for each country a resource cost, which can be measured in physical units and which we will assume to be reflected in the price charged for each unit. Suppose the resource cost of producing a tonne of rice in the LDC is greater than the resource cost of producing a tonne of identical-quality rice in the DC. Then the DC has *absolute* advantage in rice production. Similarly, the DC will also have *absolute* advantage in producing metal boxes if a typical unit can be produced within its borders at less resource cost than in the LDC.

If we take notice only of absolute advantage, it is not clear why there should be any scope for the LDC to engage in trade. After all, why should the DC buy anything from a country that is more costly (and by implication higher priced) in all that it produces? The answer lies in *comparative* advantage. To make things as simple as possible, suppose that the cost of production of each good in each country is determined entirely by the amount of the single factor labour (measured in man-hours) employed in making a unit of output. Assume also that, in any one of the countries, exactly the same amount of labour is required to produce each unit—whether it be the first or the thousandth —of any one of the outputs. To give a numerical example, imagine that 120 man-hours are required per tonne of rice in the LDC, but only 60 man-hours per tonne in the DC; and that the LDC uses 6 man-hours of labour per metal box while the DC uses only 2. Clearly, the DC has an absolute advantage in producing each output; but the principle of comparative advantage insists that we look at the *relative* production costs of rice and metal boxes in each country and compare these two ratios. If they are different, it is to the advantage of each country to specialize in making that good which, compared with the other country, it produces relatively more cheaply.

To return to our example, the ratio of absolute costs per unit of output for rice between LDC and DC is $120/60 = 2/1$, whereas the ratio of absolute costs for metal boxes is $6/2 = 3/1$. The important thing to note is that each metal box requires three times as much labour input in the LDC as in the DC but each tonne of rice requires only twice the labour. The DC has a comparative advantage in producing metal boxes: even though it is absolutely more efficient in producing both outputs, it enjoys a *greater* degree of efficiency (that is, it enjoys a greater cost advantage) compared with the LDC in metal box than in rice production. On the other hand, the LDC has comparative advantage in producing rice: it is at *less* of a cost disadvantage, compared with the DC, in producing rice rather than metal boxes.

So long as a difference exists between the absolute cost ratios, there must also be a difference between the countries in the rate at which metal box production falls when rice production is stepped up, and vice versa. In our example, the production of an extra tonne of rice in the LDC requires 120 man-hours to be diverted from metal boxes, which means a sacrifice in production of 20 boxes. In the DC, 60 man-hours would have to be diverted into increasing rice production by 1 tonne, and the sacrifice would be 30 boxes. This, of course, is only another way of seeing why the LDC has comparative advantage in producing rice. For each extra tonne of rice it produces, it sacrifices less in terms of box production than does the DC. On the other hand, production of one more metal box in the LDC requires 6 man-hours to be diverted from rice production—and a sacrifice of 1/20 of a tonne. In the DC only 2 man-hours would have to be diverted, and would involve the lesser sacrifice of 1/30 of a tonne.

Given this difference, it is now easy to see why trade will benefit both countries. From the point of view of the DC, if it can find a way of increasing the rice available to it by a tonne at a sacrifice of *less than* 30 metal boxes, it will have escaped the technical straitjacket operating on its domestic economy. From the point of view of the LDC, if it can find a way of increasing the number of metal boxes available to it by one at a sacrifice of *less than* 1/20 of a tonne of rice, then it should be happy.

Suppose the DC notices that the LDC can produce a tonne of rice for less than a cost of 30 metal boxes. If, from an initial position producing both outputs, the DC now produces 30 more boxes, it will of course be able to produce 1 tonne less of rice itself but it can offer these 30 boxes to the LDC for rice, and will be sensible to do so if it can obtain more than 1 tonne of rice in exchange. In the LDC, 30 boxes are worth, under domestic production conditions (where 30 boxes absorb 180 man-hours) 180/120 = 1.5 tonnes of rice. Since, under domestic conditions, 1.5 tonnes of rice would have to be sacrificed in the LDC to obtain another 30 boxes, it is to its advantage to trade if it can obtain the 30 boxes for less than 1.5 tonnes. Clearly, an exchange rate to the mutual advantage of the countries lies somewhere between 1.5 tonnes of rice per 30 boxes (that is, 1 tonne for 20 boxes) and 1 tonne per 30 boxes (below which it will be pointless for the DC to go).

Alternatively, suppose that the LDC notices that the DC can produce a metal box for less than a cost of 1/20 tonne of rice. If, from an initial position producing both outputs, the LDC now produces one more tonne of rice, it will have to sacrifice 20 metal boxes but can offer this tonne to the DC in exchange for boxes. In the DC, 1 tonne of rice is worth, under domestic conditions, 30 metal boxes. (Since 1 tonne of rice absorbs 60 man-hours, one metal box absorbs 2 man-hours, which implies $60/2 = 30$ boxes have to be sacrificed.) Since, under domestic production conditions, 30 boxes would have to be sacrificed in the DC to obtain another tonne of rice, it is to its advantage to trade if it can obtain the tonne for less than 30 boxes. Clearly, an exchange rate to the mutual advantage of the countries lies, as before, between 1 tonne of rice for 20 boxes and 1 tonne of rice for 30 boxes. Finally, since these arguments apply equally well to each and every tonne of rice or metal boxes each country might be making, the way to maximize the gains offered by trade is for each country to specialize completely in producing the good in which it has comparative advantage.

Diagrammatically, we can see all this by drawing the various production possibilities for each country. In the LDC, 120 man-hours are required to produce a tonne of rice and 6 man-hours for a metal box. Assuming a labour input of 6 million man-hours per year, this means a maximum of 50,000 tonnes of rice could be produced (and no metal boxes) or a maximum of 1 million metal boxes (and no rice). As we have already shown, the domestic transformation rate in production is 1.5 tonnes of rice for 30 metal boxes. Armed with this information, we can represent all the combinations of rice and metal boxes which the LDC can produce by a straight line, *AB* of constant slope (see figure 7.1(a)). If we assume an annual labour input of 2,400,000 man-hours in the DC, the production possibilities for that country can be represented by *GH* in figure 7.1(b). What our verbal argument amounts to is a demonstration that neither country, before trade, can move beyond the production possibilities whose outer boundary is marked by *AB* and *GH*. But the slopes of *AB* and *GH* represent domestic transformation possibilities in production. The countries can agree on a common international exchange rate between rice and metal boxes that lies between the slopes of *AB* and *GH*. This is represented by the slope of both *BN* and *GN*. The way to open up the maximum possible range of opportunities is for each country to specialize completely, the

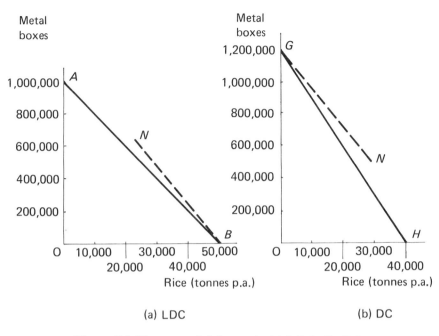

Figure 7.1 The potential for trade (a) LDC; (b) DC.

LDC at *B* and the DC at *G*, and to trade from there. Notice that *BN* and *GN* lie completely beyond the domestic production possibility frontiers. Each country therefore has the potential for enjoying a higher level of consumption than it had in the absence of trade.

So far we have discussed the principle of comparative advantage without exploring in any detail *why* different countries have comparative advantage in the production of different goods. The simplest answer to this question is that different countries are endowed in different proportions with factors of production, and that comparative advantage resides in the production of those goods that use most intensively the inputs with which the country is relatively most richly endowed. Major contributors to developing this analysis were Heckscher, Ohlin and Samuelson, and in their honour it is often called the H−O−S theory. To see how it works, let us make assumptions that rule out the possible influence of any element other than relative factor endowments that might, intuitively, seem likely to generate comparative advantage. Assume, as before, a two-country world (LDC and DC), making two goods (rice and metal boxes) with two factors of production (labour and capital, homogeneous and of identical quality in each country), using identical production functions in conditions of perfect competition in all markets, so that the full employment of all resources is guaranteed in equilibrium. Assume also constant returns to scale and identical preference patterns in each country. Suppose that the LDC is abundantly endowed with labour relative to capital and the DC abundantly endowed with capital relative to labour. Thus $(K/L)_{LDC} < (K/L)_{DC}$. Suppose also that rice is relatively labour-intensive in production and metal boxes are relatively capital-intensive. Then, drawing on our knowledge of how to construct transformation or production possibility frontiers (see Appendix 7.1), we may construct such a frontier for each of the countries as shown in figure 7.2.[3] The LDC has comparative advantage in labour-intensively produced rice, the DC in capital-intensively produced metal boxes.

In equilibrium, assuming competitive conditions, the marginal rate of transformation between rice and metal boxes will be equal to the domestic relative price ratio, represented by the slopes of P_d in each case. Closed-economy equilibrium will therefore be established at A on each frontier. If the slopes of the P_d lines before trade differ (as it is reasonable to suppose they almost always will), then the countries can work out some relative price ratio in between at which both may trade and from which both may gain. In figure 7.2 this international trading price ratio is represented by the slope of P_t. If producers in each country face this price regime rather than the former domestic prices, they will

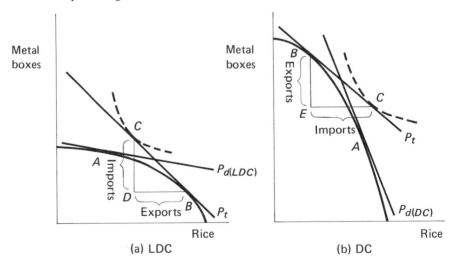

Figure 7.2 Gains from trade (a) LDC; (b) DC.

be induced to switch resources to a greater extent into producing the good in which their country has comparative advantage. Production will move from *A* in each case to *B*. Then each country will export some of the good in which it has comparative advantage (say, *BD* units of rice for the LDC and *EB* metal boxes for the DC) and import in return the good in which it is at a comparative disadvantage (*CD*(= *EB*) metal boxes for the LDC and *CE* (= *BD*) units of rice for the DC). Because of the equalities to which we have referred in the previous sentence, the two trade triangles *BDC* and *BEC* are of course equal.

The important point to notice is that each country finishes up at a point *C*, after trade, which lies *outside* its domestic production possibility frontier. By encouraging countries to specialize in the productive activities in which they have comparative advantage, therefore, trade allows every one of them to enjoy an increased opportunity to consume. This constitutes the gain from trade.

Precisely how much trade occurs (that is, precisely how the position of *C* is determined) depends upon the demand conditions prevailing in each country. The international price ratio, P_t, is determined by the interplay of both supply- and demand-side considerations, after all. If you wish, you can envisage each country's social preferences between rice and metal boxes to be represented by social indifference curves analogous to an individual's indifference curves. In each country, the position of *C* will then be determined at the point where P_t, along which both countries can trade, is tangent to its highest attainable social indifference curve. This curve is shown diagrammatically by the dashed line passing through *C* in each case. If all individuals' preferences in a country are identical, the social indifference curve is an uncontroversial representation of aggregate preferences. If preferences vary among individuals, however, social indifference curves become controversial because of the problems involved in giving proper recognition to each individual's views in the course of aggregating them all. Our general conclusions are, however, unaffected by this.

There is another developmentally interesting implication of this analysis. Before trade, the LDC produces more of the relatively capital-intensive good—metal boxes—than it does afterwards. The demand by producers for the relatively scarce input, capital, therefore falls as they start specializing in producing the relatively labour-intensive good—rice—and at the same time their demand for labour services rises. Thus, with given stocks of capital and labour, the return on capital should fall relative to labour's wage. Exactly the reverse should occur in the DC as producers specialize in the capital-intensive good. Thus, with the wage rising in the LDC but falling in the DC and the return on capital falling in the LDC but rising in the DC, relative factor rewards should tend to equalize internationally over time.

Look again now at figure 7.2 and assume that there is no objection in this case to representing social preferences by the social indifference curve.[4] You will note that in an international trade equilibrium the following conditions hold. First, the domestic marginal rate of substitution for consumption (MRS) in each country between rice and metal boxes (represented by the slope of the community indifference curve at *C* in each country) is equal to the domestic marginal rate of transformation (MRT) shown by the slope of the production possibility frontier at *B*. Second, the marginal rate at which each country in equilibrium transforms rice into metal boxes is equal to the international price ratio, and the price ratio under free trade faced by all consumers in each country. Since the MRT also represents the marginal cost of producing one unit of either output, marginal cost is equated to the price ratio in equilibrium—which is, of course, an essential characteristic of competitive equilibrium, and a condition that ensures that consumer wants are satisfied with maximum effectiveness. If competitive conditions are not met, the possibility arises of price exceeding marginal cost (as in monopoly) with the well-known consequences of a dead-weight loss to be borne by the economy. An international trade equilibrium is therefore associated with a situation of allocative efficiency.

DYNAMIC AND INDIRECT BENEFITS OF TRADE

Critics of the forgoing conventional static analysis have often charged that the assumptions underlying it are so stringent and 'unrealistic' that such theorizing cannot be of much use in the real world. Now, it must be admitted that non-uniform preferences and/or technologies, non-constant returns to scale, imperfect competition, barriers to trade and so on present complications for the basic theory to cope with and lead many to despair of its usefulness. On the other hand, even one of its most trenchant critics admits that these complications do not challenge the basic vision of the theory. (See Steedman, 1979, introductory essay: his own view, developed with J.S. Metcalfe in subsequent essays, is that its fatal flaw is its failure to deal adequately with capital as a produced means of production, particularly when we note that no sector exists in the model to produce it.)

We shall not here be drawn into this debate but instead take a different approach. We shall concede that the assumptions of the static model may not always hold but from that observation derive the comfort that this merely opens the door to considering a new range of potential benefits. Rather than assuming that resources, techniques and preferences are given as in the static analysis, we shall see how trade can introduce new resources and ideas, draw idle resources into employment and operate to change traditional preference patterns. Trade will thus be interpreted as an agent of dynamism, stimulating growth and efficiency, changing the economic framework over time rather than operating within it.

'Vent for Surplus' and 'Staple Product' Theories

Suppose first that, as seems likely, the development process in most LDCs gets under way from an initial point before trade well within the transformation curve, in other words that the country in question has the capacity to produce output in excess of domestic requirements: it has surplus capacity. The applicability to LDCs of the classical argument for trade as a vent for such surplus, is drawn out by Myint (1958). The point he makes is that international trade can overcome the narrowness of the isolated domestic market and provide an outlet for the surplus that takes the economy towards the transformation curve and increases its overall consumption potential.

Notice at the outset that the H−O−S version of trade theory could not permit a country ever to be inside its transformation curve for very long. Under the assumptions of that model, any initial imbalance between productive and consumption capacities would be equilibrated away by the smooth functioning of a comprehensive set of markets, which could be relied upon to generate any necessary adjustments through appropriate price signals. For example, Myint points out, in a country with a sparse population relative to its natural resources (in particular, land), rents would be low according to H−O−S and relatively land-using commodities would have low prices, whereas wages would be high and relatively labour-using commodities would have high prices. Since the scarce factor, labour, would thus be fully employed, there would be no surplus productive capacity. The country would be on its transformation curve.

Historically speaking, Myint reminds us, the economic framework of LDCs is a much cruder apparatus than that implied by H−O−S. Technical and capital resources are lacking, markets are not integrated, and communications are in general poor. All this restricts and fragments domestic demand and severely inhibits adjustments in the market that might lead idle resources to be put to productive use.

International trade helps to overcome this. The simplest illustration of the 'vent' at work relates to a peasant export sector in which the export crop is a traditional crop, which continues to be produced by the traditional means used in the subsistence economy. An example would be rice in south-east Asia. Here the real-world agents of trade were foreign trading companies, which provided new effective demand for rice by acting as middlemen with the world market. The result was to bring more land under cultivation. In the absence of trade, domestic requirements would not have led this land to be worked. A slightly more complex picture involves an export crop of a type not formerly grown domestically but still cultivated by traditional means.

From the point of the country involved, this analysis suggests that, contrary to the H−O−S view, export production can be increased without reducing production for domestic purposes. These exports in turn permit imports to be brought into the country to boost local consumption and investment.

Compared with the H−O−S theory, this approach also provides a more plausible explanation of how a peasant subsistence economy might start trading at all. In the H−O−S world, no surplus can exist for long. If a peasant economy is observed producing just its minimum subsistence requirements, it must be inferred in this case that it is already using all its productive resources efficiently to do so and is on its transformation curve. As we saw earlier, trade would involve the country in a reallocation of resources as it moved around its transformation curve. Export production in the area of the country's comparative advantage (an export crop) would be achieved by reducing subsistence output below the minimum level. This should not matter according to H−O−S because any gap between subsistence production and consumption could be made good by purchases out of the cash generated by exports. But suppose peasants suspect—quite rationally —that the value of their export crop might fall in world markets. Then they might not be able to earn enough to make good the subsistence shortfall. This is clearly a disincentive to undertake export crop production at all, and it becomes difficult to explain why such economies ever did enter trade.

On the other hand, if we assume surplus capacity exists right from the start, then the export crop can be produced and sold without ever endangering subsistence production. It thus is immediately apparent why the country should be happy to trade.

While this theory has considerable appeal, it should not be overplayed. It can be applied safely only to countries where resources genuinely are or were surplus to requirements, and it provides only part of the explanation for the dynamic benefits or trade (others are considered in subsequent sections).

Notice before we pass on, however, that the 'vent for surplus' theory is closely related to the 'staple products' theory, devised originally to explain the development of Canada in terms of its trade in 'staples' (natural resources) such as furs, timber and minerals. The theory focuses upon the value to LDCs of industry based on such resources, given that they may often generate a surplus of the kind Myint considers. Consideration of staple product industries, and their effects on local technology, skills, saving ratios and the stimulation of other sectors, opens the door to our section on export-led growth later.

Raised Productivity and Changing Techniques
Having isolated the way in which trade may enable a country to move towards its transformation curve, let us now assume that we are again observing a country that has reached this frontier. Here, on the other hand, let us abandon the H−O−S assumption of given technology and see how trade can benefit a country through changing and improving its productive inputs and processes. We shall be looking at 'indirect' and/or 'dynamic' benefits of trade, which can be represented by an outward shift of the transformation curve brought about by a trade-induced movement along the curve (Haberler, 1959).

The first point to note here is that trade provides a great historical short-cut for LDCs in terms of capital inputs. Left in isolation, a country would take many years to develop the skills required to build up a capital goods sector, even assuming that all the raw materials required to make capital goods were locally available. Given the central productivity-raising role of capital goods in development, such protracted delays would slow down the pace of development considerably. By trading, however, a country can import machines, vehicles, power-generating equipment and the like—important in themselves in any case but, in addition, embodying the findings of extensive and expensive research and development done in advanced nations. In a recent study, the share of capital goods in total imports was found in general to run at about 30−40 per cent in the earliest stages of industrialization, later falling back to 20−25 per cent only once the country was launched. It is of interest here that smaller countries often start with a lower ratio of capital to total imports, but, perhaps because they have a consequently slower start, they fail to reduce the ratio as rapidly as larger countries (see Batchelor, Major and Morgan, 1980, pp. 181−2).

It has often been argued, of course, that imported capital goods are inappropriate to the needs of LDCs and breed anti-developmental results. To some extent this may be true. But it must be remembered that, whatever the supposedly detrimental consequences of such capital imports, the alternative would have been very little growth for a very long time.

While this first argument may relate in some cases to the outright purchase of capital equipment, capital resources also flow into a country from investors abroad on the understanding that repayments of principal and interest, and perhaps repatriation of profits, will be made in future. Since such repayments must be made in foreign exchange, investments of this kind are contingent upon such foreign exchange earnings being sufficient to meet demand of this kind. The greater the volume of foreign trade in which an LDC engages, the more foreign exchange it may earn and the more foreign capital it can therefore hope to attract.

Notice, further, that, while new and more efficient techniques can be embodied in machines, technological know-how is also transmitted by managers and entrepreneurs who come from abroad to set up plant and, in the course of their work, pass on their skills. Similarly, public sector projects financed by foreign capital may bring experts into a country who can impart important technical skills. Contact and communication with such individuals supplies invaluable experience for local labour, managers, technicians and public servants.

Another argument presented by Haberler suggests that trade has the important indirect effect of fostering healthy competition and keeping in check inefficient monopolies. This argument would seem to have equal force whether we regard the inefficiencies as arising because a country simply has not yet been drawn into world trade or, as is more usual these days, because it has erected an array of protective tariffs and/or other barriers to trade.

Recent developments in trade theory (see Corden, 1974; Martin, 1978), present this argument in a way that makes it rather clear how trade may lead the managers of firms to apply greater effort to the efficient operation of their enterprises. It was noticed some time ago that firms could be seen as entities that organize human effort but that might vary widely in the extent to which they could actually extract effort from a given workforce, or, more accurately, from a given number of man-hours. Leibenstein (1966), who pioneered work in this area, termed the degree of success in extracting effort as *X-efficiency*, and for variations in its degree looked for an explanation to the performance of managers. The key variable in X-efficiency analysis is effort input, and we identify a reduction in managerial effort with an increase in X-*in*efficiency, since 'managers determine not only their own productivity but also the productivity of all co-operating units in the organization' (Leibenstein, 1966, p. 397). To see how this fits in with trade, notice that firms can be defined to produce marketed outputs (goods and services) and non-marketed outputs (leisure). Suppose now that, given technology, greater effort leads to greater efficiency in productivity terms, and higher profits result in greater efficiency. The cost of greater efficiency will be a sacrifice of leisure. Suppose also that managers derive positive but marginally diminishing utility from both profit and leisure, and that managerial effort can rise only as far as a given maximum. Assume, finally, that firms are initially isolated from foreign competition, either for historical or institutional (e.g. tariff) reasons, and as a consequence enjoy higher profits (perhaps based on local monopoly) for any level of managerial effort than they would if exposed to international trade.

All this can be represented on a diagram (figure 7.3). There, indifference curves are shaped to reflect our assumption that, for successive sacrifices of profit, managers require additional leisure in return, and at an increasing rate, to keep them at a fixed level of utility. I_2 represents a higher level of utility than I_1. The line OP shows how profit increases, in proportion to managerial effort, when the firm is shielded from

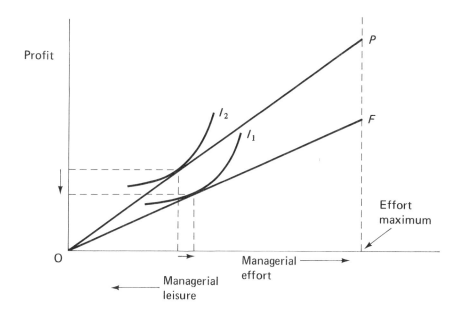

Figure 7.3 Trade and the reduction in X-inefficiency.
(Adapted from Martin, 1978, p. 276)

world competition. The line *OF* shows the profit–managerial effort relationship after the country has entered trade. As we have drawn the indifference curves (with leisure a normal good, and income effects dominating substitution effects), unhindered competition with other world producers stimulates an increase of managerial effort, which, by definition, means a reduction of X-inefficiency.

From a social welfare point of view, some weight would probably have to be given to the leisure enjoyed by managers, but for LDCs the social costs associated with a larger degree of leisure-taking are likely to be high. In particular, competition-stimulated managerial effort may well engender job-creating expansion, while isolation from international competition encourages stagnation. Other aspects of managerial effort include keeping abreast of technology, preserving flexibility and reorganizing plant—all of which contribute to long-run growth prospects and are actually the stuff of adapting to new areas of comparative advantage (see pp. 191–2).

For empirical work relating to isolation through protection, we can examine Bergsman's (1974) work on a variety of countries. For the 'small, relatively open economies' of Malaya and Norway, he attributes to X-inefficiency and monopoly returns a cost of protection to the economy of 0.4 and 2 per cent of GNP, respectively. Estimates for the large industrialized markets of Mexico and Brazil are 2.2 and 6.8 per cent of GNP, and for the smaller but protected economies of the Philippines and Pakistan, 2.6 and 5.4 per cent. These effects, he states 'seem to depend only on the level of protection; the size of domestic markets does not seem to affect them' (Bergsman, 1974, pp. 420–1). The message here appears to be that, the more isolated a country is, irrespective of size, the more are X-inefficiency and monopoly returns likely to impinge.

Even now we have not exhausted the gains that a country may come to enjoy by engaging in trade. As a final point, in the static theory, specialization involves movement along a fixed transformation curve, for techniques are given and unaffected by the move and all that actually happens is a reallocation of resources. In fact, however, trade can be seen as doing much more than this—shifting the transformation curve outwards at the same time, since the expanded market now available permits greater division of labour, learning effects, gaining productivity through increasing plant size, taking advantage of technical advances often available only in larger machines, and overcoming technical indivisibilities. All of these effects (comprising what is called the 'productivity doctrine') allow the country to enjoy increasing returns to scale; but at the same time they imply that specialization cannot be easily reversed since they require important changes in the whole structure of production, not merely a reallocation of resources. (For more on this see Myint, 1958, and his references to Adam Smith and Allyn Young; and also Gold, 1981.) This whole package of effects overlaps and interacts with influences that we noted earlier. The very plant that offers higher productivity through its size and embodied design advances, for example, is usable only because trade offers an expanded market, but is most easily obtainable through trade in the first place.

Having considered in the last two sections the sort of dynamic and indirect effects that trade can bring to a country, we pass on finally to present, briefly, a more general theoretical framework which, in a sense, is a dynamic version of the static comparative advantage approach.

Product Cycles and Technological Gaps
In the static, H−O−S theory, resources, including capital stocks, are taken as given and gain is derived from reallocating them among productive uses. In the dynamic theory, trade is seen as a means of increasing and changing the stock of productive inputs, especially capital, thereby permitting the economy to grow. So far, however, we have not explored in any detail what sorts of industry and what types of capital might be expected to promote growth in developing countries, and what changes might be expected over time.

In general, LDCs embark upon trade by exporting raw materials and primary commodities (such as agricultural produce, fuels and minerals) that are surplus to domestic requirement and are required as industrial inputs and for consumption abroad. In some cases, existing techniques might be used for export production, but in many others capital equipment is imported, and export-oriented industry, capital-intensive in production methods, forms the basis of a modern sector. Exports are either labour-intensively produced or natural-resource-rich, and the impact of the export sector on the rest of the economy depends upon the linkages it induces. Such linkages may be forward (for example, from agricultural production to food processing) or backward (as from mining to power generation to drive the machines). These effects, and others on saving, employment and income distribution, will be taken up again in the section on export-led growth, and in considering the case against trade.

This is familiar ground, but to understand how LDCs might go on to benefit further from trade through growth and structural change we need to examine their relationship, over time, to nations that may already be defined as advanced industrial countries. Notice first that characteristics of wealthy industrial nations include massive expenditure on both pure scientific and more applied research; a consequent widespread awareness of new techniques and potential for product and process innovation; large, wealthy markets often hungry for novelty; a large capital stock; a relatively highly skilled and highly paid labour force; and an ignorance or uncertainty about production conditions in LDCs.

Observe next that the 'life' of a product can be broken, conceptually, into three parts: the first stage, when it is new; a second, when it is maturing; and the last, when it is mature or standardized.

What we shall now discover is that each of these stages can be characterized by features that, when combined with our description of advanced industrial nations and our knowledge of LDCs, explains how developing countries might expect long-term trade-related growth, in addition to that based on any natural resource advantage of the kind discussed earlier.

The theory here, advanced by Vernon (1966), is restricted to products likely to be developed for high-income, high-wage economies. The reason for this is that Vernon wants to show how comparative advantage, in effect, passes out of the hands of advanced industrial nations into those of LDCs during a product's life. Since the product is, in broad terms, the same throughout the analysis, and since it must start life in an advanced nation, it must be expected that it will be a product designed for the techniques and preferences of that kind of economy.

Vernon assumes that it will be entrepreneurs in the richest and largest economies (he suggests the USA as the prime example) who will spend most on new product development. This follows from the belief that, wherever technological advance permits the opportunity to develop a new product appealing to high-income consumers, such opportunities are likely to become apparent first in the wealthiest countries. Also, countries that are already wealthy in both physical and human capital have a comparative advantage in research-intensive (that is, new) and skill-intensive goods relative to countries where capital of all forms is scarce and the feasibility of developing new goods thus is much more limited. Because of their capital wealth and high wage costs, Vernon further assumes that the search for new products will, on the processing side, also be stimulated by the desire to substitute capital for labour.

As far as the nature of new-product manufacture is concerned, it is clear that uncertainty is a pervasive factor. Producers in early production runs will not know what inputs are most suitable and how best to combine them: they must learn, and tend to go through a series of short-run 'experiments' to find out. Furthermore, they will know rather little about the dimensions of the market. For these and related reasons, there is a need for swift and effective communication between the anxious producer and his customers, suppliers—and perhaps even competitors. All this tends to lead the producers of new goods to locate production at or close to home in an environment with which they are familiar.

At the second, maturing, stage of product life, mass production methods begin to be introduced. The product can be standardized increasingly as producers learn about what the market requires (or will tolerate), and so longer runs and less frequent experimentation occurs in order to reap economies of scale. Also at this stage, the number of firms in the industry grow as the innovators' monopoly (initially protected by a now-expired patent, perhaps) is eroded. Producers therefore start to become more price-competitive and thus cost-conscious. These factors combine with the growing demand potential outside the innovating country to encourage the establishment of local production units elsewhere. While Vernon surmised that the first foreign facilities would be installed in other advanced industrial nations, it is not implausible to imagine that, even at this second stage, some products might nowadays be produced in the more industrialized developing countries. In countries where local demand could be considerable, costs (especially wages) are low and transport costs are not excessive, this would certainly make good sense—particularly if each individual producer feared that a competitor might get there before him.

All the same, as we observed at the outset, entrepreneurs in advanced industrial nations often tend to know little about production conditions in LDCs; they often fear the worst, and in any case recognize the expense involved in obtaining the information they require to give them confidence to invest. Information is not, after all, a free good, instantly available to all, as is assumed in the H−O−S model. In general, therefore, we might expect goods that began life in advanced nations to start being produced in LDCs only when, as is characteristic of the mature third stage, techniques are stable and routinized; relatively cheap unskilled and semi-skilled labour can be used; access from the LDC to international markets is easily achieved; and production can be continued even in the absence of an elaborate industrial environment.

The implications of this analysis run in a number of directions. From the point of view of developing nations, it means that, so long as more advanced nations continue to innovate and develop new products (exploiting their comparative advantage at stage 1), many LDCs can hope eventually to find themselves exploiting their own comparative advantage in manufacturing the same product both for domestic and foreign consumption. (Particularly remote, landlocked and educationally underdeveloped nations may, however, find themselves largely excluded.) This in turn stimulates their growth, broadens their industrial base and permits them to enjoy a greater volume and wider variety of consumer imports.

From the point of view of trade flows, we might expect the following sequence of events for any one of the products we have discussed. When the product is new, the technological gap between advanced nations and LDCs will lead trade to flow from the former to the latter once demand for the product is established in developing countries. As demand and production conditions make it worthwhile to set up local facilities in LDCs, the flow of trade from advanced to developing nations in the products should slow. Eventually, the originating country might find itself consuming more of the product that is produced locally—importing the residue from LDCs with their comparative advantage in standardized production. Such a sequence is known as the *product cycle*. Many such cycles are likely to be under way, and at varying stages in their progress, at any one time.

EVIDENCE ON TRADE THEORY

Perhaps not surprisingly, the results of empirical tests on trade theory are somewhat ambiguous. A consensus appears to be emerging, however, to the effect that, for definable sets of commodities and country types, particular theories seem to be particularly relevant. No single theory has proved equally successful for each set of conditions.

One recent and illuminating piece of work that shows this up rather well (Batchelor *et al.*, 1980, esp. pp. 186–91) notes first the following contrast. According to H−O−S, the relative factor endowments in a DC as compared with an LDC will result in trade between the two, leading the former to specialize in exporting capital-intensive goods. According to product cycle theory, the DC will tend to specialize in exporting goods that are most easily influenced by technical progress and are skill-intensive in their development and production. With this in mind, it becomes possible to test the two theories against each other by observing changes during development in the ratio to total exports of: (1) capital-intensive goods not requiring skilled labour, and (2) skill-intensive goods with relative capital intensity. If the H−O−S theory is correct, group 1-type goods should grow faster than group 2-type; if the product cycle theory is correct, the share of group 2-type goods should grow more rapidly than that of group 1-type goods.

Batchelor *et al.* (1980) characterize group 1 goods by 'basic metals' and group 2 by 'machinery'. Their first finding is that the share of basic metals rises, slightly, when manufacturing grows to 10 per cent of GDP (which may be taken as an index of increasing industrialization, or of development), but falls at an increasing rate thereafter. The share of machinery, on the other hand, falls until manufacturing comprises 12 per cent of GDP but rises from then on. In general, therefore, there is a transition from trends predicted by H−O−S theory to those that should be associated with product cycle theory. In the same study, the particular experience of countries at the earliest and intermediate levels of development are also separated out. For the first group, the shares of both basic metals and machinery fall as industrialization proceeds, but the latter falls lower than the former. For the second group the share of basic metals goes on falling, but the machinery share rises rapidly. Batchelor *et al.* conclude (1980, p. 191) that their findings 'are not inconsistent with our speculation that during industrialization a transition occurs from a trading pattern based mainly on relative-factor endowments along the lives suggested by the Heckscher−Ohlin theory towards a pattern based mainly on technological leads and lags along the lines suggested by the product cycle theory'.

PATTERNS OF TRADE

Having looked summarily at some of the evidence relating to various theories of trade, let us now examine briefly and broadly the patterns of world trade in recent decades. Data here are useful not only for giving a 'feel' for what goes on, but also for preparing the way for understanding some of the criticisms that have been levelled against trade in the context of development. (This forms the subject matter of the next section.)

As table 7.1 makes clear, low-income countries (the 38 nations with income per capita of less than $360 per year in 1978) have only a very small share in world trade—less than 2.5 per cent in all. The even larger group of 52 middle-income countries, while enjoying a higher per capita income range of $361−$3500 per year, still accounted in 1978 for only about a sixth of world trade. On the other hand, the group of 18 industrialized countries (per capita incomes of more than

TABLE 7.1　Shares of different types of economy in world trade, 1978

	No. in group	Merchandise[a] exports ($m)	% of world exports	Merchandise[a] imports ($m)	% of world imports
Low-income countries	38	28,749	2.27	32,073	2.44
Middle-income countries	52	179,935	14.18	231,663	17.65
Industrialized countries	18	837,956	65.97	862,455	65.71
Capital surplus oil exporters	5	94,107	7.42	49,866	3.79
Centrally planned economies	12	128,821	10.15	136,420	10.39
Total		1,269.208	100	1,312.477	100

[a] ‘Merchandise’: fuels, minerals, metals, other primary commodities, textiles, clothing, machinery, transport equipment, other manufactures

Source: World Bank *World Development Report* (1980, table 8)

$3500 per year but excluding oil exporters in this range, and centrally planned economies) engaged in almost two-thirds of the international merchandise trade transacted in 1978.

If imports and exports are broken down into their components (tables 7.2 and 7.3), we see that well over four-fifths of all low-income country exports, in value terms, are accounted for by primary commodities, and that, while this was true for middle-income countries too in 1960, the proportion had dropped to a little over three-fifths by the late 1970s. In fact, a more disaggregated analysis for middle-income countries reveals that, in that period, exports of textiles and clothing rose from 4 per cent of the total to 10 per cent, machinery and transport equipment from 2 to 9 per cent, and other manufactures from 8 to 18 per cent.

The share in overall exports occupied by primary commodities in industrialized countries is much more modest (and declining), although we should not forget that in absolute terms these countries have a much higher aggregate value of exports than other groups, so we are not talking about small magnitudes. It is in the area of manufactures (and particularly machinery and transport equipment) that industrialized countries have their greatest share of exports.

TABLE 7.2 Structure of merchandise exports

| | Share of merchandise exports accounted for by: | | | |
| | Primary commodities | | Non-primary merchandise | |
	1960	*1977*	*1960*	*1977*
	%	%	%	%
Low-income countries	83	81	17	19
Middle-income countries	86	63	14	37
Industrialized countries	34	24	66	76
Capital surplus oil-exporters	99	99	1	1

Source: World Bank *World Development Report* (1980, table 9)

TABLE 7.3 Structure of merchandise imports

| | Share of merchandise imports accounted for by: | | | |
| | Manufactures | | Non-manufactures | |
	1960	*1977*	*1960*	*1977*
	%	%	%	%
Low-income countries	55	56	45	44
Middle-income countries	62	63	38	37
Industrialized countries	43	55	57	45
Capital surplus oil-exporters	n.a.	84	n.a.	16

Source: World Bank *World Development Report* (1980, table 10)

On the other side of the ledger, for all groups of countries manufactures account for at least half the overall value of their imports, with capital-surplus oil exporters easily topping the list but middle-income countries well ahead of the others at 63 per cent.

Turning now to the direction of trade flows (table 7.4), notice that the industrialized countries take about two-thirds of the exports of all groups of countries, industrialized or not. The developing countries, conversely, take between 20 and 30 per cent of the exports of their own and other groupings.

In terms of shares and proportions, the developing countries thus seem to play a relatively subsidiary role in world trade and therefore might not be expected to enjoy gains from trade to the extent sometimes

TABLE 7.4 Direction of world trade, 1978

	Export destination:		
	Industrialized countries	Developing countries	Centrally planned economies
	(% of exporters' exports accounted for)		
Exports from:			
Low-income countries	66	23	5
Middle-income countries	67	25	5
Industrialized countries	67	23	4
Capital surplus oil-exporters	70	29	(.)

Source: World Bank *World Development Report* (1980, table 11)

predicted. But shares are not all. The volume and value of overall world trade have both risen with persistent rapidity since the Second World War. And even with only a relatively modest share of this activity available to them, developing countries have, in absolute terms, seen the value and volume of both imports and exports grow impressively.

Given the importance over time of growth rates, both for understanding domestic economy growth stimuli and for suggesting how shares in trade may change, the following points merit notice. From the point of view of the composition of trade, both imports and exports of manufactures have experienced extremely rapid growth rates during the last few decades. Batchelor *et al.* (1980) divide the world into industrial, semi-industrial and non-industrial countries. (Their footnotes on pp. 5–6 list the countries in each group.) They report that between 1950 and 1959 the annual volume growth rates of manufactured imports for these groupings were, respectively, about $9\frac{1}{2}$, 2 and 4 per cent. Between 1959 and 1971, however, these rates leaped to, respectively, about 13, 9 and 9 per cent—a particularly marked acceleration occurring in the semi-industrial grouping (which, it ought to be noted, includes Australia, New Zealand and South Africa). As for exports, the volume growth rate of manufactures here rose from $6\frac{1}{2}$ to $10\frac{1}{2}$ per cent per year between the two periods for the 11 major industrial nations. More recently, there has been growing evidence of spectacular growth rates in the export of manufactures from other countries, especially Hong Kong, South Korea and Taiwan.

Demand for primary products strengthened in the 1960s (partly reflecting Japan's ore needs as its steel industry became established), and so long as industrial production expanded in the DCs—which continued into the early 1970s—this demand was maintained. On the other hand, the fortunes of particular primary products have varied widely. Some exporters have had to cope with the displacement of natural products by synthetics. Malaysia's experience with rubber and Bangladesh's with jute are good examples. Others have faced substantial trade barriers, for example countries producing foodstuffs for the European Community.

We leave until the next few sections details on changing terms of trade which embody trends relating to changing relative values.

THE CASE AGAINST TRADE

Despite the array of arguments that can be marshalled in support of trade, there are commentators who have suggested that, far from being beneficial, trade has acted to the detriment of LDCs. In particular it has been argued that:

(1) LDCs face a much lower income elasticity of demand for their (mainly primary product) exports than that which operates for their (mainly manufactured) imports;
(2) LDCs must cope with substantial fluctuations in demand for their exports;
(3) LDCs' factor and product markets vary importantly in their nature and structure from those operating in their DC trading partner's economies.

These factors, it is said, work together, in some cases with other influences, to induce chronic balance of payments problems constraining development, a long-run deterioration in the terms of trade, and harmful 'dependence' on internationally dominant nations.

A first line of argument suggests that, if LDCs follow the precepts of classical trade theory and specialize in producing where they have comparative advantage, this will lead them towards concentrating on the production and export of primary products for use as material inputs into the manufactures of DCs. It is noted that the income elasticity of demand for primary goods is often quite low. It is also pointed out that, as they grow, not only do LDCs come to *want* finished manufactures in larger quantities, but they also *need* manufactured goods as capital and other inputs into their own productive processes. Thus, it is said, the income elasticity of demand in LDCs for imports will be much higher than the income elasticity of demand for their

exports, and thus they will quickly run into balance of payments difficulties; they will not be able to export rapidly enough to meet the
demand for imports that their export-led growth in income has
generated. This is supposed to leave LDCs with only two alternatives:
either they must grow more slowly than DCs, or they may impose tariffs
to restrict imports.

Second, it is sometimes argued that trade must bring with it, for
LDCs, a deterioration in their terms of trade. To see why this might be,
recall that the terms of trade can be represented by the ratio (P_X/P_M)
for any given country. If the price of exports falls relative to the price
of imports (which be the case even if both sets of prices are rising—but
with export prices rising less quickly than import prices), then there
will be a fall in this ratio and the terms of trade are said to have
deteriorated. In economic terms this means that the import-buying
power of a unit of exports has fallen. Now, why might trade cause
such a deterioration? It is observed that technical progress occurs both
in LDCs, producing mainly primary products, and in DCs, producing
mainly manufactures. These advances generate high levels of productivity (output per unit of input) in each type of country, but, it is said,
it is the DCs which reap most of the rewards. Why?

One reason might be the differing behaviour of wages as between
LDCs and DCs. Growth takes place in the long run to the accompani-
ment of shorter-run cyclical fluctuations. It is argued that, in the
upswing of cycles, excess demand for manufactures arises in the DCs,
and the price of manufactures (LDC imports) rises, particularly if DC
manufacturers are monopolists. On the one hand, this increases the
profitability of manufacturing in DCs, but on the other hand, trade
unions join with the pressure of market demand for labour to drive
wages up. In LDCs, the upswing also brings a rise in the profitability
of production owing to a rise in prices for primary products derived
from the excess demand for manufactures. Indeed, says Raul Prebisch,
the originator of this argument, 'prices of primary products tend to
rise more sharply than those of finished goods' (Economic Commission
for Latin America, 1950).

But it is in the downswing of the cycle that the argument bites. In the
downswing, trade union pressure once again is brought to bear in DCs,
this time to maintain wages in face of falling demand and falling prices.
Manufacturers' profits can be squeezed to some extent to accommodate
labour—but the major sufferers are LDC suppliers of raw materials.
Here three factors combine to drive primary product prices down by
more than the extent to which they had, in the upswing, risen above
finished product prices. First, productivity gains provide scope for the

price fall to occur; second, labour is not sufficiently organized, as in DCs, to protect any wage gains from being eroded; and, third, labour is in any case in such relative abundance that wages can easily be held down. Productivity gains in LDCs thus reflect in lower prices for the material inputs of DCs—thus providing manufacturers with leeway (derived from the efforts of LDCs) to pay the wages demanded by their organized labour. Over a long period many cycles will occur, and, it is argued, their cumulative effect will be to bring about a long-term fall in LDC export prices relative to their import prices.

It is also worth pointing out a connection with the balance of payments argument. There, the low income elasticity of demand for LDC exports was said to be to blame, and here too it has been argued that, since demand for LDCs exports is income-elastic, demand will expand only slowly relative to supply (relative to the rate at which demand expands relative to the supply of LDC imports) and this will mean again that export prices will rise more slowly than import prices.

In general, it is probably true to say that LDCs have been over-impressed by the strength of the terms of trade argument. Certainly (and this will be taken up again shortly) they have tended to respond actively to the main policy conclusion of the argument—that LDCs should embark upon a protectionist strategy aimed at reducing world demand for, and thus the prices of, imports of DC manufactures.

Two points of criticism will be made here. (For an extended and searching critique, see Flanders, 1964.) First, there is no conclusive empirical evidence to suggest that any particular LDC, or LDCs as a whole, must as a matter of necessity suffer a decline in their terms of trade. The terms of trade moved in favour of manufactures compared with primary products between the two world wars and thereafter until about 1970. It was during this period that critics of trade started to become vocal. The movement in favour of manufactures slowed in the 1960s and was sharply reversed between 1970 and 1974, and the terms established then remained more or less unchanged into the later 1970s (Batchelor *et al.*, 1980, p. 22). This enabled the value of market (that is, of non-centrally planned) economies' exports of primary products to rise about 250 per cent between 1971 and 1976 compared with about 160 per cent for manufactures. The danger of using aggregate terms of trade movements to argue either for or against the influence of trade on individual countries is immediately clear once these statistics are broken down even only slightly. On the one hand, this 250 per cent rise in primary exports' value represents a rise of over 400 per cent in fuels but only somewhat more than 100 per cent for food and raw materials (Batchelor *et al.*, 1980, p. 23). Developing countries naturally endowed with accessible and known fuel resources have therefore been favoured by the terms of trade shifting against manufactures.[5] Developing countries relying heavily upon food or raw material exports have simultaneously suffered. At times when the terms of trade between primary and manufactured goods in general appear to favour the latter, we might equally expect to find some countries specializing in particular areas of primary production that enable them to escape the general trend. On the other hand, the generalization that pictures a group of primary producers (LDCs) on one side of a clearly defined line and a group of manufacturing countries (DCs) on the other also obscures important realities. Some industrial countries (for example the USA and Canada) are large-scale producers and exporters of food, fuel and raw materials. Some developing countries, as we noted earlier, have very rapidly growing and exporting manufacturing sectors but also export primary commodities. These observations together mean that the effects of shifting terms of trade between primary goods and manufactures on individual countries is much less predictable than the general argument suggests.

Second, even if a deterioration does occur in an individual country, this by no means implies that it must suffer an associated welfare loss. Notice in particular that consumer preferences in LDCs may have changed in favour of imports—as a result of a change in tastes, a redistribution of income or technological progress which leads to importing goods of greater quality even if at higher prices. Changes such as these may mean that imports become much more effective in generating utility in LDCs—not only absolutely, but also relative to the utility sacrificed by not consuming goods or resources devoted to export. In fact, to be sure that a deterioration in the terms of trade, as we have defined them, *is* actually anti-developmental, it is precisely effects such as these that must be considered. (For an extended discussion of this see Meier, 1980, pp. 68–72, or Meier, 1968, chapter 3.)

We turn now to a third argument. In relation to the dynamic benefits of trade, we pointed out that trade could be seen as inducing changes that comprised not merely reversible resource allocations but perhaps irreversible changes in the structure of an economy. Irreversible specialization of this kind can be interpreted as making an economy more vulnerable than it was before. A related argument, which we shall take up here, suggests that, if countries specialize (either reversibly or irreversibly), they may anyway encounter difficulties introduced by greater uncertainty because of instability and unpredictability in export earnings.

Examining trade in non-fuel primary commodities, the World Bank assesses fluctuations in export revenues and commodity prices as one of the main problems faced by developing countries depending to any substantial extent upon selling such goods internationally. 'Large fluctuations in export revenues cannot be adequately handled by individual countries holding foreign exchange reserves and are liable to upset investment and economic growth', it asserts (World Bank, 1978, p. 19). The potential magnitude of the problem can be understood by referring initially to table 7.2, where we are reminded that developing countries as a group rely heavily on primary commodities for export revenue. Another perspective springs from realizing that developing countries supply about a third of the world exports of non-fuel primary commodities.

As far as price instability is concerned, it may induce wasteful over-investment by producers (when prices are up), or underinvestment because of uncertainty. It could also induce the development of substitute products whose price variability is less—thus reducing long-term demand for the primary good. An estimate of the degree of price instability among primary products is given in table 7.5.

Empirical work on the influence of export instability on growth has generated conflicting results. Coppock (1962), MacBean (1966) and Kenen and Voivodas (1972) were able to discover either little variation in export instability as between LDCs and DCs, or little explanatory power in product concentration and export growth trends on output growth. Glezakos (1973), however, concluded that export instability explained perhaps a quarter of the observed variations in LDCs' growth rates in the 1950s and 1960s. In similar vein, Batchelor *et al.* (1980, p. 222) find that export instability significantly depresses sources of growth in the least developed countries they investigate, and has a statistically significant negative influence on the overall rate of growth-generating investment in small developing countries.

But even if we take a rather pessimistic view about the destabilizing effects of specialization in primary goods production, this hardly constitutes an argument against trade. The obvious answer is to try to iron out the fluctuations. Stabilization schemes that attempt to do this include the Compensatory Financing Facility of the International Monetary Fund, and the Stabex programme under the Lomé Convention. (For more on price stabilization, see p. 227.)

A fourth argument against trade suggests that the techniques that tend to be used, particularly in primary export but also in manufacturing production, are in various senses anti-developmental. Since

TABLE 7.5 Primary commodities classified by degree of price instability

Index of instability[a,b]							
0–5		5–10		10–15		Over 15	
Tea	1.3	Coffee	6.5	Sugar	13.9	Copper	5.0
Bananas	1.2	Cotton	4.0	Rubber	3.5	Cocoa	2.6
		Iron Ore	3.6	Phosphate Rock	2.6	Zinc	0.7
		Maize	2.3	Rice	1.6	Fishmeal	0.5
		Logs	2.2	Palm Oil	1.4	Copra	0.4
		Tobacco	1.9	Beef	0.7	Sisal	0.2
		Tin	1.7	Wool	0.6		
		Oranges	1.4	Coconut Oil	0.5		
		Soybean Meal	0.8	Groundnut Oil	0.4		
		Bauxite	0.7	Lead	0.4		
		Manganese Ore	0.6	Lemons	0.2		
		Wheat	0.6				
		Grain Sorghum	0.5				
		Groundnuts	0.5				
		Jute	0.2				
Total	2.5		27.5		25.8		9.4

[a] The index is based on a five-year moving average of prices for 1955–76. It measures the average percentage deviation of the annual price from the five-year moving average. It does not take account of short-term fluctuations in prices.

[b] The figure shown against each commodity indicates its percentage share in total developing country exports of all primary commodities, excluding fuel, in 1975.

Source: World Bank *World Development Report* (1978, p. 20)

multinational corporations (MNCs) are often the agents responsible for introducing such activity, they tend to be identified for these and other reasons as anti-developmental in nature.

One strand of this argument explicitly assumes that the modern sector of a dualistic economy is launched on the back of foreign-financed export industry, extracting minerals or engaging in large-scale commercial agriculture. Such industry, it is assumed, employs processes not only capital-intensive in relation to traditional methods, but also relatively fixed in their technical coefficients (that is, in the precise value of their capital–labour ratios). It is also implicitly assumed that the modern sector is essentially an enclave and neither has nor induces strong linkages with the traditional sector. Under these conditions a so-called 'factor proportions problem' may arise. The problem arises in the first instance because any given capital stock can be combined in production with only one amount of labour. This is the economic meaning of the fixed coefficient assumption. If the stock of labour grows more quickly than investment proceeds, the modern sector will offer insufficient employment opportunities to an expanding workforce. Labour must therefore look for employment in the traditional sector where production techniques are assumed more flexible. But even this flexibility does not guarantee employment, since land will eventually prove a constraint and disguised unemployment will occur, reinforcing the poverty and backwardness of the sector.

In this story, trade is blamed not so much for introducing capital-intensive techniques as for leading to the employment of techniques in modern sector production that offer little prospect of substituting labour for capital, even if the real wage were to fall. Employment objectives and the prospects for on-the-job training are thus said to suffer. The problems involved become yet worse in this view if imported capital becomes increasingly labour-saving over time as a reflection of the biases of technical advance in the originating countries.

It should be said, however, that the picture envisaged here is probably too dismal. First, capital–labour ratios may not actually be fixed in the blueprint for the process; rather, lack of substitutability may reflect an unwillingness by entrepreneurs actually to allow more labour to cooperate with given capital. In a summary of the evidence on this issue, Lall (1978) concludes that 'core' processes in an industry typically run by MNCs might be made to absorb more labour by, for example, machine adaptations, increased numbers of shifts and subcontracting. (Note, though, that apparent 'under-utilization' of plant may turn out sometimes to be motivated by the rational pursuit of efficiency: see Winston, 1974.) Further, 'peripheral' processes like handling, storage and transport may also offer scope for substitution. On the whole, however, he believes that efficient technologies may indeed be fairly 'rigid' in a plausible range of economic conditions in LDCs. This tends to be reflected, he suggests, in the rather limited extent to which MNCs do actually undertake such adaptations. But, he adds, there is no strong evidence to suggest that MNCs are worse culprits in this respect than any other type of commercial organization.

A second objection relates to linkages. As envisaged by Hirschman (1958), one of the most important dynamic roles of the original export sector of industry could be to create externalities in the form of new opportunities for investment, and thus prove a fly-wheel for growth. These opportunities comprised profitable activity associated with the original industry—either supplying it (a backward linkage), or using its products as inputs (a forward linkage). As we said, the story we told implied that few such linkages would operate. While evidence on this point is fragmentary, the truth, as expected, seems to be that it depends on the industry. A considerable subcontracting network has been drawn into existence by export-oriented electronics in south-east Asia, for example (UNCTAD, 1975); but while Lall assesses that textiles shares with food processing and footwear a vast potential for backward linkages (in components) as well, the example of Hong Kong (cited in Evers *et al.*, 1977) is not altogether encouraging. Industry based on mineral extraction or plantation agriculture might by its nature be expected to offer less by way of potential linkages.

Another strand of the general argument suggests that, since techniques used in the modern sector are relatively capital-intensive, the bulk of any benefits accruing from industry there will go to the entrepreneur. If the entrepreneur is a foreigner or an MNC, profits generated locally may, further, finish up being repatriated. (Worse still, according to the proponents of this argument, many MNCs actually raise much of their capital from local institutions, and so repatriated profits may turn out to be exports of scarce local resources: see Müller in Wilber, 1979.)

Putting these comments on a broader footing, this argument again appears to turn on the particular industry involved and the techniques it employs. Its force also depends upon other ramifications. A more labour-intensive technique might threaten income distributional or employment and training objectives less than a capital-intensive process —but on the other hand, wage labour might have a lower propensity to save than capitalist entrepreneurs. Having a capital-intensive technique might in the end be the best way to promote a higher investment rate and faster long-term growth, therefore (see chapter 5). Of course, an LDC may fear the worst of both worlds, if it sees the potential for large-scale repatriation of profit from capital-intensive projects. In that case it can consider fiscal or legal action to discourage such moves—or, more positively, may try to encourage the reinvestment of profits locally.

Whether arguments relating to capital intensity, lack of factor substitutability and the general behaviour of MNCs really do contribute strongly to a case against trade is very much an open question. In some industries, for example mineral extraction, the production processes would indeed seem to offer rather limited opportunities (assuming the desirability of efficient performance) for labour–capital substitution and linkages to other parts of the economy. But this is hardly an argument against export-oriented industry of this kind, even if managed by an MNC. It is, rather, an argument for finding other ways of: (1) generating some of the benefits of a labour-intensive process (such as providing education and training at public expense rather than relying on on-the-job training and experience); and (2) ensuring that the institutions and attitudes in the economy encourage linkages to a maximum (for example by liberalizing capital markets, and improving physical communications so that the export sector becomes less of an enclave). (See Meier, 1968, especially chapter 8, for more on this.)

All the elements that we have presented as comprising the case against trade are combined in the influential work of Myrdal and, more recently, appear in what is called 'dependency theory'. Myrdal (1956) views international trade as the mechanism of international inequality. In his eyes, trade strengthens the industrial countries while the poorer countries find themselves ruined. He emphasizes the fact and the effects of the income inelasticity faced by primary goods exported by LDCs, and argues that the market will usually operate only to increase relative international inequality. The vicious circle of interconnected events that he identifies is often called the 'doctrine of cumulative causation'.

Dependency theory is avowedly Marxian in its perspective. One of its main exponents—Dos Santos (1970)—defines dependence as a situation in which one economy is conditioned by the development and expansion of another. Interdependence, the keynote of trade, becomes dependence when a dominant country experiences self-sustaining growth while the dependent country (or countries) can enjoy similar expansion only as a reflection of changes in the first economy. While this connection can, he says, have either positive or negative developmental effects, his work tends to stress the latter.

Historically, dependence is seen to have had three main forms. 'Colonial dependence' linked capital and state in establishing trading monopolies in the colonies; 'financial—industrial dependence' saw the dominance of capitalistic business in metropolitan centres extend to investment abroad to ensure their supply of raw materials. In both of these instances, production was determined by demand from already industrialized or industrializing centres. Since the Second World War, says Dos Santos, dependence has adopted a new guise, in which MNCs have started to invest in LDCs with a view to supplying internal markets.

The nature of such modern-style dependence is seen to be as follows. (1) Domestic industrial development in an LDC requires the traditional export sector, established under earlier forms of dependence, to be maintained to earn foreign exchange. But this means preserving a sector that, Dos Santos says, is characterized by rigid specialization in production, large-scale monoculture and the maintenance of political power by traditional elites—none of which is developmentally desirable. (2) Balance of payments problems are seen to be necessarily associated with industrialization promoted under these conditions because deteriorating terms of trade undermine the buying power of traditional exports, and foreign investors repatriate much of the profit made in LDCs, thus undermining the capital account. As a result, LDCs are forced to rely on the industrialized nations to provide finance to cover deficits and to supply aid. 'Foreign capital and foreign "aid" thus fill up the holes that they themselves created' (Dos Santos, 1970, p. 233). (3) The industrialized nations exercise a 'technological monopoly' because they develop and patent new machine designs, and this enables them to demand royalties before LDC companies use such equipment, even if it is already out of date.

The counter-developmental consequences of all this include a rein-forcement of economic structures directed towards extracting surplus from backward sectors, the adoption of techniques inimical to develop-mental needs, and the occurrence of increasing income inequality. In turn, these consequences limit the size and growth of the local market, says Dos Santos, because of the relatively limited employment offered by capital-intensive techniques, the extent to which domestically generated surplus is repatriated as profit, and the maintenance of traditional socioeconomic structures in the countryside.

Since we have considered these issues one by one elsewhere, we shall not pursue them again here. Decide for yourself where the weak links in the argument might arise.

PROTECTION AND INDUSTRIALIZATION

Whatever the doubts we have raised about the case against trade, it has been extremely influential in guiding LDCs in their choice of development strategies.

First, it should be noted that the burden of the anti-trade argument seems to rest on the operation of factors beyond LDCs' control. There is little or nothing that an LDC can do about the relatively low income elasticity of demand for its exports, assuming that the particular export(s) that it is best placed to trade actually have that characteristic. (Not all do.) Export instability is hard to control without large-scale international action, and appeared even more of a threat in the 1950s and 1960s than it might now. Production processes are determined largely where there are the resources to permit research and development, traditionally well away from LDCs. Furthermore, protectionist policies in the DCs against some LDC exports have certainly operated to restrict their access to large and growing markets, thus limiting the benefits LDCs might enjoy from trade. We have argued that LDCs can do much to offset these effects (which, empirically, have often proved less grave than they initially appeared) by participating in export stabilization schemes, sensitizing their own economies more to the benefits offered by trade, and using fiscal means to discourage the worst potentially anti-developmental activities of large companies. Even so, despite opportunities of this sort, LDCs have often tended to adopt an essentially defensive posture in face of what they perceive as almost exclusively external forces operating against them. They have been inclined to opt for wide-ranging protective measures (such as tariffs and import quotas), with the intention of trying to develop behind a protective barrier rather than interdependently with other growing nations around the world.

As a second point, it must be added that this inward-looking approach not only took up the lessons preached by Prebisch, Myrdal and others, but also became particularly popular at a time when the empirical data on trade seemed to support such arguments quite well. The terms of trade between manufactures and primary commodities were, in general, quite clearly shifting in favour of the former, for example; and fewer developing countries than now were in any position to see the prospect of benefiting from that.

While we have raised doubts about the case against trade, therefore, it is not impossible to understand how its appeal was established. In the remainder of this chapter we discuss the general question of protection; and notice that any doubts about protection in turn partly indict any strategy based upon protected import substitution industry. This leads us back, finally, to considering a strategy based more upon export-led growth.

PROTECTION

While a rich and varied range of justifications has been offered over the years in support of protective devices (for simplicity we shall concentrate on tariffs), hardly any stand up to close scrutiny. The one or two that deserve serious attention can, moreover, be justified only under more stringent conditions than are usually applied. And in almost all cases, alternative measures can be suggested whose potential welfare costs are less but whose effects are similar. The widespread use of protective devices cannot then be based on purely economic reasoning. Tariffs and other measures have generally proved popular, in fact, because decision-makers see, or believe they see, political gain to be made out of implementing them, or political danger in not doing so. The point is that tariffs do usually benefit one or more groups (say an industry, or organized labour) in particular ways. And if such groups are influential with decision-makers, they may threaten and cajole to see protective measures installed or maintained. Decision-makers may concede, then, even if they understand that the community at large will suffer. Too often, decision-makers fail even to understand that protection does impose costs, sooner or later, and thus they are even more susceptible to persuasion.

In this section we start with a demonstration of the welfare costs of a tariff. We then look at some of the more pertinent arguments that have been adduced in favour of tariffs, looking for links with our earlier discussion on trade as we go.

Tariff Analysis
The cost of a tariff can be demonstrated, as here, in a partial equilibrium (single-commodity) framework. To give reassurance, it can also, with greater difficulty, be shown in a general equilibrium analysis (see Kindleberger, 1968, for example), but that will be omitted here.

Look first at figure 7.4. This is a perfectly straightforward aggregate supply-and-demand diagram for a single good, adapted to take account of foreign trade considerations. It is assumed that there is an infinite price elasticity of import supply at the price, OP, at which the country can buy the good in the international market from the world's lowest-cost supplier. This reflects assumed constant costs in the exporter's industry. The domestic supply curve is shown by SS and domestic demand schedule by DD. At price OP, the pre-tariff price of the good, the quantity of it demanded domestically is OQ'''. Domestic producers are happy to supply an amount OQ at that price; the balance, QQ''', must be imported.

If a tariff of PP'' were imposed on all imports, the good would not be available to domestic consumers from international sources for less than OP'' per unit. At that price, domestic producers would be happy to supply exactly the reduced amount that, also at that price, domestic consumers would now demand. This tariff would be 'prohibitive' since, at price OP'', there would be no room left for imports. Consequently, of course, there would be no tariff revenue either.

Suppose now that a non-prohibitive tariff, equivalent to PP', were imposed. The quantity demanded domestically would fall to OQ'',

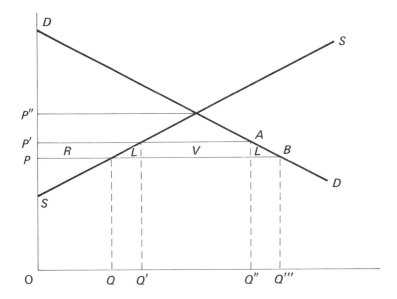

Figure 7.4 The effects of a tariff

the quantity supplied locally would rise to OQ', and the quantity of imports would shrink to $Q'Q''$. Consider the area $PP'AB$. This is a part of the consumers' surplus which lay beneath the demand curve when the price was OP. This surplus—a measure of consumers' welfare—has been reduced by the amount $PP'AB$ as a result of the tariff, but only a part of this is a total loss to the economy, and some but not all of it could in principle be given back to consumers. The area V, to start with, is the revenue collected as a result of imposing the tariff, assuming away administrative (collection) costs. It is the product of post-tariff import quantity, $Q'Q''$, and the tariff per unit of imports, PP'. This revenue could be distributed to consumers as a cash subsidy. If producers are paid more than they require to induce them to supply a given unit of output, then it is said that they receive economic rent. At the pre-tariff price, the triangular area above SS but beneath PB could be interpreted as representing producers' rents at that price. These rents increase, to the extent shown by area R, when the tariff is imposed and OP' becomes the relevant domestic price. But, in principle, rents could be taxed away by the government and again redistributed to consumers.

That leaves the areas labelled L. No one else in the economy, or elsewhere, gains from these parts of lost consumer surplus, so there is no way of 're-couping' and compensating consumers here. These triangles thus represent the so-called dead-weight loss of the tariff, the unavoidable cost that any tariff must bring with it. Such a dead-weight loss is associated with tariff protection, however attempts to justify it are made, and we must always bear that in mind, no matter how appealing the justifications might seem.[6] Let us start by considering the terms of trade argument for a tariff since the terms of trade have been at the heart of much of our recent discussion and the argument involves only a slight extension and modification of figure 7.4.

In figure 7.5 we show the aggregate supply and demand curves for a single commodity in both the importing and the exporting country.

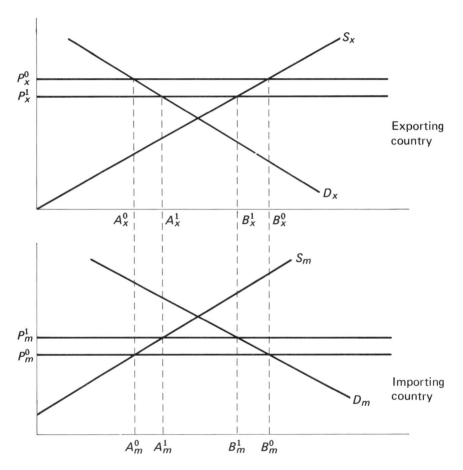

Figure 7.5 Protection and the forms of trade

(The 'importing' country could also be interpreted as either a single LDC or a group of them, the 'exporting' country as a single DC or a group of them; equally, these labels could be reversed.) We assume that trade in the commodity takes place only between the two countries shown. Before the tariff is imposed, world equilibrium is achieved at price $P_m^0 = P_x^0$. At this price, an amount $A_x^0 B_x^0$ is in excess supply in the exporting country but is exactly equal to the amount of excess demand at this price in the importing country, $A_m^0 B_m^0$. When the countries trade, excess supply and demand cancel out: exports equal imports.

Suppose now that the importing country wants to improve its terms of trade. It can achieve this if it can force down the price of the exporter's good. With this in view, assume that the importing country imposes a tariff of $P_m^0 P_m^1$. This will reduce its demand for imports to $A_m^1 B_m^1$. But the only way in which excess supply in the exporting country can be reduced to this level (equal, of course, to $A_x^1 B_x^1$) is for the price of the good to fall to P_x^1. At this price, domestic demand in the exporting country rises and the quantity supplied falls.

Notice, however, that if the supply curve of the exporter were horizontal (as we assumed in the earlier analysis), then imposing a tariff will not achieve any change in the terms of trade; it will merely reduce the volume of trade. For a small, importing LDC facing a large, exporting DC, this may well reflect the realities of the situation.

More generally, note also that improvements in the terms of trade, if available as shown in figure 7.5, can in any case be achieved only at the cost of reducing the volume of imports. A positive price effect must be weighed against a negative quantity effect. In the more advanced literature on the so-called 'optimum tariff', the exact nature of this trade-off is examined more closely but requires a lengthier and more sophisticated analysis than space permits here. (See, for example, Corden, 1974, especially chapter 7.)

Finally, remember that any country in the world can impose tariffs. Action by one country to improve the terms of trade, if successful, invites retaliation, and opens up the possibility of a tariff war from which neither country wins.

Perhaps the most widely used argument for protection in LDCs relates to so-called *infant industries*. The basis of the argument is that countries often claim to have a *potential* comparative advantage in the production of some good, but assert that their own inexperience and the long-established might of countries already more developed and industrialized than themselves prevent them from being able 'to get the industry off the ground'. Looked at more closely, the real meat of the argument lies in the claim that an industry can start to benefit from its comparative advantage only if it is protected long enough to allow it to grow, employ the services of optimal-scale capital and provide labour with the necessary skills and experience to make it competitive. The argument is an important one, and in developing it here we draw on the work of Corden (1974, chapter 9), perhaps the leading authority on protection theory in recent years.

Corden shows that there are two principal means of constructing the argument. The first suggests that protection compensates for certain market imperfections which reduce or prevent the incidence of economies that are dynamic (that is, resulting in falling costs as the time-span of production increases) and internal to the firm. The second proposes that protection is needed to achieve dynamic economies external to the firm that otherwise would not be reaped.

Taking the first argument first, recall that we have already talked about irreversible economies. It is these that Corden labels as dynamic, and his particular interest is in the falling unit costs that firms see as both management and labour learn from experience over time. Learning, of course, is equivalent to accumulating human capital. Now, if the firm would in any case reap the rewards it expected from the learning period early on in production, there is no case for protection to give it encouragement. This will happen if: (1) the firm can finance its investment at an interest rate correctly reflecting the social discount rate; (2) it has correct expectations about the returns it will obtain from its investment; and (3) there are no uncorrected divergences between social and private costs and benefits in the economy. How might these conditions fail? On (1), the firm might be unable to obtain finance commercially to cover initial losses associated with learning at a rate of interest that reflected the social desirability of undertaking the investment (in other words, the social discount rate in this case would be lower than the commercial or private rate). Reasons for this might include a capital market bias against the 'invisible' capital, learning; another capital market bias against new firms compared with established ones; and a bias against investments of the term-length required to permit learning to occur. On (2), notice that investment in learning may take some years to offer a pay-off. Observing the initially protracted learning period, particularly in economies about which they know relatively little, businessmen might have exaggerated (or over-cautious) views about the problems of production and supply, and prospects for demand. Under these circumstances, a goverment that felt (because of better local knowledge) that investors' anxieties were excessive, but understandable, might offer protection as an 'insurance policy'. On (3), businessmen might find themselves required to pay wages, for example, that they might consider excessive and that also turned out to be above the social opportunity cost of labour.

For each of these reasons, protection might be sought and offered to permit the firm and the economy to reap the desired economies of experience and learning. But as Corden points out, the first-best argument in none of these cases is a tariff. Improving the capital market is the best way to overcome capital market biases and their effects, and if that were too costly or impracticable, direct domestic subsidization is better than protection. If businessmen are poorly informed, then inform them more thoroughly—and perhaps engender confidence through a demonstrated competence in economic planning and management. Finally, if divergences exist, correct them—rather than imposing more on top.

Let us turn now to dynamic external economies. These may take a number of forms. First, a general training provided in one firm will benefit another firm or firms when the employee moves. The employee takes with him the capital asset of training and experience. But firms may be unwilling to give such training at their own cost if they believe staff will leave for jobs elsewhere, once trained. (They might instead use expatriate labour, for example.) Under these circumstances employees will be able to induce firms to train them only if the firm does not incur expense in so doing; that is, if trainees accept low wages during training. In the absence of a loan, this might be either infeasible (if the wage is a sole source of income) or undesirably uncomfortable. The difficulty is that capital markets may well be biased against making such loans, for reasons similar to those noted above. The argument for protection is thus that it will induce the employer to pay trainees a 'living wage' during training, external benefits offering an offset against the welfare cost of the tariff and capital market constraints being taken as given. Once more, however, capital market reform or labour training subsidies are both preferable policy responses.

A second potentially important external economy lies in the benefits of diffused (spread out) knowledge which the economy as a whole might derive from the experiments and advances of a pioneer, infant industry firm. Particularly in LDCs, where the value of modifying existing techniques for local conditions is recognized, protecting the pioneer might seem to have merit. On the other hand, subsidies (on research and development) can again do this job at least as well. The power of international and domestic governments in spreading information should not be underestimated, either.

Having noted the very stringent conditions that must be met even to argue reasonably on behalf of the protected infant industry, we conclude by noting a two-stage test that Corden claims such a policy would have to satisfy. These criteria are: (1) that the protected infant industry offers a sure prospect of 'growing up' and standing, eventually unprotected, on its own feet; and (2) that the appropriately discounted future cost savings achieved by the economies should be at least equal to the discounted value of the social costs incurred during the protected learning period. This is called the Mill–Bastable test (see Corden, 1974, p. 265). Given the large number of ageing 'infant industries' around the world, in countries of all kinds, we must infer that this test very often either has not been applied at all, or must have been applied with sadly inadequate estimates.

Other arguments will now be treated more summarily. The *balance of payments argument* for a tariff is based on the simple perception that, as demand for import falls, so the country's import bill will be reduced and any existing payments deficit correspondingly narrowed. On the other hand, devaluation of the exchange rate is generally considered a more appropriate and less damaging tool for this purpose. Fiscal and/or monetary policy to dampen domestic demand for imports is an alternative strategy. The two sets of policy can also be used together to encourage products to divert resources from domestic into export-oriented lines.

The *employment argument* is based on the fear that competition from abroad will undermine local employment-creating industry. If this really is true, it means that the industry is not internationally competitive, and protecting it will lead to domestic consumers having to pay a higher price for its product than they would have had to pay for the same good if it had imported in the absence of protection. Given that governments in LDCs often are concerned about employment, however, that they could use employment subsidies as one means of pursuing the objective, or indeed might well end up damaging consumer interests less than with a tariff by simply creating government jobs. Sometimes the argument may be cast in the form of claims that industry is superior to agriculture in generating productivity and externalities through learning effects. In this case we have the infant industry argument again, but couched at the level of the whole sector.

The *revenue argument* appeals for a tariff on the grounds that it will generate import duties. The attraction of this argument lies in the facts that: (1) imports usually provide a large base for taxation; and (2) import duties are easy to collect, requiring the employment of relatively few officers at ports of entry. These facts are particularly important in LDCs in which other taxation bases (income, personal or corporate) are small and where poor communications, corruption and low levels of education and literacy make their administration unreliable and unproductive (see chapter 4 and Corden, 1974, chapter 4). While revenue is an important consideration, the above argument makes it clear that governments could do much to reduce the relative attractiveness of tariffs for this purpose by raising the standards of performance and honesty elsewhere. As domestic income grows, this also provides an increasingly important base for taxation.

Finally, it is sometimes said that, because of divergences between private and social costs, modern sector activity is artificially restrained in a way that tariffs would make good. In particular, it said that modern sector wages are high relative to workers' social opportunity costs in many cases: modern sector employers have to pay a wage of value greater than the contribution that a worker would make to production if he were in the traditional sector. Because of the 'high' wage, employers' wage bills are said to be 'excessive', with the result that profit is not as great as it 'should' be, so that investment and growth consequently suffer. Protection is defended on the grounds that it will offset this distortion and permit greater profits to be earned. Underlying this argument is the belief that modern sector wages are always too high in relation to the social value of work done. But they may not be. A high modern sector wage may reflect an individual's capacity to earn quasi-rent on a scarce special talent or training, for example, rather than the activity of a trade union or the operation of minimum wage laws. Even if modern sector wages are overstated, though, this is still not an argument for a tariff. The desirable response is to remove the distortion. (This type of argument can be found in Hagen, 1958.)

We may conclude that, while protection is a widespread real-world practice, the arguments in its favour are actually far from convincing as far as the economist is concerned. We turn now to enquire into the appeal of industrialization, and place the question against the backcloth we have erected relating to international trade.

INDUSTRIALIZATION

Broadly speaking, industry can be defined to mean the application of mechanized means of production to transforming inputs into outputs. At this level of generality, industrialization may clearly be associated with agricultural output, mineral extraction and services such as transport and tourism, as well as to manufacturing. Industrialization is important for development since, by employing much more capital per man-hour or per unit of land than in traditional processes, it offers the potential of raising the productivity of all inputs used in the economy to a substantial degree.

LDCs, however, have often tended to superimpose upon this general view some rather than specific contours. In particular, they have noted that, historically, it was the countries that first experienced the rapid growth of manufacturing that are also present-day world economic leaders. It is not difficult to see, further, that high-income economies are characterized by relatively large manufacturing sectors even now. In 1978 countries with GNP per head of $360 per year or less saw manufacturing account for 13 per cent of GDP, on average; countries with GNP per head in excess of $3500 per year recorded an average of more than twice that (27 per cent); countries in between had the manufacturing contribution to GDP rise from as low as 6 per cent (Liberia, Yemen Arab Republic) to 38 per cent (Taiwan), giving an average for countries in this group of 25 per cent. Finally, there is also evidence to suggest that countries with fastest growing manufacturing sectors are also those that have the fastest overall growth rates. In the period 1970–78, the median average annual rate of growth of manufacturing in middle-income countries was 6.8 per cent, in low-income countries 4.2 per cent, and in industrialized countries 3.3 per cent. Corresponding median, average annual GDP growth rates were 5.7, 3.6 and 3.2 per cent (World Bank *Development Report*, 1980; see also Kaldor, 1966a, 1966b). Very broadly speaking, it is probably true to say that the relationship between GDP per head and the relative sectoral shares of manufacturing and primary industries are as shown in figure 7.6. Notice that we have drawn in relationships for both large and small countries (measured in terms of populations). This reflects the finding of Batchelor *et al.* (1980) that the share of manufacturing is usually 30 per cent higher in larger than in smaller countries.

While these sorts of relationships are certainly suggestive, they can hardly form the basis for informed policy-making unless we know more about why they exist. As it turns out, there are a number of hypotheses to consider. First, consider the line of causation from income to output. From the point of view of domestic consumption, it is widely agreed that rising income brings with it increased demand for manufactures as the bare essentials of food and shelter account for a decreasing proportion of consumer spending power. In general (within domestic populations as well as across countries), income growth elasticities for manufacturing output have been found to be large relative to the output of the primary goods sectors—including agriculture. Within manufacturing, moreover, it has been found (Chenery and Taylor, 1968) that there is important variation in these elasticities.

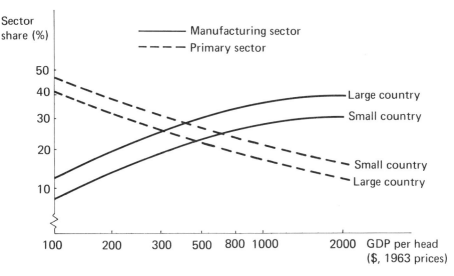

Figure 7.6 Structural change in the growing economy.
(Source: Batchelor *et al.*, 1980, p. 117)

For so-called 'early' sectors like textiles, demand response to rising incomes is most marked at the lowest income levels. For 'middle' industries such as rubber products, demand response is limited at the lowest income levels but is very pronounced once per capita purchasing power has risen beyond a critical point. 'Late' industries like metal products and consumer durables see demand growing fastest in the highest income ranges.

The hypothesis embodied here is that most countries have similar taste patterns at specified levels of income per head, but researchers in the area have concluded that supply-side factors must also be invoked. Chenery, for example, looks to economics of scale and correlations between per capita income and the ratios of physical and human capital to labour to explain why so many countries seem to have followed the same path in terms of production pattern.

A second general hypothesis draws on the technological gap type of analysis we explored earlier. It thus stresses supply-side factors where the first hypothesis rather plays them down. This approach takes the difference between per capita income in an LDC and a leading DC (say the USA) as an indication of the technological gap between the countries. The bigger the gap, it is asserted, the greater the choice of as-yet untried techniques the LDC has available to it. The LDC is a technology-borrower or imitator in this view, and since it is using processes already tried and tested elsewhere, it should be able to introduce them quickly, effectively and with impressive results for growth. As we noted earlier in the chapter, much of the innovation that LDCs borrow is likely to be in the area of manufactured products rather than primary production, since it is in the former that most research and development occurs in high-income economies.

This story is also incomplete, for it takes for granted the desire and ability of LDCs to put new techniques to effective use quickly (this depends on infrastructure and skills, among other things), and sufficient demand to make the techniques worth adopting. The latter point takes us back to the earlier hypothesis.

Finally, notice why manufacturing growth is potentially so important for the economy overall. We saw earlier that evidence does tend to suggest that countries with fastest manufacturing growth are also those with fastest aggregate growth rates. Related work notes that countries with the fastest growth rates of manufacturing output also have the fastest growth rates of labour productivity in manufacturing. This is called the 'Verdoorn law' after the economist who was one of the first to discuss it. Several arguments have been adduced which assert that causation here flows from output growth to productivity growth—prominent among them an appeal to both static- and dynamic-scale economies. Further, it is argued that, if manufacturing is growing rapidly, its demand for inputs from elsewhere in the economy will also grow rapidly; and to the extent that productivity advances occur in the production of intermediate goods that will be used elsewhere in the economy, other sectors also benefit from the experience of manufacturing. In this view, manufacturing is seen as the 'engine of growth' for the economy, and what becomes important is to find what determines manufacturing output growth in the first place.

It can of course be argued that causation runs from productivity growth in manufacturing to manufacturing and then to aggregate growth in output. In this case, the assumption is made that countries with relatively high rates of productivity advance will reflect such experience in the prices they charge both domestically and internationally. Assuming a reasonably high price elasticity of demand, this in turn should lead to rapid output growth, and assuming that productivity growth is faster in manufacturing than in other sectors, it also accounts for the relatively rapid growth of this sector.[7]

Each of these approaches takes a different position, yet combinations of them can co-exist in the same country at the same time. In different places and at different times, all are likely to have been true to varying degrees. However, each in its way establishes the importance of manufacturing in the development process, and each can contribute to an understanding of why some industrialization strategies work better than others.

Import Substitution or Export-led Growth?

With the background that we now have, it should be easy to see how import-substituting industrialization developed its appeal. On the one hand, development trade theorists were arguing that shifts in the terms of trade against primary products, the relatively low income elasticities for primary good exports and the protection of home industry by DCs were all conspiring to deprive LDCs of the full developmental benefits promised by trade. On the other hand, the sensitivity of demand for imported manufactures to rising LDC incomes appeared to pose an additional threat to the balance of payments, particularly if governments were reluctant to stem the flow by either exchange rate or fiscal and monetary policy. And so long as investment was concentrated in primary production, or even infrastructure and services, it was felt that the perceived benefits flowing from a manufacturing base could not be enjoyed. To grasp these employment-related, potentially productivity-raising benefits, and with the prospect of alleviating payments problems too, many governments saw the appeal of import-substituting industrialization, and in their zeal to implement the policy erected protective barriers in some instances for almost any local manufacturing industry that requested it.

As must be clear from our earlier discussions, such wholesale (and often *ad hoc*) protection implies little regard for the careful application of criteria required by, say, the Mill–Bastable test, and suggests that the alternative policies noted are barely considered either. More fundamentally, such a strategy also implies a misreading of history and a disregard for the predictions of well established analysis. On the first point, it does seem to be the case that, in the early stages of development, growth of primary industry is often the trigger that draws manufacturing into existence through linkages and income creation. Certainly we can see that import substitution industries proceeded apace in the early development of now-advanced industrial nations. But they sprang into existence as both supply-side factors (infrastructural and other capital, entrepreneurship, skills) and those on the demand side (growing consumer and industrial demand) exposed profitable opportunities and made possible their exploitation. This course of events is precisely the reverse of the sequence from which protected import-substituting industrialization sets out to profit. In other words, LDCs can be viewed as trying to make import substitution the 'sharp end' of an overall strategy, when history suggests that the efficient growth of such industries tends instead to be a consequence of prior change.

As far as analysis is concerned, the welfare losses associated with protection have been demonstrated; and implicit in the case supporting trade is, of course, the assertion that its benefits will be reduced to the extent that protection interferes with it.

Let us now look more specifically at the problems that can arise with protected import substitution (a classic reference here is Little, Scitovsky and Scott, 1970).

The first point to note is that protection, particularly if prohibitive, often confines the manufacturer of import substitutes to the domestic market. The strategy in any case envisaged industries setting up on the basis of domestic demand, but it can easily be seen how protection may eventually discourage any other outcome. If the country is small, the opportunities for reaping scale economies will also be limited. In a small market, moreover, minimum viable plant size may dictate that the industry be a monopoly. Furthermore, the general isolation from foreign competitive pressures opens the door to significant X-inefficiency. Even in large countries such problems may not be overcome. In some Latin American economies competition has been encouraged among domestic producers (foreign competition having been barred), with the result that opportunities for reaping scale economies have not been taken up. Import-substituting industries thus find themselves unable to compete in world markets, even if doing so offers the only prospect for their longer-run growth.

Second, import substitution has often led to a deterioration rather than an improvement in the balance of payments. On the import side, net foreign exchange losses rather than savings can easily be associated with an import-substituting industry since intermediate inputs still have to be bought abroad, capital employed may carry charges to be made in foreign currency, and project-generated incomes may themselves be spent on imported consumer goods. But this is not all. As Little *et al.* point out (1970, p. 130), the total foreign exchange cost of imports lies below the free trade level if a tariff operates. This results, compared with free trade, in fewer units of domestic currency exchanging for a unit of foreign currency: the exchange rate is 'overvalued'. Consequently, exporters are discouraged because they obtain less domestic currency for a given volume of exports than they would under free trade. Exporters also find themselves penalized to the extent that protection raises the cost of their inputs, whether obtained abroad or locally. These factors are likely to make exports less price-competitive and thus lead to a reduction in export revenue. Notice, too, that if a protected industry hopes to penetrate foreign markets as well as supplying the local one, its plans will be thwarted if the effect of protection is to encourage poor-quality workmanship or permit substantial X-inefficiency. The potential for export earnings will then not be realized.

We noted earlier that trying to lead development on by growing import-substituting industry behind tariff walls was probably a result of misreading history. The experience of LDCs bears this out. By offering protection to manufacturers and by biasing tariffs in favour of their equipment, LDCs have often provided the framework in which profits can be earned on the basis of only very limited capacity utilization. This points to a significant mis-use of scarce resources.

Agriculture in particular suffers in a number of ways. Because the exchange rate is overvalued, agricultural exporters receive less domestic currency for given output than they would in the absence of controls. Because import substitution favours manufacturing, scarce capital that might have raised returns in agriculture very substantially is not invested there. Furthermore, agricultural sector consumers suffer like everyone else from highly priced (and possibly poor-quality) domestic manufactures. This is bad enough, but the effects are more far-reaching. By raising the price of manufactures relative to agricultural goods, protection policy turns the domestic terms of trade against agriculture. In the absence of income-creating investment, this must threaten real incomes there, and a potentially large reservoir of demand for manufactures will stagnate. Protected import substitution, there-fore, can easily undermine the very process of growth that it was designed to stimulate.

Again, industries favoured by protection have tended to be capital-intensive in their production methods. This has resulted in a large proportion of the benefits of such policies flowing into the hands of capital investors rather than wage-earning labour, thus increasing income disparities. Further, where capital is invested by foreigners, a part of the benefits has been lost to the host LDC as profits are repatri-ated. Lastly, from the job creation point of view, early expansion has often been followed by long-term stagnation. Capital-intensive produc-tion does not have to run against employment, as we have noticed else-where. Growth can see to that. But when protected import substitution restricts growth prospects, then the bias against labour can be entrenched.

A final point is that manufacturing has often received a degree of what is called effective protection even greater than the nominal tariff rate might suggest. However imports are restricted, the resulting degree of protection can best be measured by the extent to which restriction causes the domestic price of imports to exceed what their price would be in the absence of the control. When we refer to a stage in the manufacturing process (rather than the commodity itself) and relate the effect of protection to value added at this stage (and not to the commodity price), we are looking at the effective rate of protection—not the nominal rate, which we have been addressing, implicitly, until now. To quote Little *et al.*, 'The effective rate of protection ... shows by what percentage the sum of wages, profits and depreciation allowances payable by domestic firms can, thanks to protection, exceed what this sum would be if the same firms were fully exposed to foreign competition' (1970, p. 39). Notice that this measure captures the degree of protection given to a manufacturing process by the entire protective structure. It thus embodies, in a more comprehensive way than the nominal rate, the extent of protection enjoyed by an industry. For our purposes here, the point to remember is that effective protection rates for manufactures are usually higher than nominal, so that all of our critique of protection and its results is further reinforced by viewing it in this way.

The general critique we have offered in relation to protected import substitution has applied with varying degrees of force in most of the countries where this strategy was applied. Of the seven countries studied by Little *et al.* (1970), Taiwan and Pakistan in the late 1950s were the first to notice the problems and limitations of the strategy, followed by India, and later (1965) Brazil and Mexico.[8] This prompted a tendency to start exploring the export markets for manufactures.

This trend held out considerable promise. As we noted earlier, trade in manufactures has consistently grown at a rapid rate in recent decades. If an LDC could concentrate in one or a few lines favoured by its comparative advantage, develop the requisite skills to ensure international standards of quality, and obtain the management to guarantee delivery, then it should be able to 'latch on' to the rapidly growing demand for manufactures world-wide. This growth, in turn, should permit economies of scale while exposure to foreign competition should minimize X-inefficiency.

For the poorest countries (in terms of resource and skill endowments) export orientation in the industrial strategy almost inevitably confines them initially to complying as best they can with the precepts of the staple product theory, perhaps supplemented by trade in distinctive local crafts and the expansion of tourism. Their best hope in relation to manufacturing is to attract the occasional 'footloose industry' seeking relatively cheap labour, although this assumes ready access to major markets. If a poor country is also small, a partial solution may be for it to join with neighbours in some sort of economic union, although the net gains from economic integration for smaller, weaker members can often prove disappointing. While this is not an altogether exciting picture, it at least steers a country clear of the disadvantages now known to accompany attempts to establish import-substituting industry at almost any cost, particularly in small economies. In the longer run, there is always the hope that new mineral discoveries may assist. For this type of country, it will be important to take advantage of any possible linkage, to try to ensure that profit repatriation is minimized (without 'scaring off' foreign investors), and to guide scarce and hard-earned surpluses into projects where social returns are assuredly highest—which of course may be infrastructural or agricultural rather than in manufacturing.

For the many developing countries less badly off than this, the picture is much brighter, and the facts of the matter have recently been examined by Tyler (1981). Looking at a set of 55 middle-income countries (those having a GNP per head of over $300 in 1977, but excluding the major industrialized nations), Tyler found that between 1960 and 1977 there was a positive and significant relationship between GDP growth and export growth for these economies. Similarly, he found strong evidence that countries enjoying the fastest rates of overall economic growth were also those with the fastest rates of growth for manufacturing exports. More specifically, he found that a 17.5 per cent increase in overall exports and a rise of about 22 per cent in manufactured exports led to a 1 per cent growth in GDP.

In their studies, Batchelor *et al.* (1980) find, overall, that export growth and investment are equally significant in explaining aggregate income growth in the least developed countries, and that exports— particularly in manufactures—are the mainspring of output growth in smaller middle-income developing countries.

Notice that growth in exports of all kinds is important in both of these studies, even though manufacturing exports turn out to be most important for the middle-income developing nations.

In the case of individual countries, the contributions to growth of exports (usually primary commodities, initially) will depend on the extent to which export production generates income that is saved and reinvested locally rather than consumed on imports; the extent to which skills and experience are provided that are subsequently used elsewhere in the economy; and the degree of linkage industry that is stimulated. If these factors work fairly strongly, we can expect the means and income to become available to make it worthwhile to undertake import substitution efficiently and without protection (apart, perhaps, from a strictly limited initial period of 'infancy'). If these effects are weak, governments may have to consider whether infrastructure needs to be strengthened and/or financial markets liberalized, and whether fiscal or monetary policy could be used to increase their impact. Finally, if the nature of the export implies large fluctuations in potential earnings, or if it must face restrictive trade barriers, then a country should probably resort to schemes to offset the effects of export instability and join in the concerted efforts of other developing countries to have trade barriers removed.

The New International Economic Order
The directions taken by theory and research in the area of international trade and development have, as we suggested earlier, reflected the experience and perceptions of developing nations *vis à vis* advanced industrial countries. At the same time, and fed by much of this theorizing, there has been a growth in the demand for what has become known as a 'New International Economic Order'—from now on abbreviated to NIEO. The term itself started to gain wide currency only after the sixth Special Session of the UN General Assembly in early 1974—a fact of some interest in itself, since as Corden (1978) remarks, much of the inspiration for the Order derived from the then relatively recent and certainly dramatic success of the OPEC cartel in raising the price of oil. By 1976, the ideas constituting the content of the NIEO had been clarified and sharpened and can be found in the Secretary General's Report to the Nairobi assembly of UNCTAD (United Nations Conference on Trade and Development), entitled *New Directions and New Structures for Trade and Development.*

The roots of the NIEO can be traced back to the growing disillusionment with what might be termed the 'existing order'. As Bhagwati (1977) puts it, the central issue for developing countries (often characterized the 'the South') in their trading relationships with the advanced industrial nations ('the North') is whether the links of trade, aid, investment and migration work to their advantage or not. In the 1950s and 1960s, thinking on this question was dominated by a perception that the existing mechanisms were primarily beneficial: even though nations, firms and individuals might be pursuing their own interests in the world economy, the result would none the less be to the advantage of the developing countries. This view emphasizes the gains from trade that we have identified and puts a benign construction upon the activities of MNCs in bringing new techniques and creating new incomes (Bhagwati, 1977, pp. 2–3). In this atmosphere, early UNCTAD assemblies stressed two aspects of trade policy: preferential access to the markets of the North for the South, and the tenet of non-reciprocity —insistence that the countries of the North should lower their trade barriers while those of the South should be permitted to maintain theirs.

As it turned out, the first of these principles was widely breached and thus achieved limited success in generating new benefits for LDCs; the second principle contained within itself the potential for damaging LDCs associated with all protective strategies—a question we have examined at length. Furthermore, North–South aid was increasingly seen as inadequate for making any real impact upon the huge 'gap' in incomes between rich and poor nations, and there was growing unease about the morality of permitting such a large gap to continue to exist. Thus, by the early 1970s there was a well entrenched feeling that neither the intent nor the impact of northern policies on the South could in the natural course of events be judged beneficial (Bhagwati, 1977, pp. 4–5). With this shift in perception among developing countries already well under way came the sudden impetus of OPEC's success.

By UNCTAD IV at Nairobi, it was possible to define fairly clearly how the NIEO might be constituted. With the maintained objective of maximizing the benefits from links with the North, the South looked for:

(1) changes that would both generally raise and stabilize fluctuations in the real prices of primary commodities;
(2) improved access for southern manufactures to northern markets;
(3) changes in the international monetary and financial system;
(4) more aid;
(5) improved access in the South to the technological innovations and capital markets of the North.

It would be difficult to argue that this 'programme' contained much that, in any general sense, could be said to be 'new' or to reflect innovative thinking. All of the issues directly or by implication raised here have been thoroughly aired before. None the less, the impact of the UNCTAD IV document has continued to be felt. In 1980 the Independent Commission on International Development Issues, chaired by former West German Chancellor Willy Brandt, produced the so-called Brandt Report, actually titled: *North–South: A Programme For Survival.* While the Report casts its net very widely, it is a central part of its thesis that drawing North and South together can and should involve establishing a NIEO. It has confidence that it is practicable to generate workable measures from the 'programme', and is optimistic that these measures can be directed towards solving world problems in the mutual interests of both North and South.

From our point of view, it is of central interest to consider how potentially successful the 'programme' outlined above might be in assisting the South—although from a strategic point of view it is as well to recognize that the potential for success depends importantly upon how much the North perceives any moves it makes to assist the South to be in its own best interests. This principle—that 'bargains must be struck which are mutually profitable and which therefore appeal also to the developed countries' interests' (Bhagwati, 1977, p. 15)—may be termed the 'principle of mutual-gain bargains'. In reality, the prospects for the NIEO would seem to depend largely upon the extent to which particular elements within it can be cast in the form of such mutual gain bargains.

But let us consider the economic arguments that surround some of the more important components of the package. In relation to primary commodity trade, two questions arise: first, whether to support or raise the real price of primary exports; and second, whether to stabilize primary export prices. It will be clear from discussion earlier in the chapter that the first issue has antecedents in the allegation that there has been (and, more strongly, in theory, must be) a secular deterioration in the terms of trade of primary products as against manufactures, and hence of commodity-producing countries as against industrial countries. We have already argued that this allegation is questionable, both theoretically and in practice, and Little (1975) (a noted development and welfare economist working as an expert for the World Bank) has argued that UNCTAD itself was founded 'on the mistaken view, which it has enshrined by constant repetition into [a] myth "that such an adverse trend in the terms of trade existed"' (1975, p. 227). The concrete form that the South has said it wishes price support to take is the indexing of commodity prices to the prices of manufactured imports to LDCs. An alternative procedure would be to apply appropriate cartel action, in the image of OPEC. On the first option, Bhagwati (1977) argues that indexation is 'crude, simplistic, inefficient, inequitable ... and virtually impracticable' (p. 14), while Kreinin and Finger (1976) point out that it also violates the principle of mutual-gain bargains since the North would always view it as an inflationary economic instrument (p. 504). As far as cartel action is concerned, Corden (1979) points out that, if commodity prices are to be raised, there must eventually be production restrictions that are agreed upon and conscientiously applied by each member. Problems of implementation here are severe and include the possibility of new producers not joining the cartel but making their own deals; existing members with-drawing or conducting private arrangements; and customers finding substitutes for the product.

Turning to price stabilization, we have seen that the evidence relating price stability to improved prospects for development is, in any case, controversial. However, to the extent that price instability is harmful, the type of measure most likely in practice to be taken to tackle it is a form of buffer stock arrangement. As Corden (1979) puts it, 'The basic idea is to establish internationally managed buffer stocks which will buy and sell particular commodities so as to keep their prices fairly stable around a trend' (p. 3). More specifically, UNCTAD has devised an Integrated Programme for Commodities, an essential element of which is a so-called Common Fund of several billion dollars which would finance commodity buffer stocks. A serious problem here is that the buffer stock managers might be mistaken in their perceptions of the price trend—failure of this kind resulting either in accumulation or exhaustion of stocks. Further, if the buffer stock managers are too optimistic about price trends, they will expect prices to rise more quickly than they actually do—with the result that a scheme might go bankrupt through paying out too much, too early.[9] Other points worth noting (Corden, 1979, pp. 4–5) are that, even if prices are stabilized, export earnings will fluctuate if instability derives from the supply side, while, as a matter of practicality, the financial investment involved in building a buffer stock large enough to make a significant impact would seem to be much larger than envisaged by UNCTAD. The Common Fund may thus be regarded as a defensible practical step, but not one that should be infused with unrealistically inflated expectations of success.

Turning now to manufactures, LDCs as a group have been pressing since the early 1960s for what is known as the Generalized System of Preferences (GSP). Under this scheme, LDCs hoped to gain freer access to the markets of advanced industrial nations as a consequence of encountering no duty on their manufactured exports to the North while calling at the same time for developed countries to charge most favoured nation (MFN) rates of duty on competitive products from other industrial countries (Kreinin and Finger, 1976, p. 495). Although this system was purportedly introduced by the EEC and Japan in 1971, and by the USA in 1976, the exceptions and restrictions that actually operate within the scheme detract in a very significant way from its generality. As Corden remarks (1979, p. 8), 'Extraordinarily, it excludes textiles and clothing, which account for much of the total exports of manufactures of developing countries.' It is improbable, therefore, that the scheme has done much to boost manufactured exports from South to North.

Supposing that all LDCs have comparative advantage in some area or areas, the search for preferential treatment seems in any case to be misplaced. What is really needed, it can be argued, is a drive to reduce permanently protective barriers of all kinds in all developed countries. Not only would the nations of the South then be able to derive the benefits of specializing in their areas of comparative advantage, but they would be able to invest with confidence in these areas in the knowledge that the developed nations would not at some future time close the door on them—a dangerous possibility for the South, given that the GSP arrangements last for only ten years. True, the labour lobby of the North is likely to object strongly to such efforts, fearing that cheaper imports from the South will lead to unemployment. But as Bhagwati (1977) has pointed out, the North may be as concerned to secure its supplies of raw materials from the South and the South is to gain access for its manufactures in the markets of the North (p. 18). This suggests a perhaps rosier prospect for a mutual gain joint deal.

We shall deal with the other elements of the package more summarily. As far as the international monetary system is concerned, the NIEO seems to envisage less exchange rate fluctuation than the world saw in the 1970s and early 1980s. Yet as Corden (1979, p. 17) reminds us, the old Bretton Woods system of fixed exchange rates was accompanied by balance of payments crises, attempted remedies for which might today include deflationary policies and sometimes reductions in aid. More fundamentally, stable, well-managed economic growth in the North would greatly reduce exchange rate fluctuations anyway, while merely fixing exchange rates may not do anything, in itself, to encourage such stability. Assuming that stable growth in their markets is what the South really wants, demands for a return to fixed exchange rates again seem misplaced. The question of aid is dealt with in Appendix 7.2. On the last point—access to North-developed technology and northern capital markets—it seems plausible to argue (Kreinin and Finger, 1976, p. 510) that both these desires can be best satisfied by noting that the MNC is the most effective vehicle for transferring technology, know-how and capital. It is not denied that MNCs can and have sometimes abused their position, but so long as the South is alert to the dangers attending MNC investment, it makes good sense to provide a welcoming climate for their operation.

By way of summary, we may say that the NIEO is an attempt to prescribe means of maximizing the benefits to be gained by developing countries from their links with advanced industrial nations. Yet there is a danger in concentrating on this strategy alone, or even predominantly. Rather like the arguments mounted against trade earlier in the chapter, the NIEO way of thinking implies a view that most of the problems of developing countries are the result of external forces and foreign decision-maker's actions. In some cases this is, at least partially, true. Governments in industrialized nations continue to bow to pressures to maintain high trade barriers against LDC manufactures (with a recent shift in emphasis from tariffs to quantitative controls); MNCs are not always innocent of the charges laid against them; market instabilities are sometimes the result of poorly formed macroeconomic policy in the North. But then, as we have seen, the LDCs themselves operate behind high protective barriers, often encourage inefficiency of resource use, and hinder rather than assist the operation of market forces. Thus, to quote Kreinin and Finger,

Economic development is essentially a process of internal transformation of society. It requires political stability, social mobility, economic incentives . . . [and] also time—probably more time than the impatient 'Third World' is willing to allow. Thus, for the most part, economic development is something that the developing countries must do for themselves . . . . It is indeed natural to find scapegoats and try to blame others for one's own failures. But in this case an indictment is worse than being unjust. Looking for faults elsewhere means that the developing countries will do less than what is optimal to clean up their own house. [Kreinin and Finger, 1976, p. 511]

CONCLUSION

This chapter has shown that the forces at work in determining a country's path of growth and development cannot properly be considered without reference to its place in the world of international trade. Under the strong assumptions characteristic of conventional trade theory, unimpeded trade brings with it resource allocation gains that should be attractive to any country. On the other hand, if these assumptions are relaxed, the door is opened to permit gains of other kinds to occur—gains that many believe are of central importance to LDCs. As we have seen, influential commentators have argued at length on behalf of the counter-developmental factors that they believe trade might promote. This in turn has encouraged protectionism and inward-looking import substitution strategies. But the evidence in favour of trade as an engine of growth, the theoretical and observed problems associated with protection and the recognition that LDCs can themselves do more, domestically, to spread the benefits of trade all indicate that an optimistic view of trade is in order.

APPENDIX 7.1 CONSTRUCTING A TRANSFORMATION CURVE

We have in this chapter referred to the 'tranformation curve', sometimes also called the 'production possibility frontier'. In this appendix
it is shown how to derive this curve from the production functions,
represented by isoquant maps, for the two commodities, rice and
metal boxes.

In figure A7.1(a) we have drawn what is called an Edgeworth box.
This box comprises two isoquant maps, with origins at O_R (for rice)
and O_{MB} (for metal boxes), which have been superimposed upon each
other. The metal box production function is upside-down in relation
to that for rice. Each production function is characterized by constant
returns to scale, but, as indicated by the differing slopes of rays from
each origin, rice is relatively more labour-intensive in production than
metal boxes. The length of each of the axes shows the total amount of
homogenous labour and capital in the economy. These inputs may be
divided in differing proportions between producing metal boxes and

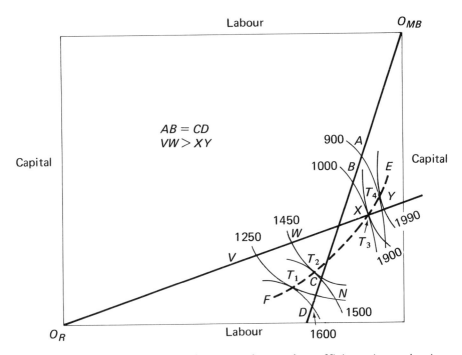

*Figure A7.1(a) An Edgeworth Box used to analyse efficiency in production:
constant returns to scale in both production functions*

rice. Each of the tangency points T_1 to T_4 is an efficient point in the senses that the economy's resources are fully employed and that any shift between such points brings an increase in the production of one output only at the expense of that of the other.

The dotted line *FE* connects these points. Were we to examine any point off this line, we should find that output of either commodity could be increased without loss of output of the other—the mark of inefficient allocation of inputs. At point *N*, for example, 1250 tonnes of rice are produced and 1500 metal boxes. However, as the figure shows, labour and capital could be reallocated to generate either 1250 tonnes of rice and 1600 metal boxes (at T_1), or 1450 tonnes of rice and 1500 metal boxes (at T_2), or in fact any output combination lying on *FE* between T_1 and T_2. As can be appreciated from the quantities attached to T_1 and T_2, they are unambiguously superior to those at *N*, and *N* is thus an inefficient point.

Without discussing preferences over various output combinations, it is not possible to say that any point on *FE* is superior to any other. What we do know is that each is an efficient point in production. Technically speaking, efficient points can be identified in the Edgeworth box by noting that they occur at tangency points between isoquants, that is, where the marginal rates of substitution between inputs in producing each output is equal.

The curvature of *FE*, given constant returns to scale in each production function, derives from the joint effects of having isoquants downward-sloping and convex to their origins, and the productive activities having different capital–labour ratios. Under these conditions, a marginal increase in the output of either commodity will at each successive increment reduce output of the other output by an increasing amount. Thus, for example, increasing metal box output from 900 to 1000 units reduces rice output by 90 tonnes, from 1990 to 1900. Increasing metal box output once more by 100 units, but this time from 1500 to 1600, will reduce rice production by 200 tonnes, from 1450 to 1250.

In figure A7.1(b) the line *FE* on figure A7.1(a) has been reproduced on a diagram whose axes are defined in terms of output rather than inputs. T_1, for example, occurs in the Edgeworth box at the tangency of the isoquants for 1250 tonnes of rice and 1600 metal boxes. It can be found at a corresponding position on figure A7.1(b) at a point determined by the (1250, 1600) output level coordinates. A similar exercise can be repeated for T_2, T_3, T_4 and *N*. The curvature of *FE* reflects the curvature of the line in the Edgeworth box. In the so-called 'output space' of figure A7.1(b), the curve becomes the transformation

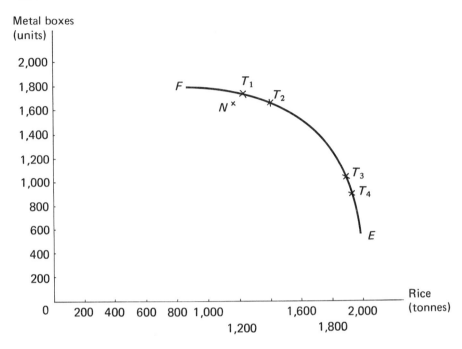

Figure A7.1(b) The transformation curve derived from A7.1(a)

curve (or production possibility frontier) between outputs. Its slope at
any point is the marginal rate of transformation between outputs. The
frontier represents the locus of efficient combinations of metal boxes
and rice that the economy can produce with the existing technology
and its given endowments of capital and labour. Points like *N*, which
lie within it, are inefficient.

This derivation has followed the lines laid down by the analysis in
the main body of the chapter. Notice however that, even if each good
were produced with techniques of similar capital–labour ratio, a
transformation curve bowed out from the origin would still occur as
long as decreasing returns to scale characterized at least one of the
production functions and was not outweighed by increasing returns to
scale in the other. In figure A7.2(a) the diagonal line across the Edgeworth box represents the capital–labour ratio of each production
process, and each production function is characterized by decreasing
returns to scale. Efficient points are marked at isoquant tangencies by
the letters *A* to *H*, and these are reproduced on the transformation
curve shown in figure A7.2(b).

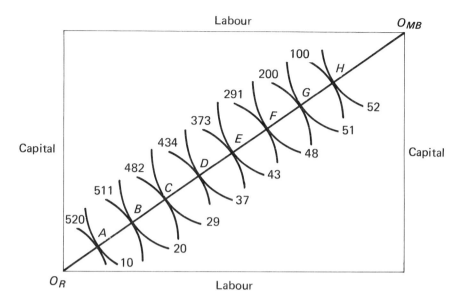

Figure A7.2(a) An Edgeworth Box used to analyse efficiency in production: decreasing returns to scale in both production functions

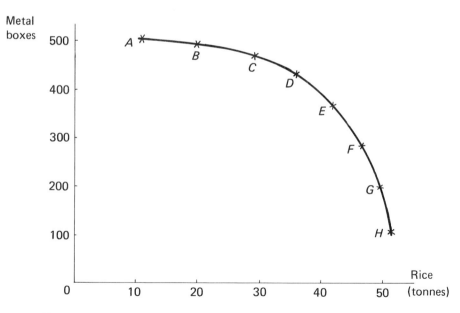

Figure A7.2(b) The transformation curve derived from A7.2(a)

At the end of chapter 4, we noted that, in addition to mobilizing capital resources domestically, LDCs could hope to rely on foreign investment and aid to assist their development. In this chapter we have been able to analyse the way in which trade brings capital goods into developing countries, and we are now in a position to consider, as an issue on its own, the distinctions between private foreign investment and foreign aid, and the rationales for each.

Let us start with some figures which place the relative importance of these flows in perspective. As table A7.1 shows, financial flows reaching developing countries can be divided into aid, direct investment, bank lending and other non-concessional flows. Definitionally, aid is distinct from the other categories in that it comprises flows that occur on concessional conditions (with respect to some or all elements of the debt-servicing package—see below) and would not have taken place through the normal working of the market. For expositional simplicity we shall lump the other categories together as 'private foreign invest-ment'—flows whose common feature is that they take place on terms determined by market forces. As far as magnitudes are concerned, it can be seen that, through the 1970s, there was a sharp decline in the proportion of net financial flows to developing countries accounted for by aid, from 42.6 per cent through a low of 29.5 per cent to 34.6 per cent. In absolute terms, non-concessional flows surpassed concessional flows in the ratio of $53.1 billion to $27.9 billion in 1979. In other words, the relatively more expensive commercial flows have dominated the picture in recent years, and not surprisingly it is the poorest countries, with least capacity to service debt on commercial terms, that rely most heavily on aid—about 85 per cent of their external finance deriving from this source.

Now, while it is by definition true that aid is concessional in its terms whereas private foreign investment is not, this by no means implies that the former is 'better' in any obvious way for LDCs. Both, in fact, are often seen as filling a 'gap'—either a savings or a foreign exchange gap—and starting with aid, we shall consider how each might do this and what their other repercussions might be.

All aid flows are forms of loan or a gift. Whatever form a loan takes, a debt arises between the aid donor and the recipient, and this debt must be serviced, or repaid over time with interest. The characteristics of a loan repayment agreement are threefold: rate of interest to be paid, length of repayment period (maturity), and initial grace period

TABLE A7.1 Structure of net financial flows to developing countries

	% share of total					Total ($b)
	1970 %	1974 %	1978 %	1979 %		1979
Aid	42.6	44.1	29.5	34.6		27.9
Bank lending (incl. private export credits)	27.0 ⎫	36.8 ⎫	40.9 ⎫	32.1 ⎫		26.0 ⎫
Direct investment	19.3 ⎬ 57.4	3.3 ⎬ 55.9	13.9 ⎬ 70.5	16.7 ⎬ 65.4		13.5 ⎬ 53.1
Other non-concessional	11.1 ⎭	15.8 ⎭	15.7 ⎭	16.6 ⎭		13.6 ⎭
	100.0	100.0	100.0	100.0		81.0

Source: OECD, *Development Co-operation 1980 Review*; reproduced in Bird and Gutmann (1981)

during which no repayment of principal is required. A 'loan' that never need be repaid and has zero interest is a grant: it is not a loan but a gift. Although the terms and conditions attaching to loans can vary widely, a grant element embodied in any loan can be found by calculating the present value of the service charges over the life of the debt discounted at today's market interest rate and subtracting it from the dollar value of the aid flow received today. In the case of a commercial loan, the various components of debt servicing would be such that this calculation would yield a zero grant element. It would not be aid at all. The lower is the interest rate and the longer the maturity of the debt and any grace period, the greater the grant element will be.

From the point of view of the recipient, the essence of grant element calculations is to identify the difference between the financial terms actually faced and those that would be enforced on a commercial loan. This 'relative attractiveness' approach may need modification, however, if constraints are imposed upon the use of the loan by the donor. Such constraints are called aid-tying and may take two forms. First, a donor may insist that aid finance be spent on goods or services that either it or its nominees produces. This is called 'procurement tying' and reduces the value of the aid to the extent that donor producers may be more expensive or qualitatively inferior in their products compared with other suppliers in world markets. Alternatively, a donor may require that aid funds be devoted to particular types of project (junior schools or village hospitals, for example), which may have special political appeal at home. The value of aid is undermined here to the extent that the social rate of return associated with such project-tied flows falls below the returns that they could have earned on other projects in the economy.

From the point of view of LDCs, the principal rationales for aid have to do with absolute urgent need on the one hand and, more generally, with development-impeding resource constraints on the other. We shall only mention in passing the aid flows destined to meet the needs arising from natural disaster and civil strife. Usually such aid largely comprises food, medicaments and temporary shelter. While in the long run this might be viewed as a contribution to human capital in the country, it is probably better to see it as an emergency filip to maintain consumption at a minimally tolerable level.

Returning to our central theme of mobilizing capital, the main argument given in favour of aid is that development is often impeded by either inadequate domestic savings or insufficient foreign exchange. The so-called two-gap model on which this argument is based assumes at its simplest that increases in output are related through fixed capital —

output and import–output ratios to easily calculable investment and import requirements. If it is further assumed that the aggregate savings ratio is fixed and that exports, determined by world conditions, form a fixed proportion of demand for aggregate output, it is easy to see how either gap might arise. On the one hand, domestic savings might be insufficient to generate the investment required to support a desired or target growth rate—given the fixed relationship between output growth and capital accumulation. On the other hand, export revenues earned in foreign exchange might be insufficient to allow the country to buy the imports it requires to support the target growth rate, given the fixed relationship between output growth and an increasing import volume.

Aid may assist with either gap—but notice an important asymmetry. Increased domestic saving can close the savings gap but, because exports are determined by world conditions, can do nothing about the foreign exchange gap. Increased foreign exchange, however, may not only fill the foreign exchange gap but can also close the savings gap. The larger of the gaps acts as the constraint that actually 'bites'. If the savings gap dominates, the answer to some extent could be said to lie in the hands of the country in question. Is it really doing all it can, it may be asked, to save? If the foreign exchange gap dominates, there may well be less that the country can do to help itself, but this still does not justify filling the whole gap with aid. Instead, it might be better to supply aid equivalent to the *excess* of the foreign exchange over the savings gap—and then, again, to examine the possibilities for increasing domestic savings to close that gap.

While gap analysis assumes fixities, much of the thrust of the last paragraph was concerned with the possibility of changing at least one of them: the savings ratio. An important part of the business of economic development should be to tackle, rather than merely accept, some of the assumed fixities of the model. In particular, why accept that X units of capital must always be required to raise output by one unit? Greater efficiency in production, technical progress and the improved quality of co-operant inputs should all, in the longer run, help to reduce the capital–output ratio and so permit greater growth, even with given savings. Furthermore, a broadening and compositional change in the structure of the economy should permit a reduction in the volume of imports needed per unit of output. Such changes might also increase the share of exports in output, thus releasing the foreign exchange constraint from that angle.

Underlying all of this, we have two broad arguments running in opposite directions. In favour of aid, we have the proposition that the ratios we have assumed fixed cannot be altered rapidly, so that, particularly if essential imports become more expensive or staple exports weaken in their earning power, countries may, during a period of adjustment, be left with little or no growth prospects. In these circumstances, aid can be seen as oiling the wheels of adjustment and maintaining growth. (This is very much what was attempted in the period of adjustment to higher oil prices.) Against aid, there is the counter-proposition that loans on 'soft' terms encourage the acceptance of fixities that it is the business of developing countries to try to change. Attempts to stimulate growth or promote adjustment will founder, it is suggested, because 'hand-outs' will only help to maintain the belief that changes are difficult or impossible.

It is, in fact, the question of attitudes encouraged that forms an important part of discussion on aid and private foreign investment (PFI). As we have already noted, project-tied aid may finish up supporting schemes that are wasteful in the sense that resources of a similar value could have earned a higher return elsewhere. This may weaken the determination of governments actually to discover where the highest social returns lie. More generally, Bauer (1974) notes that aid helps perpetuate individuals' perceptions that opportunities and resources for advancement can be initiated only by others. Aid may thus negate one of the central drives of development, self-motivation, at the very grass roots.

If, alternatively, we look at PFI we are necessarily concerned with flows in search of an internationally competitive return. This is obviously true in the case of direct foreign investment, which will be undertaken by rational businessmen only if the profit rate promised in a developing country compares well with those obtainable elsewhere. This is also true of commercial bank lending, since countries would not be able to borrow in the market unless they undertook debt-service obligations in line with those faced by other customers in the international market.

Since, in the case of direct investment, foreign businessmen will be anxious to maximize profit, they will use local and imported resources as efficiently as possible, which not only is desirable in itself but also may give rise to beneficial demonstration effects among the local community of entrepreneurs. More fundamentally still, if entrepreneurship and management skills have barely developed at all, PFI can fill a human resource gap unnoticed by the standard two-gap analysis.

In fact, once we start thinking in terms of 'gaps', it is clear that we need not restrict ourselves to two gaps at all. The managerial or skilled labour gap can constrain growth at least as effectively as a scarcity of savings, for example, and may 'bite' harder if such savings as there are cannot quickly be converted into human capital on a sufficient scale. Another 'gap' may be a budgetary one: a certain amount of government spending on general infrastructure may be a prerequisite for growth in the earliest stages of development, and taxation the only means of raising funds. Given the difficulty of raising revenue from personal income and wealth levies in many LDCs (see pp. 94–7), PFI has the important advantage of providing a new, corporate base for taxation.

We noted in the body of the chapter how foreign investment is the vehicle for bringing new technology into LDCs; how it may have important 'spin-off' through training local employees who can later take their skills to other locations in the economy; how it creates new employment; and how it generates new incomes that not only alleviate poverty but also may be partially saved to contribute to the growth effort. In principle, aid could do all of this too, but the question is, would it do so as effectively? We have argued that in practice it is unlikely to, since PFI is undertaken with all the pressures of the market and profit maximization to sharpen its cutting edge. On the other hand, we have also seen that protected import substitution industry in its turn may have a poor efficiency record, and PFI in this context may therefore lose much of the efficiency-generating and productivity-raising potential it brings with it. Evidence to suggest that PFI might indeed have been less effective in promoting growth than aid is adduced by Papanek (1973).

As for filling the foreign exchange gap, Streeten (1969) has argued that, whatever the claims of aid, PFI can probably not achieve a large and sustained transfer of foreign exchange resources to developing countries. While willing to admit the many merits PFI offers, he is uneasy about a dilemma that many LDCs must face. This dilemma arises because LDCs must choose between allowing continued new PFI and limiting it. If it is their aim to encourage the retention locally of current profits, LDCs will permit foreign business to undertake additional new investment for as long as they wish. However, if, as seems likely, the rate of return on foreign capital is higher than the growth rate of national income, this process will lead to foreign capital growing faster than national income. With a constant capital–output ratio, foreign ownership of local capital must thus grow faster than domestically owned capital. In the limit, alienation of the capital stock may continue until foreign interests own it all, and at this point profit repatriation becomes unavoidable, in the absence of government intervention.

Suppose, then, that governments tried to limit this process before it had run its full course. This, unfortunately, is no real answer either, says Streeten, because foreign businesses will no longer have need to retain profits locally (no further investment opportunities being allowed to them), and from this point on remittances of profit and repatriation of capital will have to be financed, in foreign exchange, out of much-needed export revenues.

There are ways out of this dilemma. Foreign capital might be admitted, for example, on terms that required some degree of local share in ownership, right from the start. Alternatively, it might be hoped that the stimulative effects of PFI and general development advances could combine to achieve fast enough export growth to keep at bay any serious balance of payments problems arising from remittances and repatriation of capital. Some countries will be better placed than others to fulfil these hopes.

Notice, finally, on this point that the balance of payments can also come under pressure from debt-servicing the concessional loans provided under aid. PFI is not alone in generating balance of payments problems, and critics of aid are quick to point this out. Since aid usually flows directly into locally owned capital resources (agricultural and infrastructural uses dominate), the alienation problem does not, however, arise.

FURTHER READING

The subject of trade has been at the heart of economics since its earliest beginnings. The relationships between trade and growth and development have similarly generated literatures of long-standing. As a consequence, the subject matter of this chapter necessarily represents only the briefest summary of a range of protracted and heated debates which have been conducted at many levels.

A lucid up-to-date and accessible text which clearly presents the pure theory and also considers many of the issues canvassed here is Meier (1980). A slightly dated but still very worthwhile reference is Meier (1968). General texts in the area of international trade include Caves and Jones (1973); Södersten (1971); and, for a treatment using the modern techniques of duality, Dixit and Norman (1980). Standard references on protection and policy are Corden (1971, 1974); Little,

Scitovsky and Scott (1970); and Batchelor, Major and Morgan (1980)— a valuable theoretical and empirical up-date of Maizels (1963).

A clear and concise coverage of issues relating to aid can be found in Hawkins (1970), and a more recent presentation of the area is contained in Bird and Gutmann (1981). Chenery and Strout (1966) wrote the seminal article on the two-gap model. One of the classic treatments of PFI is MacDougall (1960), a paper that provides a simple analytical framework for discussing most of the important points and, in its penultimate paragraph, gives an important hint on the relevance of the theory to LDCs. Streeten (1969) gives a useful discussion of the pros and cons of PFI. Bauer (1974) should be consulted for the case against aid.

NOTES

1 Notice that mechanized means of production can be used as much in agriculture as in manufacturing. 'Industry' may therefore include agro-industry.

2 This is not to suggest that industry cannot develop in the absence of international trade. In a closed, dual economy model, for example, it is logically coherent to envisage the growth of industry so long as capitalists know how to design and construct reproducible capital, the requisite raw materials are available domestically, the agricultural surplus can be mobilized to induce them to install capital, and local demand for industrial output is sufficient to make investment worthwhile. Some large countries (the USA, for example) have grown and industrialized rapidly on the basis of domestic interregional trade.

3 The frontiers will be even more sharply bowed if decreasing returns to scale occur for both countries but could bow inwards for part or all of their length in the presence of increasing returns.

4 In fact, since all individuals face the same prices, irrespective of their preferences, the mere fact that preferences cannot always be aggregated diagrammatically does no fundamental harm.

5 A few of the developing countries where oil production has expanded sharply in recent years are Indonesia, Malaysia, Philippines, Nigeria, Angola, Zaire, Gabon, Cameroon and the Ivory Coast (see for example *The Economist*, 5 December 1981, pp. 89–90).

6 Remember, of course, that we identified a wide range of dynamic gains from trade that a country might experience but that cannot be captured in comparative static analysis of the kind we have used here. Protection can reduce the benefits in this direction quite obviously: we actually raised the issue in passing when discussing X-inefficiency, and in general we would expect protection to permit or even encourage production inefficiency

because of the insulation it provides against world competition. This is taken up again in the section on import substitution.

7 The whole of this debate is treated in much more detail in Cornwall (1977, especially chapters 6 and 7).

8 In the many studies now carried out, there has been widespread agreement that protected import substitution policy generally brings with it harmful effects—even in the cases where the strategy has been associated with economic growth. See for example Donges (1976) for a summary.

9 I am indebted to H.W. Arndt for this point.

8

Inequality and Poverty

When we discussed the meaning of development in the Introduction, we suggested that development required growth but that growth in itself was not ultimately enough. The reason we have stressed growth is that the expansion of economic activity is necessary to offer the greatest potential for fulfilling human aspirations—and, if population is growing, is necessary to prevent an actual narrowing of opportunity for the majority. Having said that, growth can hardly be considered developmentally desirable if its fruits go in their entirety to a small minority and if the long-term prospects for any change in this distributional pattern are poor.

In this chapter we explicitly recognize distributional goals and discuss a number of the major issues in this area. We start by asking how a distribution of income might be described analytically, and discover (1) that two quite different concepts of income distribution must be distinguished; and (2) that measures of the degree of inequality present in a distribution turn out to be treacherously lacking in objectivity. We then proceed to discuss some of the more important distributional theories, first in isolation and then in relation to growth. In particular, we shall want to know whether growth must lead to greater inequality, and whether redistributive policies to reduce inequality might reduce the growth rate.

Finally, we notice that there is a further distinction to be made between *relative income inequality* (which can occur even in economies where no one is poor) and the degree of *absolute poverty* (which might exist in economies where everyone has a very similar, low income). Perhaps the major normative aim of development economics is to find ways of alleviating the extent and degree of absolute poverty, but this may not be at all the same thing as looking for means of reducing relative inequality. (For example, an upward shift of the whole income distribution will alleviate poverty but do nothing to change relative inequality.) We shall see that growth seems the best route to take towards alleviating absolute poverty, even if it does not guarantee reduced relative inequality.

DEFINITIONS AND MEASUREMENT

The distribution of income can be viewed from two main angles. On the one hand, the *functional distribution of income* considers how income is distributed among the factors of production. On the other, the *personal* (or size) *distribution of income* looks at how income is distributed among persons or families in an economy.

The functional distribution is considered widely in the theoretical growth literature, in which a common measure of the distributional consequences of growth is taken to be the change in the relative factor shares in national income. In a two-factor model such as Solow's, the relative shares of capital and labour are found in the ratio:

$$\frac{rK}{wL} = \frac{\text{profit per unit of capital} \times \text{quantity of capital}}{\text{wages per unit of labour} \times \text{quantity of labour}}.$$

The functional distribution is most helpful for our understanding of the personal distribution if the economy can be divided into functional groupings (classes) of people like labourers and capitalists, and if it is reasonable to assume that each class is relatively homogeneous, internally, with respect to incomes, but that they vary in significant ways from each other. As it happens, we now know that the greater part of overall inequality in LDCs stems from variations in the payments to labour for its services. Thus, while the determinants of the functional distribution will be discussed shortly, our main emphasis will be on the personal distribution. It is to measures of inequality in that distribution that we now turn.

The distribution of incomes over persons or families is exactly similar in principle to the distribution of examination marks over a class of students. It can be represented diagrammatically by a curve (see figure 8.1 for two examples) and its dimensions captured or described by the commonly used statistics, mean and variance (and sometimes less commonly used statistics, skewness and kurtosis). The mean gives us an arithmetic average of all the individual incomes in the population; the variance, a measure of the extent to which actual incomes are spread out around the mean.

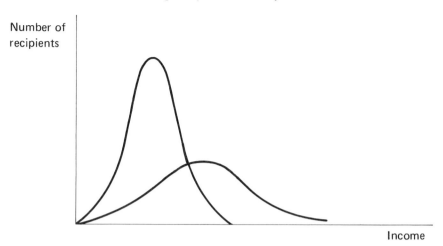

Figure 8.1(a) Two normal distributions

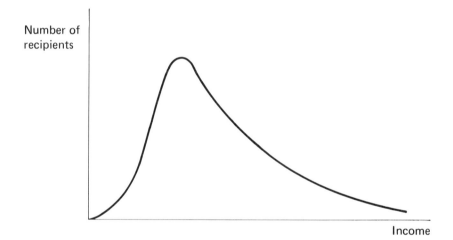

Figure 8.1(b) A distribution skewed to the right

While this is fairly straightforward, the real difficulties start to arise when we try to look for summary measures to reflect the degree of inequality embodied in a distribution. Inequality relates, in essence, to the dispersion present in an entire distribution—irrespective of whether the distribution mean is located a high or low level. But from a developmental point of view, we may be just as interested in the absolute amounts of income received in each part or, more often, some particular parts of the distribution. Measures concerned only with dispersion are called 'relative inequality measures'. Those that take account of absolute amounts of income are embodied in the absolute income and absolute poverty approaches.

Relative Inequality Measures
The most widely used tool in the analysis of relative inequality is the Lorenz curve (see figure 8.2). The Lorenz curve can be built up from observations upon each person's or household's income, or constructed in a more rough-and-ready way from knowledge of the income shares received by various fractiles (say poorest 10 per cent, poorest 20 per cent, ...) of the population. (As will be seen, it presents identical distribution data in an alternative way from that shown in figure 8.1.)

In constructing the Lorenz curve, we start by drawing two axes of equal length: OA to represent cumulative percentages of total income,

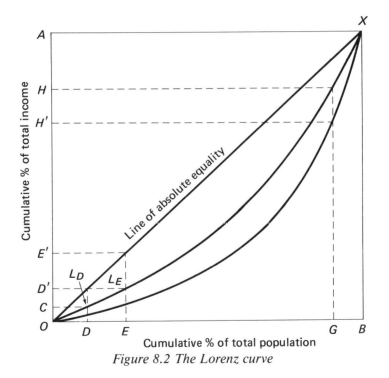

Figure 8.2 The Lorenz curve

and *OB* to represent cumulative percentages of total population. The 'box' is completed (for reasons we shall see later) by drawing *AX* and *BX*, also of equal length. Look first at the straight diagonal line *OX*. This is called the line of absolute equality. To see why, notice that, whatever fraction of the population is observed, this fraction will be found by reference to *OX* to have command over an exactly identical fraction of national income. For example if *OD* represents some chosen 10 per cent of the population, it receives 10 per cent ($= OD'$) of national income. Further, $OE = 20$ per cent $= OE'$; and so on. Since this can happen only if every person or household has the same income, there is no dispersion in the distribution whatever and hence 'perfect equality'.

Suppose we now go to an LDC and find that the poorest 10 per cent of the population, *OD*, receive a proportion of national income represented by *OC* on the cumulative income axis: in other words, less than 10 per cent. Then L_D will be a point on the Lorenz curve for this country. Similarly, if the poorest 20 per cent, *OE*, receive *OD'* ($= 10$ per cent of national income), L_E will be another point on the curve. This exercise can be repeated for all proportions of the population, starting with the poorest person or family. The distance *OG* represents the bottom (or 'poorest') 90 per cent of the population, and *OH* the proportion of national income they receive.

As must be clear from this exercise, the Lorenz curve must always lie beneath the line of absolute equality, and because the percentage measures on each axis are in cumulative terms, the curve must also be concave to it as shown.

It is fairly easy to see that, the farther from the line of absolute equality an entire Lorenz curve lies, the lower will be the proportion of national income received by any given fraction of the population, working up from the poorest. Looking at the outer of the two Lorenz curves in figure 8.2, even the 'poorest' 90 per cent of the population receive *OH'* rather than *OH* as their share in national income.

Having established an understanding of the Lorenz curve, we can now build on it in a number of directions. First, we shall note that manipulation of figure 8.2 can lead to the derivation of a single statistic, *the Gini coefficient*, which is often used to measure the degree of inequality in a distribution. Second, we shall review some of the other indices of inequality found in the literature, derived using data underlying the Lorenz curve. Third, we shall discover that all apparently objective measures of inequality actually embody value judgements based on social preference for one type of distribution rather than another. The Lorenz curve is instrumental in showing this.

Let us start with the Gini coefficient. This coefficient measures the ratio of the area between the line of absolute equality and the Lorenz curve to the total area of the triangle *OXB* beneath the line of absolute equality. (It can now be seen why we drew in the line *BX*: it permits us to talk about the triangle *OXB*.) The larger is the area between the straight line *OX* and the Lorenz curve under consideration, the greater is the Gini coefficient. Now, we noted a moment ago that, the farther an entire Lorenz curve lies from *OX*, the lower will be the proportion of total income received by any part of the population, where we start counting from the poorest household. It seems reasonable to go on to say that, if we consider a distribution A, in which the poorest 5%, 10%, ..., 90%, ... of the population each receives a higher share in national income than similar fractiles receive in another distribution B, then of the two distributions, A has the lower degree of overall relative inequality. The Gini coefficient related to distribution B will be higher than that to A, and in general, the higher the Gini coefficient calculated in association with any distribution, the more unequal the distribution is said to be. The great advantage of the Gini coefficient is that it captures in a single number (between 0 and 1) the result of ranking all persons' or households' incomes and comparing them with each other.

Our second point relates to alternative measures of relative inequality based on information used for constructing the Lorenz curve. These include: (1) the *range* of a distribution—the gap between the highest and lowest income levels; (2) the *relative mean distribution*—the proportion of total income represented by summing the absolute values of the difference between each person's income and the overall mean; (3) the *variance*—obtained by squaring the differences between each individual's and mean incomes, then summing, and dividing the whole by the number of persons; (4) the *coefficient of variation*—which is simply the square root of the variance divided by mean income; and (5) the *standard deviation of logarithms*—which involves taking the logarithms of individual and mean incomes, squaring the difference between the logarithms and summing the squares, dividing by the number of individuals, and taking the square root of the resulting number.

The additional operations that successive measures involve are associated with problems of interpretation related to simpler formulations. The range looks only at extreme observations and abstracts from potentially important features of income variation in between. The relative mean deviation gets over this by looking at the whole distribution, but registers no change in its value (that is, it suggests no change in the degree of inequality) when income is transferred between individuals—even from poorer to richer—on one side of the mean. Variance changes when any transfer occurs, but its value also depends upon that of the mean—a feature undesirable in pure measures of relative inequality and removed in the mean independent measures of coefficient of variation and standard deviation of logarithms. Compared with even the last three, the Gini coefficient is an improvement, since it resorts neither to arbitrary squaring procedures nor to comparisons with a mean whose significance is actually not self-evident.

The third and most fundamental point (hinted at in the last paragraph) is that apparently objective measures such as these turn out to be anything but objective. The best way to arouse your suspicions about their credentials is to ask you to look at table 8.1. There, the Gini coefficient, standard deviation of logarithms and coefficient of variation measures are shown for the income distributions in five developing countries. While Mexico comes off worst and Sri Lanka is third whichever index is used, India is ranked most equal of the five by the standard deviation of logarithms, second best by the Gini coefficient, and second most unequal by the coefficient of variation. Other variations in ranking can be seen in the cases of Barbados and Puerto Rico.

This puzzle was tackled by Atkinson (1970). What he explored was the insight that different indices of inequality implied different social welfare judgements about the relative desirability of alternative distributions of income. For example, we noted earlier that the relative mean deviation index was unaffected in its value as a measure of inequality by income transfers between people on the same side of the mean. Most of the other measures, however, changed in value when such transfers were made. The relative mean deviation index thus

TABLE 8.1 Variations by index in ranking of income distributions according to inequality

Country	Year	Gini coefficient	Standard deviation of logarithms	Coefficient of variation
India	1950	0.410 (2)	0.305 (1)	0.901 (4)
Sri Lanka	1952–53	0.427 (3)	0.341 (3)	0.876 (3)
Mexico	1957	0.498 (5)	0.395 (5)	1.058 (5)
Barbados	1951–52	0.436 (4)	0.383 (4)	0.842 (2)
Puerto Rico	1953	0.394 (1)	0.317 (2)	0.783 (1)

Source: Atkinson (1970)

embodies a view of social welfare, or a value judgement, that we should be concerned about the increased impoverishment of the already poor only if income removed from them were transferred into the hands of people whose income level lay above the mean. Other indices, however, that change in value if any transfer occurs between poor and less poor have embedded in them the different judgement that we should be concerned about the increased impoverishment of the poor if income taken from them were passed on to anyone at a higher income level, irrespective of whether they lay above or below the mean. Similar variations in underlying value judgement can be found upon comparing almost any pair of indices.

Despite such variation in the social value judgements underlying the indices, the ranking of income distributions by Lorenz curve (where the curves lie in relation to each other) and their ranking by any social welfare function will be identical so long as:

(1) the respective Lorenz curves nowhere intersect;
(2) the social welfare function is symmetric and quasi-concave.

(Condition (2) is actually a very general specification of the social welfare function; cf. Kakwani, 1980, chapter 4. Atkinson himself used a more restrictive formulation.) The technicalities of the argument need not concern us here, but even without intensive thought, it should not be surprising to find that condition (1) is often violated; Lorenz curves do, in practice, often intersect. When this occurred, Atkinson showed that two social welfare functions could always be found that would rank the distributions in different ways.

This, then, is the key to the puzzle. Since different social welfare functions generating different social value judgements underlie different indices of inequality, the incidence of intersecting Lorenz curves immediately offers the potential for different indices to rank the distributions represented by the curves in different ways. Figure 8.3 shows two such intersecting curves. By inspection we can see that the distribution represented by curve *A* would be viewed as less unequal by the Gini coefficient. On the other hand, a measure attaching greater weight to inequality specifically at the bottom of the distribution might indicate less inequality in the distribution represented by curve *B*.

The upshot of this discussion is that the comparison of income distributions according to their degree of inequality is much less straightforward than the business of calculating summary indices may make it appear. Thus, to talk about 'increasing' or 'decreasing' relative inequality in a country's income distribution over time may require

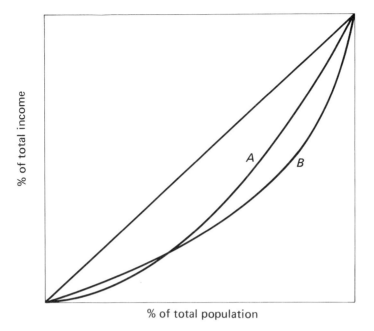

Figure 8.3 Intersecting Lorenz curves

considerable elaboration about the measure(s) used. Ambiguity, ultimately, should not surprise us, for as Sen (1973) remarks, 'the concept of inequality has different facets which may point in different directions' (p. 48). But we should not despair. Making explicit the value judgements underlying measures used is one solution. Atkinson suggests another route. He proposed that conventional measures should be rejected in favour of another type of measure, which explicitly contains a parameter that captures the degree of aversion to inequality felt by society. While this certainly brings the whole issue out into daylight, however, an important difficulty here is devising a satisfactory process for accurately determining this degree of aversion.

Absolute Income Approach
While a heated, protracted and highly technical debate has surrounded the measurement of relative income inequality, discussion of the absolute income approach has been on a rather smaller scale and more or less limited to the development literature. In this approach, the

focus for measurement is upon the actual incomes received by individuals rather than differences between them. Under such measures an improvement in general is said to have occurred when any individual, all other things equal, sees his income rise; and the poorer the individual to receive a given income increase, the greater the improvement is often said to have been.

This general formulation has been adapted in various ways, notably by Ahluwalia and Chenery (1974). They divide the income distribution into quintiles (the poorest 20 per cent grouped under the numerical label '5'; the next poorest 20 per cent under '4'; and so on) and take as their measure of the increased welfare of each group the rate of growth of its income. The overall welfare improvement experienced by society G is then defined as a weighted sum of the growth of income of all groups:

$$G = w_1g_1 + w_2g_2 + w_3g_3 + w_4g_4 + w_5g_5$$

where the values of the w_i can be adjusted to reflect a social judgement on the relative desirability of each group's receiving the fruits of income growth. In particular, if we think that poorer groups would benefit most from a given increment in income, it makes sense to have $w_5 > w_4 > w_3 > w_2 > w_1$, and if we were concerned only with the fortunes of the poorest quintile, we could set $w_5 = 1$ and all the other weights equal to zero. Such a system of 'poverty weights' permits us to observe the extent to which overall income growth assists or conflicts with distributional and poverty objectives.

We leave until later comment about measuring poverty as such. We now pass on to an examination of distributional theory.

THE NEOCLASSICAL THEORY OF INCOME DISTRIBUTION: A BRIEF SUMMARY

In chapter 2 we recalled that, under the 'neoclassical' assumptions of perfectly competitive markets and constant returns to scale in the production function, (1) wage rate and rate of return on capital would be equated to the marginal products of labour and capital, respectively; and (2) the incomes of these two factors (in a two-input world) would exactly exhaust the product available for distribution.

In this type of world it is relatively easy to see how, in principle, the distribution of income is determined. Each individual is assumed to have some endowment of resources (physical, financial, intellectual), and his income can be found by multiplying each of these resource amounts by their marginal products. For greater precision, we need to know more about relative resource endowments, the nature of the technology and patterns of demand.

Under the generally neoclassical assumptions in chapter 1 we showed what would happen to relative factor prices as the aggregate capital–labour ratio varied. Under the same conditions, we shall go a step further here and show how the nature of the technology has to be examined, in addition, if we are to understand how changes occur in one of the simplest measures of income distribution, the relative shares in total income of aggregate capital and labour.

Recall first the neoclassical result from chapter 1 that a rise (fall) in K/L would be associated with a rise (fall) in w/r. This can be alternatively expressed by saying that a rise (fall) in K/L will be associated with a fall (rise) in r/w.

Now, the expression for the relative shares of capital and labour in national income is:

$$\frac{rK}{wL} = \frac{\text{profit per unit of capital} \times \text{quantity of capital}}{\text{wages per unit of labour} \times \text{quantity of labour}}.$$

This can be rewritten as the product of two ratios:

$$\frac{r}{w} \times \frac{K}{L}.$$

Clearly, the relationship established in production between these two ratios will be crucial for determining the relative factor shares.

The missing link that we now need to explore is the elasticity of substitution, σ (sigma). The definition of this elasticity is:[1]

$$\sigma \equiv - \left[d\left(\frac{K}{L}\right) \middle/ \left(\frac{K}{L}\right) \middle/ d\left(\frac{r}{w}\right) \middle/ \left(\frac{r}{w}\right) \right].$$

In words, σ measures the proportional change that occurs in (K/L) when there is a small proportional change in (r/w). The intuition behind σ can be grasped by thinking of an aggregate isoquant (see figure 8.4(a)). With labour measured on the vertical and capital on the horizontal axis,[2] the 'flatter' isocost line BB' represents a lower r/w—that is, a higher w/r—than does AA'. Further (as a reflection of our analysis in chapter 1), AA' is associated in equilibrium with a technique of lower K/L—i.e. higher L/K—than is BB'.

Let us turn now to figure 8.4(b). Here AA' and BB' are reproduced as in figure 8.4(a), but an isoquant of different shape appears. This isoquant is much more sharply curved. Comparing figures 8.4(a) and (b), it will be noticed that for a similar difference between, or change

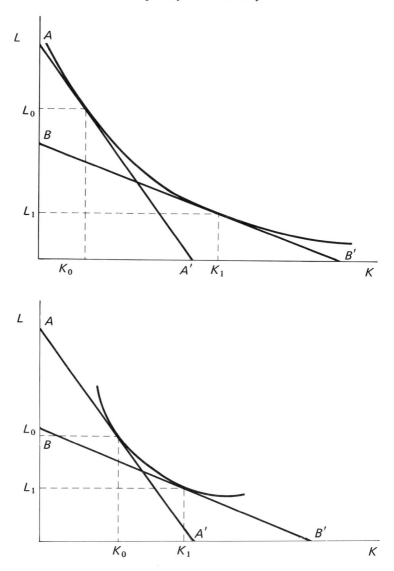

Figure 8.4 Deriving the elasticity of substitution (σ) from the aggregate isoquant

in the value of, r/w, changes of quite different proportion have occurred in the equilibrium (K/L) ratios. In the case of figure 8.4(b), the quantity response, $d(K/L)/(K/L)$, is much less than in figure

8.4(a). Since $d(r/w)/(r/w)$ is in each case the same, a glance back at the definition of σ reveals that the value σ takes will vary with the curvature of the isoquant. If the proportionate response in K/L to a relative price change is large, then σ will be large; if the response is small, then σ will be small.

Thus σ captures, in terms of a number that can be measured, the curvature of the isoquant, and since the degree of this curvature reflects the ease with which inputs can be substituted for each other, σ gives us a measure of the flexibility of the technology.

This in itself is important, but it has particular significance for our factor shares ratio. If $\sigma = 1$, this reflects the fact (look at the definition to convince yourself) that a given proportionate rise (fall) in r/w will be associated with a fall (rise) in K/L of identical proportions; in other words, σ can be equal to 1 only if $d(K/L)/(K/L)$ and $d(r/w)/(r/w)$ are equal to each other. In this case, factor shares will be unaffected by changes in the relation between profit and wage rates since techniques will alter in response to the changed factor price relativity in an exactly offsetting way.

Suppose now that $\sigma < 1$. This would be the case if the technology were inflexible to an extent which meant that a given proportionate change (say, 5 per cent) in r/w would be associated with a change of lesser proportions (say, 4 per cent) in K/L. Given that r/w and K/L move in opposite directions, this would mean that if r/w fell—perhaps because of the introduction of minimum wage legislation which raised w relative to r—K/L would not be able, for purely technological reasons, to rise by a similar proportion. In turn, therefore, the overall value of rK/wL would fall—capital's share in national income would fall relative to that of labour's; or, alternatively, labour's share would rise relative to that of capital.

Finally, if $\sigma > 1$, any given proportionate change in r/w would be associated with a greater proportionate change in K/L. In this case, a rise in w relative to r would reduce r/w by less than K/L would rise in response—and so capital's relative share would increase.

In principle, σ can take any value between zero (where no substitution possibilities at all, at a given output level, are permitted by the technology) and infinity (where capital and labour are perfect substitutes). By construction, $\sigma = 1$ in the Cobb–Douglas production function and must be constant (though not at unity) in the constant elasticity of substitution production function.

Empirically, the values of σ that have been found in practice vary quite widely. Cline (1975) reports that, for the manufacturing sectors of the Philippines, Argentina and Chile respectively, studies have estimated σ to be well above unity, about unity and about 0.33 (see Williamson, 1971; Katz, 1969; Behrman, 1972). In work on 20 manufacturing industries in Venezuela, Sines (1979) finds σ to range from 0.353 to 1.378. Studies of the agricultural sector suggest elasticities in that area of perhaps unity or rather more. Morawetz (1974) concludes that no useful generalization is possible. Recall also that Lall's (1978) survey of evidence on techniques used by MNCs left him with the view that efficient processing probably did involve a fairly 'rigid' set of techniques.

We have spelled this analysis out in some detail because the results it embodies are often employed in the development literature without much elaboration. (See, for example, Cline, 1975, p. 36; Chenery *et al.*, 1974, p. 75.) Important points can easily escape our attention in the absence of background like this. However, while an understanding of the meaning of σ is important from the point of view of interpreting the thrust of parts of the literature, it should not be thought that the neoclassical distribution theory in which it fits can be applied without hesitation to developing countries. We have questioned most of the growth model built on largely neoclassical assumptions, and the related distribution theory is similarly prone to criticism.

The assumptions of the model envisage a world of perfectly informed, smoothly working markets in which market-determined equilibrium prices are established equal to the marginal cost of production. In fact, the confined nature of many markets in LDCs encourages monopoly (particularly under protection), with the result that price will lie above marginal cost; furthermore, labour markets are characterized by the non-equilibrium feature of a labour surplus and the prevalence of institutionally determined wages; capital markets are often subject to quantity rationing and, because of fragmentation, are relatively poor conveyors of information; and the international trading sector is influenced by interferences such as tariffs and import quotas.

At this point we introduce an alternative theory of the functional distribution which takes as its cue anxieties about the helpfulness of placing changes in the ratio of capital and labour (both homogeneous and qualitatively unchanging by assumption) at the centre of the stage. In a famous article, Kaldor (1955) complains that the neoclassical theory 'focuses attention on a relatively unimportant feature of a growing economy' (p. 91). Accumulation does not, he says, take the form of 'deepening' the structure of capital at a given state of knowledge (that is, merely increasing K/L in the absence of technical progress), but rather attempts to keep pace with technical advance and growth in the labour force.

Kaldor then turns to building his own Keynesian distribution theory. Its importance lies in the fact that it relates factor shares to aggregate savings propensities and so can be used to interrelate growth, distribution and changes in income distribution. Kaldor divides income into wages, W, and profits, P, and assumes that the wage-earners' marginal propensity to save (s_w) is less than that of capitalists (s_p). Investment is assumed to be exogenously determined. Thus:

$$Y \equiv W + P$$

$$I \equiv S$$

$$S \equiv S_w + S_p = s_w W + s_p P$$

where S_w and S_p are aggregate savings out of wages and profits, and proportional saving functions are assumed. Then

$$I = s_p P + s_w (Y - P)$$

$$= (s_p - s_w) P + s_w Y$$

so that

$$\frac{I}{Y} = (s_p - s_w) \frac{P}{Y} + s_w \tag{8.1}$$

and

$$\frac{P}{Y} = \frac{1}{s_p - s_w} \frac{I}{Y} - \frac{s_w}{s_p - s_w}. \tag{8.2}$$

Thus, if we know the propensities to save, the share of profits in income can be found simply by reference to the ratio of investment to output. The share of wages in income is what is left. In an extreme but often cited case it may be assumed that $s_w = 0$, in which case (8.2) simplifies to

$$P = \left(\frac{1}{s_p} \right) I,$$

which by assumption leaves workers to spend all they earn and, according to the model, raises the total profit of capitalists by the identical amount that they spend on investment goods. On the same assumption, and supposing that I/Y and s_p remain constant, the wage share also remains constant even though real wages increase automatically with increasing output per man.

But despite rising real wages for labour 'capitalists perpetuate their economic positions: the more they have, the more they invest and accumulate, the more profits they earn, the more they can save and reinvest, the more capital gains they reap, and so the spiral goes on' (Sahota, 1978, p. 22). Growth and rising real incomes for all result, of course, from the operation of a Keynesian multiplier with rising investment.

Engaging though this theory appears, it is no less immune from criticism than the neoclassical. As we pointed out in chapter 5, the determinants of investment are many and varied, and to assume the investment rate given exogenously begs too many questions, both of cause and effect. Furthermore, the model becomes indeterminate (impossible to solve uniquely) once the number of income classes rises to three or more. This in turn makes it hard to apply in the many-income-class world of the size distribution of income.

DETERMINANTS OF THE PERSONAL DISTRIBUTION OF INCOME

As we remarked earlier, an income distribution over persons can be represented by curves such as we might find in seeking the frequency distribution of examination marks over a class. Our task in this section is to try to understand the factors determining the shape of the curve that represents this distribution. From explanations drawing primarily on the distribution of ability, we proceed to consider the influence of random chance and rational choice under varying attitudes to risk. In recent years, frameworks such as these have come to be dominated by the views of the human capital theorists, here pressing their claims to explain distributional patterns rather than growth performance. But the human capital approach is not without its critics, and other work has asked what determines variations in educational investment in the first place and whether demand for education and the nature of labour market must also be drawn in.

The first theory we consider relates the distribution of income to that of individual abilities. It was assumed by the early theorists of this school that natural abilities were normally distributed over a large population of individuals, and the theory hypothesized that incomes, more or less directly determined by ability, would have a similarly normal distribution. Now, by observation, it gradually became clear that personal income distributions often had a tendency to be lognormal (that is, symmetric in the logarithms of income but in its absolute values skewed to the right) rather than normal. One reason for this might be that, even though intelligence quotients are distributed normally, the attributes connected with different degrees of earning power may not be. To explain the finding in another way, R. Gibrat devised what is known as the 'law of proportional effect'. In his analysis, Gibrat assumed an initial distribution of income (which could be completely equal), then worked out the effect upon it of subjecting individual incomes to random percentage changes, independent of the income level. Under these circumstances, he found, a lognormal distribution would always be generated. Gibrat's analysis has been shown to have technical defects, but while these can be corrected for, the economist is likely to worry more that this type of stochastic approach tells him little about human behaviour or rational choice, and their role in shaping the distribution.

Milton Friedman supposes that individual choice among different occupations is determined by individual attitudes towards risk.[3] Individuals can be classified as either risk-lovers or risk-averters. This classification is defined in terms of the relationship between utility and income. If an individual's marginal utility of income rises as income increases (see figure 8.5(a)), he is defined as a risk-lover; if it falls with rising income (see figure 8.5(b)), he is defined as a risk-averter. To see why this is so, suppose an individual has an income of Y_1, and has the opportunity either of not gambling and keeping this income intact for certain, or of engaging in a gamble that offers a 50–50 chance of incomes Y_0 (if he loses) and Y_2 (if he wins), where the mean or expectation of Y_0 and Y_2 is Y_1. To see whether he will gamble (and qualify as a risk-lover) or not (to qualify as a risk-averter), we must compare the utility he will derive on the one hand from Y_1 for certain and, on the other, from the risky prospect of identical expected income.

Looking at figure 8.5(a), we see that, if an individual's marginal utility of income rises consistently, the utility he derives from the certain prospect of Y_1 is U_1 while that associated with the risky prospect is:

$$\tfrac{1}{2}U(Y_0) + \tfrac{1}{2}U(Y_2) = \tfrac{1}{2}U_0 + \tfrac{1}{2}U_2 = U_E.$$

Since $U_E > U_1$, he will derive greater utility from the prospect of taking a gamble whose expected income is Y_1 than from not gambling. He is a risk-lover. If, as in figure 8.5(b), the individual's marginal utility of income falls consistently, $U_1 > U_E$ and the individual would choose the certain prospect of Y_1 rather than the risky prospect. He is risk-averse.

Broadly speaking, the shape of the overall income distribution will depend in this view on the distribution of attitudes towards risk in a society. Suppose most individuals are risk-averse in a society but a minority are risk-lovers. The income distribution for each class is normal, but that of risk-lovers is much more spread out and has a higher mean. If the two are added together a distribution skewed to

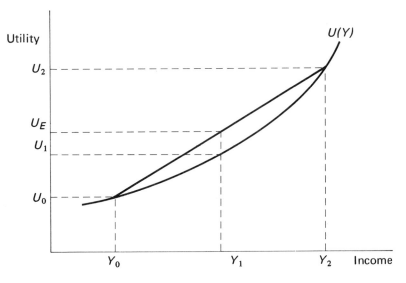

Figure 8.5(a) The utility function of a risk-lover

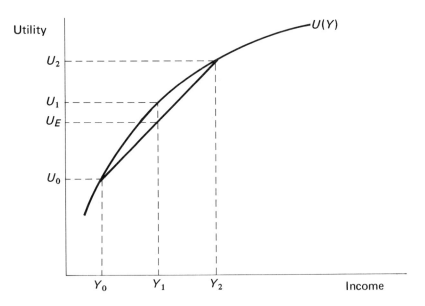

Figure 8.5(b) The utility function of a risk-averter

the right emerges (see Bronfenbrenner, 1971, pp. 58–9, for a simple demonstration).

Friedman's appeal to the exercise of rational choice is taken over and extended by human capital theory—to the point where it all but eclipses its parent analysis. (The judgement is Sahota's 1978, in an excellent survey of the area.) Indeed, Fields (1980) identifies the human capital model as 'the main theory of the size distribution of income' (p. 129), albeit now one that is much under fire. We have already explored in detail (in chapter 6) how human capital theory postulates that individuals invest in themselves as the result of rational optimizing decisions based on estimates of discounted, expected values of future costs and benefits. Mincer (1958) may be taken as a seminal analysis in this context.

Mincer assumes (by contrast with the ability theorists) that all individuals have identical ability, and equal opportunity to enter any line of work. These assumptions rule out any influence on the income distribution from these directions. Training time, however, varies from one occupation to another, and each year of training is assumed to reduce an individual's earning span by a year. Training costs are made to vary positively with length of training. Mincer then looks for the ratio of annual earnings of individuals differing by, say, x years of training. He finds that, if all individuals equalized the present value (PV) of their expected lifetime earnings when they were choosing their occupations, (1) those who chose to take more training command higher annual pay; (2) the difference between actual annual earnings is larger for any given difference x, the higher is the discount rate used, because of the greater sacrifice involved in initially postponing earning activity; (3) the actual earnings difference also increases with decreases in the length of work-life, because initial costs must be recouped more quickly; and (4) the difference in earnings between individuals relates not only to the *differences* between them in time spent training (see point (1)), but also to the absolute number of years for which each has been trained. This can be best understood through Mincer's illustrative example of two pairs of individuals for each of which $x = 2$. His conclusion is that the relative earning differences between a pair with ten and eight years of training are larger than those between a pair with four and two years of training. The difference between the earnings ratios is, however, slight, and Mincer adopts as a constant for all two-year differences the ratio between the earnings of a person with two years' training and one with none. This means that annual earnings corresponding to various levels of training differing by the same length x must differ by a multiplicative constant. This constant converts any given training distribution into an earnings distribution. Even if the former were normal and thus symmetric, Mincer finds, the latter would necessarily turn out to be positively skewed.

Despite the obvious appeal of the human capital approach, we must view it these days as a stepping-stone towards understanding rather than as a final destination. As Cline (1975) points out, the limitations of the model start to appear once we consider a startling implication of it which Mincer did not explicitly state: namely, that all incomes are in reality equal. Observed differences are statistical illusions arising from the fact that a high-income recipient will have been on the job a shorter time than his low-income cohort. As we saw, the model by construction requires the present value of expected lifetime earnings—the definition of permanent income—to be equal for all. This is plausible within the human capital theorists' generally competitive framework but much less so in the conditions prevailing in most LDCs. In particular, family background and inherited material wealth need to be additionally considered as causes of the human investment on the supply side, while it should be recognized that the demand for labour (barely considered at all by much human capital theory) can also contribute significantly to our understanding of the overall picture.

On the first point, let us follow Meade (1964, 1976) in defining inheritance in terms of genetic make-up, parental training, social contacts and inherited property. All of these endowments (dubbed 'fortunes' by Meade) interact to influence incomes and the accumulation of both physical and human capital. For example, the already rich are better placed than the poor to evaluate the relative merits of alternative financial investments, and better placed to take the greater risks with which higher returns are associated. They are also better able to afford the educational opportunities for themselves and their children that, together with their social contacts, ensure better jobs—particularly if educational qualifications are used as a screening device. Notice that many of the features described here imply the existence of market imperfections (imperfect information important among them), which human capital theory assumes away.

Turning now to the demand side, we find that a number of commentators have suggested that the proportion of the population receiving low incomes depends at least as much on the availability of and access to well-remunerated jobs as it does on the availability of education and training. The human capital theorists seek greater income equality through equalizing the amounts of education enjoyed by a population. (Remember it was differences here that generated inequality in Mincer's view.) This competing school suggests that lack of demand for skills and/or the availability of most work in only low-paying sectors—irrespective of education—may hold the key to distributional policy.

One authority here, Thurow (1975), suggests that the distribution of wages over the employment spectrum is determined primarily by the attributes of particular jobs. While Thurow's explanation of each job wage stresses the marginal product of the job, Cline is more persuaded that organized industrial jobs often have relatively high wages reflecting union activity in the sector; government jobs are also well remunerated (perhaps because of the influence of elites or minimum wage legislation); but traditional agriculture is characterized by an institutionally determined, low subsistence wage. This profile of job openings and associated wages defines the earnings distribution in a way that changes only with changes in the structure of the economy. Thurow views the labour force as a queue awaiting job opportunities, their position in the queue determining which type of job they may take. If educational attainment is viewed as a screening device, formal qualifications (related to length of schooling) can be seen as determining position in the queue. In this framework it is no good, from the point of view of distribution, to allow everyone to spend longer in the education system, for wage relativities are fixed by the job structure. The only result of increasing education will be to raise the level of qualification that higher paid jobs can demand.

Other commentators have argued that job profiles of the type just analysed provide clear evidence of labour market segmentation. Fields shows that such a conclusion is not always permissible. He points out that the key to labour market segmentation theory is really the claim that such markets are 'restrictive in the sense that some individuals are prevented from acquiring more education moving to higher-paying locations, or in other ways taking action aimed at increasing their attractiveness to the market' (Fields, 1980, p. 131). In other words, while the human capital theorists assume no bar to individual optimization, the labour segmentation school concentrates on the conditions that constrain and interfere with such optimizing behaviour. The operation of such constraints restricts the equalizing tendencies implicit in intersectoral and geographical mobility and, in the particular instance of a dualistic economy, may prevent workers ever escaping from low-paid underemployment in the traditional sector.

This section has been dominated by considerations relating to the earnings of labour. Notice, however, (1) that rich and poor alike in many LDCs also receive property incomes; and (2) that within the agricultural sector important inter-country variations in distribution may arise as a reflection of differing tenural arrangements on the land.

Looking at (1) first, suppose that society can be broken into two classes—rich and poor.[4] The difference between the two resides in their initial capital stocks—$K_R > K_P$. On the other hand, each receives the same wage per period, w, for any labour services rendered, and each earns the same interest rate r on his capital. Under these circumstances, it can be shown how changes in inequality in the distribution of income depend quite specifically upon saving behaviour.

Suppose first that both types of individual have similar fixed saving propensities, s, out of each type of income. Then the poor man saves in any given period

$$S_P = s(rK_P + w)$$

and the rich man saves

$$S_R = s(rK_R + w).$$

By definition, savings in any period constitute the additional capital accumulated in that period (dK_i/dt, $i = P, R$). Thus, the proportional change or percentage growth rate in capital assets ($dK_i/dt)/K_i$, can be found as

$$s\left(r + \frac{w}{K_P}\right) \quad \text{and} \quad s\left(r + \frac{w}{K_R}\right)$$

for the poor and rich man, respectively. Since $K_R > K_P$, $w/K_R < w/K_P$, and so

$$\frac{dK_P/dt}{K_P} > \frac{dK_R/dt}{K_R};$$

that is, the poor man's capital grows more rapidly than the rich man's, and so their capital stocks and incomes move towards each other over time, leading to an equalizing tendency in the distribution of income. Suppose next that saving occurs (as in the extreme Kaldor model) only out of property income at rate s, while all wages are consumed. (The difference here is that the population is divided according to income class, both receiving wages and property income, rather than according to factors provided, as in Kaldor's model of labourers and capitalists.) Then

$$S_P = srK_P = \frac{dK_P}{dt}$$

and

$$S_R = srK_R = \frac{dK_R}{dt}$$

Thus

$$\frac{dK_P/dt}{K_P} = sr = \frac{dK_R/dt}{K_R}$$

and the income distribution remains unchanged over time.

Finally, if the propensities to save from wages, s_w, and property income, s_k, are different but both positive, then

$$S_P = s_k r K_P + s_w W = \frac{dK_P}{dt}$$

and

$$S_R = s_k r K_R + s_w W = \frac{dK_R}{dt}$$

so that

$$\frac{dK_P/dt}{K_P} = s_k r + s_w \frac{w}{K_P}$$

and

$$\frac{dK_R/dt}{K_R} = s_k r + s_w \frac{w}{K_R}.$$

If $s_k > s_w > 0$ (the basic Kaldor assumption), capital stocks and incomes will converge, but if $s_k > s_w = 0$, then the income distribution will not tend to equalize.

Turning now to point (2), take as an example an entrenched landlord and tenant system. This may engender considerable inequality within the agricultural sector if landlords take large surpluses for themselves, as rent, and leave tenants with only subsistence income. In turn, workers on the land may find their incomes to be much below those of industrial workers. Land reform, on the other hand, may give owner-ship of parcels of land to former tenants, the distribution of income within the sector coming to depend then upon varying quality of land, and the owner's willingness and ability to work it more productively and to innovate upon it. If land reform leads to a general rise in agricultural incomes and this rise occurs more rapidly than income increases elsewhere, we should expect greater overall equality.

This sort of thinking has been one of the main forces behind the so-called 'Green Revolution', with its emphasis on raising rural incomes through the use of irrigation, modern farming machinery and high-yielding varieties of staple crops. Such 'Green Revolution' innovations require land reform in most cases if their beneficial effects are to be maximized. For more on this, see chapter 9.

Clearly, we are moving here into the area of policy-induced changes in the income distribution. While it must be recognized that government policy (through taxing, subsidies, land reform, tariffs and the like) can influence the distribution of income, we leave these considerations until later. Next, we look at the connections between growth and income distribution.

LINKS BETWEEN DISTRIBUTION AND GROWTH

Following the useful distinction made by Cline (1975), this section will consider, in turn, the effects of growth on distribution and the effects of distribution on growth. It must be expected that influences flowing in both directions will do so simultaneously. Since development is taken these days to be reflected both in growth and distributional experience, we are at the heart here of the sub-discipline.

Influence of Growth on Distribution
One of the most deeply entrenched hypotheses of economic development is the suggestion that distribution will become more unequal with growth. This proposal was given perhaps its most influential form by Kuznets (1955). He argued that, as real income per head increased from the lowest levels, the personal distribution of income would become more unequal but that at some critical point in the middle-income range it would start tending back towards equality again. Diagrammatically (see figure 8.6) there would be, he suggested, a U-shaped relationship between income per head and an index of the relative equality of the income distribution. To gauge changes in relative inequality, Kuznets inspected the changes, over time, of the income shares received by upper and lower quintiles of the distribution for the USA, England and Germany.

We shall examine the extensive empirical work done on this relationship later, but it is important to understand that Kuznets did not present

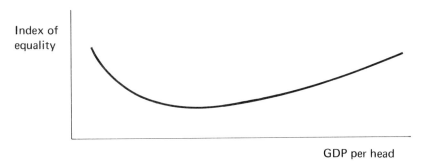

Figure 8.6 The Kuznets relationship

his findings merely as a statistical association. He attempted to explain his findings theoretically. Most of this section will be devoted to examining the theoretical contributions both of Kuznets and of those who have followed.

Kuznets identified two groups of forces working from growth to influence distribution, one related to the concentration of savings in the upper income brackets, the other to the changing structure of the economy. On the first point, Kuznets argues that, if the relatively rich do most or all of the saving in an economy, then with economic growth 'the cumulative effect of such inequality in savings would be the concentration of an *increasing* proportion of income-yielding assets in the hands of the upper groups—a basis for larger income shares of these groups and their descendants' (Kuznets, 1955, p. 7). (In terms of our analysis on p. 265, this is equivalent to saying that s_k and s_w for the poor man are both zero but for the rich man are positive. Here, $(dK_P/dt)/K_P = 0$, but $(dK_R/dt)/K_R > 0$.) This argument is reinforced if we also consider the interactions between physical and human capital analysed by Meade.

On the second point, Kuznets argues that, if inequality in the traditional sector is less than that in the modern, and if modern sector growth is the key to rising real incomes, then the increasing weight of modern sector population means an increasing share for the more unequal of the two sectoral distributions.

These arguments explain the increasing inequality, but to explain the tendency, later, towards greater equality once more, they have to be thrown into reverse. Kuznets suggests that counteracting forces on savings concentration may include a general broadening in the income-generating industrial base and a consequent long-run decline on the returns to property, and policy intervention to limit such concentration. On structural change, he concludes that the major offset to widening overall inequality lies in the rising income share often found to be flowing to the lower income groups in the increasingly large modern sector.

Kuznets's arguments have considerable intuitive appeal, although as Cline (1975, p. 369) demonstrates, the structural change element needs to be treated with particular caution. Kuznets's approach does not, however, establish the inevitability of the U-shaped pattern. That has been done, using the coefficient of variation, by Swamy (1967); the Gini coefficient, by Knight (1976) and Fields (1980); log variance, by Robinson (1976); and both Gini coefficient and income shares, by Lydall (1977).

Fields's proof (1980, pp. 40–56) is built on the observation that overall growth, ΔY, in an economy assumed to be dualistic can be decomposed in the following way:

ΔY = (growth due to modern sector growth) + (growth due to traditional sector growth)

= [(effect of modern sector *enlargement*) + (effect of modern sector *enrichment*)

+ (*interaction* of modern sector enlargement and enrichment)]

+ [*traditional* sector enrichment effect].

Enlargement-derived growth springs from a sector including a larger proportion of the economically active population; enrichment-derived growth, from the increasing average incomes of workers in a sector.

In general, the modern sector enlargement effect is greater, the greater is increased modern sector employment and the size of the modern–traditional wage differential; the modern sector enrichment effect is greater, the faster modern sector wages are rising and the more important the modern sector is as an employer; and the traditional sector enrichment effect is greater, the faster traditional sector wages rise and the more important the sector is as an employer.

Dualistic development can then be classified in three limiting cases. In modern sector enlargement growth, development is achieved via expanding the size of the modern sector and holding wages in each sector constant, but with modern sector wages higher. In modern sector enrichment growth, numbers and wages in the traditional sector remain fixed and higher incomes flow only to a fixed number of persons in the modern sector. Traditional sector enrichment growth envisages the benefits of growth flowing in equal proportions to all in that sector.

The first of these strategies is that which 'most closely reflects the essential nature of economic development as conceived by the existing literature' (Fields, 1980, p. 47). In this case, the simplest way of viewing the result is to take as our measure of inequality simply the income share to the poorest 40 per cent of the population. When the modern sector is relatively small, most of the population still live in the traditional sector where incomes are relatively low and, by construction, static. The poorest 40 per cent thus see no change in their absolute incomes, but as overall income grows through modern sector enlargement, so their share in the whole falls. Eventually, however, the modern sector grows large enough to account for 60 per cent of the population, and progressively accounts for more and more of it. The poorest 40 per cent thus start to benefit from growth and their share rises.

Fields also shows that the Gini coefficient follows a similar course but starts to reduce in value (betokening a reduction in relative inequality according to the value judgements it embodies) before the share of the poorest 40 per cent starts to rise.

While this result is important for establishing the conditions under which we can be certain of observing the Kuznets relationship, it is equally important to note that, whether Gini coefficient or the share of poorest 40 per cent is used as the measure, inequality unambiguously rises under modern sector enrichment growth and falls under traditional sector enrichment growth. Given that real-world development need be neither of the modern sector enlargement type nor, indeed, a pure version of any one of the three types analysed (mixtures being a possibility), we should not necessarily expect to find the Kuznets relationship always appearing in practice. The evidence is surveyed later.

Before we proceed to the evidence, we shall examine briefly some of the other forces that might link growth to distribution.

One school of thought points to the increasing heterogeneity of industries and labour skills that usually accompanies growth. Since structural change of a more or less complex kind seems to accompany all growth, the increasing heterogeneity implicit in that change certainly requires attention. The usual argument is that, at least in the short run, those who already have, or can obtain early, scarce skills needed for growth industries will be able to command a quasi-rent on their specialized labour services. For those who are trained on the job locally, the force of this argument will rather depend upon the extent to which trainees are required and enabled to bear training costs and the degree of mobility subsequently open to them (see chapter 6).

In the longer run, we should expect the essentially short-run phenomenon of quasi-rent to disappear in relation to any given skill in any case. It has been suggested, however, that originally scarcity-justified payments of this kind might become entrenched in the longer term. Instead of competitive forces being permitted to erode high wages, it has been suggested that high-wage sectors may sometimes become 'protected' by collective bargaining agreements in industries with strong unions or by the policies of MNCs wishing to show themselves favourably disposed to local employees (see Harberger, 1971, p. 563).

Johnson (1973) argues that distributional outcomes will differ with increasing job heterogeneity, depending on the nature of preferences in the society. In a society where all members felt strongly and similarly about the relative desirability of different jobs, we would expect, says Johnson, that those who did jobs uniformly regarded as unpleasant would be able to require, successfully, high cash incomes to compensate them. Supposing a country at the earliest stages of development to have such tastes, the appearance of a wider range of jobs than before (with modern sector jobs uniformly regarded as desirable) might thus be expected to lead to increasing inequality. On the other hand, suppose that education, structural change and modernization lead to a much greater diversity of views on the relative desirability of jobs. Then people would allocate themselves among occupations according to their own tastes and, 'we would find a tendency towards equality of incomes, but also a segregation of the population into those who traditionally did another (the tradition resting on personal tastes)' (Johnson, 1973, pp. 212–13).

Let us now focus more precisely upon education. If human capital accumulation assists with growth on the one hand and if inequality is explained primarily in terms of unequal educational opportunities on the other, both growth and distributional objectives should be sensitive to increasing educational expenditure, particularly if channelled in the direction of those who would not otherwise receive much (or any) education. In this case it is perhaps appropriate to view the growth and distributional effects as simultaneous results of the independent source of change, the education system. At the same time, though, growth from physical capital accumulation and growth of demand for exports could be seen as the start of a process that subsequently makes it possible to broaden the scope of education. Assuming education can be relied on to be a beneficial influence, spending on the education system should then reinforce the growth tendencies already operating and simultaneously should permit the fruits of growth to be divided up at minimum cost to distributional goals.

On a less optimistic note, recall that, in relation to spending on education, whether undertaken by private individuals or the state, rates of return on investment can turn out to be much lower than expected. Even for just growth objectives to be effectively met, careful manpower planning and an assessment of the optimum structure of education may well be necessary. As far as distributional objectives are concerned, we saw earlier in this chapter that inequality may spring as much from the employment profile or job structure as from supply-side considerations. And even on the supply side it is now recognized that cultural, genetic and material inheritance factors can still leave their mark on earnings performance, even if all have equal access to the education system.

An entirely different group of arguments relates domestic inequality to an LDC's position internationally. A first, widely canvassed hypothesis here is that foreign investment must increase the inequality of the distribution at the same time as it promotes growth. We can think of circumstances when it might—when $\sigma > 1$, for example, as the capital–labour ratio is raised by foreign investment and labour's share in national income falls; or if foreign investment is associated with a strategy of modern sector enrichment growth; or (as we see in a moment) if foreign investment occurs in a context of protected import substitution. On the other hand, we think of other conditions in which it might not. If foreign investment were directed wholly towards traditional sector enrichment, it would not. If a strategy of modern sector enlargement growth were already well under way, it might not. And as Cline (1975) points out, under normal neoclassical assumptions, labour's share in national income will be raised relative to that of capital when foreign investment occurs because more jobs will be created and at the same time wages will rise relative to the return on diminishingly scarce capital. This should reduce inequality in the size distribution so long as: (1) foreign investment does not supplant investment that would otherwise have occurred domestically; and (2) foreign investment does not induce an increased degree of skewness in the distribution of labourers' incomes by increasing the income differentials between skilled and unskilled.

A second focus for discussion here is the effect on distribution of import substitution industrialization. We noted in the last chapter that such a strategy, pursued behind a tariff wall, had the effect of disadvantaging the majority of the population in most LDCs—those resident in the agricultural sector. It was argued that the terms of trade were turned in this strategy against agricultural goods, leaving recipients of agricultural incomes less well off in real terms, and that, simultaneously, protection permitted substantial profits in the modern sector to go hand in hand with inefficiency. The implications for distribution of achieving growth in this way are clear. But, as we also noted, growth through industrialization can take other forms and their distributional consequences may be quite different.

The framework of dependency theory has also been used to analyse distributional issues. It, too, identifies foreign investment, with its capital-intensive techniques, as a source of inequality, particularly when the vehicle of investment is the MNC. Furthermore, import substitution policies are now admitted by some in this school (Sunkel, 1973, for example) to have produced only another version of the 'centre-and-periphery' type of world generated initially by development through primary export expansion. In such a picture, both international and internal inequality are seen to be inevitable.

As a final note, recall that if a minority already holds most of the capital assets in a country, its growth is likely to be reflected disproportionately in their incomes and those of their descendants who inherit their wealth. In other words, the distribution of income, particularly in the early stages of growth and in the agricultural sector, is likely to reflect the initial distribution of assets or wealth, especially land. The nature of the distribution of incomes as growth and structural change occur will, in this light, depend partly on the saving habits of the rich and partly on the extent to which they and their descendants can 'switch' their capital into uses where highest returns continue to be offered.

Influence of Distribution on Growth

It is fairly easy to show, using the apparatus of the aggregate consumption and saving functions, that the implications for growth of different income distributions might vary substantially.

Suppose first (see figure 8.7) that the aggregate consumption function takes the form suggested by Keynes: that it has a positive intercept and declining MPC. Consider now two two-person economies, E and U, each with the same aggregate consumption function. Let the incomes of the rich and poor in each society be, respectively, Y_{RE} and Y_{PE}, and

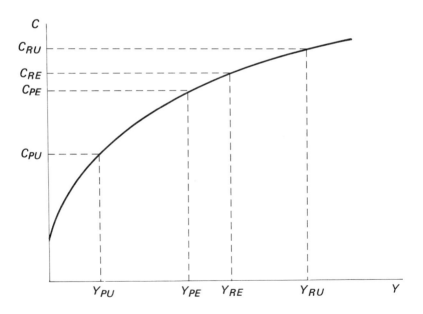

Figure 8.7 Aggregate consumption function: diminishing marginal propensity to consume

Y_{RU} and Y_{PU}.[5] Suppose that $Y_{RE} < Y_{RU}$ and $Y_{PE} > Y_{PU}$ (see figure 8.7). Since incomes in E are less widely dispersed than in U, we shall say E has a more equal distribution of incomes than U.

Suppose now that the growth rate depends either exclusively or importantly upon the domestic saving rate—because of the capital investment it permits. What difference does the distribution make?

In U, total consumption is $(C_{PU} + C_{RU})$; in E $(C_{PE} + C_{RE})$. Now by inspection we can see that the total consumption in U is less than that in E, and since each country has the same income, this means total saving and thus growth rate will be greater in U than in E.

This sort of argument has led many to look with hope rather than despair upon relatively unequal distributions on income and to caution against redistribution in favour of the poor. Ignoring for a moment the argument that alleviating absolute poverty might be considered a desirable goal in itself, let us notice however that the argument will not go through anyway if the consumption function is linear. In this case (see figure 8.8), $(C_{PU} + C_{RU}) = (C_{PE} + C_{RE})$, and no amount of redistribution can make any difference to saving and growth. At this level the argument devolves, then, on the nature of the aggregate consumption function.

As Cline (1972) has argued, however, this is not quite all. Redistribution of income could influence growth in ways other than through the savings ratio, through what are called 'demand composition

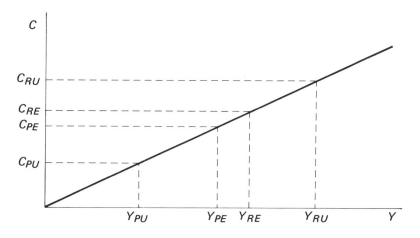

Figure 8.8 Aggregate consumption function: constant marginal propensity to consume

effects'. Here, the crucial assumption is that the poor have a different pattern of consumption behaviour from that of the rich, so that transferring income from rich to poor will change the overall demand structure of the economy. In particular, it is argued that the poor will tend to spend on 'basic' rather than 'luxury' goods. Such goods, it is said, need to be imported much less than luxuries, thus freeing foreign exchange to finance other imports which can contribute directly to growth. Furthermore, the mass market potential and the relative homogeneity and divisibility of basic goods offer greater scope for scale economies to be reaped in local production than do luxuries. Finally, the production of basic goods will, it is suggested, be relatively labour-intensive in processing, again freeing scarce capital for use elsewhere. Each of these arguments is open to question. The relatively poor might be no less prone to import than the rich, even where basics are concerned, and if import substitution is already well under way, there may be little opportunity for further import reduction. Economies of scale gained in producing basics might have to be weighed against losses of scale economy in producing goods favoured by the rich. And there is no reason in logic why basic goods should necessarily be more labour-intensive in production than luxuries.

As for other factors, we noted in chapter 6 that nutrition could bear significantly upon labour productivity and that increasing the nutritional value of the food intake of the poor could therefore be viewed as an investment in human capital by society. Redistribution from the already well-nourished rich could play its part here. Finally, to the extent that increasing relative and absolute affluence encourage parents to plan for smaller families, redistribution may assist in raising income per head in the long run.

Evidence

In this section we give a brief critical review of the evidence that has been produced to examine the relationships between growth and income distribution. We start with the Kuznets hypothesis.

Tests of this hypothesis take two forms. The first and most widely performed takes 'spot' observations on GDP per head and some index of inequality for a wide range of countries at different stages of development. Using this cross-section of observations, it then goes on to make inferences about the relationship, over time, between changes in inequality and changes in income level. The second type of test looks at the experience, over time, of individual countries and, with observations on income and inequality for a sequence of periods, gives direct information on how changes occur.

For cross-sectional work Kuznets (1955, 1963) and Kravis (1960) arrived early on the scene with relevant data, and were followed with much larger samples by Adelman and Morris (1973), Paukert (1973), Ahluwalia (1974, 1976), Chenery and Syrquin (1975) and Lydall (1977). Working over these data in various ways, these commentators concluded among them that, on average, developed countries were characterized by less inequality than were LDCs; while, among the LDCs themselves, it was the poorest that exhibited on average the least inequality. This seems to provide substantial support for the U-shaped relationship, but on closer examination it can be seen that the pattern is actually much less clear.

A first critical point relates to use of data, a second to the inferences permissible from them. On the former, the conclusions reached above were based on relationships observed between the average level of inequality and average GDP per head in groups of countries bracketed together according to GDP per head. Once observations are made upon income–inequality relationships on a country-by-country basis (following the rule that the best results always derive from making use of all information available), it becomes obvious that, within any group of countries, relative inequality varies at least as much as between groups. Fitting a line to this, disaggregated data still lead to the conclusion that the highest levels of relative inequality arise in countries with low to middle levels of income, but because variation around the line is so great it can hardly be claimed to be a good predictor. Another way of putting this is to say that inter-country variation in income explains only a relatively small part of inter-country variation in inequality. This, therefore, raises an important question-mark over the extent to which the U-shaped relationship can be interpreted as defining a very precise relationship between inequality and income levels in any given country. Other factors must also be given due weight.

On the question of inferences, it is possible to go from cross-sectional relationships (assuming they exist) to statements about changes in relationships over time only if we assume or believe that every country will or must go through the same course of developmental experience. Suppose, however, that there is in actuality a variety of paths that a country might follow (see Sundrum, 1974, for a full taxonomy). Then each point on the cross-country U-curve could actually be tracing out a path over time that might or might not be U-shaped. Individual observations at particular points on each path could generate, in cross-section, a rather convincing U-shape. But the cross-section U-shape itself is no guarantee that each country must follow the same path (see figure 8.9).

To assure ourselves of the strength or weakness of the Kuznets

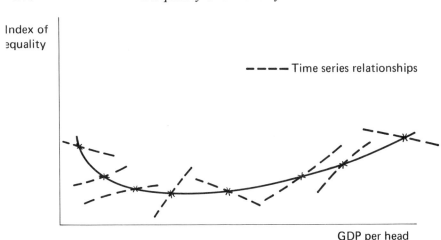

*Figure 8.9 A U-shaped cross-sectional relationship based on non-U-shaped
time–series relationships*

hypothesis, we need therefore to look at the path of the inequality
associated with income growth in individual countries. In an exhaustive
survey of studies on more than 20 LDCs, Fields (1980) concludes that
'According to the best available data, it appears that inequality rose in
seven countries ..., fell in five ..., and exhibited no unambiguous
trend in one ...' (p. 94). These very mixed results are similar to those
found in the multi-country studies of Weisskoff (1970), and Ahluwalia
(1974). The latter study also reveals, separately, that both improvements and deteriorations in relative inequality can be seen both in
rapidly and slowly growing countries.

We are thus led to the unavoidable conclusion that, as foreshadowed
by the theory, relative inequality might actually change in any direction (or even not change at all) as growth proceeds. We need to know
more about the framework in which aggregate income is rising before
we can predict how individual incomes will change relative to each
other. On this score we have already mentioned a number of possibilities: inherited resources, extent and structure of education, government
intervention, nature of comparative advantage, technology and so on.

One of the most famous pieces of empirical work in this area was
performed by Adelman and Morris (1973). Having examined political
and socio-cultural influences as well as economic ones, although
sometimes in a qualitative rather than a quantitative way, they attri-

buted to the human resource improvement rate (measured by school enrolments) the major influence on income distribution. Next most important was what they called 'direct government economic activity' —fiscal policy, tariffs and so on. After these, they saw as other important influences the strength of socioeconomic dualism, potential for economic development, GNP per head and the strength of the labour movement.

Adelman and Morris's study has been criticized from a number of angles which must leave us cautious about their conclusions. But in independent studies by Ahluwalia (1974, 1976), Chenery and Syrquin (1975) and Chiswick (1971), education-related factors are again found to have a significant impact upon inequality. Expanding school enrolments seems to produce greater equality; inequality of educational attainment seems to foreshadow inequality in earnings. Ahluwalia and Chenery and Syrquin both find that, the smaller the share of agriculture in overall production, the greater the inequality in income distribution—a reflection, Fields feels, of his modern sector enlargement form of growth (1980, p. 76). Chenery and Syrquin identify the extent of dualism (mirrored, for them, in the share of primary exports) as a significant contributor to inequality (cf. Adelman and Morris, 1973), while Ahluwalia notes that inequality tends to increase with population growth and to decrease with urbanization and the degree of commitment to socialist objectives in policy-making. Growth in income, as such, is found to have little explanatory power.

POVERTY

When we talked about 'the poor' in the last section, we really meant the *relatively* poor. Yet as we said at the start of the chapter, the relatively poor might still be, in absolute terms, quite well off. The purpose of this section is to focus on the absolutely poor. Assuming that there are others in the economy much better off, then the absolutely poor will also be relatively poor. But that is not the main thrust here. The absolutely poor are absolutely impoverished even if there is no relative inequality at all—in which case all will be equally absolutely poor.

MEASURES OF POVERTY

As it turns out, devising a poverty measure can involve complications just as with relative inequality. As has often been pointed out in the literature (see for example Sen, 1976; Kakwani, 1980, chapter 15; Fields, 1980, chapter 2), poverty measurement presents two distinct problems. The first is to identify 'the poor' as a group, the second is to determine the intensity of poverty suffered by that group.

The first problem involves choosing some criterion of poverty, the most common example of which is a 'poverty line', defined in real per capita income terms.[6] 'The poor' are then those who fall below that line. Conceptual problems abound even at this stage. Given the fact of income-sharing within the family, and sometimes beyond it into the extended family, we might question whether we should look at individual or at family incomes. Again, if we think of the real content and implications of poverty—hunger, exposure to the elements, disease— there is the question of whether more meaning attaches to measuring income or to direct measures of minimum nutritional intake, or mortality. Further, income measures give an idea of what could be consumed rather than what *is* consumed—yet it is the latter that impinges directly upon poverty. Finally, poverty lines defined in terms of a common currency (say, US dollars) using official exchange rates have been shown to give a much distorted view of international comparisons of absolute poverty. Exchange rates that correspond to purchasing power parity (Kravis, 1960) are much preferable. (For more on these points see Fields, 1980, chapter 5, and references in Sen, 1976, p. 219.)

Suppose that we can agree on some poverty line in a country, call it P. Then 'the poor' are those who fall below it. But what of the intensity of poverty, which we shall index by P, in the country? Perhaps the most widely used measure here is the head count ratio, call it H. This shows the percentage of the total population identified as poor. The problem with this measure is that, for any given number of persons below the poverty line, its value is insensitive to changes in the *amount by which* their conditions place them below the line. In other words, the poor could, on average, be just below or far below the line, and H would not register any distinction between these two situations. Implicit in using H, therefore, is a value judgement that we do not care more about the one situation than the other. A further difficulty with H is that if it is also insensitive to transfers of income within the group of poor. The very poorest well below the line could have their income even further reduced to benefit people only just below the line, and H would again be unchanged.

In response to these two defects, alternative measures have been suggested. To meet the first difficulty, the 'poverty gap' measure is sometimes used. This adds up all the individual amounts by which persons or families fall short of the poverty line, and will clearly increase, for any given number of poor, if any one of them becomes poorer, all other things equal. This measure does not, however, meet the second difficulty. If $1 were transferred from the poorest family to one that was less poor but still below the line, the overall poverty gap would increase by $1 in respect of the first family but fall by $1 in respect of the second. The two would cancel out, and neither H nor the gap measure would change. Use of either H or a gap measure implies that we are not concerned about such transfers—but if we think we should be, we must look for some other index.

Faced with this task, Sen devised a measure that is based on axioms that ensure that neither of the problems implicit in H arises—or, to put it positively, that guarantee sensitivity to the number of poor and also to both the extent of group shortfall beneath the poverty line and to transfers among the poor. This measure, which may be called P_S, can be written

$$P_S = H[I + (1 - I)G]$$

where H is the head count ratio, the percentage of people below the poverty line; I (the 'income gap ratio') gives the percentage of their mean shortfall from the poverty line; and G is the Gini coefficient of the income distribution among those with incomes below the poverty line. (For a full rationale of this measure see Sen, 1976, p. 227; and for diagrammatic representations of it, see Sen, 1976, p. 226 or Kakwani, 1980, p. 333.)

Sen gives no illustrations of his measure, but Kakwani shows that P_S can be rewritten

$$P_S = \frac{H}{\bar{P}} [\bar{P} - \mu^*(1 - G)]$$

where the only new symbol is μ^*, which represents the mean income of the poor. This is closely related to another measure which he independently derives, and which we shall call P_K:

$$P_K = \frac{H}{\mu} [\bar{P} - \mu^*(1 - G)].$$

Where Sen expresses the poverty gap as a percentage of the poverty level $\bar{P}$, Kakwani writes it as a percentage of μ, the mean income in the economy. A simpler but less comprehensive measure from Kakwani, which does not take account of income inequality among the poor, is $H(\bar{P} - \mu^*)/\mu$.

Armed with these indices, Kakwani calculates poverty indices for both Malaysia and India. For the measure defined at the end of the last paragraph, he finds Malaysia with a value of 0.055 and India with one of 0.119. This implies that 5.5 per cent (Malaysia) or 11.9 per cent (India) of total income would have to be transferred from non-poor to poor to eliminate poverty in each country—that is, to bring the poor up at least to the poverty line. In another exercise, he examines urban and rural poverty in each country by using P_k. In each case urban poverty is found to be much less intense than rural, P_k in urban and rural Malaysia taking values of 0.0185 and 0.1232 respectively, and in India values of 0.0692 and 0.1751.

Many, perhaps, would argue that poverty is self-evident and that overly fine distinctions may tend to distract from the urgency of the fundamental problem faced by LDCs. We shall now pass on to consider the determinants of poverty, but it is worth remembering that policy measures designed to attack the problem can be precisely formulated only if the dimensions of the problem have been clearly defined. That was the purpose of dwelling on measurement issues to start with.

THE CHARACTERISTICS OF POVERTY GROUPS

While the above discussion led to statistical measures of poverty, an additional dimension of understanding can be gained through examining attributes that most commonly characterize groups in absolute poverty.

In a widely reported study, Ahluwalia (1974) defines the poor as those in the bottom 40 per cent of the income distribution—a relative measure, certainly, but one that, given the countries examined, would contain large elements of absolutely poor. He concludes: (1) that the poor are disproportionately located in rural rather than urban areas—at least 70 per cent of the poor are to be found in this sector, mostly gaining a living from agriculture; (2) that, in terms of employment status, the bulk of the poor are self-employed farmers (including both owner—cultivators and tenant farmers); and (3) that the problem of poverty is inseparably linked to the availability of land in rural areas, and in both sectors to the availability of capital assets in general.

Notice here that Ahluwalia specifically plays down the importance of wage labour and the implied significance of employment in this context. This does not, of course, invalidate any connections that the structure of labour earnings might have for the overall distribution.

All of Ahluwalia's findings are borne out in a wide-ranging international comparison of poverty group characteristics performed by Fields. Additionally, however, he finds that the incidence of poverty declines with educational attainment, usually rises with family size, and, depressingly, often hits hardest at families headed by workers in the prime of their earning life.

Findings such as these help in defining target groups most in need of the aid of poverty-alleviating policies. On the other hand, as Fields remarks, for any given characteristic outlined above (including rural location, self-employed status, low level of educational attainment), only a proportion of people or families with such characteristics will actually be poor. And even though the proportion may be 'large', policies directed solely according to, say, one or two such characteristics will benefit some who are not poor and exclude others who are.

POVERTY AND GROWTH

Suppose for a moment that we knew for sure that the historical experience of a country could be truthfully reflected in a Kuznets type of U-shaped curve in which the share of the poorest fractiles in total income declined as real incomes per head grow. Must this imply that there had been an absolute decline in the incomes of the poor? Clearly it could. (One example of such experience can be found in relation to the decline of the Indian cotton industry in face of the then technologically advanced competition from Lancashire.) But on the other hand, it need not. The poor will see a decline in their relative share if the rich benefit from growth more rapidly than they do. But this could happen with poor incomes static or even increasing—so long as the incomes of the rich rise more quickly.

Even if we observe a Kuznets-type relationship, therefore, we cannot infer that the poor have become absolutely poorer, and still less that growth in incomes is the cause of increasing poverty in such a case. Yet in their 1973 study, Adelman and Morris concluded not only that the U-shaped Kuznets type of relationship was a characteristic of development (a conclusion we have questioned), but also that LDCs must expect increasing impoverishment to accompany the early stages of growth. To be fair, they reached their conclusion only after much more extensive and sophisticated analysis than can be suggested here. But their methods have been questioned, and the logic of the argument we have just presented demands that we explore a little more deeply the actual links between poverty and growth.

Looking first at cross-section evidence (while bearing in mind its limitations for inferences about changes over time), Ahluwalia (1976) found that the elasticity of the absolute income of the poor with respect to GNP itself per head was both positive and rising as GNP itself increased. This was true whether the poor were defined as the poorest

20, 40 or 60 per cent and irrespective of whether data were drawn from a sample of 60 countries of all kinds or were restricted to a smaller sample of developing countries only. This finding also proved to be consistent simultaneously with increasing relative inequality. Ahluwalia concludes that, 'while the cross-country evidence points to unequal benefits from growth, it does not support the hypothesis of a prolonged decline in absolute incomes for the poor as development proceeds' (1976, p. 335).

But what does time-series analysis reveal? Here, the most comprehensive survey of recent evidence can again be found in Fields (1980). He examines the experience of 13 developing countries for which reliable poverty measures could be calculated for two or more points in time. He summarizes his results as follows:

The best available absolute poverty measures for each of [the] countries suggest that absolute poverty was alleviated in varying degrees in ten . . . and that poverty worsened in three . . .

We would expect that countries with moderate to rapid rates of aggregate economic growth would succeed in upgrading the economic condition of significant numbers of their people—this is the so-called trickle-down theory. The evidence is generally consistent with this view. In nine countries' experiences, growth led to demonstrable improvements in the economic position of the poor (Bangladesh, Brazil, Costa Rica, Pakistan, Puerto Rico, Singapore, Taiwan, Thailand and Mexico), and in one country nongrowth did not (India). On the other hand, three countries' experiences run contrary to the predictions of the trickle-down theory: Argentina and the Philippines because they grew substantially but do not appear to have alleviated poverty during the years in question; and Sri Lanka, which grew slowly yet did substantially lessen poverty. [Fields, 1980, pp. 170–4]

Before any final assessment can be made of the relationship between poverty and growth, we shall need evidence from a larger number of countries based on their experience over more prolonged periods. But even the results we already have are suggestive. They certainly should not be taken as grounds for leading to any general presumption that growth is incompatible with developmental objectives related to the alleviation of poverty. And they do little to support the case for de-emphasizing growth as a worthy goal in the general context of development planning. On the other hand, even the few instances we have before us make it clear that growth in itself is not a sufficient condition for alleviating poverty. But this is not an argument against growth. It can be interpreted as an argument against the slow rates of growth that many LDCs have experienced—the implication being that only with faster growth rates can we reasonably expect to see any substantial impact upon the plight of the poor. Alternatively, it can convincingly be viewed as an argument for making changes to the socioeconomic and institutional structure of countries as the means of permitting the impact and benefits of growth to be felt more readily by the poor. We take up the policy implications in the next section.

POLICY

Were any LDC able simultaneously to achieve a relatively rapid growth rate, a reduction in the degree of relative income inequality and substantial alleviation of the plight of the absolutely poor, few would contest that it was experiencing unambiguous developmental advance. Such performance is by no means impossible, either theoretically or according to the record of developmental experience. But it is fairly unusual, and for a time the postwar optimism associated with confident predictions of trickle-down growth gave way in the 1960s and 1970s to pessimism that growth inevitably brought in its wake worsening relative inequality and perhaps even intensifying impoverishment.

As it has turned out, extreme pessimism about the concomitants of growth seems to have been no more justified than the over-optimistic view that growth would rapidly bring benefits to all, whatever the economic conditions and socioeconomic structure in which development might have to proceed. In this chapter we have examined a number of policy alternatives that governments might pursue in attempting to achieve a balance between distributional, poverty and growth objectives. Such a review has relevance to all LDCs. Any individual country must decide for itself how much weight it wishes to place upon one objective compared with others. But both the rational determination of that choice and the potential for success in achieving the desired balance depend on a knowledge of the main policy options and their probable effects in each direction.

A clear and illuminating discussion of the options here is given by Ahluwalia (1974). He reminds us that each market in the economy interacts with every other to generate from a given initial distribution of resources the level and growth of income for every group in society. Within this nexus, the state of technology plays a crucial part. Governments may intervene to influence either the resource distribution—the 'ownership and control of assets', or the operation of factor and commodity markets, or, by taxation, subsidy and public provision, to adjust the distributional consequences of the market at work. They might also intervene to influence technology.

We may start by considering intervention in factor markets, built on the desire to promote growth, distributional aims and poverty objectives by raising employment. Here, it is the functional distribution of income that occupies our attention.

In dual-sector models of the kind we examined in chapter 3, it was the availability of surplus labour at a wage at or near the fixed institutional wage in the traditional sector that, given an initial capital stock, permitted uninterrupted growth. The threat to growth was the danger of rising real wages in the modern sector.

More generally, a fall in the real cost of labour to firms relative to the price of capital is predicted, under neoclassical assumptions, to lead to an increase in employment. (Diagrammatically, the isocost line will be tangent to the highest attainable isoquant at an equilibrium point where techniques are now more labour-intensive.) With given capital working with a greater flow of labour services, higher output should also be achieved. Considering the extent to which distortions overstate labour costs and understate the price of capital in many LDCs, it can be argued that policy intervention, operating on either labour or capital prices, could create new employment opportunities (with beneficial distributional effects) and at the same time promote growth.

In the labour market, governments can reduce employers' labour costs either by directly operating on the wage paid to labour or by paying an employment subsidy to firms. In either case we will assume the price of capital constant, so that such intervention amounts to raising the value of (r/w). Assuming additional output results from such interventions, what of the distributional consequences? Clearly, the answer depends importantly on the nature of the technology as reflected in the value of σ.

In the case of direct pressure on labour's wage (by, for example, doing away with minimum wage laws), we can employ our analysis from earlier in the chapter to conclude that a rise in r/w will raise labour's share in income only if $\sigma > 1$. If $\sigma < 1$, labour's share will fall and, worse still, the total value of wages in the economy may also fall—and will do if the additional men employed or man-hours worked in the new equilibrium less than offset the wage rate reduction.

While labour is not made to suffer directly if employers are subsidized to employ more labour at cheaper rates, the additional employment thus induced again depends on the value of σ and will be smaller, the smaller is σ. The distributional benefits achieved through new employment are thus dependent on the technology but whether they will be great or small must be weighed against the total budgetary cost of the subsidy, which, of course, is applied to all labour. The distributional benefits must, then, be weighed against the value of alternative uses to which the subsidy could have been put by the government.

For these and other reasons Ahluwalia cautions against too vigorously attacking institutionally fixed wage minima. Indeed, if σ were relatively low, and, additionally, output relatively insensitive to reductions in labour input, governments interested in shifting the distribution in favour of labour could consider allowing wages to rise. Output and employment would fall by a small amount, but labour's share and total wages could rise substantially.

Raising r/w can alternatively be achieved by raising the price of capital, wages constant. In their anxiety to induce capital investment, LDCs have frequently suppressed interest rates and offered a range of rebates, incentives and 'tax holidays' which effectively subsidize the cost of capital. Removing such instruments of policy is certainly one course open to LDCs, but it can be argued that in most cases more effective means of dealing with the capital side are available.

We noted in chapter 4 that capital market fragmentation could result in modern capital-intensive industries being favoured by access to capital at low interest rates while smaller, labour-intensive industries might be excluded from the market, or admitted to it only if they took up high-interest loans. By freeing up the capital market—providing equal access to it for all—the door could be opened for the more traditional labour-intensive industries (farmers and urban small producers, for example) to expand more rapidly, thereby offering employment opportunities at a faster rate. As the experience of Korea suggests, growth might well be strongly assisted at the same time by such action.

Operating on relative prices in factor markets can change the functional distribution as reflected in factor shares. To get to grips with the personal distribution, we have to tackle the distribution of income-earning assets (physical and human capital) over the population. As Ahluwalia points out, if all income units (households) were equally endowed with every type of asset (such as land, machines and skills), the personal distribution would also tend to equality. It is because asset concentrations, by contrast, are a characteristic of many economies that income distributions are so unequal. We noted the substance of this argument when looking at the analyses of Kaldor, Stiglitz and Meade.

Policies can be formulated with respect both to physical and human capital. If the main form of capital in an economy is land, and if it is the concentration of land into a few hands that initially determines and subsequently perpetuates income inequality, then redistribution of land—land reform—must be a prime candidate for achieving income-equalizing objectives.

Reform may involve simply a redistribution of the existing land— tenurial reform to remove ownership from landlords and place it in the hands of smallholders, or expropriation from existing owners to put the land in state hands as the collective property of the people. Alternatively, reform may involve rural development programmes: inducing changes in the nature of agriculture by directing investment on to the land to improve its productivity and raise the incomes of agricultural workers.

Growth will suffer through land reform if the new system leads to lower levels of productivity than were achieved under the old. Tenurial reform offers the prospect to landholders of enjoying the benefits of a more direct relationship between input of effort and reward received. But productivity still may not rise unless institutional structures (such as crop failure insurance schemes and lending agencies) and co-operant inputs (including irrigation and high-yielding varieties) can be organized to encourage and enable the smallholder to make the best of the new conditions. Redistribution of land in this way is best done, therefore, only if complementary rural development programmes are simultaneously planned. (For more on all this, see chapter 9.)

As far as collectivization is concerned, growth objectives may be easily met if state-supplied, mechanized means of production and planned large-scale farming in general permit productivity gains formerly unobtainable. Certainly, as an economic device, it may well be more effective than the market or landlord-and-tenant system in garnering the surplus for use and investment elsewhere. The distributional effects must depend entirely upon the decisions of the state.

We have already discussed human capital at length elsewhere. Suffice it to say here that education appears to have the potential both to promote growth, by broadening the base of necessary but scarce skills, and of providing a means of alleviating poverty for those who can gain access to it. Its impact upon equality remains an open question and must be seen in the context of job profiles and the structure of employment on the demand side, and in conjunction with inherited 'fortune' on the supply side.

When we looked at the characteristics of poverty, we drew attention to the fact that effective policy for its alleviation must require a rather fine degree of selectivity. If we add to that requirement a desire to act as quickly as possible (extreme poverty, after all, implies death), then the most useful policy instrument is probably the direct provision of consumption goods. Examples might include subsidized nutrition programmes in villages known to be impoverished, or extensions to rural water supplies to reduce the threat of disease. These, and other examples of such provision in the general area of public infrastructure (such as electrification), not only hit at poverty directly but also operate in favour of growth by creating a healthier, stronger labour force and an overall framework in which productivity may be raised.

One general problem relating to the operation of consumption support schemes aimed at closely defined poverty groups is delivery; it is necessary only to listen to the complaints of aid donors who have seen food go astray for evidence of that.

Both consumption subsidies of this kind and rural investment, which we said needed to accompany land reform, imply raising resources from elsewhere. Abstracting from the possibility of aid, this means applying a progressive tax structure. Taxing the rich to subsidize the poor is, of course, the most direct instrument of redistribution. But what form should the tax structure take?

Taxes can be direct (on income or wealth), or indirect (embodied in goods and services purchased for consumption or investment). In developing countries, the latter dominate because a worthwhile and workable base for personal income tax can usually be found only in the modern and government sectors (and may be small), while inheritance and land taxes are often difficult to administer because of the political power and access to legal contest that the wealthy may threaten. If the wealthy have a higher marginal propensity to save than the poor, and if their savings are productively invested, the distributional gains achieved by progressive income taxation need also to be weighed against possible losses in growth resulting from the reduced investment rate.

As far as progressivity in indirect taxation is concerned, it is necessary to identify the income and price elasticities associated with commodities to be taxed to permit discrimination between different classes of consumer.

Progressive taxation to raise revenue for subsidies is one matter, but imposing taxes (and using subsidies) to induce demand pattern changes is quite another. We are already familiar with this, the last instrument of redistribution that we shall consider. A tariff is a tax that raises the price local consumers must pay for an imported good above that which they would otherwise have to pay. It places the locally made import-competing product on a (relatively) more favourable price footing with such imports and is aimed at switching domestic demand from the foreign-made product to the local one. We have already noted in the last chapter that one aim of tariff protection is to stimulate additional employment locally—but we also noted the potential changes for long-term growth and the way in which agriculture has often been made to suffer for modern sector inefficiency.

Intervention to block imports is only one aspect of this type of policy, however. Some industries (such as building and services) tend to be inherently labour-intensive in production, and if the price of their product can be subsidized (or the price of capital-intensively produced goods taxed), then the argument is that demand can be switched increasingly towards labour-intensive goods, the employment creation rate can be rapidly raised, and distributional objectives can thus be met. Clearly, the potential success of such thinking depends upon the actual degree of demand sensitivity to relative price changes.

Enough has now been said to indicate that meeting the objectives of rapid growth, equalizing income distribution and reduced impoverishment actually requires a careful and informed choice of policy instruments. No single instrument will do, and each of the several chosen may operate against one objective at the same time as it helps to achieve another.

A final point worth noting is that policy formulation on the scale implied in this section also suggests fairly extensive planning. Planning— by which was envisaged more rather than less government intervention —held out great promise to LDCs two or three decades ago. But the hard experience of the ensuing years has shown that our own ignorance of how economies work and what the future holds, and weaknesses at the point of implementation, have together conspired to make planning a much less certain vehicle for success than had been hoped. Johnson (1962) has argued cogently that much can be said for helping markets to work better rather than intervening in attempts to counteract perceived imperfections, and the thrust of some of Friedman's arguments centres on the dangers of increased destabilization that policy intervention may bring. With those thoughts in mind, goverments should perhaps more often consider the implications for their objectives of not intervening at all.

CONCLUSION

This chapter has taken us through the heartlands of recent developmental debate and experience. We have shown that neither the concepts nor the measurement of inequality and poverty are straightforward, but that careful discussion in these areas can lead to a sharper understanding of what developmental objectives actually mean. One important lesson is always to be aware of value judgements that lie embedded in the words and measures we use. We have also shown that the relationships between growth, distribution and poverty are complex—and must vary from one economy to another. There can be no absolute presumption that growth is either harmful or helpful to other developmental objectives. Much will depend upon the initial conditions from which development begins; even more, perhaps, will depend upon the policies that governments pursue. On the other hand, there is little evidence that growth positively increases impoverishment, and rather more that it leads to its alleviation. Policies that explicitly or implicitly play down growth and efficiency may well finish up scoring poorly on the distributional objectives that they set out to meet.

FURTHER READING

A lucid, readable and wide-ranging analysis of this whole area can be found in Fields (1980). Fields not only surveys the conceptual and measurement issues raised here, but also examines all the available evidence on interactions between growth, distribution and poverty—including several detailed case studies. For more on the measurement side, Atkinson (1970) is a seminal paper and is best read in Atkinson (1973), where a non-mathematical summary accompanies the taxing technical analysis presented in the original. Kakwani (1980) presents a slightly less demanding proof of Atkinson's result, and his book tackles in great depth, and with many extensions, the measurement problems we have examined. On theories of the distribution of income, Bronfenbrenner (1971), Johnson (1973) and Lydall (1979) are all valuable general references, but Kaldor (1955) is still the best place to start. Sahota (1978) should be consulted for leads on the personal distribution. For distribution in the context of development Kuznets (1955) is basic; Cline (1975) is an excellent survey but could be usefully supplemented by Frank and Webb (1977). On poverty look at Sen (1976) for the theory—especially sections 1, 6 and 7. On policy, and for a flavour of the whole debate, read Chenery *et al.* (1974), with its contributions by Ahluwalia, Chenery and others and a number of country studies.

NOTES

1 Because the proportionate change expressions always move in opposite directions, the ratio of the changes is necessarily negative. Purely out of convention, σ is usually given a positive value, and so the whole expression

has to be preceded by a minus sign—minus a negative value being a positive one.

2 As in chapter 1, we are referring here to aggregate capital and labour.

3 Notice that risk is 'insurable' in the sense that the probabilities of various outcomes are known in advance, and by pooling enough risky opportunities, the actuarial value (expected or mean income from) the outcome can be reduced to a 'certainty equivalent'. By contrast, uncertainty permits no such calculation (see Johnson, 1973, p. 216).

4 We follow here the exposition of Bronfenbrenner (1971, pp. 79–80) in relating work done by Stiglitz (1967) and paraphrased by R. Lucas.

5 The argument works equally well for classes of rich and poor, assuming that our individual persons can be taken as representative of their class and that the rich never constitute a larger class of persons than the poor.

6 To give a few examples, Ahluwalia (1974) chose annual per capita incomes of $50 and $75 at 1971 prices to make international comparisons; Anand (1973) defined the poverty line for Malaysia at that time as 25 Malaysian dollars per person per month; Dandekar and Rath (1971) proposed a figure of Rs15 per head per month for the rural and Rs22.5 for the urban poverty line (see Kakwani, 1980, chapter 15 for the latter two).

9

Agriculture

This book has been organized within the framework of a broad 'functional' classification; that is, we have looked at the theories of saving, investment, trade and so on and, other than in chapter 3 have not given much emphasis to a sectoral classification of activities. It is not denied that further illumination into the development process might be gained by looking at the sectoral divisions 'industry', 'manufacturing', 'services', 'the financial sector', 'agriculture' and the like, and the relationships among them. On the other hand, it is not possible to do everything in a short book. What we have done already is to draw attention to the work of Chenery and his associates (chapter 1, p. 9) and work in a similar vein in connection with trade and industrialization. This work has a much more 'sectoral' flavour about it, and in this chapter we also adopt this approach by looking more closely at the specific characteristics and place of agriculture in development. None the less, many of the arguments to be raised will be found to contain 'echoes' of the general work we have already done.

   The most obvious rationale for studying the agricultural sector is its size relative to the rest of the economy. Particularly in low-income LDCs, agriculture may account for at least half of GDP while the percentage of the labour force located in the sector characteristically exceeds 70 per cent in low-income and 50 per cent in middle-income developing countries. There are also conceptual reasons for wishing to examine agriculture. A homogeneous, traditional agricultural economy can be viewed as the starting point from which development must proceed. Questions thus need to be asked in relation to how the transformation to a multi-sectoral, heterogeneous, modern economy can be effected. We have already taken many steps towards answering these questions, but this chapter will enable us to review them from a different angle. Furthermore, we now have the chance to explore in greater depth the reasons for and effects of the 'Green Revolution'.

A MODEL TO FOCUS IDEAS

In our basic model we noted that income per head would rise in a single-commodity economy (just like a homogeneous, agricultural economy) if:

(1) savings per head rose, given the population growth rate and state of technology;
(2) the population growth rate fell, given the savings rate and state of technology;
(3) technical progress occurred, given population growth rate at the savings rate.

When we adapted the basic model for use in our chapter on human resources, we noted that, in the absence of technical progress, a 'low-level equilibrium trap' might arise if a population explosion accompanied growth in income per head, assuming that the saving rate could not be raised sufficiently to prevent the *nk* schedule from passing through the *sf(k)* schedule from beneath.

Here we shall examine a model that reaches the same sort of conclusions but, by building on one or two extra assumptions, also provides further insights. The model is also useful for answering (in a way in some respects consonant with the Ranis–Fei approach) the troublesome question of where the modern sector's initial capital stock might be found. In the absence of foreign trade, a domestic surplus of production over consumption is an essential prerequisite for the capital accumulation that is needed for growth. Our model here suggests the conditions under which such a surplus may be generated.

The model we present here was devised by Jorgenson (1961, 1967). He abstracted from the possibility of disguised unemployment defined in terms of a zero marginal product of labour and assumed a simple production function in which output derives from three factors: land (D), labour (L), and a trend factor[1] reflecting the influence of productivity-raising, neutral technical advances. The production function is assumed to take the form:

$$Y(t) = e^{Mt}D^{\alpha}(t)L^{\beta}(t) \qquad \alpha + \beta = 1 \qquad (9.1)$$

Now notice that the first derivative of output with respect to labour input can be found as follows:

$$\frac{dY(t)}{dL(t)} = e^{Mt}D^{\alpha}(t)\beta L^{(\beta-1)}(t)$$

$$= \beta e^{Mt}D^{\alpha}(t)\frac{L^{\beta}(t)}{L(t)}$$

$$= \beta \frac{e^{Mt}D^{\alpha}(t)L^{\beta}(t)}{L(t)}$$

$$= \beta \frac{Y(t)}{L(t)}. \tag{9.2}$$

This is of course the marginal product of labour and must be positive as long as Y and L are positive and $\beta > 0$, which is assumed to be the case.

Recall further that, in general, the elasticity η of any variable, x, with respect to another variable, y, is given by the expression:

$$\eta_{xy} = \frac{dx}{dy}\frac{y}{x}$$

where η_{xy} is defined as the percentage change or response in x to a given percentage change in y. Substituting $Y(t)$ for x and $L(t)$ for y, we see that

$$\eta_{YL} = \frac{dY(t)}{dL(t)}\frac{L(t)}{Y(t)}.$$

But we know that

$$\frac{dY(t)}{dL(t)} = \beta\frac{Y(t)}{L(t)}.$$

So, substituting again,

$$\eta_{YL} = \beta\frac{Y(t)}{L(t)}\frac{L(t)}{Y(t)}$$

$$\therefore \eta_{YL} = \beta. \tag{9.3}$$

Suppose, as Jorgenson does, that land is a fixed stock. D will then not change over time and is therefore not regarded as a function of t in the way in which we represented it in (9.1). Taking the natural logarithms of (9.1) under this assumption, we have

$$\ln Y(t) = \ln(e^{Mt}) + \ln(D^{\alpha}) + \ln[L^{\beta}(t)]$$

$$\therefore \ln Y(t) = Mt + \alpha \ln D + \beta \ln L(t). \tag{9.4}$$

Notice now another general rule of differentiation:

$$\frac{d(\ln x(t))}{dt} = \frac{1}{x}\frac{dx}{dt} = \frac{\dot{x}}{x}.$$

Taking derivatives with respect to time for all parts of (9.4) and applying this rule,

$$\frac{d(\ln Y(t))}{dt} = \frac{d(Mt)}{dt} + \frac{d(\alpha \ln D)}{dt} + \frac{d[\beta \ln L(t)]}{dt}$$

$$\Rightarrow \frac{\dot{Y}(t)}{Y(t)} \quad = M + \beta\frac{\dot{L}(t)}{L(t)}. \tag{9.5}$$

This simply says that the proportional growth rate of agricultural output, which we shall call 'food', is derived from the contribution of M, the productivity-raising rate of technical progress, and the product of labour force growth with the elasticity of output with respect to labour.

To show how this bears upon changes in food output *per head*, we need to recall another relationship:[2]

$$\frac{\dot{y}(t)}{y(t)} = \frac{\dot{Y}(t)}{Y(t)} - \frac{\dot{L}(t)}{L(t)}. \tag{9.6}$$

Put another way, the proportional growth rate of food output per head is the difference between the growth rate of output and the growth rate of labour. Less formally, the faster the labour force grows relative to any given growth rate of output, the more slowly must food output per head grow.

Combining (9.5) and (9.6), it is clear that

$$\frac{\dot{y}(t)}{y(t)} = M + \beta\frac{\dot{L}(t)}{L(t)} - \frac{\dot{L}(t)}{L(t)}. \tag{9.7}$$

This is the crucial relationship that we want to study. It can be interpreted as follows. The first two terms on the right-hand side of the equation show how labour force growth and technical advance contribute to output and its growth. The final term, however, captures the fact that the growing labour force must also be fed. Thus the growth rate of food output (and income) per head must be seen as the result of subtracting from the growth of output the growth in consumption arising from labour force growth. Equation (9.7) can be rewritten (dropping the function-of-t notation) as

$$\frac{\dot{y}}{y} = M - (1-\beta)\frac{\dot{L}}{L}. \tag{9.7a}$$

To study this relationship and its implications for development, assume now that the *growth rate* of the labour force, $\dot{L}/L$, rises as food income per head rises. Assume further that, once income per head reaches some critical value, $\bar{y}$, the growth rate of the labour force ceases to rise further, and that at $\bar{y}$ and all values of $y > \bar{y}$, the labour force grows at a *constant* rate, v. Adopting the notation used earlier in the book, let $\dot{L}/L \equiv n$. Then these assumptions can be expressed as follows:

$$n = f(y) \qquad\qquad (9.8)$$

where

$$f'(y) > 0 \qquad \text{for values of } y < \bar{y}$$

and

$$f'(y) = 0 \qquad \text{for values of } y \geqslant \bar{y}.$$

It should be clear that, when $y \geqslant \bar{y}$, $n = v$. All of this is shown in figure 9.1. We may now rewrite (9.7a) as follows:

$$\frac{\dot{y}}{y} = M - (1 - \beta)n$$

or

$$\frac{\dot{y}}{y} = M - (1 - \beta)f(y). \qquad\qquad (9.7b)$$

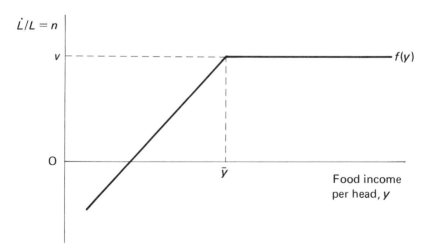

Figure 9.1 The relationship between population growth and per capita food income in Jorgensen's model of the agricultural sector

A final assumption now needs to be made. At $\bar{y}$, the population in the agricultural sector are regarded as having sufficient food. It is assumed that this is the result of the operation of their own preferences —which is equivalent to saying that at $\bar{y}$ the income elasticity of demand for food in this sector falls from unity to zero. At values of $y < \bar{y}$, all extra food is consumed; at values of $y > \bar{y}$, any extra food produced is not consumed. The importance of reaching and exceeding $\bar{y}$ should therefore be apparent. It is only beyond $\bar{y}$ that production exceeds consumption and a surplus becomes available for investment.

There are now two possible types of outcome. Suppose first that we consider values of $y \geqslant \bar{y}$; in other words, values of y for which $f(y)$, the labour force growth rate, is at its maximum, v. In figure 9.1 these are points to the right of $\bar{y}$. Then at such points,

$$M - (1-\beta)f(y) = M - (1-\beta)v$$

One possibility here is that

$$M - (1-\beta)v > 0;$$

that is, productivity-raising technical advance and the productive efforts of labour together combine to produce food output that is growing at a faster rate than the rate at which the growing labour force consumes it, even though the labour force is growing at its maximum rate, v. Since $M - (1-\beta)v$ is equal to the growth rate of food output per head when the population growth rate is at its maximum, the condition that $M - (1-\beta)v > 0$ is equivalent, for the reasons just given, to saying that food output itself must be rising.

Conversely, if we consider the case where

$$M - (1-\beta)v < 0,$$

the interpretation is that, even though y is high enough initially to support a labour force growth rate of v, the consumption growth rate outstrips the production growth achieved by technical advance and labour effort, and so output and food income per head must fall.

Now turn to consider values of $y < \bar{y}$, where $f(y)$, the labour force growth rate, is below its maximum. Here we are looking at points in figure 9.1 to the left of $\bar{y}$. If $[M - (1-\beta)v] > 0$ (the first possibility examined above), then it must also be the case that $[M - (1-\beta)f(y)] > 0$ for *any* value of $f(y)$. The reason simply is that v is the *maximum* value $f(y)$ can take, so that when $f(y) < v$, a *smaller* quantity is being subtracted from M in the square brackets than $(1-\beta)v$. But if $[M - (1-\beta)v] > 0$, it must then be the case that $[M - (1-\beta)f(y)] > 0$. The first positive conclusion we reach, therefore, is that when

$[M - (1-\beta)v] > 0$, y will rise uninterruptedly from any initial value that it might take, below or above $\bar{y}$, and will continue to rise indefinitely. As a corollary, the smaller is $f(y)$—that is, the lower is y—the higher will be the expression in the square brackets and the higher therefore will be the growth rate of food income per head. As $f(y)$ rises in response to the increase in y, this growth rate will slow down as increasingly large values of $(1-\beta)f(y)$ are subtracted from M. In the end, $f(y) = v$, and growth proceeds at a constant positive rate, generating a surplus once $\bar{y}$ is passed.

Suppose, however, that we had $[M - (1-\beta)v] < 0$. Then, as we saw, y must fall from any point above $\bar{y}$. The second conclusion is built upon the point to which it falls. Once y has fallen below $\bar{y}$, $f(y)$ can also fall—to below v. Since y is falling, and $f(y)$ with it, $[M - (1-\beta)f(y)]$ can now start to rise from whatever negative value it originally took because successively smaller values of $(1-\beta)f(y)$ are being subtracted from M. Eventually, y will take a value low enough to bring M and $(1-\beta)f(y)$ into equality, so that the expression in the square brackets will become zero. Since this tells us, according to (9.7b), the growth rate of food output per head, we know that at this point y will be stationary—with Y and L both growing at the same rate and y not growing at all. We will call this point y_T. Clearly there is no surplus here since $y_T < \bar{y}$. Notice finally that if y is very low indeed (below y_T) and $f(y)$ accordingly small, $[M - (1-\beta)f(y)]$ could rise as far as y_T but no further, for at values of $y > y_T$, we have already seen that y must fall when $[M - (1-\beta)v] < 0$. We denote y_T with a 'T' because it represents another low-level trap.

The message from this analysis is clear. The path to sustained growth at the potential for development lies in ensuring that $[M - (1-\beta)v] > 0$, in other words, that labour inputs and productivity-raising advances can together produce output fast enough to offset the rate at which agricultural sector consumption is growing even when labour force growth is at its maximum. Only then can a surplus of resources be made available for use elsewhere—where 'elsewhere' may be thought of as the modern sector. If $[M - (1-\beta)v] < 0$, two obvious alternatives are available: raise M relative to $(1-\beta)v$, or reduce v so that $(1-\beta)v$ falls relative to M (or, of course, both). The first strategy amounts to seeking ways of raising productivity, the second to population control programmes, the third to a combination of the two. In the first case, technical progress seems to be the obvious source to exploit—except that in the absence of a capital input as specified in the production function it is unclear how such advances may be envisaged as occurring. Much technical progress is, after all, embodied in equipment.

An alternative suggestion might be to think of education (provided in schools financed by aid, perhaps) permitting higher performance levels of labour as a reflection of investment in human capital. The provision of infrastructural capital such as irrigation (again aid-funded, perhaps) could have the same effect. In the second case, it would be necessary to consider the factors influencing the motivation of families to increase or decrease their average size and the potential for applying (and having successfully adopted) contraceptive devices.

One reason for the starkness of the alternatives presented here is the rather 'tight' way in which the model is specified. The simplicity of the formulation can be justified in terms of the ease with which it generates results and insights, but can be criticized to the extent that it misleads by its omissions. Productivity in agriculture has risen slowly in many LDCs precisely because investment in capital there has taken second place to investment elsewhere, so the implications of incorporating capital in the production function really should not be ignored. This in turn requires that a satisfactory theory should have something to say about the determination of such investment. Again, it is unsatisfactory to regard the stock of land under cultivation as always fixed. In sparsely populated countries, population growth might be accommodated by spreading cultivation into formerly virgin land, with D growing as a consequence in (9.1). (This cannot go on for ever, of course, and in many countries the fixed stock assumption is justified.) Further, the assumption of a step-reduction in the elasticity of demand for food in the agricultural sector (from unity to zero) is a very crude device. This income elasticity is valued, according to widespread empirical work on Engel curves, somewhere between 1 and 0 in most cases and falls steadily as income per head rises. A more comprehensive model would endogenize this process (see Dixit, 1973). Finally, nothing is said about transferring the surplus to the non-agricultural sector. Jorgenson's model tells us how the surplus can be generated but not how to ensure its effective transfer and deployment. These are matters to which we shall return later.

AGRICULTURE AS AN INSTRUMENT OF DEVELOPMENT

USES OF THE SURPLUS OUTSIDE AGRICULTURE

We have just seen that increasing productivity in agriculture has a crucial role to play in ensuring that a surplus of food will be generated. Before we explore further how productivity may be raised, however, the next essential step is to review why it is important not only to generate but also to expand the agricultural surplus. This provides extra motivation for analysing productivity-raising strategies in the next section.

To understand why expanding the agricultural surplus has so much to contribute, we must view agriculture in relation to the other parts of the economy. What we are about to do, in fact, is to identify what has been called agriculture's 'instrumental' role—that is, its part in serving the ends of development by assisting in the growth of *other* sectors, in particular manufacturing, which have in turn been viewed as the locomotives of economy-wide development.

In this light we noted as far back as chapter 3 that the agricultural surplus was needed to feed the modern sector labour force, on the assumption that the modern sector could not feed itself. We also noted that, if the withdrawal of labour from agriculture at any point resulted, through a positive marginal product of labour, in a reduction of food output, food would start to become scarce for the modern sector labour force. Productivity increase in agriculture, reflected in an outward shift of the total product curve in the Ranis–Fei diagrams and a positive value of M in Jorgenson's model, is therefore required if growing food scarcity is to be prevented from turning the terms of trade against the modern sector and thereby slowing or halting its growth as capitalist profits are eroded. Lewis (1954, p. 173) was well aware of this from the outset—as well as its corollary that success in raising agricultural productivity could be expected on the other hand to raise subsistence income and hence exert pressure on modern sector wages. The problems could be simultaneously escaped, however, 'if rising productivity in the subsistence sector is more than offset by improving terms of trade' (p. 174).

That part of the agricultural surplus that is exchanged for modern sector consumer goods is called the *marketable* agricultural surplus. We have already seen that it serves the purpose of feeding the modern sector workforce, but it is of at least equal importance to notice that this process of exchange also provides a market for modern sector goods. In a closed economy it is the only source of demand for modern sector goods beyond the modern sector itself. The greater is agricultural productivity, the greater will be the agricultural surplus and the greater, therefore, the potential market for modern sector goods. We have noted elsewhere the way in which small markets can encourage monopoly and inefficiency, while larger (and better, growing larger) markets can permit both static and dynamic economies of scale to be reaped. Growth in the agricultural sector thus encourages growth elsewhere, and, to the extent that it is built upon locally produced

productivity-raising capital equipment, exerts demand upon the producers of investment goods as well as the producers of consumption
goods.

Another part of the agricultural surplus, as we have already observed,
generates the basis of the capital stock that can be used by the modern
sector to set the process of development, via investment and reinvestment, in motion. This is called the *investible agricultural surplus*.
Once again, the greater is agricultural productivity, the more surplus
there will be available to finance production in the modern sector.

Finally, the instrumental role of agriculture in the open economy
must be noted. In the absence of higher agricultural productivity a
developing country may be forced to import food to meet the needs of
its non-agricultural labour force as workers move away from food
production. There is a serious opportunity cost in terms of the goods
and materials that could, alternatively, have been imported with the
same foreign exchange. Higher agricultural productivity thus permits
foreign exchange to be 'saved', or, more accurately, to be used for
other productive non-food imports vital for development. Assuming
no domestic food shortage, higher agricultural productivity could
increase the surplus by enough to allow food (or other agricultural
products) to be exported. This would actually earn the country foreign
exchange which would be used to buy imports subsequently.

EXTRACTING AND DEPLOYING THE SURPLUS

It is fairly easy to see how much of a contribution the agricultural
surplus can make to development. We should, however, note that the
surplus must in some way be transferred, and will fulfil its potential
only if successfully deployed.

On the question of effecting the intersectoral transfer, it is sometimes
assumed that a landlord class, to whom the agricultural surplus accrues
as rent, sees and grasps the opportunities to invest in modern sector
activity. Dixit (1973, p. 342) has expressed scepticism on this score,
pointing out that this view puts an implausibly heavy burden upon the
perspicacity and entrepreneurial drive and skills of the landlord group.

If the institutionally oriented landlord argument is to be discounted,
at least four other alternatives might be considered. The first two, the
'Marxist–Leninist' and 'market-oriented' approaches, are analysed
by Owen (1966).

Describing the Marxist–Leninist approach, Owen points to direct
state intervention in organizing and operating collective farms as the
core of an attempt to maximize the surplus. Combined with this is the

strategy of *requisitioning*, that is, relying upon the physical direction of agricultural produce to state procurement agencies to allocate farm output to the non-agricultural sector. This direct, quantity-control approach (a manifestation of central planning) has to be contrasted with the 'market-oriented' picture. Here, agriculture is assumed to comprise a profusion of price-taking, competitive, family farming units whose productive activity is aimed primarily at permitting them to acquire, by exchange, the goods and services produced by the non-agricultural sector. To complete the picture, the non-farm sector is assumed increasingly to be characterized by concentration and monopoly in its markets. The key to understanding the transfer mechanism here is to note the assumption that technical progress raises productivity in both sectors. The asymmetry in market forms, however, results in the benefits of progress passing disproportionately into the hands of the non-agricultural sector. In the farm sector, it is supposed, the pressure of competitive conditions hastens the diffusion (or spread) of new techniques, shifting the sectoral supply curve outwards and resulting in an increased market supply of food at a lower market price. On the other hand, it is argued that farmers as consumers are denied compensating gains from technical progress in the modern sector, because producers there have the monopoly power to lay more prolonged claim to the benefits of their higher productivity.

This latter proposition may be viewed as a 'turning terms of trade' argument, agriculture seeing any productivity gains it makes penalized by the operation of monopoly power elsewhere. Another form that this argument takes (and this is our third alternative) is to suppose that the modern sector is protected by tariff and quota. As we noted in our chapter on trade, one effect of this will be to turn the terms of trade against agriculture since agriculture must now pay more, in terms of its produce, for any non-agricultural good that it wishes to acquire. This can be viewed as raising modern sector real incomes and, assuming a positive (and preferably rising) marginal propensity to save there, should increase resources available for investment—the appearance of the 'investible surplus'.

While protection of industry is, of course, equivalent to taxing agriculture, governments finally may simply resort to direct taxation of farm incomes to mobilize the surplus for modern sector use.

Developing countries have, in general, been rather successful in transferring the agricultural surplus elsewhere, especially by means of protecting the non-agricultural sector. But as we noted in chapter 7, protection has often been associated with such inefficiency in the modern sector that the developmental potential of transferring the surplus has not been realized. None the less, as we noted there, the dangers inherent in protected import substitution industrialization are now widely appreciated, and together with that advance has gone another, of equal importance for agriculture. To that we now turn.

While it cannot be denied, and must not be forgotten, that agriculture has a role to play through its intersectoral links, too much emphasis on this instrumental approach can lead to the neglect of efforts to develop the agricultural sector for the sake, directly, of its own population. As we noted at the beginning of the chapter, the majority of the population in LDCs still lives in the agricultural sector; it is in that sector that we would expect the comparative advantage of many developing countries to lie; and it is there that poverty in its most intense form can often be found. Much more thought has been devoted more recently, therefore, to raising rural incomes, creating rural employment and reducing inequality both within agriculture and between agriculture and non-agriculture. The achievement of higher levels of productivity is again an objective here, but a simultaneous aim has been to ensure that at least some of the benefits of higher productivity should in this case accrue to rural workers. It is this sort of thinking that has given rise to what is often called 'The Green Revolution'.

To put the Green Revolution in perspective, note first of all that productivity can in principle be raised, with higher incomes for all, by exploiting what may be called the *extensive margin of cultivation*. Here a population of given size can be envisaged, raising productivity by putting an increasingly large area of land under cultivation by moving into formerly unfarmed territory. The land–labour ratio rises and, in addition, we would expect the ratio of output to labour to rise. This is not the margin with which we shall be concerned here, although it could be of importance in the more sparsely populated LDCs, especially in Africa. In this section we shall concentrate upon the means of exploiting the *intensive margin*, that is, achieving higher output per man from a given stock of land by working it harder or 'better'.

We could think of three ways in which exploiting the intensive margin may serve developmental ends, although in practice the strategies may well be used in combination. Rearrangement of land holdings may achieve a distribution of land–labour ratios across holdings that raises productivity at the same time as creating new employment. Second, innovations may be used that (1) are, at least initially, labour-displacing and thus, by definition, may raise labour productivity; and/or (2) are most effective on larger holdings. Most mechanized innovations can be classed in this way. Finally, scale-neutral innovations can be used to raise output and productivity, in this case without any apparent threat to employment. These innovations, those most readily associated with the Green Revolution, include high-yielding crop varieties (HYV), chemical inputs including fertilizers, and special cultivation practices. In contrast with the second type of innovation, these techniques should be equally effective whether on large plots or small.

Looking first at the question of redistributing land, notice that Sternberg (1971) claims that most agricultural production in LDCs is characterized by systems in which there is a wide spectrum of holding size and land–labour ratios. In Latin America, for example, he suggests that in the 1960s land area per worker could be as little as 5 per cent of the national average in some units, yet as much as 12 times the national average elsewhere. Large differentials in land–labour ratios were also found in the Philippines, but in South Asia the difference between extremes could be as small as a factor of two or three (Sternberg, 1971, p. 464). In such cases, it has often been found that intensity of land use varies inversely with holding size, and Sternberg concludes that, if land and labour were recombined in proportions reflecting their general availability in the agricultural sector as a whole, both inputs could be employed more productively. Clearly, rearrangement of land holdings to reduce the variation in land–labour ratios should be able to create more rural employment opportunities, a desirable end in itself and one with the potential of alleviating rural poverty, reducing inequality and tempering the strength of 'push' factors behind rural–urban migration in countries where urban unemployment is already widespread. On the other hand, as Chenery *et al.* (1974) have pointed out (chapter IV), land reform of this kind also has the potential for reducing productivity and output at least in the short run. This will particularly be the case if large estates have been efficiently run in the past while governments fail to provide beneficiaries of the redistribution with back-up in terms of advice and education, or to provide complementary inputs in the form of marketing, credit facilities, seeds and fertilizers (Chenery *et al.*, 1974, p. 79).

The second means of exploiting the intensive margin—which we shall broadly characterize as 'mechanization'—may appear to have less developmental advantages than the other two. While mechanization offers the almost certain promise of much improved yields, it also seems to threaten the livelihood of those who have worked as either wage labour or tenant farmers using labour-intensive means. A mechanized commercial farm will operate with a higher capital–labour ratio and offer less employment to wage-earners. In the landlord–tenant case, the landlord may perceive that his returns can be increased by employing tractors, but only if tenants are evicted to permit amalgamation of plots so that the indivisible tractor input can be used to maximum effect. Employment, poverty and distributional problems may all, therefore, seem to be a probable short- to medium-term consequence.

On the other hand, Singh and Day (1975) have investigated the apparent paradox of mechanization on family-run farms—by choice—in a labour surplus environment, the Punjab, and discover that mechanization may, in fact, offer a variety of important advantages. First, family labour may be plentiful at some times of the year but scarce at others. Although an overview suggests a labour surplus, therefore, surpluses are in fact seasonal, and when labour is scarce machines are now being used to deal with the types of task that none the less must be done. When labour is abundant, however, traditional labour-intensive methods are still employed. Second, specified agricultural operations (land preparation, sowing, harvesting, etc.) must be done at specified times—or else they cannot be done at all (for example, harvesting cannot be done at sowing time because there is no crop to harvest). Now, Green Revolution innovations, which we have yet to discuss in detail, call for better land preparation and additional cultivation, or, in general, an intensification of traditional tasks requiring greater use of power. If such power cannot be provided either by traditional animal draft or by labour, machines are the only option left. Finally, even if mechanization were shown to be developmentally objectionable in some ways, Punjabi farmers none the less were impressed by its cost-effectiveness. As Singh and Day show (1975, p. 681), while operating costs per tractor hour exceeded costs per bullock hour by a factor of at least 10, the tractor could complete a task that either machine or animal could perform between 10 and 30 times as quickly.

By itself, mechanization may indeed run the danger of appearing anti-developmental. Yet it offers great advantages, and as Singh and Day also show (1975, pp. 670–1) need not at least over some time horizons even reduce employment, since more efficient methods should raise yields, total output and thus the derived demand for labour. In the Punjab, tractors combined with an upsurge in the use of nitrogenous fertilizers, and better water supplies to double output and treble the marketed surplus between 1952 and 1965. While employment initially fell, the increased yields and total output eventually led to a labour use level 5 per cent higher at the end of the period than the start.

We turn now to the Green Revolution itself. In a sense, the key to identifying Green Revolution techniques is to seek those innovations that, in particular, are *scale-neutral*. However large or small a plot of land, a better seed (a HYV), the application of a fertilizer or pesticide or the use of a new cultivation practice should, all other things being equal, have the *same* proportional effect in raising output. Thus, all landowners should be able to see equal proportional increases in food production, irrespective of the size of their holding. All then should be able to benefit by an equal proportional amount. This seems to be true in a way that tractorization was not.

The benefits promised by the Green Revolution are easy to identify: higher yields, higher increases and more opportunities for employment associated with raising such yields. Ahmad (1972) suggests that yield increases may range from 50 to 300 per cent using HYV. On the question of employment, he points out that labour requirements in growing a rice HYV could lead to a 60 per cent growth in labour requirements because of: (1) the very labour-intensive cultivation practices involved (extreme care in seedling-picking, line transplanting, regular application of fertilizers and pesticides and so on) and (2) the multiple cropping that such practices permit. On the question of incomes, he adds that not only can more food be produced for direct rural consumption, but that higher productivity also opens the door to the achievement of higher cash incomes which can be used to buy consumer goods produced in the modern sector.

While the benefits promised by the Green Revolutions were (and are) spectacular, it has to be said that in many instances problems have arisen that require a more sober appraisal of its success. Some classes of rural worker (small cultivators, share-croppers and the landless) are said not to have benefited at all; rural income inequality has worsened; fears of unemployment and eviction have grown.

Looking first at the question of size of farm operation, it has been found in the Maharashtra region of India that small farmers can achieve growth rates of output twice as high as those with more land. On the other hand, for results as impressive as these, farmers need to be able to obtain and effectively deploy important but 'lumpy' complementary capital inputs, often associated with providing water for their land (such as tube wells and pumping sets). This requires careful organization and cooperation among small farmers, something that may often be hard to achieve. In the absence of such efforts, however, the small farmer may find himself incapable, financially, of raising the capital necessary to obtain the irrigation required for HYV cultivation. Operations of a larger-size may well find mobilizing capital much easier (Ahmad, 1972, pp. 16–17).

Turning to the question of the organization of labour on the land, it has often been pointed out that, if traditional landlord–tenant arrangements continue to prevail, it is hard to see how HYV could be introduced. Holdings are in these cases cultivated by tenants and share-croppers on the basis of crop-sharing agreements. The use of HYV would in these cases require much greater labour input, but would be uncompensated by commensurate reward since landlords could be expected to take most of the increased output as their share. On the other hand, we have already noted that HYV are likely to be particularly successful when combined with mechanized inputs such as tractors and threshers. If landowners choose to maximize profit by operating only on large holdings where machines are at their most effective, tenants and share-croppers will be denied the opportunity of renting smaller-sized holdings into which the larger blocks could have been divided. In cases where tenants did work smallholdings in the past but existing or new landlords wish to amalgamate plots, the Green Revolution may be associated with widespread eviction. (This occurred, for example, in the irrigated central area of Luzon in the Philippines: see Ahmad, 1972, pp. 19–20.)

Not surprisingly, the sort of difficulties raised in the last paragraph led many commentators to call for land or tenurial reform as a condition for the success of Green Revolution techniques. If a country's objectives are socialistic, reform might lead towards a framework implied in the Marxist–Leninist picture discussed earlier in the chapter, with collective farms acting as the operational units within which the new technology is applied. If a country is aiming, by contrast, to encourage individual enterprise, reform is more likely to have as its objectives the desire to ensure security of tenure, and the strengthening of mechanisms to permit rewards to be associated with individual effort. It will often also be necessary to provide instruction about new techniques, access to credit and marketing support. To cite one example here, Fleming (1975) points out that in Kenya, providing security of tenure has been seen for decades as the 'essential prerequisite to increased productivity' (p. 49). Elsewhere, Sternberg reports that in Japan, Iran, Taiwan and the United Arab Republic an immediate increase in income resulted from the change in status from tenant to owner (or member of a cooperative), or from increased security of tenure. There was no need in these latter also to appeal to the Green

Revolution as such, but there is little doubt that such changes can do much to assist the Green Revolution in achieving its objectives.

As presented so far, it should be clear that the coming of the Green Revolution might well herald increasing rural relative inequality. For, although it is true that Green Revolution techniques are scale-neutral in production, it could be the case that some landholders are better able to benefit from HYV than others, while in other instances the adoption of HYV could even coincide with mechanization in a way that, temporarily at least, increases the absolute poverty of disadvantaged groups. We conclude this analysis with a discussion of one other factor that can be of great importance in the agricultural sector: attitude to risk. And we can show how the relatively high degree of risk aversion among smaller farmers may help to explain increasing relative inequality as diffusion of the new techniques proceeds.

It has been appreciated for some time that, if two farmers are faced with a new technique, their responses to it may differ markedly, depending upon how close each one lives on the one hand to a 'minimum physiologic level of living' (MPL) and on the other to a 'minimum desired level of consumption' (MDL) (see Miracle, 1968, p. 295). MDL lies above MPL and is determined largely by cultural factors. Farmers would always like to have consumption at least equal to MDL but most of all fear falling below MPL, since consumption below MPL implies death. Assume that two farmers sell the same proportion of their output but that one enjoys a consumption stream at a higher level than the other. (We may imagine that the higher consumption stream is associated with a larger landholding.) Two cases can then be considered.

If both farmers lie above the MPL, but one of them is only barely above it, then, faced with a new technique, the one farther above the MPL is more likely to adopt the innovation. The reason? Adopting a new technique is perceived to be fraught with uncertainty: neither farmer knows how the upper and lower limits of his output and consumption when using the innovation will compare with the limits to which he is accustomed from using existing techniques. For the farmer with the lower-level income stream, the fear that the lower limit might fall below the MPL is greater than that experienced by the higher-income farmer.

Assume now that both lie, again, above the MPL but that this time one is *also* above the MDL while the other is just below it. In this case, neither farmer will think it very probable that adopting the new technique will lead to catastrophe (that is, to a decline in income below

MPL), but the one with the lower income stream may now perceive, in adopting the new technique, the possibility of rising above the MDL. Since the other is already above the MDL we may surmise that in this case the higher-income farmer is less likely to be the innovator than the lower-income farmer.

Although the comparison is instructive, most attention in the literature has focused upon the first case—where the better-off farmer is said to be the more likely innovator because of the justified fear of catastrophe on the part of the less well off. Often the argument is couched in terms of the degree of risk aversion among smaller farmers. As Feder and O'Mara (1981) put it, 'Since the new technology is perceived as (and sometimes indeed is) more risky, and provided that smaller farmers are more risk averse, it is argued that smaller farmers will be less inclined to adopt the innovation' (p. 60).[3] As is clear from the quotation, the attitude-to-risk analysis of the question is frequently made to turn on the relationship between risk aversion and farm size. (In the earlier discussion, one could easily imagine the smaller farmer, in danger of dropping below the MPL, having a greater aversion to the risks associated with innovation than the larger.)

On closer examination, however, it turns out that risk aversion can be argued to be a deterrent to the adoption of new techniques by small farmers only to the extent that adoption involves fixed costs. In their study, Feder and O'Mara concentrate solely upon exploring the implications for adoption patterns of having farms of various size worked by risk-averse farmers in a given area. Other than for their farm size, the farmers are assumed to be identical in all respects—their utility functions, cost structures, access to credit and inputs and so on. Variation in these latter factors could, of course, also influence adoption patterns, but generally only in a fashion that would serve to accentuate the results of the simpler model.

Feder and O'Mara identify three fixed cost elements: (1) financial and time costs associated with acquiring all the information related to cultivating HYV; (2) transaction costs associated with applying for and acquiring loans to finance innovatory techniques; (3) costs incurred through having to wait for innovatory inputs in the period before distribution networks are running smoothly. Given the assumed variability in farm size and the pressure of risk aversion, it is shown that the effect of these fixed costs is to lead larger farmers to jump in first, with experimental plots of increasing area, while smaller farmers delay adoption until the larger landholders have already experienced high yields over a number of seasons. This result conforms with widely observed phenomenon that adoption rates and the sequence of adoption decisions are indeed related to farm size.

Several interesting points can be made about Feder and O'Mara's results. First, the pattern of diffusion of the innovation generated by a simulation based on their model takes an S-shape (see figure 9.2). The proportion of all potential adopters who initially jump in is small, and grows at a positive but only slowly increasing rate in the early stages. These early adopters provide the externality or community service, however, of 'showing how it is done' to all the other farmers in the area. As they learn by doing, everyone else observes their successes (and problems) and their uncertainty is in turn reduced. After the passage of a few seasons, therefore, the rate of adoption quickens markedly as knowledge and confidence in the innovation grows. Eventually only the more highly risk-averse or externally constrained are left using the old technique, and the adoption rate slows down until all (or almost all) have been 'converted'. Such a pattern of diffusion has been widely observed in many contexts (see, for example, Davies, 1980), and it is comforting to see it replicated here.

Second, this diffusion pattern necessarily implies an initial worsening of relative rural inequality since, in the early stages, the larger land-owners receive higher incomes than before while smaller farmers see no rise in their incomes until they adopt the new approach. As an

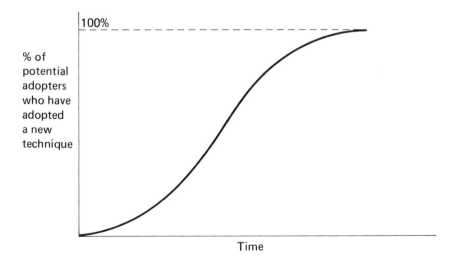

Figure 9.2 A diffusion curve for a new technique of production

increasing proportion of farmers adopts the innovation, however, relative income inequality eventually falls again.

Third, to the extent that fixed adoption costs constitute the reason for lags in innovation, it is clear that policy-makers should address themselves to reducing such costs. An effective extension service can reduce the costs of acquiring information; simplified loan procedures can help to cut out 'red tape' transaction costs; distribution channels can be improved with the needs of the smaller farmer a special priority.

To conclude this section, let us recall that the promise of the Green Revolution lay in its scale neutrality as compared with the scale-dependent benefits of mechanization in exploiting the intensive margin. We have seen, however, that mechanization can help Green Revolution techniques to maximize their potential, and in the long run may do so even without inducing increased rural unemployment. On the other hand, fixed cost elements in the actual business of adopting new techniques can lead to a temporary worsening of rural income inequality, if the widely observed characteristic of farmer risk-aversion is present. Furthermore, the success with which the fruits of Green Revolution techniques can be widely distributed may very often depend upon not only the size of landholdings but also on the arrangements under which land is worked. Land reform may indeed be a prerequisite for a successful revolution.

CONCLUSION

This chapter has explored the way in which an agricultural surplus might be generated, and the way in which that serves to allow agriculture to act in its instrumental role in promoting development. Bearing in mind the danger that this view of agriculture could lead to a neglect of the interests of that sector in its own right, we have tried to show why Green Revolution techniques have been considered of particular importance for LDCs. Productivity could be raised simply by adopting more capital-intensive methods. A greater surplus would be generated, but given the evictions and rural unemployment that this approach could bring about, it has not been considered the best approach to the problem when viewed from the perspective of the agricultural sector alone. Land reform by itself can go some way to raising productivity and achieving a more equal distribution of income, but clearly it will achieve the ends both of raising yields and output, and of improving equity if it is combined with land-augmenting innovations. If applied in an appropriate structure of landholding arrangements and with the necessary support of technical advice, credit and marketing services, Green Revolution technology can not only benefit the rural populace in all its parts but also raise productivity in a way that should enable agriculture, in addition, to fulfil its instrumental role.

Jorgenson's papers (1961 and 1967) not only have a model of the agricultural sector (which we have outlined) but also integrate the agricultural sector with the non-agricultural. The papers are not easy but represent an important part of the 'neoclassical' tradition of development economics and have been widely discussed. Dixit (1973) is an excellent critical review and forms the basis for some of the analysis in this chapter. Another key contribution is Nicholls's (1963) paper on the agricultural surplus as a factor in economic development, and Streeten (1967) is among the writers who have classified the uses to which the surplus might be put in the form adopted here. Important general works in the area include Johnston and Kilby (1975) and Mellor (1966).

Much has been written about the Green Revolution, but in addition to the references in the text, students would find it particularly rewarding to consult Griffin (1974) and Day and Singh (1977)—the latter a much more detailed account of the methods and findings embodied in the study reported in this chapter.

1 As equation (9.1) shows, the impact of technical advance is captured by the term e^{Mt}. Students familiar with continuous compounding formulae will recognize e as the number 2.718, which can be shown to be the year-end value to which a principal of one unit of currency will grow if interest at the rate of 100 per cent per year is continuously compounded. More generally, when e is raised to the power rt (that is, when we examine a term e^{rt}), we have an expression that indicates the value to which a unit quantity of any kind will grow if compounding occurs continuously at r per cent per year for t years. Looking at this statement differently, r represents the instantaneous rate of growth of e^{rt}, where, at any point in time t, e^{rt} can be interpreted as the value to which our unit quantity has grown since the compounding process began, that is, since $t = 0$. In this case, we have written M in place of r, where M represents the growth attributable to productivity-raising technical advance that could be applied to any unit of

inputs. Since the production function is written multiplicatively, this then applies to all input units.

Notice finally that 'ln' stands for 'natural logarithm', logarithms to the base e. Thus in the same way that $\log_{10}100 = \log_{10}10^2 = 2$, $\ln_e e^{Mt} = Mt$. (See equation (9.4).)

2 This can also be derived from the logarithmic differentiation rule for:

$$\ln y(t) = \ln Y(t) - \ln L(t)$$

$$\therefore \frac{d \ln y(t)}{dt} = \frac{d \ln Y(t)}{dt} - \frac{d \ln L(t)}{dt}$$

or

$$\frac{\dot{y}(t)}{y(t)} = \frac{\dot{Y}(t)}{Y(t)} - \frac{\dot{L}(t)}{L(t)}.$$

3 One implication of this is that the smaller farmer is relatively disadvantaged when it comes to enjoying the potential benefits offered by new techniques. If larger farmers do innovate while smaller farmers do not, relative income inequality will increase.

10

Conclusion

This book has had as its aim a desire to provide a framework in which the study of development can be pursued in a logical and structured fashion. We have had to be selective to maintain the fairly sharp lines of direction that make the study of an area manageable, and the thrust of these concluding remarks is that the end of this book should be treated only as another beginning.

From a theoretical point of view, a number of leads suggested throughout this book deserve pursuing. First, many authorities would probably wish to stress disequilibrium phenomena as being at the heart of economic development. (For a recent overview of this approach, see Nugent and Yotopoulos, 1979.) We started, in choosing Solow's model, with an essentially 'neoclassical world in which change is gradual, marginalist, non-disruptive, equilibrating and largely painless' (Nugent and Yotopoulos, 1979, p. 542). On the other hand, we could have set out with an emphasis not so much on the equilibrating, harmonizing mechanisms of smoothly working markets but rather on the 'jolt and backwash effects' of development which induce the dualistic type of economy we have studied, with development benefits trickling up and not down. A major problem of exposition with this type of approach is that there is no unified theory of disequilibrium— nor, indeed, is there ever likely to be. What we have tried to do instead is to show where disequilibrating tendencies might have their roots.

In general, for example, we have drawn attention to the high degree of imperfection in many markets in LDCs, and particularly to the ways in which poor information undermines the capacity of markets to work well. Two specific examples are also worth mentioning. We discussed in chapter 5 the conditions under which a growing market economy might move persistently away from equilibrium, contrary to Solow's predictions. And in chapter 8 we saw that factors such as educational attainment could determine an individual's place in the queue for modern sector jobs. This view is contrary to the homogeneous-labour assumption of Solow and the homogeneous-traditional-labour assumption of Lewis. Disequilibrium theorists say that one consequence of this will be to upgrade educational or skill requirements for all modern sector jobs, thus displacing the less well qualified (however able or suitable) and creating new urban unemployment.

On the other hand, to the extent that the more highly qualified are traditional sector migrants, their departure leaves traditional agriculture no more capable than before of raising productivity relative to the modern sector.

On another tack, much more could be said about the role of money and financial institutions in LDCs (see McKinnon, 1973, and Drake, 1980, for expositions in this area). It is rapidly becoming recognized that economic development requires a parallel maturing in financial structures (see Myint, 1973, chapter 5, for a view on this), and that this in turn calls for considering the definition of 'money' and a study of its arrival, and its changing role as development proceeds. A study of these aspects also links up with the disequilibrium approach, since it is the presence of money in a market economy that is blamed by many economists these days (see Clower, 1965, for a seminal statement) for creating the conditions for disequilibrium to arise.

Third, the whole question of planning for development is an area of detailed study. We have talked about cost–benefit analysis, manpower planning and policy-making to reconcile conflicting developmental objectives. But we have not discussed explicitly what planning might actually comprise, whether there is a good case for it, what techniques are involved, and what the difficulties of implementation would be. The first two questions are essentially theoretical in flavour and revolve around judgements relating to the relative strengths and weaknesses of the market with its imperfections and planning procedures with theirs. (A good introduction to this discussion is Johnson, 1962.) The third question involves developing an understanding of often complex mathematical methods underlying input–output analysis and linear and non-linear programming, and is best treated separately anyway. (See Todaro, 1971, for a short and lucid account of this area.) The fourth question is founded primarily on administrative and organizational issues, and discussion here tends to explain why planning has often failed to live up to its promise. (See Waterston, 1965, for a comprehensive coverage.)

Again, in the area of international trade we left on one side most of the discussion on the balance of payments and policy tools to manage it.

This sort of list could be extended almost indefinitely: the economics of uncertainty has much to contribute, as we saw in our sections on entrepreneurship and income distribution (see also Miracle, 1968); energy economics and the economics of natural resources are important fields on their own now (see Smil and Knowland, 1980; Dorner and El-Shafie, 1980; and Dasgupta and Heal, 1979, for further reference); the study of the economics of corruption has an obvious relevance for some LDCs; and so on.

One final note requires separate attention. Space has not permitted much here by way of case studies. As it is, one of the major difficulties in presenting the economics of development is that no general statement worth making is likely to hold everywhere; yet to say that every country requires separate study before anything useful can be said about it is a denial of the generality of economic principles. One resolution of this problem can be found in 'cluster analysis'—in which countries are grouped according to their similarity in a range of specified, measured characteristics. This approach is taken in the empirical work of Batchelor *et al.* (1980) and permits them to make stronger empirically valid statements than would otherwise be possible—albeit at the cost of generality in cover.

As a general proposition, however, the best understanding of development requires a familiarity both with theory and with country experience. The two complement each other. If the theory is worth having it will be illuminating at least to some extent in most countries, but if its users are adept, they will want to massage and qualify the theory in light of their observation. While there is no substitute for direct experience, case studies are extremely valuable for giving a 'feel' for the actualities of development, and at least one desirable extension of study in this field would be to read a number. (A good place to start might be the individual studies of Brazil, Mexico, India, Pakistan and Taiwan and the Philippines undertaken, respectively, by Bergsman, King, Bhagwati and Desai, Stephen Lewis, and Hsing, Power and Sicat for the OECD in connection with Little, Scitovsky and Scott's (1970) comparative study of those countries. See also Lim (1975) for Malaysia; Fields (1980) for case studies on Costa Rica, Sri Lanka, India, Brazil, the Philippines and Taiwan; and any recent catalog of World Bank publications for country studies of economies as widely varied as Chile, Chad and the Comoros, Guatemala, Ivory Coast and the Yemen Arab Republic.)

It is sometimes tempting to think in terms of constructing a truly general model of economic development; yet after several decades of research in the area, the prospect seems increasingly like a mirage. The model would need as a minimum to be dynamic, multi-sectoral, open to international influences, and capable of generating disequilibria and the conditions for resolving them. This is a very tall order and even if it were ever built, such a model would probably be technically inaccessible to most practitioners and policy-makers. By contrast, the strategy of this volume has been to start with the simplest integrated growth model we have and work up from there. Many avenues have been left virtually untouched or wholly unexplored. To seek them out is now the reader's prerogative.

Bibliography

Adelman, I. and Morris, C.T. (1973), *Economic Growth and Social Equity in Developing Countries*, Stanford University Press, California.

Ahluwalia, M. (1974), 'Dimensions of the Problem', in Chenery *et al.* (1974).

Ahluwalia, M. (1976), 'Inequality, Poverty and Development', *Journal of Development Economics*, 3, 307–42.

Ahluwalia, M. and Chenery, H. (1974), 'The Economic Framework', in Chenery *et al.* (1974).

Ahmad, Z.M. (1972), 'The Social and Economic Implications of the Green Revolution in Asia', *International Labour Review*, January, 9–34.

Anand, S. (1973), 'The Size Distribution of Income in Malaysia', Part I. Development Research Center, World Bank, Washington DC.

Anderson, C.A. and Bowman, M.J. (1967), 'Theoretical Considerations in Educational Planning', *The World Year Book of Education*, 1967. *Educational Planning* (J.A. Lauwereys *et al.*, eds); reprinted in M. Blaug (ed.) (1968), *Economics of Education*, vol. 1, Penguin, Harmondsworth, pp. 351–82.

Arndt, H.W. (1981), 'Economic Development: A Semantic History', *Economic Development and Cultural Change*, 29 (3), 457–66.

Arrow, K., Chenery, H., Minhas, B. and Solow, R. (1961), 'Capital–Labour Substitution and Economic Efficiency', *Review of Economics and Statistics*, 43, 225–48.

Atkinson, A. (1970), 'On the Measurement of Inequality', *Journal of Economic Theory*, 2, pp. 244–63.

Atkinson, A. (ed.) (1973), *Wealth, Income and Inequality*, Penguin, Harmondsworth.

Baron, C. (ed.) (1980), *Technology, Employment and Basic Needs in Food Processing in Developing Countries*, Pergamon, Oxford.

Baster, N. (ed.) (1972), *Measuring Development*, Frank Cass, London.

Batchelor, R.A., Major, R.L. and Morgan, A.D. (1980), *Industrialisation and the Basis for Trade*, Cambridge University Press.

Bauer, P. (1974), 'Foreign Aid, Forever?' *Encounter* (March); reprinted in G. Meier (1976), *Leading Issues in Economic Development*, Oxford University Press.

Becker, G.S. (1960), 'An Economic Analysis of Fertility', in *Demographic and Economic Change in Developed Countries*, a Conference of the Universities–NBER Committee for Economic Research, Princeton University Press.

Becker, G.S. (1964), *Human Capital. A Theoretical and Empirical Analysis with Special Reference to Education*, Princeton University Press.

Behrman, J. (1972), 'Sectoral Elasticities of Substitution between Capital and Labour in a Developing Economy: Time Series Analysis in the Case of Postwar Chile', *Econometrica*, 40 (2), 311–26.

Berelson, B. and Haveman, R.H. (1980), 'On Allocating Resources for Fertility Reduction in Developing Countries', *Population Studies*, 34 (2), 227–38.

Bergsman, J. (1974), 'Commercial Policy, Allocative and X-Efficiency', *Quarterly Journal of Economics*, 88, 409–33.

Bertrand, T. and Squire, L. (1980), 'The Relevance of the Dual Economy Model: A Case Study of Thailand', *Oxford Economic Papers*, 32, 480–511.

Bhagwati, J.N. (ed.) (1977), *The New International Economic Order: The North–South Debate*, MIT Press, Cambridge, Mass.

Bhalla, A.S. (1971), 'The Role of Services in Employment Expansion', in W. Galenson (ed.), *Essays on Employment*, ILO, Geneva.

Bhatia, R. (1967), 'A Note on Consumption, Income and Taxes', IMF Departmental Memoranda, DM/67/70; cited in Mikesell and Zinser (1973), p. 21.

Bird, G. and Gutmann, P. (1981), 'Foreign Aid—The Issues', *National Westminster Bank Quarterly Review*, August, 36–51.

Blaikie, P. (1975), *Family Planning in India: Diffusion and Policy*, Edward Arnold, London.

Blake, D.J. (1973), 'Unemployment: the West Malaysian Example', *UMBC Economic Review*, 11, 36–45; reprinted in Lim (1975).

Blaug, M. (ed.) (1968), *Economics of Education* (2 vols), Penguin, Harmondsworth.

Blaug, M. (1970), *An Introduction to the Economics of Education*, Penguin, Harmondsworth.

Blaug, M., Layard, R. and Woodhall, M. (1969), *Causes of Graduate Unemployment in India*, Allen Lane, the Penguin Press, London.

Blyth, C. (1969), 'Primitive South Pacific Economies: Their Consumption Pattern and Propensity to Save out of Cash Income', *Economic Record*, 45, 354–71.

Bottomley, A. (1963), 'The Premium for Risk as a Determinant of Interest Rates in Underdeveloped Rural Areas', *Quarterly Journal of Economics*, November, 637–47.

Branson, W. (1979), *Macroeconomic Theory and Policy* (2nd ed.), Harper and Row, New York.

Bromley, R. (1978), 'The Informal Sector: Why is it Worth Discussing?' *World Development*, 6 (9/10), 1033–9.

Bronfenbrenner, M. (1971), *Income Distribution Theory*, Macmillan, London.

Brunhild, G. and Burton, R.H. (1974), *Macroeconomic Theory*, Prentice-Hall, Englewood Cliffs, NJ.

Buchanan, N. (1945), *International Investment and Domestic Welfare*, New York.

Bulletin of the Oxford University Institute of Economics and Statistics (1972), Symposium, vol. 34, pp. 1–153.

Caldwell, J.C. (1977), 'The Economic Rationality of High Fertility: An Investigation Illustrated with Nigerian Survey Data', *Population Studies*, 31, 5–28.

Cassen, R.H. (1976), 'Population and Development: A Survey', *World Development*, 4 (10/11), 785–830.

Caves, R. and Jones, R. (1973), *World Trade and Payments*, Little Brown, Boston.

Chelliah, J., Baas, H. and Kelly, M. (1975), 'Tax Ratios and Tax Effort in Developing Countries, 1969–71', *IMF Staff Papers*, 22, 187–205.

Chenery, H. (1960), 'Patterns of Industrial Growth', *American Economic Review*, 50 (March), 1–28.

Chenery, H. and Strout, A. (1966), 'Foreign Assistance and Economic Development', *American Economic Review*, 56 (September), 679–733.

Chenery, H. and Syrquin, M. (1975), *Patterns of Development 1950–70*, Oxford University Press.

Chenery, H. *et al.* (eds) (1974), *Redistribution with Growth*, Oxford University Press.

Chenery, H. and Taylor, L. (1968), 'Development Patterns among Countries and over Time', *Review of Economics and Statistics*, 50 (November), 391–416.

Chiswick, B. (1971), 'Earnings Inequality and Economic Development', *Quarterly Journal of Economics*, February, 21–39.

Clark, C. (1945), 'Public Finance and Changes in the Value of Money', *Economic Journal*, 55, 371–89.

Cline, W. (1972), *Potential Effects of Income Redistribution on Economic Growth: Latin American Cases*, Praeger, New York.

Cline, W. (1975), 'Distribution and Development: A Survey of Literature', *Journal of Development Economics*, 1, 359–400.

Clower, R. (1965), 'The Keynesian Counter-Revolution: A Theoretical Appraisal', in F. Hahn and F. Brechling (eds), *The Theory of Interest Rates*, Macmillan, London.

Coale, A. and Hoover, E. (1958), *Population Growth and Economic Development in Low Income Countries*, Princeton University Press.

Coppock, J. (1962), *International Economic Instability: The Experience After World War II*, McGraw-Hill, New York.

Corden, M. (1971), *The Theory of Protection*, Oxford University Press.

Corden, M. (1974), *Trade Policy and Economic Welfare*, Oxford University Press.

Corden, M. (1979), *The New International Economic Order: A Cool Look*, Thames Press, London.

Corden, M. and Findlay, R. (1975), 'Urban Unemployment, Intersectoral Capital Mobility and Development Policy', *Economica*, 42, 59–78.

Cornwall, J. (1977), *Modern Capitalism. Its Growth and Transformation*, Martin Robertson, Oxford.

Cuca, R. (1980), 'Family Planning Programs and Fertility Decline', *Finance and Development*, 12, 37–9.

Dandekar, V. and Rath, N. (1971), *Poverty in India*, Indian School of Political Economy, Poona.

Dasgupta, P. and Heal, G. (1979), *Economic Theory and Exhaustible Resources*, Nisbet/Cambridge University Press.

Dasgupta, A. and Pearce, D. (1972), *Cost–Benefit Analysis*, Macmillan, London.

Davies, S. (1980), *The Diffusion of Process Innovations*, Cambridge University Press.

Day, R.H. and Singh, I. (1977), *Economic Development as an Adaptive Process*, Cambridge University Press.

Denison, E. (1967), *Why Growth Rates Differ: Postwar Experience in Nine Western Countries*, Brookings Institution, Washington DC.

Dixit, A. (1973), 'Models of Dual Economies', in J.A. Mirrlees and N. Stern (eds), *Models of Economic Growth*, IEA/Macmillan, London.

Dixit, A. and Norman, V. (1980), *Theory of International Trade*, Cambridge University Press.

Donges, J. (1976), 'A Comparative Survey of Industrialization Policies in Fifteen Semi-Industrial Countries', *Weltwirtschaftliches Archiv*, 626–57.

Dorner, P. and El-Shafie, M. (1980), *Resources and Development: National Resource Policies and Economic Development in an Interdependent World*, University of Wisconsin Press/Croom Helm, London.

Dos Santos, T. (1970), 'The Structure of Dependence', *American Economic Review*, 60 (Papers and Proceedings), 231–6.

Drake, P.J. (1980), *Money, Finance and Development*, Martin Robertson, Oxford.

Easterlin, R. (ed.) (1980), *Population and Economic Change in Developing Countries*, Universities–NBER Committee for Economic Research Conference Report, University of Chicago Press.

Economic Commission for Latin America (1950), *The Economic Development of Latin America and its Principal Problems*, United Nations, New York.

Edwards, E. and Todaro, M. (1973), 'Educational Demand and Supply in the Context of Growing Unemployment in Less Developed Countries', *World Development*, 1 (3/4), 107–17.

Evers, B., de Groot, G. and Wagenmans, W. (1977), 'Hong Kong: Development and Perspective of a Clothing Colony', Progress Report 6, Development Research Institute, Tilburg, Netherlands (mimeo); cited in Lall (1978).

Feder, G. and O'Mara, G. (1981), 'Farm Size and the Diffusion of Green Revolution Technology', *Economic Development and Cultural Change*, 30(1), 59–76.

Fei, J.C.H. and Ranis, G. (1975), 'A Model of Growth and Employment in the Open Dualistic Economy: The Cases of Korea and Taiwan', *Journal of Development Studies*, 11(2), 32–63.

Fields, G.S. (1980), *Poverty, Inequality and Development*, Cambridge University Press.

Fisher, I. (1930), *The Theory of Interest*, Macmillan, London.

Flanders, M.J. (1964), 'Prebisch on Protectionism: An Evaluation', *Economic Journal*, 74, 305–26.

Fleming, J.T. (1975), 'Tenurial Reform as a Prerequisite to the Green Revolution', *World Development*, 3(1), 47–58.

Frank, C. and Webb, R. (1977), *Income Distribution and Wealth in the Less Developed Countries*, Brookings Institution, Washington DC.

Freedman, M. (1961), 'The Handling of Money: A Note on the Background of the Economic Sophistication of Overseas Chinese', in T.H. Silcock (ed.), *Readings in Malayan Economics*, Eastern Universities Press, Singapore.

Friedman, M. (1957), *A Theory of the Consumption Function*, NBER/Princeton University Press.

Friend, I. (1966), *The Propensity to Consume and Save in Argentina*, Buenos Aires.

Friend, I. and Taubman, P. (1966), 'The Aggregate Propensity to Save: Some Concepts and their Application to International Data', *Review of Economics and Statistics*, 48 (May), 113–23.

Galenson, W. (1963), 'Economic Development and the Sectoral Expansion of Employment', *International Labour Review*, 88, 505–19.

Ghatak, S. (1978), *Developmental Economics*, Longman, London.

Glezakos, C. (1973), 'Export Instability and Economic Growth', *Economic Development and Cultural Change*, 21, 670–8.

Gold, B. (1981), 'Changing Perspectives on Size, Scale and Returns: An Interpretive Survey', *Journal of Economic Literature*, 19(1), 5–34.

Griffin, K. (1969), *Underdevelopment in Spanish America*, Allen & Unwin, London.

Griffin, K. (1974), *The Political Economy of Agrarian Change*, Macmillan, London.

Gupta, K. (1970), 'On Some Determinants of Rural and Urban Household Saving Behaviour', *Economic Record*, 46, 578–83.

Haberler, G. (1959), *International Trade and Economic Development*, National Bank of Egypt Fiftieth Anniversary Commemoration Lectures, Cairo; reprinted in G.M. Meier (ed.), *Leading Issues in Economic Development* (1976) (3rd ed.), Oxford University Press.

Hacche, G. (1979), *The Theory of Economic Growth*, Macmillan, London.

Hagan, E.E. (1958), 'An Economic Justification of Protectionism', *Quarterly Journal of Economics*, 72, 496–514.

Harberger, A. (1971), 'On Measuring the Social Opportunity Cost of Labour', *International Labour Review*, 103, 559–79.

Harbison, F. (1977), 'The Education–Income Connection', in C. Frank and R. Webb, *Income Distribution and Growth in the Less Developed Countries*, Brookings Institution, Washington DC.

Harris, J.R. and Todaro, M. (1970), 'Migration, Unemployment and Development: A Two-Sector Analysis', *American Economic Review*, 60, 125–42.

Harrod, R. (1939), 'An Essay in Dynamic Theory', *Economic Journal*, 49, 14–33.

Harrod, R. (1948), *Towards a Dynamic Economics*, Macmillan, London.

Hart, J.K. (1973), 'Informal Income Opportunities and Urban Employment in Ghana', *Journal of Modern African Studies*, 11, 61–89.

Haveman, R.H. (1976), 'Benefit–Cost Analysis and Family Planning Programmes', *Population and Development Review*, 2(1), 37–64.

Hawkins, E. (1970), *The Principles of Development Aid*, Penguin, Harmondsworth.

Henderson, J. and Quandt, R. (1980), *A Mathematical Approach* (3rd ed.), McGraw-Hill, Kogakusha, Tokyo.

Hicks, N. and Streeten, P. (1979), 'Indicators of Development: the Search for a Basic Needs Yardstick', *World Development*, 7, 567–80.

Higgins, B. (1959), *Economic Development*, Constable, London.

Hirschleifer, J. (1958), 'On the Theory of Optimal Investment Decision', *Journal of Political Economy*, 66, 329–72.

Hirschman, A. (1958), *The Strategy of Economic Development*, Yale University Press, New Haven, Conn.

Houthakker, H. (1961), 'An International Comparison of Personal Savings', *Bulletin of the International Statistical Institute*, 38, 56–69.

Houthakker, H. (1965), 'On Some Determinants of Saving in Developed and Underdeveloped Countries', in E.A.G. Robinson (ed.), *Problems in Economic Development*, Macmillan, New York.

International Labour Organization (1974), *Sharing in Development: A Programme of Employment, Equity and Growth for the Philippines*, ILO, Geneva.

Johnson, D. and Chiu, J. (1968), 'The Savings–Income Relation in Under-developed and Developed Countries', *Economic Journal*, 78 (June), 321–33.

Johnson, H.G. (1962), *Money, Trade and Economic Growth*, Allen & Unwin, London.

Johnson, H.G. (1969), *Essays in Monetary Economics*, Allen & Unwin, London.

Johnson, H.G. (1973), *The Theory of Income Distribution*, Gray-Mills, London.

Johnston, B. and Kilby, P. (1975), *Agriculture and Structural Transformation: Economic Strategy in Late-Developing Countries*, Oxford University Press.

Jones, H.G. (1975), *An Introduction to Modern Theories of Economic Growth*, Nelson, London.

Jorgenson, D. (1961), 'The Development of a Dual Economy', *Economic Journal*, 71, 309–34.

Jorgenson, D. (1967), 'Surplus Agricultural Labour and the Development of a Dual Economy', *Oxford Economic Papers*, 19(3), 288–312.

Jorgenson, D. and Griliches, Z. (1967), 'The Explanation of Productivity Change', *Review of Economic Studies*, 34, 249–83.

Kakwani, N. (1980), *Income Inequality and Poverty: Methods of Estimation and Policy Applications*, World Bank/Oxford University Press.

Kaldor, N. (1934), 'The Equilibrium of the Firm', *Economic Journal*, 44, 60–76.

Kaldor, N. (1955), 'Alternative Theories of Distribution', *Review of Economic Studies*, 23, 83–100.

Kaldor, N. (1963), 'Taxation for Economic Development', *Journal of Modern African Studies*, 1(1), 7–13.

Kaldor, N. (1966a), *Strategic Factors in Economic Development*, Cornell University Press, Ithaca, New York.

Kaldor, N. (1966b), *Causes of the Slow Rate of Growth of the United Kingdom: An Inaugural Lecture*, Cambridge University Press.

Katz, J. (1969), *Production Functions, Foreign Investment and Growth: A Study Based on the Argentine Manufacturing Sector, 1946–1961*, North-Holland, Amsterdam.

Kelley, A. and Williamson, J. (1968), 'Household Saving Behaviour in the Developing Economies: The Indonesian Case', *Economic Development and Cultural Change*, 16(3), 385–403.

Kenen, P. and Voivodas, C. (1972), 'Export Instability and Economic Growth', *Kyklos*, 25(4), 791–804.

Kilby, P. (ed.) (1971), *Entrepreneurship and Economic Development*, Free Press, New York.

Kim, Y.C. and Kwon, J.K. (1977), 'The Utilization of Capital and the Growth of Output in a Developing Economy: South Korea', *Journal of Development Economics*, 4, 265–78.

Kindleberger, C. (1968), *International Economics* (4th ed.), Irwin, Homewood, Illinois.

Knight, J. (1976), 'Explaining Income Distribution in Less Developed Countries: A Framework and an Agenda', *Bulletin of the Oxford Institute of Economics and Statistics*, August, 161–79.

Kravis, I. (1960), 'International Differences in the Distribution of Income', *Review of Economics and Statistics*, 42(4), 408–16.

Kravis, I. et al. (1978), *International Comparisons of Real Product and Purchasing Power*, Johns Hopkins University Press, Baltimore.

Kreinin, M.E. and Finger, J.M. (1976), 'A Critical Survey of the New International Economic Order', *Journal of World Trade Law*, 10(6), 493–512.

Kuznets, S. (1955), 'Economic Growth and Income Inequality', *American*

Economic Review, 45, 1–28.

Kuznets, S. (1963), 'Quantitative Aspects of Economic Growth of Nations: VIII, Distribution of Income by Size', *Economic Development and Cultural Change*, 11 (2II) 1–80.

Laidler, D. (1974), *Introduction to Microeconomics*, Basic Books, New York.

Lall, S. (1978), 'Transnationals, Domestic Enterprises and Industrial Structure in Host LDCs: A Survey', *Oxford Economic Papers*, 30(2), 217–48.

Landau, L. (1969), 'Differences in Saving Ratios Among Latin American Countries', PhD dissertation, Department of Economics, Harvard University; reproduced in condensed form in H. Chenery (ed.) (1971), *Studies in Development Planning*, Harvard University Press.

Lecraw, D.J. (1978), 'Determinants of Capacity Utilization by Firms in Less Developed Countries', *Journal of Development Economics*, 5, 139–54.

Leff, N.H. (1979), 'Entrepreneurship and Economic Development: The Problem Revisited', *Journal of Economic Literature*, 17, 46–64.

Leibenstein, H. (1966), 'Allocative Efficiency vs. X-Efficiency', *American Economic Review*, 56, 392–415.

Leibenstein, H. (1974), 'An Interpretation of the Economic Theory of Fertility: Promising Path or Blind Alley?' *Journal of Economic Literature*, 12(2), 457–79.

Leibenstein, H. (1978), *General X-efficiency Theory and Economic Development*, Oxford University Press.

Lele, U. and Mellor, J.W. (1981), 'Technological Change, Distributive Bias and Labour Transfer in a Two-Sector Economy', *Oxford Economic Papers*, 33, 426–41.

Lewis, W.A. (1954), 'Economic Development with Unlimited Supplies of Labour', *Manchester School of Economic and Social Studies*, 22, 139–91.

Lewis, W.A. (1955), *The Theory of Economic Growth*, Allen & Unwin, London.

Lewis, W.A. (1958), 'Unlimited Supplies of Labour: Further Notes', *Manchester School of Economic and Social Studies*, 24, 1–32.

Lim, D. (ed.) (1975), *Readings on Malaysian Economic Development*, Oxford University Press.

Little, I. (1975), 'Economic Relations with the Third World—Old Myths and New Prospects', *Scottish Journal of Political Economy*, 22, 223–35.

Little, I. and Mirrlees, J. (1974), *Project Appraisal and Planning for the Developing Countries*, Heinemann, London.

Little, I., Scitovsky, T. and Scott, M. (1970), *Industry and Trade in Some Developing Countries: A Comparative Study*, OECD and Oxford University Press, London.

Lotz, J. and Morss, E. (1967), 'Measuring "Tax Effort" in Developing Countries', *IMF Staff Papers*, 14, 478–99.

Lydall, H. (1979), *A Theory of Income Distribution*, Oxford University Press.

Lysy, F. (1980), 'Investment and Employment with Unlimited Labour: The Role of Aggregate Demand', *Journal of Development Economics*, 7(4), 541–66.

MacBean, A. (1966), *Export Instability and Economic Development*, Allen & Unwin, London.

MacDougal, G. (1960), 'The Benefits and Costs of Private Investment from Abroad: A Theoretical Approach', *Economic Record*, 36, 13–35.

McKinnon, R.I. (1973), *Money and Capital in Economic Development*, Brookings Institution, Washington DC.

McKinnon, R.I. (ed.) (1976), *Money and Finance in Economic Growth and Development*, Marcel Dekker, New York.

McKinnon, R.I. (1977), 'Money and Credit in Semi-Industrial Less Developed Countries', mimeo. A revised version of this paper is McKinnon (1981).

McKinnon, R.I. (1981), 'Financial Repression and the Liberalisation Problem within Less Developed Countries', in S. Grassman and E. Lundberg (eds), *The World Economic Order: Past and Prospects*, Macmillan, Hong Kong.

Machlup, F. (1962), *The Production and Distribution of Knowledge in the United States*, Princeton University Press.

Maddison, A. (1970), *Economic Progress and Policy in Developing Countries*, Allen & Unwin, London.

Maizels, A. (1963), *Industrial Growth and World Trade*, Cambridge University Press.

Marglin, S. (1967), *Public Investment Criteria: Studies in the Economic Development of India*, George, Allen and Unwin, London.

Martin, J. (1978), 'X-inefficiency, Managerial Effort and Protection', *Economica*, 45, 273–86.

Matthews, R.C.O. (ed.) (1980), *Economic Growth and Resources: Proceedings of the 5th World Congress of the I.E.A.* (held Tokyo, 1977), vol. 2: *Trends and Factors* (gen. ed. E. Malinvaud), Macmillan, London.

Meade, J.E. (1962), *A Neo-Classical Theory of Economic Growth* (2nd ed.), Allen & Unwin, London.

Meade, J. (1964), *Efficiency, Equality and the Ownership of Property*, Allen & Unwin, London.

Meade, J. (1976), *The Just Economy*, State University of New York Press, Albany.

Meier, G. (1968), *The International Economics of Development*, Harper and Row, New York.

Meier, G. (1980), *International Economics, The Theory of Policy*, Oxford University Press, London.

Mellor, J.W. (1966), *The Economics of Agricultural Development*, Cornell University Press, Ithaca, New York.

Mikesell, R. and Zinser, J. (1973), 'The Nature of the Savings Function in Developing Countries: A Survey of the Theoretical and Empirical Literature', *Journal of Economic Literature*, 11, 1–26.

Mincer, J. (1958), 'Investment in Human Capital and Personal Income

Distribution', *Journal of Political Economy*, 66, 281–302.

Miracle, M. (1968), '"Subsistence Agriculture": Analytical Problems and Alternative Concepts', *American Journal of Agricultural Economics*, 50, May, 292–310.

Miracle, M.P., Miracle, D.S. and Cohen, L. (1980), 'Informal Savings Mobilization in Africa', *Economic Development and Cultural Change*, 28, 701–24.

Modigliani, F. (1965), *The Life-Cycle Hypothesis of Saving—Part III*. Presented at the 1st Econometric Society Congress, Rome.

Morawetz, D. (1974), 'Employment Implications of Industrialization in Developing Countries: A Survey', mimeo, IBRD Staff Working Paper no. 170, Washington DC.

Moser, C. (1978), 'Informal Sector or Petty Commodity Production: Dualism or Dependence in Urban Development?' *World Development*, 6 (9/10), 1041–64.

Myint, H. (1958), 'The "Classical" Theory of International Trade and Underdeveloped Countries', *Economic Journal*, 68, 317–37.

Myint, H. (1973), *The Economics of the Developing Countries* (4th, rev., ed.), Hutchinson, London.

Myrdal, G. (1956), *An International Economy*, Harper, New York.

Nicholls, W.H. (1963), 'An "Agricultural Surplus" as a Factor in Economic Development', *Journal of Political Economy*, 71(1), 1–29.

Nugent, J. and Yotopoulos, P. (1979), 'What Has Orthodox Development Economics Learned from Recent Experience?' *World Development*, 7, 541–54.

Nurkse, R. (1959), *Patterns of Trade and Development*, University of Stockholm, Stockholm.

Owen, W. (1966), 'The Double Developmental Squeeze in Agriculture', *American Economic Review*, 56(2), 43–70.

Papanek, G.F. (1973), 'Aid, Foreign Private Investment, Savings and Growth in Less Developed Countries', *Journal of Political Economy*, 81, 120–30.

Paukert, F. (1973), 'Income Distribution at Different Levels of Development: A Survey of Evidence', *International Labour Review*, 108, August/September, 97–125.

Perlman, M. (1981), 'Population and Economic Change in Developing Countries', *Journal of Economic Literature*, 19, 74–82.

Please, S. (1967), 'Saving through Taxation: Reality or Mirage?' *Finance and Development*, 4, 24–32.

Polak, J. (1943), 'Balance of Payment Problems of Countries Reconstructing with the Help of Foreign Loans', *Quarterly Journal of Economics*, 57, 208–40.

Popenoe, O. (1969), 'A Study of Malay Entrepreneurs', *Quarterly Journal of the Institute of Technoloji MARA*, 1(3), September, reprinted in Lim (1975), 350–9.

Prebisch, R. (1950), *The Economic Development of Latin America and its Principal Problems*, UN Dept of Economic Affairs (Economic Commission for Latin America), New York.

Preston, S.H. (1980), 'Causes and Consequences of Mortality Decline in Less Developed Countries during the Twentieth Century', in R. Easterlin (ed.), *Population and Economic Change in Developing Countries*, National Bureau of Economic Research, New York.

Purcal, J.T. (1975), 'Employment Patterns in the Rice-growing Areas of West Malaysia', in D. Lim (ed.), *Readings on Malaysian Economic Development*, Oxford University Press.

Ranis, G. and Fei, J. (1961), 'A Theory of Economic Development', *American Economic Review*, 51(4), 533–65.

Robinson, S. (1971), 'Sources of Growth in Less Developed Countries: A Cross Section Study', *Quarterly Journal of Economics*, 85, 391–408.

Robinson, S. (1976), 'A Note on the U Hypothesis relating Income Inequality and Economic Development', *American Economic Review*, 66, 437–40.

Rozenthal, A.A. (1970), *Finance and Development in Thailand*, Praeger, New York.

Sahota, G. (1978), 'Theories of Personal Income Distribution: A Survey', *Journal of Economic Literature*, 16 (March), 1–55.

Sato, K. (1966), 'On the Adjustment Time in Neoclassical Growth Models', *Review of Economic Studies*, 33, 263–8.

Schultz, T.P. (1980), 'An Economic Interpretation of the Decline in Fertility in a Rapidly Developing Country: Consequences of Development and Family Planning', in R. Easterlin, *Population and Economic Change in Developing Countries*, National Bureau for Economic Research, Chicago.

Schultz, T.W. (1961), 'Investment in Human Capital', *American Economic Review*, 51, 1–17.

Scott, M. Fg., Macarthur, J. and Newbery, D. (1976), *Project Appraisal in Practice: The Little–Mirrlees Method Applied to Kenya*, Heinemann, London.

Sen, A. (1967), 'Isolation, Assurance and the Social Rate of Discount', *Quarterly Journal of Economics*, 81, 112–24.

Sen, A. (1968), *Choice of Techniques: An Aspect of the Theory of Planned Economic Development* (3rd ed.), Basil Blackwell, Oxford.

Sen, A. (ed.) (1970), *Growth Economics*, Penguin, Harmondsworth.

Sen, A. (1973), *On Economic Inequality*, Oxford University Press.

Sen, A. (1976), 'Poverty: An Ordinal Approach to Measurement', *Econometrica*, 44(2), 219–30.

Sines, R. (1979), 'Sectoral Elasticities of Substitution between Labour and Capital in Venezuelan Manufacturing: A Cross-Sectional Micro-Analysis', *World Development*, 7(1), 79–82.

Singh, I. and Day, R. (1975), 'A Microeconometric Chronicle of the Green Revolution', *Economic Development and Cultural Change*, 23, 661–86.

Singh, S.K. (1971), 'The Determinants of Aggregate Savings', Domestic Finance Division, IBRD', mimeo. See also S.K. Singh (1975), *Development Economics: Theory and Findings*, D.C. Heath, Lexington, Mass.

Smil, V. and Knowland, W. (1980), *Energy in the Developing World: The Real Energy Crisis*, Oxford University Press.

Snyder, D. (1974), 'Econometric Studies of Household Saving Behaviour in Developing Countries: A Survey', *Journal of Development Studies*, 10(2), 129–53.

Södersten, B. (1971), *International Economics* (1st ed.), Macmillan, London.

Solow, R.M. (1956), 'A Contribution to the Theory of Economic Growth', *Quarterly Journal of Economics*, 70, 65–94.

Solow, R.M. (1957), 'Technical Change and the Aggregate Production Function', *Review of Economics and Statistics*, August, 39, 312–20.

Solow, R.M. (1970), *Growth Theory, An Exposition*, Oxford University Press.

Squire, L. and Van der Tak, H. (1975), *Economic Analysis of Projects*, World Bank/Johns Hopkins University Press, Baltimore.

Steedman, I. (1979), *Fundamental Issues in Trade Theory*, Macmillan, London.

Sternberg, M.J. (1971), 'Agrarian Reform and Employment: Potential and Problems', *International Labour Review*, May, 103, 453–76.

Stewart, F. and Streeten, P. (1971), 'Conflicts between Output and Employment Objectives in Developing Countries', *Oxford Economic Papers*, 23(2), 145–68.

Streeten, P. (1967), 'The Frontiers of Development Studies: Some Issues of Development Policy', *Journal of Development Studies*, 4, 2–24.

Streeten, P. (1969), 'Nouvelles Manières d'aborder le problème de l'investissement privé dans les pays en boie de dèveloppement', *Revue de la Société d'Études et d'Expansion*, 238; reprinted in J. Dunning (1972), *International Investment*, Penguin, Harmondsworth.

Sundrum, R. (1974), 'Development, Equality and Employment', *Economic Record*, 50, 430–42.

Sunkel, O. (1973), 'Transnational Capitalism and National Disintegration in Latin America', *Social and Economic Studies*, 22(1), 132–76.

Swamy, S. (1967), 'Structural Changes and the Distribution of Income by Size: The Case of India', *Review of Income and Wealth*, Scries 13, 155–74.

Tait, A., Gratz, L. and Eichengreen, B. (1979), 'International Comparisons of Taxation for Selected Developing Countries, 1972–76', *IMF Staff Papers*, 26, 123–56.

Thirlwall, A.P. (1974), *Inflation, Saving and Growth in Developing Economies*, Macmillan, London.

Thirlwall, A.P. (1978), *Growth and Development* (2nd ed.), Macmillan, London.

Thurow, L.C. (1975), *Generating Inequality*, Macmillan, London.

Todaro, M.P. (1969), 'A Model of Labour Migration and Urban Unemployment in Less Developed Countries', *American Economic Review*, 59(1), 138–48.

Todaro, M.P. (1971a), *Development Planning: Models and Methods*, Oxford University Press.

Todaro, M.P. (1971b), 'Income Expectations, Rural–Urban Migration and Employment in Africa', *International Labour Review*, 104, 387–414.

Todaro, M.P. (1976), 'Urban Job Expansion, Induced Migration and Rising Unemployment. A Formulation and Simplified Empirical Test for LDCs', *Journal of Development Economics*, 3, 211–25.

Tyler, W. (1981), 'Growth and Export Expansion in Developing Countries: Some Empirical Evidence', *Journal of Development Economics*, 9, 121–30.

UNCTAD (United Nations Conference on Trade and Development) (1975), *International Subcontracting Arrangements in Electronics Between Developed Market-Economy Countries and Developing Countries*, United Nations, New York.

UNIDO (United Nations Industrial Development Organization) (1972), *Guidelines for Project Evaluation*, United Nations, New York.

Vernon, R. (1966), 'International Investment and International Trade in the Product Cycle', *Quarterly Journal of Economics*, 80, 190–207.

Wai, U.T. (1957), 'Interest Rates outside the Organized Money Markets of Underdeveloped Countries', *IMF Staff Papers*, 6, 80–125.

Waterston, A. (1965), *Development Planning: Lessons of Experience*, Johns Hopkins University Press, Baltimore.

Weisskoff, R. (1970), 'Income Distribution and Economic Growth in Puerto Rico, Argentina and Mexico', *Review of Income and Wealth*, Series 16, 303–32.

White, B. (1976), 'The Economic Importance of Children in a Japanese Village', in M. Nag (ed.), *Population and Social Organization*, Mouton, the Hague.

Wilber, C. (1979), *The Political Economy of Development and Underdevelopment*, Random House, New York.

Williamson, J. (1968), 'Personal Saving in Developing Nations: An Intertemporal Cross-Section from Asia', *Economic Record*, 44, 194–210.

Williamson, J. (1969), 'Income Growth and Savings', *Philippine Economic Journal*, 8(1), 54–74.

Williamson, J. (1971), 'Relative Price Changes, Adjustment Dynamics and Productivity Growth: The Case of Philippine Manufacturing', *Economic Development and Cultural Change*, 19(4), 307–26.

Winston, G.C. (1974), 'The Theory of Capital Utilization and Idleness', *Journal of Economic Literature*, 12, 1301–20.

World Bank (1979), *Brazil: Human Resources Special Report*, World Bank, New York.

World Bank (various years), *World Development Report*, World Bank/ Oxford University Press.

Author Index

Subject Index